CAMBRIDGE COMMENTARIES ON
WRITINGS OF THE JEWISH AND CHRISTIAN WORLD
200 BC TO AD 200
VOLUME I PART 2

Jews in the Hellenistic World

CAMBRIDGE COMMENTARIES ON
WRITINGS OF THE JEWISH AND CHRISTIAN WORLD
200 BC TO AD 200

General Editors:

P. R. ACKROYD
A. R. C. LEANEY
J. W. PACKER

1 i *Jews in the Hellenistic World: Josephus, Aristeas, the Sibylline Oracles, Eupolemus* – J. R. Bartlett
1 ii *Jews in the Hellenistic World: Philo* – R. Williamson
2 *The Qumran Community* – M. A. Knibb
3 *Early Rabbinic Writings* – H. Maccoby
4 *Outside the Old Testament* – M. de Jonge
5 *Outside the New Testament* – G. N. Stanton
6 *Jews and Christians: Graeco-Roman Views* – M. Whittaker
7 *The Jewish and Christian World 200 BC to AD 200* – A. R. C. Leaney

JEWS IN THE HELLENISTIC WORLD: PHILO

RONALD WILLIAMSON

Senior Lecturer in
New Testament Studies
University of Leeds

CAMBRIDGE UNIVERSITY PRESS

Cambridge
New York New Rochelle
Melbourne Sydney

Published by the Press Syndicate of the University of Cambridge
The Pitt Building, Trumpington Street, Cambridge CB2 1RP
32 East 57th Street, New York, NY 10022, USA
10 Stamford Road, Oakleigh, Melbourne 3166, Australia

First published 1989

Printed in Great Britain at
the University Press, Cambridge

British Library cataloguing in publication data

Jews in the Hellenistic world. – (Cambridge
commentaries on writings of the Jewish
and Christian world 200BC to AD200;
v. 1, pt 2).
Philo
1. Greek literature. Jewish writers,
BC200 – AD200 – Critical studies 2. Judaism.
Documents, to 200 – Critical studies
I. Williamson, Ronald
880.9′8924

Library of Congress cataloguing in publication data

Williamson, Ronald.
Jews in the Hellenistic world: Philo/Ronald Williamson.
p. cm. – (Cambridge commentaries on writings of the Jewish
and Christian world, 200 BC to AD 200; v. 1, pt 2)
Includes selections from Philo's Greek works, translated into English.
Bibliography.
Includes index.
ISBN 0 521 30511 X. ISBN 0 521 31548 4 (pbk)
1. Philo, of Alexandria. I. Philo, of Alexandria. Selections.
English. 1989. II. Title. III. Title: Philo. IV. Series.
B689.Z7W54 1989
181′.06–dc19 88–23432 CIP

ISBN 0 521 30511 X hard covers
ISBN 0 521 31548 4 paperback

VN

Contents

Note: The numerical references above are those used in the Loeb Edition of Philo's Works.

General Editors' Preface

The three general editors of the Cambridge Bible Commentary series have all, in their teaching, experienced a lack of readily usable texts of the literature which is often called pseudepigrapha but which is more accurately defined as extra-biblical or para-biblical literature. The aim of this new series is to help to fill this gap.

The welcome accorded to the Cambridge bible Commentary has encouraged the editors to follow the same pattern here, except that carefully chosen extracts from the texts, rather than complete books, have normally been provided for comment. The introductory material leads naturally into the text, which itself leads into alternating sections of commentary.

Within the severe limits imposed by the size and scope of the series, each contributor will attempt to provide for the student and general reader the results of modern scholarship, but has been asked to assume no specialised theological or linguistic knowledge.

The volumes already planned cover the writings of the Jewish and Christian World from about 200 BC to AD 200 and are being edited as follows:

1 i *Jews in the Hellenistic World: Josephus, Aristeas, The Sibylline Oracles, Eupolemus* – John R. Bartlett, Trinity College, Dublin

1 ii *Jews in the Hellenistic World: Philo* – R. Williamson, University of Leeds

2 *The Qumran Community* – M. A. Knibb, King's College, London

3 *Early Rabbinic Writings* – H. Maccoby, Leo Baeck College, London

4 *Outside the Old Testament* – M. de Jonge, University of Leiden

5 *Outside the New Testament* – G. N. Stanton, King's College, London

6 *Jews and Christians: Graeco-Roman Views* – Molly Whittaker, University of Nottingham

A seventh volume by one of the general editors, A. R. C. Leaney, *The Jewish and Christian World 200 BC to AD 200*, examines the wider historical and literary background to the period and includes tables of dates, relevant lists and maps. Although this companion volume will preface and augment the series, it may also be read as complete in itself and be used as a work of general reference.

P.R.A. A.R.C.L. J.W.P.

Preface

I should like to express my deep gratitude to the Cambridge University Press for allowing me the privilege of contributing this volume on Philo of Alexandria as the second part of the volume on *Jews in the Hellenistic World* in the series Cambridge Commentaries on Writings of the Jewish and Christian World 200 BC to AD 200. I should also like to thank very much the three editors for their considerable help. A special word of thanks must be offered to Canon John Packer, who has given enormous encouragement to me and has provided substantial help just when help, in difficult circumstances, was most needed.

The reader will notice that in the case of the three chapters on 'Philo's doctrine of God', 'Philo's Logos doctrine' and 'Philo's allegorical exegesis of Scripture' there is more introduction and less commentary on selected passages, whereas in the chapter on 'The ethical teaching of Philo' the commentary on selected passages exceeds the introduction. The reason for this is that, while Philo wrote continuously on ethical matters in at least six treatises, making it possible to select extended passages for commentary, his thoughts and ideas on other subjects occur intermittently over vast distances in his many treatises. It should, perhaps, be added that, in the case of his employment of the allegorical method of exegesis, there is almost no paragraph in the whole of his works where it is absent. This fact, however, also makes it difficult to select compact groups of passages from his works to illustrate his procedure.

Having read the great works on Philo by eminent Philonists such as Drummond, Wolfson and Goodenough, to name only some of the most famous, and having taken part in international seminars at SNTS conferences, with the modern generation of distinguished Philo experts, I realise how inadequate this small volume is and how lamentably it fails to do justice to its subject. However, if it helps some students to discover Philo, to realise his importance and to want to go on to study more of his works, then I shall feel it has served its limited purpose.

The reader of Philo's works will, like the man referred to in one of Philo's treatises, be 'nourished with peace' and will depart from his reading 'having gained a calm, unclouded life, a life of true bliss and happiness'.

I should like the reader to note that, while the translation of the selected passages is my own, I have been helped greatly by the translation in the Loeb edition; by that, in four volumes, made by C. D. Yonge (London and New York, 1854) in Bohm's Ecclesiastical Library; and by the volumes of the French translation (by various translators) published under the patronage of the University of Lyons: *Les Œuvres de Philon d'Alexandrie*, Vol. I (Paris: Editions du Cerf, 1960).

Finally, I wish to extend my warmest thanks to Miss B. Spensley, who kindly undertook the task of checking that the Philo quotations in the commentary passages corresponded accurately to the translated sections of text.

Abbreviations

Abr.	*De Abrahamo*	On Abraham
⋆*Aet. Mund.*	*De Aeternitate Mundi*	On the Eternity of the World
⋆*Agric.*	*De Agricultura*	On Agriculture
Cher.	*De Cherubim*	On the Cherubim
Conf. Ling.	*De Confusione Linguarum*	On the Confusion of Tongues
Congr.	*De Congressu Eruditionis Gratia*	On the Unity of Study
⋆*Decal.*	*De Decalogo*	On the Decalogue
Det. Pot. Ins.	*Quod Deterius Potiori insidiari soleat*	The Worse is wont to ambush the Better
Deus Imm.	*Quod Deus sit Immutabilis*	On the Unchangeableness of God
Ebr.	*De Ebrietate*	On Drunkenness
⋆*Flacc.*	*In Flaccum*	Against Flaccus
Fug.	*De Fuga et Inventione*	On Flight and Discovery
Gig.	*De Gigantibus*	On the Giants
Jos.	*De Josepho*	On Joseph
Leg. All.	*Legum Allegoriae*	Allegorical Interpretation of the Law
⋆*Leg. Gaj.*	*Legatio ad Gaium*	The Embassy to Gaius
Migr. Abr.	*De Migratione Abrahami*	On the Migration of Abraham
Mut. Nom.	*De Mutatione Nominum*	On the Change of Names
⋆*Omn. Prob. Lib.*	*Quod omnis Probus Liber sit*	Every good Man is free

Op. Mund.	*De Opificio Mundi*	On the Making of the World
Plant.	*De Plantatione*	On Planting
Poster. C.	*De Posteritate Caini*	On the Posterity and Exile of Cain
★*Praem. Poen.*	*De Praemiis et Poenis*	On Rewards and Punishments
★*Prov.*	*De Providentia*	On Providence
★*Quaest. in Gn. (Ex.)*	*Quaestiones in Genesin (Exodum)*	Questions and Answers on Genesis (Exodus)
Rer. Div. Her.	*Quis Rerum Divinarum Heres sit*	Who is the heir of Divine Matters
Sacr. AC.	*De Sacrificiis Abelis et Caini*	On the Sacrifice of Abel and Cain
Sobr.	*De Sobrietate*	On Sobriety
★*Som.*	*De Somniis*	On Dreams
★*Spec. Leg.*	*De Specialibus Legibus*	On the Special Laws
★*Virt.*	*De Virtutibus*	On the Virtues
★*Vit. Cont.*	*De Vita Contemplativa*	On the Contemplative Life
Vit. Mos.	*De Vita Mosis*	On the Life of Moses

Note: Quotations from the volumes marked★ from the Loeb Classical Library are reproduced by kind permission of William Heinemann Ltd (UK and British Commonwealth excluding Canada). Permission to reproduce excerpts from the above volumes in the USA and Canada has kindly been granted by Harvard University Press.

Since the New English Bible did not seem a suitable source for the biblical quotations used in a volume on Philo, they are largely translated directly from the Septuagint or taken from the Revised Version or Revised Standard Version.

Introduction: Philo's life and work

Life. Philo is usually referred to as Philo the Jew (Philo Judaeus) or Philo of Alexandria, a city of the Jewish Dispersion in Egypt. We do not know the exact dates of his birth and death, but in one of his writings he refers to himself as among the 'aged' who have grown 'grey' (*Leg. Gaj.* 1), by Jewish reckoning sixty or seventy. Later in this same work he speaks of his (advanced) 'age' (*ibid.* 182). He describes a visit in AD 40 by a delegation of Jews from Alexandria to the Roman Emperor Caligula in Rome to complain about anti-Jewish hostilities on the part of the Egyptian citizens of Alexandria which occurred in AD 38. From this we may deduce that Philo was between sixty and seventy in AD 40 and was therefore born *c.* 30 BC. His lifetime thus extended over a period from the time of Herod the Great, including that of some of the great Jewish rabbis (Hillel, Shammai and Gamaliel) and Paul; in particular, he was a contemporary of Jesus of Nazareth, of whom, however, he makes absolutely no mention. In *Leg. Gaj.* 299 he refers to Pontius Pilate and the incident involving the placing of 'shields coated with gold' in Herod's palace in 'the holy city' (cf. Josephus, *War* II.9.2 (169ff.)). He describes Pilate as 'naturally inflexible, a blend of self-will and relentlessness', and as stubbornly refusing to meet the Jews' request for the removal of the shields. He also describes 'the briberies, the insults, the robberies, the outrages and wanton injuries, the executions without trial constantly repeated, the ceaseless and supremely grievous cruelty' which characterised the governorship of Pilate, but makes no mention of the trial and crucifixion of Jesus of Nazareth, a silence which is an indication of the unimportance to contemporary Judaism of the career of the Jew recognised by Christians as the Messiah and regarded by them with such reverence and devotion.

We know almost nothing about the personal and domestic life of Philo. We do not even know if he was married, though two passages in the *Legatio ad Gaium* perhaps imply that his experiences with women – and perhaps with a wife – had not been particularly happy. In the first (*Leg. Gaj.* 39) he writes: 'A wife has great power to paralyse and seduce her husband and particularly if she is a wanton, for her guilty conscience increases her wheedling.' In the second (*ibid.* 61) he states: 'love as they say is a fickle passion, and therefore none of its endearments are stable'. These comments, so much like Proverbs, may have little biographical value, but Philo makes a number of references to relationships between parents and children which may reflect his own experiences as a father; however, that he *was* a married man with a family we do not know for sure.

He seems to have belonged to a rich and influential Jewish family, and was to become an esteemed leader of the Alexandrian Jewish community, of such eminence that he was chosen to lead the five-man delegation to the Roman Emperor Caligula which he describes in the *Legatio ad Gaium* and to which he refers in the *In Flaccum*. From Josephus we learn that his brother Alexander was rich and that his nephew was deeply involved in the political and military affairs of the Roman Empire.

Jew or Greek? Much discussion has taken place on the extent to which Philo remained truly Jewish, an orthodox Jew. It has been said: 'It is significant that Philo could assimilate so much from Hellenism and still consider himself a Jew'; 'Was he a *Greek* Jew, or, might one more properly speak of him as a Jewish *Greek*?' The writer of the second of these quotations could also, however, say 'no Jew in history ever surpassed Philo's loyalty to Judaism', and also 'If at times it seems to be Judaism, rather than the Jews, to whom his loyalty is addressed, nevertheless that loyalty is beyond all denial.'

Philo certainly thought of himself as a good Jew, a Jew by religion and not just by race. He describes himself as a scholar of Moses (*Spec. Leg.* 1.345) and as one of 'the disciples of Moses' (*Rer. Div. Her.* 81), and in his own mind was as far removed as it is possible to be from those described in *Conf. Ling.* 2 as 'persons who cherish a dislike of the institutions of our fathers and make it their constant study to denounce and decry the Laws'. Philo wrote his treatises to refute these 'impious scoffers'.

Philo's place on the deputation to Caligula shows that he was not regarded by the Alexandrian Jewish community as either an outsider or an heretic. The sole purpose of the deputation was to protest against attacks on Jewish beliefs and practices and, in particular, the desecration of the local synagogues by the introduction into them of images of the emperor.

When Philo asks the question (in *Leg. Gaj.* 194) 'For what religion or righteousness is to be found in vainly striving to show that we are Alexandrians, when we are menaced by the danger which threatens a more universal interest, the corporate body of the Jews?', it shows that Philo was a Jew first and an Alexandrian only second.

Philo believed Judaism to be a universal religion, capable of attracting and winning 'the attention of all, of barbarians, of Greeks, of dwellers on the mainland and islands, of nations of the east and the west, of Europe and Asia, of the whole inhabited world from end to end' (*Vit. Mos.* II.20); but it did not, in Philo's view, achieve this universality by any abandonment of its fundamental beliefs and practices. In the sections following on the one just quoted Philo speaks of the Jewish respect for the seventh day and the solemn annual celebration of the Day of Atonement (*Vit. Mos.* II.21–4).

It might perhaps have been expected that Philo, because of his practice of the allegorical exegesis of the Old Testament, and in the light of his philosophical tendencies, would have felt it in order to advocate an abandonment of certain Jewish practices, especially perhaps the rite of circumcision. In fact, while he sees it as possessing a symbolic meaning, there is nothing in the opening paragraphs of the *De Specialibus Legibus* to suggest that he saw any good or sufficient reason to abandon the practice ridiculed by others (even though its observance by the Egyptians might have been a good enough reason in itself for doing so). But in *Migr. Abr.* 92 Philo makes it quite clear that an understanding of the symbolic meaning of the law regarding circumcision should not lead to that law's being repealed.

Philo lived at a time when the Temple in Jerusalem was still standing. That Temple Philo, according to his statement in *Prov.* 64, had visited at least once, 'to offer up prayers and sacrifices'. It is possible, as has been suggested, that Philo regarded the physical Temple as a hindrance to the spiritual cult, but he never actually says so, and it is more likely that he regarded the worship of the Jerusalem Temple as symbolic of a greater, spiritual worship, but as indispensable to Judaism all the same (though in fact the synagogue played a larger part in Philo's own worship, since he was a citizen of Alexandria). In *Migr. Abr.* 92 he says: 'Why, we shall be ignoring the sanctity of the Temple and a thousand other things, if we are going to pay heed to nothing except what is shown to us by the inner meaning of things' (that is, excessive allegorism, or an exclusively allegorical interpretation of the Scriptures, is dangerous). There are a great many references to the Jerusalem Temple in the course of the *Legatio ad Gaium* and the *In Flaccum*: for example, the statement (*Leg. Gaj.* 157) that the Emperor Augustus ordered perpetual sacrifices for himself to be offered there and that 'these sacrifices are maintained to the present day and will be maintained for ever'. Philo clearly did not expect the total destruction of the Temple which occurred in AD 70. Another interesting reference to the Temple is to the sacrifices offered in it on behalf of Caligula, 'as a prayer of hope for victory in Germany' (*Leg. Gaj.* 356).

But, as will be shown below, Philo, although he participated in, and does not appear in any way overtly to have objected to, the sacrificial ritual of the Temple, also interpreted sacrifice as a symbol for prayer, and presented prayer as a sacrifice superior to that of bodies of animals, and regarded the universe as the true Temple in which the Logos, as High Priest, ministered.

Philo always speaks with great reverence for the Jewish Sabbath, though he also feels free to interpret it symbolically. In *Vit. Mos.* 216 he says of Sabbath observance: 'Even now this practice is retained, and the Jews every seventh day occupy themselves with the philosophy of their fathers, dedicating that time to the acquiring of knowledge and the study of the truths of nature.' He adds: 'For what are our places of prayer throughout the cities but schools of prudence and courage and justice and also of piety, holiness and every virtue by which duties to God and men are discerned and rightly performed?' The Pentateuch was the section of the Old Testament read serially on the Sabbath in the synagogues of Judaism. It is quite possible that Philo gave some instruction as part of the synagogue services, since much of his work has a homiletical flavour and character. Many of his treatises could have begun their life as synagogal homilies on lections from the Alexandrian synagogue lectionary. Philo would by no means be the first theological writer to have presented in another form material first used by him in sermons.

There are many passages in Philo's works which reveal him as a man of deep piety and delicate spirituality. In *Leg. Gaj.* 210 he describes the Jewish nation as one which zealously guards its own customs, as others do, but which is distinguished by its belief that 'the laws are oracles vouchsafed by God'. He continues, with reference to the Jews, 'having been trained in this doctrine from their earliest years, they carry the likenesses of the commandments enshrined in their souls'. No reader of Philo can reasonably doubt that the Law of Moses was enshrined in *his* soul. Its study was his perpetual delight, if we are to judge from the quantity and quality of his writings in exposition of it. The way in which Philo refers to the synagogues of Alexandria in, for example, the *Legatio ad Gaium* shows that they were for him meeting-houses for prayer and study to which he was a regular, weekly visitor. It was to protect those very synagogues from defilement by the introduction into them of images of the Roman Emperor that Philo led the delegation to Rome described by him in the *Legatio ad Gaium*. Whatever the peculiarities and eccentricities of Philo's particular theological and philosophical viewpoint, at times apparently distant from orthodox Judaism, there can be little doubt that, as is often the case with radical, eccentric Christian theologians, the man behind them was, deep down, a devout, orthodox Jew.

Philo's loyalty was both to his fellow Jews, in Alexandria and Palestine (remarks he makes in the *Legatio ad Gaium* and the *In Flaccum* show that he was equally concerned about the desecration of the Temple and the defilement of the synagogues of Palestine), and to Judaism and its doctrines.

What he thought about the Temple is revealed by a passage in the *Legatio ad Gaium*. When he is telling of the news of Caligula's intention to defile the Temple with a statue of himself as Zeus, he asks: 'Shall we be allowed to come near him and open our mouths in defence of the houses of prayer to the destroyer of the all-holy place? For clearly to houses less conspicuous and held in lower esteem no regard would be paid by one who insults that most notable and illustrious shrine whose beams like the sun's reach every whither, beheld with awe both by east and west' (*Leg. Gaj.* 191; see also *ibid.* 292, etc.).

Philo and Alexandria. Philo is frequently referred to as Philo of Alexandria. He is known to us, therefore, by a Greek, and not a Jewish, name and by reference to a city founded by Alexander the Great (a city which by its very name constituted a memorial to the great Emperor and a reminder of him), who introduced into it a colony of Jews. Philo was almost certainly born in Alexandria. He refers to it, with evident pride, as 'our Alexandria' (*Leg. Gaj.* 150). Of Caligula Philo wrote (*Leg. Gaj.* 338): 'he was possessed by an extraordinary and passionate love for Alexandria'. An intense affection for Alexandria, if not for all Alexandrians, can also be detected in Philo's writings.

Alexandria has been called the 'metropolis' of Egypt. It was a city which, for intellectual culture, had outstripped Athens in the period in which Philo lived. Within the Roman Empire Alexandria was second only to Rome itself, and that only in political terms. It possessed what we would call a university, the museum and a vast library of over 400,000 volumes. As a centre of Judaism it had an enormous importance – Philo estimated (perhaps overestimated) its Jewish population as more than a million, outnumbering that of Judaea. He speaks of 'the many myriads of the Alexandrian Jews' (*Leg. Gaj.* 350). He mentions its many synagogues, in which every Sabbath the Pentateuch was read from the Greek version or translation known to us as the Septuagint (LXX) and made in the city (Philo gives an interesting account of the making of the Septuagint in *Vit. Mos.* II.26–44).

The Jewish citizens of Alexandria had achieved a high degree of prosperity. The personal circumstances of Philo's family can alone have made it possible for him to become the highly educated person he undoubtedly was. Philo describes the occupations of some of the Jews living in Alexandria. He refers to 'tradespeople', including 'husbandman, shipman, merchant, artisan' (*Flacc.* 57).

It is interesting to note that, while no written work has come down to us from the Jewish community in Rome, Philo's works, themselves numerous, represent only a part of the literary activity and output of Alexandria. Philo can speak of Egypt (admittedly in his account of the persecution of the Alexandrian Jews by Flaccus) and the Egyptians as 'the greatest of his possessions' (*Flacc.* 158), and of Alexandria as 'that great city or multitude of cities' (*ibid.* 163).

The Jews of Alexandria seem to have been the most thoroughly hellenised of the Diaspora. In fact, it has been suggested that in the period in which Philo lived Alexandria *was* hellenism. If that is true, as it probably is, then Philo lived within a Jewish community exposed intimately to the most complete expression of hellenistic culture existing in his day.

Philo the statesman. Philo became involved in political life on more than one occasion. He looks back, in the opening paragraphs of the third book of the *De Specialibus Legibus*, to the time when he had 'leisure for philosophy and for the contemplation of the universe and its contents' (*Spec. Leg.* III.1). But, he adds regretfully, he was 'plunged . . . in the ocean of civil cares' (*ibid.* 3). His most painful involvement in the political, or civil, affairs of the Jews in Alexandria came in AD 38 and in the years immediately afterwards. After Egypt became part of the Roman Empire, relationships between Jews, Greeks and Egyptians deteriorated to the point of overt hostility, and with the accession of Caligula in AD 37 anti-Jewish hostility – what we now mistakenly call anti-*Semitism* – developed into the first imperial pogrom, or a pogrom conducted in the name of Rome. The Emperor wished to be regarded as a god, and so regarded himself, commanding that images of himself as a god should be erected in all religious meeting-places in the Empire, including Alexandria. The Jews in Judaea, helped by an understanding governor (Petronius, the legate of Syria), escaped from the – to them – impossible demand to place an image of the Emperor, a statue in fact, in their holy Temple. But in Alexandria, according to Philo, Flaccus, the Roman prefect, was persuaded by the non-Jewish residents of the city to support their anti-Jewish feelings by representing the Jewish opposition to the placing of the emperor's image in their synagogue as a sign of political disloyalty to the Emperor. Flaccus did not, unfortunately for the Jews in Alexandria, handle the matter with the same good-will and understanding shown by Petronius in Judaea towards the Jews there. To secure their rights and to convince Caligula that opposition to images did not involve any political disloyalty, the Jews sent a deputation to Rome headed by Philo. Philo has written two works about the situation of the Jewish community in Alexandria at the time Flaccus was governor there and about the deputation's visit to Rome and its meeting with the Emperor: his *In Flaccum* and his *Legatio ad Gaium*.

In the *In Flaccum* Philo accuses Flaccus of proclaiming that the Jews in Alexandria were 'foreigners and exiles': that is, that they were deprived of civil rights. On the issue of the erection of statues and images of emperors in synagogues and the Temple the Jews had to wait until after the death of Caligula and the accession of Claudius. Only then was this particular requirement rescinded.

The immediate reaction to the policy of Caligula and the actions of Flaccus was twofold. There was a diplomatic response: this took the form of the deputation to Rome, a five-man team of senior Jews with the intellectual Philo as its leader, whose aim was to secure, if possible, the restoration of the *status quo ante*. Philo's *Legatio ad Gaium* contains many interesting statements about that situation as it involved and affected the inhabitants of the Roman Empire. The Empire Caligula inherited from Tiberius is described as 'the sovereignty of the whole earth and sea, not gained by faction but established by law, with all parts, east, west, south, north, harmoniously adjusted, the Greek in full agreement with the barbarian, the civil with the military, to enjoy and participate in peace' (*Leg. Gaj.* 8). The Empire, Philo says, extended over the greater part of the inhabited world, 'the world, that is, which is bounded by the two rivers, the Euphrates and the Rhine, the one dissevering us from the Germans and all the more brutish nations, the Euphrates from the Parthians and from the Sarmatians and Scythians, races which are no less savage than the Germans' (*ibid.* 10), the 'us' indicating that Philo and his fellow Jews in Alexandria regarded themselves as citizens or subjects of the Empire of Rome. They were certainly not part of the world occupied by 'brutish nations' or savages. Within this great Empire, which extended 'from the rising to the setting sun both within the ocean and beyond it', if we are to judge from Philo's comments, the Jews shared in a society based on a rule of law, which extended freedom to its citizens, and in particular freedom to worship in their own way, so long as loyalty was given to the Empire and the Emperor. Philo's case to Caligula seems to have been based, to judge from his account in the *Legatio ad Gaium*, on the record of Rome in offering, above all, equality to all Roman citizens and subjects: 'In these days the rich had no precedence over the poor, nor the distinguished over the obscure, creditors were not above debtors, nor masters above slaves, the times giving equality before the law' (*ibid.* 13). People, until things began to go wrong under Caligula, enjoyed 'freedom from grief and fear' (*ibid.*). But, as Philo puts it elsewhere: 'Slavery to the free is a thing most intolerable. To avoid it sensible people are eager and ready to die and gladly run any risk in contending with those who menace them with enslavement. But an irresistible enemy is also something intolerable, and when both despotic power and hostility are combined in the same person, who can resist one to whom his authority has given the power to act unjustly and his implacable enmity the disposition to show no consideration?' (*Praem. Poen.* 137). The description there of the hostile despot sounds very like Philo's delineation of Caligula, but when the confrontation came in AD 38 the Jews did resist. They did so first, however, by an appeal to the Empire's past record of good government and toleration. Philo says at one point, 'the best and greatest art is the art of government which causes the good deep soil in lowlands and highlands to be tilled, and all the seas to be safely navigated by merchant ships laden with cargoes to effect the exchange of goods which the countries in desire for fellowship render to each other, receiving those which they lack and sending in return those of which they carry a surplus' (*Leg. Gaj.* 47). But Rome had done more than that. The Roman Empire, according to Philo – and especially the Roman Empire in what he regards as the golden age of Augustus (an emperor whom Philo describes as one 'who in all the virtues transcended human nature' and who was justly entitled to 'the veneration which was received also by those who followed him' (*ibid.* 143)) – had its praiseworthy aspect. In a later passage, Augustus is called by Philo the 'best of the emperors' (*ibid.* 309). In his eulogy of Augustus Philo describes him as 'the Caesar . . . who healed the pestilences common to Greeks and barbarians, pestilences which, descending from the south and the east, coursed to the west and north, sowing the seeds of calamity over the places and waters which lay between' (*ibid.* 145). Then follows a lengthy description of the many benefits bestowed upon the citizens and subjects of the Empire by Augustus. Among the achievements of the great Emperor was his reclamation of 'every state to liberty' (*ibid.* 147) and his enlargement of 'Hellas' by 'many a new Hellas' and his hellenisation of 'the outside world in its most important regions' (*ibid.*). Augustus was annoyed, according to Philo, if anyone addressed him as a god – unlike Caligula, who expected it. Augustus also approved of the Jews, 'who he knew full well regarded all such things with horror' (*ibid.* 154). He knew from his experience of the Jewish community 'on the other side of the Tiber' in Rome that the Jews met in 'houses of prayer' each Sabbath and took collections to send to Jerusalem to pay for sacrifices in the Temple. But this did not make him deprive the Jews of their citizenship or take any violent measures against them or their synagogues. In fact, Philo says, 'so religiously did he respect our interests' that he 'adorned our Temple through the costliness of his dedications' and ordered sacrifices to be offered there at his own expense (*ibid.* 155–7).

However, under Caligula things took a sudden turn for the worse. He was a man 'beside himself with vanity, not only saying but thinking that he was God' (*ibid.* 162). The Egyptians, who, according to Philo, used the title of God to apply to 'the indigenous ibises and venomous snakes and many other ferocious wild beasts' (*ibid.* 163), did not hesitate to use it of the Emperor, who 'supposed that he really was regarded by the Alexandrians as a god, since they incessantly used plainly and without any indirection terms which other people commonly employ when speaking of God' (*ibid.* 164). Because of this, Caligula was persuaded that the attack on the Jewish synagogue by the Alexandrians, made out of hostility towards the Jews, was really prompted by a sincere regard for him as Emperor and a genuine reaction against what the Alexandrians regarded as Jewish irreverence towards him. Philo then describes the part played in stirring up hatred towards the Alexandrian Jews by a man called Helicon (*ibid.* 166ff.), and refers to a 'supplication' prepared by the Jews and sent to the Emperor by the hand of King Herod Agrippa I (grandson of Herod the Great, appointed ruler of Judaea in AD 41) and to an 'epitome' of it which the Jews decided to present to the Emperor.

While Philo and the other four members of the deputation were in Rome, news came to them of the imperial order for a 'colossal statue to be set up within the inner sanctuary' (*ibid.* 188). This was to be dedicated to Caligula 'under the name of Zeus'. This news naturally caused great consternation among the members of the deputation, who 'stood there speechless and powerless in a state of collapse with our hearts turned to water' (*ibid.* 189). The attitude of the Jews in the face of the threat to the sanctity of their holy Temple is shown by the words Philo attributes to the deputation: 'Well so be it, we will die and be no more, for the truly glorious death, met in defence of laws, might be called life' (*ibid.* 192). In other words, Roman rule could be endured, and indeed enjoyed, for the many benefits it conferred, so long as it did not involve any interference with the Jews' religious beliefs and practices and, in particular, any desecration of their synagogues or the Temple by images of 'divine' emperors. Philo's words reveal another aspect of Jewish belief which he obviously shared – confidence that God would not abandon his Chosen People: 'But let our souls retain indestructible the hope in God our Saviour, who has often saved the nation when in helpless straits' (*ibid.* 196). Philo, and the Jewish community of Alexandria, were convinced that God would come to the aid of his People and protect them from the hostility of the Egyptians and the blasphemous intentions of Caligula.

The root of the problem, as far as Caligula was concerned, was, in words attributed by Philo to the bringers of the tragic news: 'He wishes to be thought a god and has supposed that the only dissentients will be the Jews, on whom he can inflict no greater injury than the ruin of the sanctity of their Temple' (*ibid.* 198). Philo makes it clear that 'the Jews would willingly endure to die, not once but a thousand times, if it were possible, rather than allow any of the prohibited actions to be committed' (*ibid.* 209), because, while 'all men guard their own customs', this is 'especially true of the Jewish nation' (*ibid.* 210). Such an attitude springs from the belief that 'the laws are oracles vouchsafed by God, and, having been trained in this doctrine from their earliest years, they [the Jews] carry the likenesses of the commandments enshrined in their souls' (*ibid.* 210). 'Still more abounding and peculiar', Philo goes on, 'is the zeal of them all for the Temple' (*ibid.* 212), as is shown by the fact, he explains, that the death penalty 'without appeal' is passed on Gentiles who 'penetrate into its inner confines'. But at many points in the *Legatio ad Gaium* – and especially in the speech placed on the lips of the Jewish elders in Judaea to Petronius, the Roman governor of Syria – we see Philo expressing the view, held by him and no doubt by many Jews, both in the Dispersion and in Palestine, that the Jews are ready to be peaceful and law-abiding subjects of the Roman Empire. All that they ask for is that their Temple should be kept 'as we received it from our grandparents and ancestors' (*ibid.* 232). The elders, in the speech attributed to them by Philo, describe their 'twofold motive: respectful fear of the Emperor and loyalty to the consecrated laws' (*ibid.* 236). So great is their dread of the desecration of the Temple that any seeing the statue being carried in procession to the Temple would, they say, be 'transformed to stone', like those who looked on 'the Gorgon's head' (*ibid.* 237–8). The final request put to Petronius was for the right to send a deputation to the Emperor asking for at least 'our right to be no worse treated than all the nations, even those in the uttermost regions, who have had their ancestral institutions maintained' (*ibid.* 240).

The heart of Philo's own understanding of the matter is a

conviction that historical precedent, especially in the reign of Augustus, supports a plea for Roman non-interference in Jewish religious beliefs and practices.

According to Philo, Petronius, impressed by the case put to him by the Judaean elders and not unsympathetic to it, helped their cause by delaying the construction of the statue, a case of God's whispering to him, as a good man, 'good decisions' (*ibid.* 245), though he did not grant the Judaeans their request for an embassy. Then, according to Philo, Petronius wrote to Caligula explaining and excusing the delay.

When Agrippa later visited Caligula, he was told that the Jews were alone among 'every race of men' in refusing to acknowledge the divinity of the Emperor, a refusal which meant that they were 'courting even death' (*ibid.* 265). But Agrippa voices, in his speech to Caligula, the Jewish viewpoint: 'This Temple, my lord Gaius', he says, 'has never from the first admitted any figure wrought by men's hands, because it is the sanctuary of the true God' (*ibid.* 290). Then follows a description of the nature of images and idols, paralleled in other works of Philo, in which Agrippa says: 'the works of painters and modellers are representations of gods perceived by sense, but to paint or mould a likeness of the invisible was held by our ancestors to be against their religion' (*ibid.*). The strength of Jewish feeling on the subject – a feeling which there is no reason to doubt was shared by Philo himself – is expressed in a later section of Agrippa's speech, when he says: 'Thus no one, Greek or non-Greek, no satrap, no king, no mortal enemy, no faction, no war, no storming or sacking of the city, nor any existing thing, ever brought about so great a violation of the Temple as the setting-up in it of an image or statue or any hand-wrought object for worship' (*ibid.* 292).

Philo describes how the Emperor Tiberius ordered Pilate to remove the shields that had been dedicated to him 'in the holy city', something which the Jews regarded as an 'infringement of their traditions' which violated 'the customs which throughout all the preceding ages had been safeguarded without disturbance by kings and by emperors' (*ibid.* 299ff.), and when they had been removed, Philo notes, 'both objects were safeguarded: the honour paid to the emperor and the policy observed from of old in dealing with the city' (*ibid.* 305). Here again we meet an expression of the view that Jews, even in Judaea, could remain loyal subjects of the Emperor and true to their ancestral beliefs and practices so long as their pure monotheism was not compromised by the placing of images and statues, for which a divine status was claimed, in their places of worship (on Philo's understanding of the Jewish doctrine of God, see below, pp. 28–102). We can, therefore, imagine the horror experienced by Philo and his fellow Jews when the object to be placed in the Temple was 'a colossal statue' of Caligula as Zeus, which was to be placed 'in the inmost part of the Temple in the special sanctuary itself, into which the Grand Priest (*ho megas hiereus*) enters once a year only' (*ibid.* 306).

Philo tells us – though it is difficult to say how true this is – that the great Augustus, when told about the Jewish Temple's having 'no work of man's hands, a visible effigy of an invisible being', marvelled and paid it honour. Naturally this enlightened attitude on the part of Augustus was attributed by Philo to the fact that Augustus had 'not taken a mere sip of philosophy but had feasted on it liberally': that is, like Petronius (*ibid.* 310). Philo regarded Augustus, at least in the idealised conception of him in his own mind, as an adherent of Judaism, who 'gave orders for a continuation of whole burnt offerings every day to the Most High God' (*ibid.* 317). Philo calls Augustus 'this philosopher second to none' and says that he 'reasoned in his mind that within the precincts of earth there must needs be a special place assigned as sacred to the invisible God which would contain no visible image, a place to give us participation in good hopes and enjoyment of perfect blessings' (*ibid.* 318). Philo holds up Augustus to Caligula as 'an instructor in piety' (*ibid.* 319). For such an instructor Julia Augusta also had a temple built with no image in it, because, although women, according to Philo, comprehend only what their senses perceive, she gained such clarity of vision that her mind 'apprehended the things of mind better than the things of sense and held the latter to be shadows of the former' (*ibid.* 320). It seems that for Philo, alongside traditional, orthodox Judaism, there was a philosophical outlook on life, involving the recognition of the purely spiritual nature of the Transcendent, in which one day, Philo believed, all mankind would share. In *that* Judaism the idealised Augustus, Julia Augusta and Petronius – among, no doubt, many others – had already participated.

In Agrippa's letter, as recorded by Philo, reference is made yet again to the concern felt by Jews 'that the ancestral institutions be not disturbed' (*ibid.* 327). Agrippa speaks of his relationship to Rome as freedom from a bondage but asks that the physical bondage which has been removed should not be replaced by an even worse kind, spiritual bondage, the violation of Judaea and its Temple. Agrippa explains to Caligula that 'unless my homeland is guarded unscathed from every kind of mischief and the Temple is untouched' he cannot remain Caesar's friend without being a traitor to his people (*ibid.* 328). How serious the situation was felt to be for the Jews under Caligula is indicated by what Philo says about Agrippa's feelings after he had sent his letter to the Emperor. He appreciated that 'the danger which had fallen upon him was no trifle but one which involved the expulsion, enslavement and wholesale spoliation of the Jews who dwelt not only in the Holy Land but everywhere through the habitable world' (*ibid.* 330). The Roman view of the Jewish attitude, as Caligula exemplified it, is revealed in Philo's explanation of the Emperor's reaction to Agrippa's letter. He accused Agrippa of 'over-complaisance to his compatriots, who stood alone among mankind in their recalcitrance and refusal to accept his deification' (*ibid.* 332).

Philo describes Caligula's mind as occupied by 'the idea of godship' and speaks of his notion of 'the worship due to him' (*ibid.* 338). He then tells how the 'inconstancy' of Caligula's conduct particularly affected 'the Jewish race' and how he filled the Jewish synagogues, first in Alexandria and then elsewhere, 'with images and statues of himself in bodily form' (*ibid.* 346). Philo says that he wished to take over the Temple in Jerusalem and convert it into 'a temple of his own to bear the name of Gaius, "the new Zeus made manifest"' (*ibid.*; Leaney 1984: 112, 137–40). Philo's own reaction to this intention on the part of Caligula is revealed by his next words: 'What is this that you say? Do you, a mere man, seek to annex also ether and heaven, not satisfied with the sum of so many mainlands, islands, nations, regions, over which you assumed sovereignty? And do you deem God worthy of nothing in our world here below, no country, no city, but even this tiny area hallowed for him and sanctified by oracles and divine messages you propose to take away, so that in the circumference of this great earth no trace or reminder should be left of the reverence and honour due to the truly existing veritable God?' (*ibid.* 347).

Philo then proceeds to give an account of the meeting of the deputation with the Emperor (*ibid.* 349ff.). (An account is also given in Josephus, *Ant.* XVIII.8.1; see Bartlett 1985: 187.) Philo characterises the case to be heard as 'of the greatest importance', and says of it that 'nothing has been heard of it for four centuries'. He makes it clear, however, that, despite the seriousness of the issue, Caligula had no intention of dealing with it fairly, but revealed himself as a 'ruthless tyrant' (*Leg. Gaj.* 350). The 'tragedy which was aimed against our whole nation was to be performed with us who were present as the immediate victims' (*ibid.* 351). At first, when the delegation actually met Caligula, it seemed, according to Philo, as if he might act in a mild and kindly way, but the greeting given by the Jews was met with the sarcastic question 'Are you the god-haters who do not believe me to be a god, a god acknowledged among all the other nations but not to be named by you?' (*ibid.* 353). The 'exceptional honours' which Caligula desired, and which Philo admits were perhaps deserved, if by anyone, by Augustus (*ibid.* 149), could certainly not be paid to Caligula. But it is clear that, even in the case of Caligula, the Jewish attitude of god-hatred – that is, their reverence for the one true God, which allowed them to worship no man as a god – did not involve hatred of the Emperor as such; nor did the extremely high regard in which Augustus was held involve any infringement of their monotheism or any breach with their refusal to worship idols or men.

Caligula's address to the Jewish deputation Philo describes as 'a sin even to listen to' (*ibid.* 353). It delighted, however, the supporters of the Emperor who were opposed to the Jewish viewpoint (*ibid.* 354). One of these, a man called Isidorus, seeing that Caligula 'was delighted at being addressed as of more than human nature' (*ibid.* 355), then accused the Jews of failing to offer sacrifices on behalf of the Emperor, and made it clear that he included all Jews within his accusation. To this the members of the deputation responded with an indignant denial. It is interesting to note that Isidorus' 'My Lord', in his address to Caligula, is *despota*, that of the deputation *kurie Gaie*. Caligula conceded that the Jews had in fact, as they asserted, offered many sacrifices for him. He pointed out, however, that the Jewish sacrifices were offered 'to another'. The blunt words 'you have not sacrificed to me' make clear what the crime of the Jews was, as Philo understood the Emperor's mind. Caligula really did regard himself as in some sense divine. The Jewish reaction to Caligula's words was, not surprisingly, one of 'profound terror' (*ibid.* 357). Caligula's contempt for his Jewish visitors was shown by the fact that, while they were attempting to plead their case before him, he engaged in a survey of some new premises he was having constructed for himself. Philo indicates the other major difficulty the Jews encountered: 'when the person on trial is accused by a judge and that one of such eminence, he must needs hold his peace' (*ibid.* 360). The silence maintained by the Jews, Philo explains, was necessary also because 'our customs and laws muzzled the tongue and closed and stitched up the mouth' (*ibid.*). Caligula then proceeded to mock the Jews for their refusal to eat pork, an abstention which the delegation asserted as due again to their 'different customs' (*ibid.* 362). Then, after further mocking, Caligula asked to hear about the Jews' claim on the subject of 'citizenship'. It is interesting that at this point in Philo's account of the interview with Caligula no direct mention is made of the question of the violation of the Alexandrian synagogues. Presumably what Philo and his colleagues started to say before Caligula interrupted them involved the claim 'we are Alexandrians' (*ibid.* 194), and that they were, therefore, entitled to the rights and freedoms accorded to other, non-Jewish Alexandrians, and in particular the right to live without any interference in their religious beliefs and practices. But Caligula persisted in refusing to hear them out, and it was a 'mangled and disjointed' case that the delegation was able to put to the Emperor. Finally, however, the Emperor relented and conceded that the Jews seemed 'to be people unfortunate rather than wicked . . . in refusing to believe that I have got the nature of a god' (*ibid.* 366–7). He then dismissed the delegation. His final words to them, however, indicate that more was at stake than the issue of their citizenship. The claim the Emperor made to possess the divine nature (*phusis*) indicates that the question of placing his image in Jewish synagogues – images of a divine being in a place where God and the gods (as Caligula conceived them) were worshipped – was still an issue with which the delegation was concerned.

Some words Philo uses at this point in his account of the interview granted by Caligula to the Jewish delegation remind us of the Greek title of the *Legatio ad Gaium* and its underlying subject. What we know as the *Legatio ad Gaium* is known in the majority of manuscripts as the *Peri aretōn* (*Concerning the Virtues*). The virtues Philo has in mind are those of God, a God who takes care of his People, just as he did when he took compassion on the delegation by turning Caligula's spirit to mercy (*pros eleon*), and relaxing him into a 'softer mood' (*ibid.* 367). This was God's response, Philo tells us, to the delegation's supplication to 'the true God that he should restrain the wrath of the pretender to that name'. Right at the beginning of the *Legatio ad Gaium* Philo notes that 'some have come to disbelieve that the Deity takes thought for men, and particularly for the suppliants' race which the Father and King of the Universe and the Source of all things has taken for his portion' (*ibid.* 3). This portion of mankind is, of course, the Jewish nation, Israel. Although, after the opening paragraphs, Philo is occupied with a narrative of events in Alexandria and in Rome, it is a major concern of his to show that, despite their suffering of misfortunes, God in the end punishes the perpetrators of evils, especially of those evils which afflict his People. Thus, after the farcical interview between Caligula and the Alexandrian Jewish delegation, the mocking of the Jews, the blasphemies against God's name and, especially, the affront to Judaism implicit in Caligula's 'desire of the deification to which he supposed the Jews alone did not assent and could not pledge themselves to subscribe' (*ibid.* 368), there was a palinode, a counter-story or reversal-story, to tell, though unfortunately no copy of this has come down to us among Philo's works (see *ibid.* 373). It may well have told of Caligula's death as a punishment from God, perhaps in a way similar to the narrative of Flaccus' death in the *In Flaccum*, and of the reversal of Caligula's policy by Claudius (see the two edicts of Claudius recorded in Josephus, *Ant.* XIX.5).

Philo ends the *Legatio ad Gaium* by saying that the delegation would have accepted martyrdom if it would have helped towards a 'restoration of our institutions' (*Leg. Gaj.* 369). Indeed, death for such a cause would have been chosen gladly 'as being immortality'. Philo expresses regret that 'the fate of all the Jews everywhere should rest precariously on us five envoys' (*ibid.* 370), for he appreciated that whatever decision the Emperor made regarding Alexandria would affect every Jewish community in the Roman Empire: 'What other city will keep tranquil or refrain from attacking its fellow inhabitants, what house of prayer will be left unscathed, what kind of civic rights will not be upset for those whose lot is cast under the ancient institutions of the Jews?' (*ibid.* 371). All this reminds us that the issues which exercised the minds of the delegation and which prompted their trip to Rome were two: the violation of Jewish synagogues, and the violation of civic rights hitherto enjoyed by Jews under Roman rule. The danger facing Judaism that Philo and his four colleagues were seeking to avert was the danger of the loss of 'their peculiar laws' and 'the rights which they enjoy in common in every city' (*ibid.* 371). Others who had been giving some kind of support to the delegation in the end gave up and left in fear, 'knowing full well the longing which he [Caligula] cherished for being acknowledged as a god' (*ibid.* 372); and even Philo and his fellow delegates were 'dragged down and submerged in the depths' because of 'the enmity which Gaius had for the whole nation of the Jews' (*ibid.* 372–3).

A strikingly different account of the events of Caligula's reign from that implied by the *Legatio ad Gaium*, and in particular of the experiences of the Jewish community in Alexandria when Flaccus was the prefect of Alexandria and Egypt, is given in the *In Flaccum*. (See below, pp. 7 and 17. See also Josephus, *Apion*, in Bartlett 1985: 182–8.)

Philo and the future. Philo's ideas, his hopes and beliefs, about the future are of great interest and importance both in relation to the question of the depth and integrity of his Jewishness – it has been suggested that there is no eschatology in the Old Testament sense in his writings – and in relation to the subject of his role as an apologist for Judaism.

The main work of his to which the reader must go for an explanation of his eschatological beliefs is the *De Praemiis et Poenis*, which has been said to be 'the treatise in which his eschatology is most fully worked out'. But there are statements in other treatises, especially in the two volumes of his *De Vita Mosis*, which should not be overlooked.

The *De Praemiis*, after some preliminary remarks on the structure of the oracles delivered through Moses, proceeds to describe the rewards for obedience to the Law and the punishments for disobedience. Philo then describes how God has bestowed many honours on mankind, among them 'hope, the fountain-head of the lives which we lead' (*Praem. Poen.* 11). Various kinds of worldly benefits are listed and condemned, the only kind of hope which is approved being hope 'in God', since it is God who alone brings man into existence and is 'the sole power which can keep him free from harm and destruction' (*ibid.* 13). A passage in the *De Agricultura* makes it clear that Philo believed that 'land and water and air and fire, and all plants and animals which are in these, whether mortal or divine, yea and the sky, and the circuits of sun and moon, and the revolutions and rhythmic movements of the other heavenly bodies, are like some flock under the hand of God its King and Shepherd', but also that 'this hallowed flock he leads in accordance with right and law, setting over it his true Word and Firstborn Son, who shall take upon him its government like some viceroy of a great king' (*Agric.* 51). The hope of the Jew, for Philo, is grounded in his belief in the divine government of the universe and, in particular, in belief in the direction of the universe by the Logos (on Philo's Logos doctrine, see below, pp. 103–43.).

Philo, to return to the *De Praemiis*, using Enoch as his Old Testament model, affirms that 'no one should be thought a man at all who does not set his hope on God' (*Praem. Poen.* 14). Now, hope is a virtue which implies belief in a time still to be; it is an eschatologically orientated virtue. Alongside hope, in the first triad or trinity of virtues described by Philo, is 'repentance', the rewards of which are 'a new home and a life of solitude' (*ibid.* 16). The third virtue, 'justice', receives the reward of 'salvation amid the general destruction' and a role in the 'second creation' (*ibid.* 22), statements at least couched in the language of eschatology. It might be thought, however, when Philo goes on to say 'Belief in God, life-long joy, the perpetual vision of the Existent – what can anyone conceive more profitable or more august than these?' (*ibid.* 27), that he is no longer thinking in traditional, Old Testament, Jewish terms of the future; it is correct, at this point, to regard his thought as of a kind within which eschatology has been displaced by a form of intellectual mysticism owing more to Hellenism than to Judaism. But, after describing the second, higher, trinity of virtues represented by Abraham, Isaac and Jacob, Philo describes the rewards given to the houses of Abraham and Isaac, and in particular the privilege granted to Jacob's children of founding the nation of Israel, which became in time 'a great multitude' (*ibid.* 66). He next describes the punishment meted out to Cain and the Levites under Korah, and then turns to the subject of the rewards granted to those who keep the Commandments. First, there is victory over enemies (*ibid.* 79). Philo interprets this allegorically to mean the happiness which accompanies the harmony of mouth and heart and hand, but then, quite suddenly, extends his thought to embrace the concept of a harmony which includes, as well as the internal harmony of man's self, a harmony between man and a tamed wild animal kingdom.

Though Philo does not at this point quote any particular Old

Testament passage, he probably had in mind Isa. 11: 6–9 (although some have doubted if Philo 'appealed' to Isaiah) and also perhaps Job 5: 23 and Hos. 2: 18. It is possible that a passage in the Sibylline Oracles (III.788; see also Bartlett 1985: 35ff.) also influenced him. He looks forward to the time when the ferocity of the wild animals will disappear and they will respect man and become docile and affectionate domestic pets. Even 'scorpions and serpents and the other reptiles will have no use for their venom'. Man will be able to move, even among crocodiles, hippopotami and the 'formidable animals' of the sea, 'sacrosanct and inviolate' (*ibid.* 90). That will be God's reward to the virtuous, the goal to which, employing his Logos as its guide, he will bring his created world.

Philo's vision of the End, then, includes the thoroughly biblical idea of the ending of the 'primary war' through the change which will make the wild beasts 'tame and amenable' (*ibid.* 91). The end of the 'primary war' will be followed, Philo suggests, by the ending of the war of man against man, for men will be shamed by the animals' abandonment of savagery into an abandonment of their own war-like and violent passions. It is interesting to note that Philo sees this state of affairs as one in which man's essential nature – 'gentle and kindly' – will be displayed. Drawing upon the words of Lev. 26: 6, which are quoted almost verbatim, Philo states that war 'will dissolve' (*ibid.* 92–3). Even if there are those who persist in bellicosity, they will be defeated by the power of virtue, which is 'majestic and august and can unaided and silently allay the onsets of evils, however great' (*ibid.*). Philo, in this section of the *De Praemiis*, quotes the words of Num. 24: 7 (LXX): 'there shall come forth a man'; this 'man' will 'subdue great and populous nations'. But some of those who persist in war will be overcome, not by a human leader, but by 'swarms of wasps'. So, for Philo, peace will be established among the nations of the earth.

In addition to peace, a second blessing, wealth and prosperity, will be bestowed on mankind by God. This will be both material and spiritual. To justify his description of this future bliss Philo refers to a number of passages in Leviticus and Deuteronomy (e.g., Lev. 26: 3, 4; Deut. 11: 13, 14; 28: 12). The harvests will be so great, he says, that sometimes no one will trouble to gather in the crops but will leave them 'unhusbanded and unhoarded' for all who wish to use them. Of course, for Philo it is the case that 'those who possess stored up in heaven the true wealth whose adornment is wisdom and godliness have also wealth of earthly riches in abundance' (*Praem. Poen.* 103–4). The Jewish people will be so rich, in those last days, that they will have no need to borrow money from moneylenders, but will in fact lend to whole nations. The prosperity that God will confer will be crowned by the gift of fertility: 'no man shall be childless and no woman barren, but all the true servants of God will fulfil the law of nature for the procreation of children'. Each family 'will be a plenitude with a long list of kinsfolk'. In addition, no one who obeys the divine Law will die an early death or be denied any stage of human life assigned by God to the human race (cf. Isa. 65: 20). Even at the end, when he reaches the last stage, man will be 'the neighbour of death or rather immortality' and will pass from 'that truly goodly old age to leave a great house of goodly children to fill his place' (*Praem. Poen.* 108–10). Here 'immortality' is understood, in Jewish terms, as the possession of a plentitude of offspring. Other blessings too, which will be God's reward for the virtuous, are described – life with no time or room in it for sin, the good life made easy by God, life delivered 'by the mercy of its Saviour' from evil, and also freedom from bodily infirmity or disease (except when it is sent as a reminder of mortality or as a corrective), together with complete efficiency and perfection of every part of the body (so that 'a mind purged clean of every spot' will dwell within a healthy body). Freed from bodily ailments and 'troublesome sensations', the mind of the virtuous man will drink deep 'of the strong wine of God's beneficent power' and feast on 'holy thoughts and doctrines'. In this state 'the wise man's mind is a palace and house of God'. Such a mind possesses personally 'the God who is the God of all; this again is the chosen people' (*ibid.* 117–23), redeemed from slavery to vices and lusts. So Philo reaches the end of his catalogue of the rewards which God will one day bestow upon his People, 'good men, men who fulfil the laws by their deeds, which blessings will be accomplished by the gift of the bounteous God, who glorifies and rewards moral excellence because of its likeness to himself' (*ibid.* 126).

The second part of the *De Praemiis et Poenis* is headed *Peri arōn*, (On Curses), and describes the fate which will befall 'law-breakers and transgressors'. In this part Philo closely follows Leviticus and Deuteronomy, describing first famine caused by the destruction of crops or by the action of enemies. Earth will become sterile, seasons will not come and go as they should, there will be neither rain nor dew. Philo interprets Lev. 26: 19 and Deut. 28: 23 to mean that earth and heaven will be turned into brass and iron and fail to perform their proper functions. He also sees in the mention of brass and iron a reference to the weapons of war and the destruction of crops and food-supplies caused by war. Alluding to Deut. 28: 24, he says that the earth will bear dust and that powder will descend from heaven, choking and destroying life. So people will starve and even be driven to cannibalism: 'The story of Thyestes will be child's play compared with the monstrous calamities which those times of terror will bring about' (*Praem. Poen.* 134). The wicked will, in those days, have 'a great longing for survival' in order to experience 'miseries measureless and ceaseless all beyond hope of cure'. They will set aside the escape suicide affords because 'their appetite for supreme misery' will never be satisfied (*ibid.* 135). Another of the punishments God will inflict on the disobedient will be enslavement, to the free 'a thing most intolerable' (*ibid.* 137). In this paragraph, when he refers to 'despotic power and hostility . . . combined in the same person', Philo may have had his people's experiences under Caligula in mind (see above, pp. 7–18). The punishment of those who disobey God's Laws will, then, include subjection to 'enemies who do not shrink from ruthlessness' (*ibid.* 138). Surrender to such despotic rule will be forced on them by famine and hunger, the lesser evil being accepted in order to escape from the larger ones. All that they have possessed, made or acquired, even wives, will be taken from them, and their attempted defence against hostility will prove totally ineffectual. No success will attend any of their endeavours, but they will all be thwarted by evil practices or actions which their abandonment of God's service consummates: 'For these are the wages of impiety and disobedience' (*ibid.* 142).

Bodily diseases of every kind will also, Philo explains (*ibid.* 143–51), form part of the terrible fate the disobedient will suffer. Punishment by the sword, from which there will be no escape, will be inflicted; everyone will take to flight in the attempt to survive, each taking thought only for himself, but even if human enemies are eluded, 'wild beasts more ferocious than men' will attack (an allusion perhaps to Lev. 26: 22). Cities will be demolished, and 'all the calamities, whether described in the Law or not' (an allusion to Deut. 28: 61), will occur, followed by total and utter despair created by terrors so appalling that 'in the morning they will pray for evening and in the evening for morning through the palpable miseries of their waking hours and the horrible dreams which appear to them in sleep' (*Praem. Poen.* 151) – all these punishments will be heaped upon the disobedient.

However, proselytes will prosper, teaching others that it is virtue that God welcomes, even when it 'springs from ignoble birth', and that 'He takes no account of the roots but accepts the full-grown stem, because it has been changed from a weed into fruitfulness' (*ibid.* 152). It has been suggested that Philo is alluding to the words of Deut. 28: 43, taking the word *proselutos* (LXX) to mean 'proselyte' in the technical sense. Philo promises, then, to the convert to Judaism – the man who accepts its moral law and its philosophical ideas and ideals – a 'place in heaven' (cf. Deut. 28: 43, 'higher and higher'), while the Jew who disobeys God's Law will be rejected by him and will be dragged and carried down 'into Tartarus itself' (*ibid.* 152). Philo, in other words, like Paul in some of his epistles (and other New Testament writers), distinguishes between the empirical Israel and the true Israel, the latter for Philo being understood not in terms of physical descent but in terms of obedience to the Law, and he thinks that converts to the Jewish way of life will be examples to all men to bring them to 'a wiser mind' and to the knowledge that God welcomes virtue whatever its ethnic roots. This passage on the essential nature of the true Judaism should be read in conjunction with what Philo says in the *De Vita Mosis* about the universality of Judaism before a full understanding can be arrived at of Philo's view of the future.

The *De Praemiis* then includes material, based on the Book of Leviticus (e.g., Lev. 26: 43; cf. 2 Chron. 36: 21), on the sabbaths which the earth which has been desolated will then enjoy. The desolations occurred because of the disobedience to the Law regarding the Sabbath/sabbaths (what Philo describes is a Jewish community that has forgotten its traditional obligations to God and man), but when they are complete a period of sabbath rest will follow, in which a renewal of the land and its people will take place. Though prompted by a recollection of the words of Isa. 54: 1, Philo is led into a description of how the soul full of vice is feeble and weak and 'near to death', but when it has become barren and infertile it is transformed into 'a pure virgin', and receives the 'divine seed' and brings forth new life, a life full of virtues (*ibid.* 159–60). So Philo holds out some hope for the disobedient Jews. The future, even for them, is not entirely black or empty. If they respond to the example of goodness to be seen in the lives of the proselytes and repent, if they accept the punishments they have suffered for turning away from the faith of their fathers to 'polytheistic creeds which finally lead to atheism' as 'a warning rather than as intending their perdition' and are prompted by them to repent sincerely, then they will find God to be a merciful Saviour who has bestowed on mankind as his chief gift 'kinship with his own Word' (*ibid.* 162–3). There is a similarity between Paul's argument in Rom. 9–11 about the creation of jealousy among the unbelieving Jews by the faith of the Christian Gentiles and the ultimate salvation of all Israel, and Philo's argument here that the disobedient Jews may be prompted to repent and return to their old faith by the sight of the virtuous life of the Gentiles converted to Judaism.

Disobedient, apostate Jews, even those dwelling 'in the uttermost parts of the earth', will be set free, and when this has happened those scattered in Greece and other parts of the world 'will arise and post from every side with one impulse to the one appointed place, guided in their pilgrimage by a vision divine and superhuman unseen by others but manifest to them as they pass from exile to their home' (*ibid.* 164–5). Some have seen in this statement an allusion to the Jewish expectation of a personal Messiah, but, even if an expectation of *the* Messiah (as distinct from men 'anointed' by God for particular tasks) existed in Judaism at this time (and was not rather the invention of Christianity), it is unlikely that Philo was thinking here in such terms. It is probable that he had in mind the kind of guidance given to the Israelites at the time of the Exodus, when a cloud followed the travellers to guide them, a cloud which was 'the vision of the Godhead, flashing rays of fire' (*Vit. Mos.* II.254). Philo certainly intended to indicate a belief that the returning pilgrims would receive divine guidance for their journey, but there is no hint of a belief in a personal Messiah who would go before, or behind, the People.

Philo then describes three intercessors (the word he uses is *paraklētos*: cf. John 14: 16, 26), which the returning nation would have to plead with for mercy from the Father – the kindness of God, the holiness of the founders of the race, and their own penitence. Their arrival would witness the restoration of ruined cities and the regeneration of barren land, the return of prosperity on so unprecedented a scale that there would be no room left for envy, the wealth available would be so great. 'Everything will suddenly be reversed', Philo affirms (*Praem. Poen.* 169). The curses endured by the Jews will be turned against their enemies, who have not understood that their temporary prosperity was meant only as 'a lesson to others' – that is, to the Jews who have lapsed from their traditional beliefs and practices. The sight of the good fortune of their enemies was intended by God to be 'a medicine to save them from perdition'. So the penitent *lapsi* will enter into a life of prosperity in their ancestral homeland, while the enemies of Israel will realise how wrong they have been in their estimate of the members of the Jewish nation, who in fact are men of 'high lineage retaining sparks of their noble birth', which, when fanned into a flame, shine forth gloriously (*ibid.* 170–1).

By the time the reader has reached the end of the *De Praemiis* he can understand why Philo's eschatology has been described as one which is limited to the vision of a brilliant future for Israel. But what Philo has to say about the future in the *De Vita Mosis* is an important qualification of this judgement, since some of his statements there seem to express a belief in a universalised Judaism in which non-Jewish nations can and will share. In the opening sections Philo distinguishes the Law of Moses from the laws and constitutions of other nations, noting, for example, that among other nations there is no case of one that honours the institutions of another, whereas 'not only the Jews but almost every other people, particularly those which take more account of virtue, have so far grown in holiness as to value and honour our laws' (*Vit. Mos.* II.17). He claims that Moses' Laws are 'firm, unshaken, immovable, stamped, as it were, with the seals of Nature herself', and he hopes that 'they will remain for all future ages as though immortal, so long as the sun and moon and the whole heaven and universe exist' (*ibid.* 14). Then, after an account of the translation of the Hebrew Scriptures into Greek on Pharos, Alexandria, Philo tells of the annual festival of thanksgiving for the LXX version of the Laws, which are 'shown to be desirable and precious in the eyes of all . . . and that too though our nation has not prospered for many a year', during which period it was only natural that 'their belongings' should be 'under a cloud' (*ibid.* 43). It is what Philo says next that is of special interest: 'But, if a fresh start should be made to brighter prospects, how great a change for the better might we expect to see' (*ibid.* 44). Then comes a remarkable expression of eschatological and universalistic faith: 'I believe', Philo affirms, 'that each nation would abandon its peculiar ways, and, throwing overboard its ancestral customs, turn to honouring our laws alone' (*ibid.* 44). Unlike the laws of other nations, the

Laws of Moses 'attract and win the attention of all, of barbarians, of Greeks, of dwellers on the mainland and islands, of nations of the east and the west, of Europe and Asia, of the whole inhabited world' (*ibid.* 20). But as the passages in the *De Praemiis* noticed earlier (see above, pp. 18–21) make clear, the nations will continue to exist, even when they honour the Law of Moses, as distinct entities with their own languages. See, especially, *Praem. Poen.* 95, where it is said that the 'man' spoken of in Num. 24: 7 (LXX) 'will subdue great and populous nations' (cf. the views expressed in the Sibylline Oracles III.751–8: see Bartlett, 1986: 35ff.). God, for Philo, is a God who 'brings to perfection the gifts which he loves to bestow' (*Agric.* 173), who is concerned with the ultimate destiny of 'whole regions and nations', who presides over the rise and fall of nations and who, after Greece has been succeeded by Macedonia, and nations such as the Persians, Parthians and Egyptians, cities such as Carthage and continents such as Europe and Asia have enjoyed prominence, will, according to a 'divine plan which most call fortune', bring the life of mankind to the goal of 'a single state, enjoying that best of constitutions, democracy' (*Deus Imm.* 173–6; cf. *Jos.* 135–6; *Agric.* 45). For Polybius the circlewise motion of time is eternal, but not for Philo. In the *Legatio ad Gaium*, as we saw above, Philo expresses great admiration for the Roman system of government (*Leg. Gaj.* 8–14), based on a rule of law which for Polybius was perfect; but it did not represent for him the perfect society of the End. That would be a divine commonwealth of nations, with different languages and separate ethnic identities, united in a single state governed by the Law of Moses. That ideal may at present be a dream, but in real life the ascendancy of certain nations is also only, as it were, a passing dream, to be succeeded by the realisation of the ideal of a perfect society.

Hope, therefore, was an important virtue for Philo. In *Abr.* 7 he states that 'the first step towards the possession of blessings is hope'. Later in the same work he states: 'Faith in God, then, is the one sure and infallible good, consolation of life, fulfilment of bright hopes, dearth of ills, harvest of goods, inacquaintance with misery, acquaintance with piety, heritage of happiness, all-round betterment of the soul which is firmly stayed on him who is the cause of all things and can do all things yet only wills the best' (*ibid.* 268). So, for Philo, authentic faith in God produces hope that 'the hidden future' seen by the prophet Moses (*Vit. Mos.* II.269), who before his death prophesied to each tribe 'the things which were to be and hereafter must come to pass', will in fact occur. Indeed, some of these things 'have already taken place', though 'others are still looked for, since confidence in the future is assured by fulfilment in the past' (*ibid.* 288).

1. Philo's doctrine of God

Faith in God. There is a doctrine of God in Philo's works, for he was a philosophical theologian (or a theological philosopher) of a very high order. But, although the Philonic doctrine of God is coherent and consistent, it is not presented in a systematic way, for Philo was not merely a theologian or a philosopher. He was an ardent believer, a devout worshipper, a charismatic exegete, and he wrote with the fervour of a mystic. What personal religion meant to him is shown by his words in *Quaest. in Ex.*II.51, 'For the beginning and end of happiness is to be able to see God.' Explaining, in *Leg. Gaj.* 4, that the name 'Israel' means 'he that sees God' (presumably *ish* (man), *ra* (see – from *ra'ah*), *el* (God)), he adds: 'to see him seems to me of all possessions, public or private, the most precious'. Philo can say, in *Quaest. in Gn.*IV.4: 'the limit of happiness is the presence of God, which completely fills the whole soul with his whole incorporeal and eternal light' and 'for the soul to be separated from the contemplation of the Existent One is the most complete of evils'. The definition of faith in *Abr.* 268 also gives a clear idea of what belief in God meant to Philo: 'Faith in God, then, is the one sure and infallible good, consolation of life, fulfilment of bright hopes, dearth of ills, harvest of goods, inacquaintance with misery, acquaintance with piety, heritage of happiness, all-round betterment of the soul which is firmly stayed on him who is the cause of all things and can do all things yet only wills the best.' Man, Philo believed, 'is the recipient of a privilege which gives him distinction beyond other living creatures, that, namely, of worshipping him that IS' (*Som.* I.35). In *Decal.* 108–10 Philo describes those who devote themselves wholly to the service of God and those who devote themselves wholly to the service of mankind, 'lovers of men' and 'lovers of God', as both coming 'but halfway in virtue'. Only those who 'win honour in both departments' achieve wholeness. Philo's doctrine of God, or rather the God in whom he believed, confronted him with urgent ethical imperatives. 'Lovers of God', if the God loved is himself a 'lover of men', cannot escape the obligation and duty to be 'lovers of men'.

Figuratively speaking, 'the pious and worthy life of virtuous man is the food of God' (*Quaest. in Gn.* IV.9). Without doubt, food for God, by a life of piety and virtue, is what Philo wanted to be.

God in the Scriptures. Philo's doctrine of God is unambiguously grounded in the Jewish Scriptures and, in particular, in the Pentateuch. It depends a great deal, therefore, upon his understanding of Moses and his interpretation of Moses' teaching. This is not surprising, since for Philo Moses 'the theologian was all-wise' (*Quaest. in Ex.* II.74; see below, pp. 54–9, on the place of Moses in Philo's doctrine of God). In *Spec. Leg.* I.32 Philo suggests that there are two main questions which the 'genuine philosopher' must consider: 'One is whether the Deity exists, a question necessitated by those who practise atheism, the worst form of wickedness, the other is what the deity is in essence.' As his guide in seeking answers to these two questions, Philo follows Moses, whom he describes as 'of all men the best suited to be the revealer of verities' (*Decal.* 18) and 'the explorer of nature which lies beyond our vision' (*Mut. Nom.* 7). Moses represented, to Philo, one who had both 'attained the very summit of philosophy' and 'been divinely instructed in the greater and most essential part of Nature's lore' (*Op. Mund.* 7).

Philo was very much concerned, in all that he wrote, to combat atheism ('the source of all iniquities' (*Decal.* 91) and 'the worst form of wickedness' (*Spec. Leg.* I.32)) and polytheism (whose proponents 'do not blush to transfer from earth to heaven mob-rule, that worst of evil polities' (*Op. Mund.* 171)), and to commend the particular brand of philosophical theism which he had developed. For Philo there were various kinds of atheists. There were those who entertained doubts about the eternal existence of God. Then there were 'the bolder sort' who audaciously declared that 'the Deity does not exist at all, but that it is a mere assertion of men, obscuring the truth with myth and fiction' (*Op. Mund.* 170). There were also whose who said that 'nothing exists beyond this world' and that it is 'uncreated' (*Som.* II.283). They, according to Philo, 'postulate in God a vast inactivity' (*Op. Mund.* 7) or go further and assert that the uncreated cosmos is 'without guardian, helmsman or protector' (*Som.* II.283). In *Migr. Abr.* 178–9 Philo refers to the 'Chaldaeans' and says of them: 'These men imagined that this visible universe was the only thing in existence, either being itself God or containing God in itself as the soul of the whole.' Elsewhere, in *Abr.* 69, Philo says that the Chaldaeans 'glorified visible existence, leaving out of consideration the intelligible and invisible' and that 'they concluded that the world itself was God, thus profanely likening the created to the Creator'. It has been suggested, no doubt correctly, that when Philo says that Abraham (celebrated in Judaism as the hero who broke away from polytheism for a monotheistic faith) migrated from materialistic pantheism to theism he is attacking not the Chaldaeans but rather the Stoic materialistic pantheists of his own day. The attack on the 'Chaldaeans' is for Philo an important element in his defence of Jewish monotheism against the threats to it contained in philosophies contemporary not with Abraham but with himself. There is, therefore, a polemical note in much of Philo's theological writing. His defence of Jewish monotheism and spirituality against what was to him atheistic pantheism and materialism frequently consisted of attack.

Idols and idolatry. In *Spec. Leg.* 1.28 Philo refers to the 'personages, which the myth-makers have invented' and by means of which they have spread 'delusion' and created a powerful threat to the truth by the fabrication of 'new gods', in order that the 'eternal and really existing God might be consigned to oblivion'. He goes on to describe the seductiveness of idols and idolatry with their accompanying poetry and music. He had earlier referred, somewhat scathingly, to the way in which sculptors fashioned gods, 'as they are supposed to be' (*ibid.* 21–2), in human form, and cited the prohibition of idolatry in Exod. 20: 23 as justification for his critique of idols and idol-making. To the Roman Emperor (see above, p. 12), Philo addresses the words, 'For the works of painters and modellers are representations of gods perceived by sense, but to paint or mould a likeness of the invisible was held by our ancestors to be against their religion' (*Leg. Gaj.* 290). Philo here appears to concede that there are perhaps 'gods' perceived by the senses – powers at work in the universe – which can be represented by idols, but that in sharp contrast to these lesser gods is the supreme God, whose transcendence renders him incapable of portrayal in wood or stone by even the most skilful of idol-makers. In the *De Decalogo*, in a section on idolatry, Philo refers to the horror of horrors, image-makers offering prayers and sacrifices to their own creations (*Decal.* 72), even though such creations are utterly lifeless, unable to see, hear, breathe, taste, speak, walk, totally incapable of any activity (*ibid.* 74; cf. Isa. 44: 12–20). Philo frequently refers to the worship of animals by the Egyptians, who, unlike any other nation known to him, 'have advanced to divine honours irrational animals' (*ibid.* 76), going to an excessive extreme by choosing the fiercest of animals, lions, crocodiles and the venomous asp, to which they have devoted 'temples, sacred precincts, sacrifices, assemblies, processions and the like' (*ibid.* 78). After listing other animals sacred to the Egyptians, Philo asks: 'What could be more ridiculous than all this?' (*ibid.* 79). It has been suggested that Philo should have known – and did in fact know – that intelligent pagans did not worship the cult object before which they made their devotions, but that Jewish propaganda misrepresented it. Philo almost certainly knew that Egyptians did not bow down *to* the animals *before* which they bowed down, but only to the gods they represented, but to have admitted that in his writings would have served only to weaken his *apologia* on behalf of Judaism. In *Leg. Gaj.* 139 Philo refers to the deification of the kings of Egypt and to the way in which his fellow-Alexandrians, except for the Jews, acknowledged them as gods. The *Legatio ad Gaium* is therefore an apologetic work in which he defended – and commended – the Jewish views of God against both the idolatrous Emperor-worship of the Roman world and the idolatrous worship of animals by the Egyptians.

God's championship of his People. Within the generally apologetic writings of Philo there is a subtle mingling of Jewish theology and Greek philosophy, but in most cases Philo succeeds in constructing a restatement of Jewish belief in the language of the world of Greek philosophy without allowing the latter to submerge or extinguish or supplant the former. In some cases, however, there does appear to be a substitution of philosophical concepts and tenets for elements of orthodox Jewish theology, in a form which suppresses the latter and elevates the former and assigns to the borrowings from the philosophers a position of exclusive supremacy. But the God Philo writes about is still the God of the Jews. An aspect of Jewish belief in God which is present here and there throughout Philo's writings is the conviction that God is the God of history and that he intervenes in the history of his People to save them by his mighty acts. In *Decal.* 47 Philo affirms: 'whatever God says is not words but deeds'. What Philo says about the deliverance of the Israelites at the Red Sea sounds very much like the language of an orthodox and patriotic Jew. He speaks of the hymns sung beside the Red Sea 'in honour of the wonders there wrought' and of how 'at the command of God the sea became a source of salvation to one party and of perdition to the other'. Then follows a poetic description of the miracle, characterised as a 'wonderful sight and experience, an act transcending word and thought and hope' (*Vit. Cont.* 85–7).

The *In Flaccum* closes with a section in which Philo describes the execution of Flaccus by the Roman Emperor and asserts that Flaccus' fate showed that God was still watching over his People. Describing the horrific assassination of Flaccus, Philo comments: 'For it was the will of justice that the butcheries which she wrought on his single body should be as numerous as the number of the Jews whom he unlawfully put to death' (*Flacc.* 189). The final sentence reads: 'Such was the fate of Flaccus also, who thereby became an indubitable proof that the help which God can give was not withdrawn from the nation of the Jews.' It has been noted that Philo had earlier said (*ibid.* 121) that the Jews, when they heard of the capture and imprisonment of Flaccus, said: 'We do not rejoice, O Lord . . . at the punishment meted to an enemy, for we have been taught by the holy laws to have human sympathy.' Philo appears, it has also been pointed out, to gloat over the misery of Flaccus in his fall, exile and death with a repulsive vindictiveness, but the *In Flaccum* certainly shows that Philo believed God to be the one who 'takes care for human affairs' (*ibid.* 102), especially the affairs of the Jews, and intervenes as 'the champion and defender of the wronged, the avenger of unholy men and deeds' (*ibid.* 104). God for Philo is a God who gives the suffering Jews a glimpse of cheering hopes that Thou wilt amend what remains for amendment, in that Thou hast already begun to assent to our prayers' (*ibid.* 124), and who lets them see the downfall of their enemy, Flaccus, close at hand, 'to give them a clearer picture of swift and unhoped-for visitation' (*ibid.*). In the case of the *Legatio ad Gaium*, a lively and powerful piece of invective against the Roman Emperor, we do not possess the 'palinode', promised at the end, which, after the description of 'the cause of the enmity which Gaius had for the whole nation of the Jews' (*Leg. Gaj.* 373), probably gave an account of the death of Gaius, and perhaps of the change of imperial policy under Claudius – events interpreted almost certainly, like Flaccus' unhappy fate, as proof that God had not deserted his People (see above, p. 17). Philo, at one point, tells how the Jewish delegation, as they attempted to put their case to Gaius, pleaded with God to restrain the Emperor's wrath. He comments: 'And God taking compassion on us turned his spirit to mercy' (*Leg. Gaj.* 367). At the end of the *De Praemiis* Philo described the curses with which God will visit those who have disobeyed his Law, the punishments attached to disloyalty. Such curses will be effected by God in accordance with his words as recorded in Scripture (for example, Lev. 26: 19, Deut. 28: 23). Among the punishments to be meted out is an encounter with 'wild beasts more ferocious than men, formidably equipped with their native weapons, whom God when he first made the universe created to put fear into those who could take the warning and to punish inexorably the incorrigible' (para. 149).

In the concluding sections of his description of the eschatological reversal of fortunes that God will bring about, Philo states that 'God will turn the curses against the enemies of the penitents' (Deut. 30: 7). The 'enemies' in question have been mistaken in thinking that their heritage is indestructible and that their opponents will remain 'firmly established' in 'unchanging adversity' (*Praem. Poen.* 169). But those who have proved persistent enemies of the People of God will 'begin to reap the rewards of their cruelty' (*ibid.* 171). It is doubtful if Philo saw even Caligula's reign as the sign of the End, but he certainly believed that Israel would be rescued by God from unchanging adversity and Rome punished for her persecution of the Jewish saints. God, then, is for Philo a God who acts: 'it belongs to God to act' (*Cher.* 77). And in the opening paragraphs of the *Legatio ad Gaium* Philo laments the fact that in 'the present time . . . some have come to disbelieve that the Deity takes thought for men, and particularly for the suppliants' race which the Father and King of the Universe and the Source of all things has taken for his portion' (*Leg. Gaj.* 3).

Philo had no doubt whatever that 'the true God' (*ibid.* 366) was the God of the Jewish Scriptures. There is no comparison between him, 'the truly existing veritable God', and 'the new Zeus made manifest' (*ibid.* 346–7), the Emperor deified. In the course of what he said to the Emperor Philo stated, with regard to the Temple in Jerusalem: 'This temple, my Lord Gaius, has never from the first admitted any figure wrought by men's hands, because it is the sanctuary of the true God' (*ibid.* 290). In *Som.* 1.35 he affirms: 'man is the recipient of a privilege which gives him distinction beyond other living creatures, that, namely, of worshipping him that IS' (see above, p. 28). And for Philo, as for Judaism as a whole, monotheism means believing that one God and one God only is to be worshipped. It is this conviction that lies behind all the polemic in Philo's works against polytheism, idolatry and Emperor-worship.

God answers prayer. Philo also retained his Jewish belief in God's ability and readiness to answer prayer. In *Migr. Abr.* 122 he speaks of God as a personal being who 'does not turn his ear away' from men's supplications. To Moses God says: 'I am of a kindly nature and gracious to true suppliants' (*Vit. Mos.* I.72). God is the God of 'suppliants' (*ibid.* I.36, where in fact the adjective, *hikesios* (of suppliants), applied by classical authors to Zeus, is applied by Philo to Yahweh). According to *Det. Pot. Ins.* 95, God 'accepts our suppliant souls'. God is also, according to Philo, 'the gracious Being who assents to prayers' (*Vit. Mos.* II.5). One of the kinds of prayer offered by Philo himself is for the long life of good men living in an honoured city (*Sacr. AC* 124): 'I pray that their years may be prolonged to the utmost.' He defines prayer as 'an asking for good things' (*Agric.* 99) and indicates what it is that in his view is the best thing to ask for: 'Good sirs, the best of prayers and the goal of happiness is to become like God' (*Decal.* 73). Philo also refers to the part played by the Jewish High Priest in seeking to propitiate God with 'supplication and intercession' on behalf of the universe as well as on behalf of the human race (*Spec. Leg.* I.97) and as the 'intercessor for the sinners' (*ibid.* I.244). In the course of his life of Moses, Philo says that 'God, in high approval of his spirit, which loved the good and hated evil, listened to his prayers' (*Vit. Mos.* I.47). Moses 'prays that he may learn from God himself what God is' (*Fug.* 164), thus providing a model for the rest of men of the highest form of prayer.

God the Creator. Philo's God is, of course, the Creator of the universe, of whom it may be said: 'For all things are possible to God, who does not need time at all in order to create' (*Quaest. in Gn.* II.47), such is his miraculous, divine, creative power. One of the five things Philo believed that Moses' account of the creation of the world teaches its readers is 'that the world came into being', against those who hold that it is 'without beginning and eternal' (*Op. Mund.* 171). The whole of his treatise *De Opificio Mundi* is devoted to an exposition of the Creation story, a story which he believed shows that the cosmogony and philosophy of Moses were those of Plato and the Neo-Pythagoreans; a story which affirms unambiguously that God is, and is from eternity, that he really is One, and 'that he has made the world, and has made it one world, unique as himself is unique, and that he ever exercises forethought for his creation' (*Op. Mund.* 172). Philo's Jewish view of God in relation to the universe is vigorously expressed in *Poster. C.* 175. There he states that 'it is the act of a sober and well-ordered reason to acknowledge God as the Maker and Father of the universe, but the assertion that he himself is the author of everything that concerns the life of man is that of one who is being ruined by drunkenness and sottishness'. In *Leg. All.* I.5 Philo says that 'God never leaves off making' and that 'it is the property of God to make'. God is frequently called by Philo 'the Maker' and also 'the Artificer', as in *Migr. Abr.* 41. According to *Migr. Abr.* 131, God is the Being to whom 'all things owe their being'. Philo affirms that God is the One who 'gives being to what is not and generates all things' (*Rer. Div. Her.* 36) – an affirmation of the Jewish belief in creation *ex nihilo*. Philo also calls God the 'Cause' (*Deus Imm.* 116) or 'the Highest of causes' (*Som.* I.190), or the 'Cause of All' (*Decal.* 64). 'The transcendent source of all that exists is God', Philo states in *Decal.* 52. God is, then, for Philo, 'the Maker of all', and he adds that 'if anyone renders the worship due to the Eternal, the Creator, to a created being and one later in time, he must stand recorded as infatuated and guilty of impiety in the highest degree' (*Spec. Leg.* I.20). A little later (*ibid.* I.30), Philo describes God as 'the Framer and Maker of all things' and as 'Lord of created beings'.

Philo also insists that God's goodness was his motive in creating the world. In *Cher.* 27 he states: 'Through his goodness he begat all that is.' In *Quaest. in Gn.* II.13 Philo records God's statement that 'the cause of creating the world was the goodness and kindness in Me'. In *Op. Mund.* 21 he asserts that the power by which the universe was made was 'true goodness' and that the Father and Maker of all, who is that true goodness, 'grudged not a share in his own excellent nature to an existence which has of itself nothing fair and lovely, while it is capable of becoming all things'. In *Leg. All.* III.78 he says: 'For all things in the world and the world itself is a free gift and act of kindness and grace on God's part' (the same word for free gift', *dōrea*, is used by Paul in Rom. 5: 15 and the same word for 'grace', *charisma*, as used in 1 Cor 12: 31 of the 'gifts' of the Holy Spirit). In *Deus Imm.* 108 Philo says that 'if anyone should ask me what was the motive for the creation of the world, I will answer what Moses has taught, that it was the goodness of the Existent, that goodness which is the oldest of his bounties and itself the source of others'. The 'potency' by means of which God 'ordered and marshalled the whole realm of being', Philo says in *Migr. Abr.* 182–3, 'is nothing else than loving-kindness'; or, as he puts it in *Cher.* 127, 'the final cause of the building is the goodness of the architect'.

Connected with what Philo says about God as a Creator who is motivated to create by his goodness and love is what he says about God's providential care of his creation. One of Philo's treatises, the *De Providentia*, only part of which survives in Greek, attempts to answer arguments against belief in Divine Providence. Philo ends it with the statement that what he has written provides 'solid grounds for believing that God takes care of human affairs' (*Prov.* II.72). In *Op. Mund.* 9 Philo claims that 'it stands to reason that what has been brought into existence should be cared for by its Father and Maker'. In *Sobr.* 63, referring to God as containing all things but being contained by none, he speaks of 'his special providence' which 'watches over and cares for' the universe. In *Rer. Div. Her.* 301 God 'steers the common barque of the world, in which all things sail; he guides that winged chariot, the whole heaven'. God, for Philo, is 'the All-leading God' (*Migr. Abr.* 175), a God whose 'invisible powers', which hold the universe together, reach from the ends of the earth to heaven's furthest bounds and are 'chains that cannot be broken' (*ibid.* 181). God is also described by Philo as 'the overseer of the All' (*Abr.* 71). In *Vit. Mos.* I.67 Philo interprets the angel of the Burning Bush as 'a symbol of God's providence, which all silently brings relief to the greatest dangers, exceeding every hope'. Ps. 23: 1 is applied to God by Philo in *Agric.* 50ff., where he says that the contents of the universe 'are like some flock under the hand of God its King and Shepherd'. The passage opens with Philo's statement 'Indeed, so good a thing is shepherding that it is justly ascribed not to kings only and wise men and perfectly cleansed souls but also to God the All-Sovereign.' In *Spec. Leg.* II.198 God is said to be 'the Parent and Father and Saviour of the world and all that is therein, who has the power and the right to nourish and sustain us by means of these or without these'; and Philo illustrates the nature of God's providental care by reference to the feeding of the Israelites with manna in the wilderness. Such was God's bountiful goodness that the Israelites reverenced him and worshipped him 'with the hymns and benedictions that are his due'.

The Fatherhood and love of God. God is not merely the Creator of the universe for Philo; he is, as he puts it in *Spec. Leg.* IV.180, 'the Maker and Father'. He is 'the Father of all' (*Conf. Ling.* 63; cf. *ibid.* 144). The statement (*ibid.* 145) that 'they who live in the knowledge of the One are rightly called "sons of God"', implies that the possibility of becoming sons of God the Father exists for men, even though first they may need to become 'sons of his invisible image, the most holy Word' (*ibid.* 147).

The love of God for mankind is described in *Som.* I.90–1 as the love of 'the universal Father', who is all-seeing. Yet, even though he can see everything we are, 'the One gracious Being will be found gracious'. Philo then explains that if we expose our sins to God's sunlight and repent, then our soul has 'gained cleansing and benefit and has appeased the just wrath of the convicting wielder of the lash who was standing over it'. Later in the same treatise, (*Som.* I.112) Philo interprets Exod. 22: 26 as referring to the fact that, 'by reason of his compassion for our race', God, who is 'greatest and most present to help', sends his 'all-illuminating rays' to heal the disorders of man's soul. In *Praem. Poen.* 166–7 it is said that one of men's intercessors with God, who is here called 'Father', is 'the clemency and kindness of him to whom they appeal, who ever prefers forgiveness to punishment'. One of the other intercessory agencies is the movement in men towards reconciliation and to find favour with God 'as sons may with their father'. The loving-kindness of God is stressed again in *Spec. Leg.* I.308, where it is said that he 'takes pity and compassion on those most helplessly in need, and does not disdain to give judgement to strangers or orphans or widows. He holds their low estate worthy of his providential care, while of kings and despots and great potentates he takes no account.' Here is a description of God's compassion which owes a very great debt to the prophetic tradition of Israel, and to prophets such as Amos and Hosea in particular, and which compares closely with that of Philo's Palestinian contemporary, Jesus of Nazareth. Of orphans and widows he says (*ibid.* I.310) that 'they are not denied the hope that is greatest of all, the hope in God', and he adds that God 'in the graciousness of his nature does not refuse the task of caring for and watching over them in this desolate condition'.

Philo often speaks of God as 'God the Saviour' (e.g. *Abr.* 176, in an account of the rescue of Isaac in the story of Gen 22) and elsewhere as the Saviour of mankind: 'But God, moved by pity for mankind whose Saviour and Lover he was' (*ibid.* 137). In the *Quaestiones* Philo frequently alludes to 'the loving friendship and care of God' (*Quaest. in Ex.* II.18). In *Quaest. in Gn.* II.75, commenting on Gen. 9:26, he says: 'He gave his beneficent grace and largess with peculiarly abundant magnificence.' Earlier (*ibid.* II.15), he uses the phrase 'by the grace of the Father' (the divine flood washes away sensible and corporeal things), and later, in *Quaest. in Gn.* IV.180, he says: 'since he is blessed and gracious and propitious, he does not judge created beings in accordance with his greatness but in accordance with theirs'. According to *Quaest. in Gn.* III.3, 'all things are the gift and grace of God'.

Man knows God's existence, not his essence. Man can know only *that* God exists. He cannot know *what* he is in essence. That is something which human reason cannot penetrate. To ask about 'the essence of the Existent Being' is to embark upon 'a quest of that which is beyond matter and beyond sight' (*Poster. C.* 15). There seems to be a contradiction here within Philo's thought on his doctrine of God, but it is only apparent, for he believed that, though God's essence is beyond the reach of man's intellectual ability, his existence and his activities are knowable. But just as man 'is not even able to look upon the beams of the sun', so man's sight 'could not have borne the rays that pour from him that IS' (*Abr.* 76). All that man can apprehend of God is the fact of his existence: 'He is not apprehensible even by the mind, save in the fact that he is' (*Deus Imm.* 62). Having warned his readers against supposing that 'the Existent which truly exists is apprehended by any man', he goes on to explain: 'for we have in us no organ by which we can envisage it' (*Mut. Nom.* 7). 'Nothing that can give assurance', Philo writes in *Leg. All.* III.206, 'can give positive assurance touching God, for to none has he shown his nature'; and he continues: 'In a word, who can make any positive assertion concerning his essence or quality or state or movement? Nay, he alone shall affirm anything regarding himself since he alone has unerringly exact knowledge of his own nature.' For man to be able to know God's essence would involve his possessing knowledge, omniscience, equal to God's. Even knowledge of God's existence, knowledge that God exists, is the result of 'clear intuition rather than demonstrated by arguments carried on in words' (*Poster. C.* 167). Created beings cannot perceive 'the God who IS'. 'For it is quite enough for a man's reasoning faculty to advance so far as to learn that the Cause of the Universe is and subsists. To be anxious to continue his course yet further, and enquire about essence or quality in God, is a folly fit for the world's childhood' (*ibid.* 168). Philo goes on at once to explain how it is that the unknowable God *is* known, not directly but indirectly. Commenting on Exod. 33: 23, he says: 'all that follows in the wake of God is within the good man's apprehension, while he himself alone is beyond it, beyond, that is, in the line of straight and direct approach, a mode of approach by which (had it been possible) his quality would have been made known; but brought within ken by the powers that follow and attend him; for these make evident not his essence but his subsistence from the things which he accomplishes' (*ibid.* 169). Philo, not surprisingly, makes frequent reference to Exod. 33: 12ff., where Moses asks to see God but is allowed to see only his back (see *Mut. Nom.* 9). In *Spec. Leg.* I.32 Philo explains that while it is relatively easy to answer the question whether the Deity exists, the question 'what the Deity is in essence' is not only difficult but perhaps impossible to solve. In *Leg. All.* III.97ff. Philo speaks of how the 'first men' tried to find out 'how we came to conceive of the Deity'. What he goes on to say indicates that for Philo knowledge of God is, as it were, 'by means of a shadow cast'; it is a case of 'discerning the Artificer by means of his works'.

A logical consequence, for Philo, of the fact that God's essence cannot be apprehended by man is what he says about the namelessness of God. Having said that it should be no surprise that men, who cannot know their own minds, cannot apprehend the Existent, Philo goes on to say: 'It is a logical consequence that no personal name even can be properly assigned to the truly Existent' (*Mut. Nom.* 11). Philo cites as evidence for this conclusion the words of Exod 3: 14, where God says to Moses: 'I am he that is' (*egō eimi ho ōn*) (*ibid.*; see pp. 40–2).

In *Som.* I.64ff., commenting on Gen 22: 3–4, Philo interprets the incident as meaning that Abraham cannot actually 'reach him who is in very essence God, but sees him from afar', and then he adds the qualifying statement 'or rather, not even from a distance is he capable of contemplating him; all he sees is the bare fact that God is far away from all Creation, and that the apprehension of him is removed to a very great distance from all human power of thought' (*ibid.* 66), and he refers to God in the final paragraph of the section (*ibid.* 67) as 'God for whom no name nor utterance nor conception of any sort is adequate'. Referring again to Exod. 3: 14 in *Som.* 1.231, Philo explains God's words in reply to Moses' question 'whether he has a name' ('I am he that IS') as given so that 'since there are not in God things which man can comprehend, man may recognise his subsistence'. He has just explained that God 'has no proper name' since 'it is not the nature of him that IS to be spoken of, but simply to be' (*ibid.* 230). Philo is here alluding to Exod. 6: 3, and indeed all that he says about the namelessness of God reflects the practice of the Septuagint in using titles, *theos* and *kurios*, in place of the personal divine name, and the tradition represented in the Hebrew text of the Old Testament of vocalising the Tetragrammaton YHWH with the vowels of a divine title such as *Adonai*. The original pronunciation of the name YHWH is unknown: there are strong but not fully valid arguments for 'Yahweh'. To Philo God had to remain nameless, or rather his name had to remain hidden from man, because a name, to the Hebrew or Jewish mind, expresses the inmost essence of the thing or person named. That, however, is something, in the case of God, which the human mind cannot adequately conceive or human language adequately express. God is *sui generis*, and men can speak of him, therefore, only by analogy, as, for example, Father or Shepherd or King, and for the most part in negative terms such as immortal, invisible, incorruptible, unchangeable and incomprehensible – the obverse of the qualities possessed by man and the creation. God is unnameable or nameless, because he 'belongs to no class or kind' (*Leg. All.* 1.36); 'He belongs to no type'; 'He is One and incorruptible and unchangeable' (*ibid.*, 51).

The namelessness of God required Philo, when speaking of him without concessions to human needs (in relation to prayer and personal piety), to refer to him, in highly philosophical language, as *ho ōn*, 'He who IS' (*Deus Imm.* 110), and other variants of that expression. The simple form of the expression has both Platonic and biblical associations. In a slightly extended form it is applied by Plato to the world of Ideas or Forms. In Exod. 3: 14 (LXX) the simple phrase *ho ōn* is applied to God. So Philo was applying to God, as nameless and as essentially Pure Being, a phrase he met in the Septuagint, though he departed from Plato's usage in applying it to God alone (and not, as Plato did, to the Ideas).

Philo also uses expressions to denote God which carry within them suggestions of the impersonal being of the Deity. This occurs when he designates God, using the neuter, impersonal form, *to on* ('that which exists') or *to ontōs on* ('that which really exists'). Philo uses the simple *to ōn* in *Gig.* 52 and also in *Poster. C.* 28, *Mut. Nom.* 27, and *Som.* I.230, whereas the fuller *to ontōs ōn* is used in *Congr.* 51 (where God is also called 'the best'). Philo also warns: 'Do not suppose that the Existent which truly exists [*to pros aletheian on*] is apprehended by any man' (*Mut. Nom.* 7). All that 'the comrades of the soul' who are able to 'hold converse with intelligible incorporeal natures' do is, refusing to compare God with any form of created being, to dissociate him from every category, since 'his being is apprehended as simple being, without other definite characteristic' (*Deus Imm.* 55).

In using these philosophical terms for God Philo is emphasising God's transcendence. God is not merely another being; he is Pure Being. He really exists. But Philo occasionally also alludes to the biblical name of God, YHWH (see above, p. 40) to affirm his belief in God's transcendence. In *Vit. Mos.* II.203 he cites the Lev. 24: 15 (LXX): 'he that nameth the name of the Lord let him die', as a warning which shows that naming is worse than cursing God's name. He is almost certainly thinking of the 'holy name of the Deity' (*ibid.* 208), which he alludes to earlier (*ibid.* 114) when he refers to the name incised in the gold crown of the high priest, 'a name which only those whose ears and tongues are purified may hear or speak in the holy place, and no other person, nor in any other place at all'. 'That name', he goes on (*ibid.* 115), 'has four letters'. Later in the same treatise (*ibid.* 132) Philo again refers to the golden plate above the priest's turban on which, he says, 'the graven shapes of four letters, indicating, as we are told, the name of the Self-Existent, are impressed, meaning that it is impossible for anything that is to subsist without invocation of him'. So, despite all that he has said about the namelessness of God, there is for Philo a name which belongs to God and to God alone. Here again we have an example of Philo combining his Jewish piety with his philosophical understanding of reality, a mingling of a metaphysician's ontology with a Jewish theologian's reverence for God. What he says about the impropriety of naming God is in part a protest, prompted by his Jewish feelings of awe before the numinousness of God reinforced by the appreciation he has gained from Greek philosophy of the existence of absolute or necessary Being, against the use of the exalted name of God carelessly, too frequently or at inappropriate times.

The transcendence of God. God, for Philo, is, as he is for Judaism, transcendent. In his account of the creation of the world Philo described God, 'the active Cause', as 'transcending virtue, transcending knowledge, transcending the good itself and the beautiful itself' (*Op. Mund.* 8). 'God is above and over all generated creatures' (*Quaest. in Gn.* IV.2). In *Conf. Ling.* 170 Philo quotes from Homer's *Iliad* in support of his view. Having said that 'no existing thing is of equal honour to God', he quotes the words:

> It is not well that many lords should rule;
> Be there but one, one king. (*Iliad* II.204, 205)

In *Sacr. AC* 93 Philo expresses his belief in God's transcendence as follows: 'The gulf that separates God from what comes next to him is one of kind and nature.'

One aspect of God's transcendence is his temporal priority, or rather his existence before and beyond time and creation. As Philo puts it in *Migr. Abr.* 183, 'He is before all creation; his goings are outside it; nor is he present in any of the things that come after him.' This priority of God applies to him also, in relation to the Logos. In *Quaest. in Gn.* II.62 Philo speaks of God as 'the pre-Logos God' and affirms that he is 'superior to every rational nature' and 'above the Logos'. God, according to Philo, 'has no likeness even to what is noblest of things born' (*Gig.* 42). 'The Lord is my light' in Ps. 27: 1 really means, according to Philo's exegesis, that God is 'the archetype of every other light, nay, prior to and high above every archetype, holding the position of the model of a model' (*Som.* I.75). So, those who 'have truth for their fellow-traveller' and who have been admitted by her into the infallible mysteries of the Existent 'do not overlay the conception of God with any of the attributes of created being' (*Deus Imm.* 61). Scripture, according to Philo, addresses thus those who through forgetfulness of their blessings have lost the spirit of thankfulness: 'if thou rememberest thine own nothingness in all things, thou wilt also remember the transcendence of God in all things'. God, then, is 'high above both place and time' (*Poster. C.* 14). According to *Quaest. in Ex.* II.68, 'the Deity is above the propitious and the creative and every other power', and Philo goes on to explain that 'In the first place [there is] he who is elder than the one and the monad and the beginning' and that then, secondly, comes 'the Logos of the Existent One'.

Involved in the transcendence of God is his self-sufficiency. Frequently Philo insists that God is in need of nothing: 'He that IS is in need of no one' (*Leg. All.* III.181); 'For neither God, who is full, nor supreme and consummate knowledge, needs anything' (*Det. Pot. Ins.* 54); 'He gains benefit from nothing, seeing that he is neither in need of anything nor does any exist capable of adding to his superiority in all things' (*ibid.* 55); 'God needs nothing' (*Deus Imm.* 7). Rather, God is 'full of himself and is sufficient for himself' (*Mut. Nom.* 27). He 'possesses all things, but needs nothing' (*Vit. Mos.* I.157). Philo stressed this truth about God partly because he was influenced by Aristotle's view that the relationship between an agent and a patient (one who is acted upon) involved reciprocity. This could, however, not be so for God. If God is entirely self-sufficient his actions do not depend in any way at all upon the patient (see below, pp. 45–8).

God's omnipresence. Another aspect of God's being which receives considerable attention in Philo's works, in his own special terms, is that of his omnipresence. In *Poster. C.* 14 Philo simply says 'He filled the universe with himself', though here we also meet the kind of statement that abounds in Philo's treatises: namely, that God 'is contained by nothing, but transcends all'. *Sacr. AC* 67 contains the statement 'He who is here exists also there and elsewhere and everywhere, for he has filled all wholly and entirely and left nothing where his presence is not.' It is an impropriety exceeding 'the bounds of ocean or of the universe itself', Philo says in *Conf. Ling.* 134, to suppose that God comes or goes, ascends or descends, or moves in any way. The application of such language of motion to the Deity is a case, Philo explains, of the application by Moses of 'human terms to the superhuman God' in order to make the truth easier for men to understand (*ibid.* 135). 'But', Philo concludes, 'God fills all things; he contains but is not contained. To be everywhere and nowhere is his property and his alone' (*ibid.* 136). It would be absurd to say that God, who is the Creator, was contained within anything he had made. Yet, on the other hand, 'he is everywhere'. This is possible, Philo suggests, 'because he has made his powers extend through earth and water, air and heaven, and left no part of the universe without his presence'. God, in his pure essence, the aspect of him 'which transcends his Potencies', cannot be conceived of in spatial terms, though that Potency of his by which he has made and ordered the universe, the Potency called God (*theos*), 'holds the whole in its embrace and has interfused itself through the parts of the universe' (*ibid.* 136–7). When spatial language is used of God by Philo, it is used in a very special sense. In *Leg. All.* I.43 Philo urges his readers not to allow such fables as to imagine that God tills the soil or plants gardens (a reference to Gen. 2: 8). In the next section he explains that 'not even the whole world would be a place fit for God to make his abode, since God is his own place, and he is filled by himself, and sufficient for himself, filling and containing all other things in their destitution and barrenness and emptiness, but himself contained by nothing else, seeing that he is himself One and the Whole'. God, for Philo, is omnipresent, but not in a materially spatial sense, since 'this divine nature which presents itself to us, as visible and comprehensible and everywhere, is in reality invisible, incomprehensible, and nowhere' (*Conf. Ling.* 138). His omnipresence must not be expressed in the spatial terms used of movement, since none of these 'are applicable to God in his aspect of pure being' (*ibid.* 139). Such language is incompatible with 'our' (i.e. Philo's) 'conception' of him – an intellectual conception, as the verb used (*epinoeitai*, 'is conceived of'), shows.

God's perfection and sinlessness. God is, of course, utterly sinless and perfect in his goodness. According to *Decal.* 81, he is the 'primal and most perfect good, from whom as from a fountain is showered the water of each particular good upon the world and them that dwell therein'. He is superior, therefore, to the Platonic Idea of the Good, since he is not merely the Idea but the reality of the Good beyond the Idea (see below, p. 45). In *Op Mund.* 88, in fact, Philo can say that God transcends virtue and even 'the good itself and the beautiful itself'. Here is a Jewish thinker who knows Platonism well, who appreciates its beauty and truth, and yet wishes to claim that the best of Platonism – and more – is contained within Judaism, its theology and piety. God, for Philo, is himself 'the good' or 'the truly Good' (*Gig.* 45), but he is not merely the Platonic Idea of the Good. 'God alone is happy and blessed, exempt from all evil, filled with perfect forms of good, or rather, if the real truth be told, himself *the* good, who showers the particular goods on heaven and earth' (*Spec. Leg.* II.53).

As 'the Good', God is naturally perfect: 'all perfection and finality belong to One alone' (*Rer. Div. Her.* 121). 'To God nothing is uncertain and nothing is unattainable' (*Quaest. in Gn.* II.54). His perfection is complete, Philo continues, 'For that blessed and most happy One does not admit any likeness or comparison or parable; nay, rather he is beyond blessedness itself and happiness and whatever is more excellent and better than these.' According to *Cher.* 86, 'his nature is most perfect', so much so that 'he partakes of nothing outside himself to increase his excellence'. In *Det. Pot. Ins.* 54 God is described as 'full', in the sense of complete. Philo continues: 'He gains benefit from nothing, seeing that he is neither in need of anything nor does any exist capable of adding to his superiority in all things' (*ibid.* 55), for everything God has is perfect to start with (*ibid.* 56). One of the reasons given by Philo for believing in the 'simplicity' of the divine nature is that if God were composite anything added would be either superior, inferior or equal to him. 'But there is nothing equal or superior to God. And no lesser thing is resolved into him' (*Leg. All.* II.3). In *Spec. Leg.* I.277 God is described as 'the primal good, the consummation of perfection, the perennial fountain of wisdom and justice, and every virtue'. Sometimes Philo speaks of God's perfection using the biblical terms 'holy' and 'holiness', as in *Sacr. AC* 101, where he speaks of 'God the uncreated, the unchangeable, the immortal, the holy and solely blessed', in *Praem. Poen.* 123, where he speaks of 'the chosen people' as 'holy even as he is holy', and in *Som.* I.254, where the One to whom Hannah dedicates her son is described as 'the Holy One'. In *Quaest. in Gn.* IV.130 Philo suggests that those who genuinely love God thank and praise him who 'fills all things with his powers for the salvation of all' and can call him 'holy, blessed Creator, all-mighty, God of truth'. Such a God is, it goes without saying, totally and utterly without sin. 'Not to commit any sin at all', Philo states, is the property of God, and perhaps also of a divine man (*Virt.* 177) – a passage of some considerable interest to students of Christological statements in the New Testament about the sinlessness of Jesus of Nazareth. (Philo was almost certainly thinking of 'Our most holy Moses' (*ibid.* 175).)

Linked with all that Philo says about God's perfect goodness and sinlessness is his belief, to which he gives expression many times, that God cannot be, and is not, the cause of evil in the universe. 'God', he says, 'is the cause of good things only; and of nothing at all that is bad, since he himself was the most ancient of beings and the good in its most perfect form' (*Conf. Ling.* 180). According to *Quaest. in Gn.* I.68, 'the Deity is not the cause of evil'; and later Philo states: 'no longer may one say that the Deity is the cause of all things, good and evil, but only of the good' (*ibid.* 78). In *Prov.* II.53 he states his belief categorically and unambiguously: 'For nothing evil at all is caused by God' (Philo has been referring to earthquakes, thunderbolts and pestilences). Yet there are places where Philo's language does appear to contradict this frequently stated view and to attribute even the creation of evil to God. In *Leg. All.* III.104–6 he does seem to attribute to God the creation of the evils that befall men as well as the goods they enjoy. Commenting on Deut. 28: 12 and 32: 34–5 he says that with God there are 'treasuries as of good things, so also of evil things'. He does state that the treasury of good things, like God himself, is one, whereas there are many treasuries of evil things, 'for countless too are those that sin'. In defence of God, he notes that Scripture teaches that God opens the treasury of good things, but closes that of evil, even when men do not deserve it. God at least 'gives time for repentance and for the healing and setting on his feet again of him who had slipped'. Philo had a clear awareness of the problem of evil, as it is dealt with in the philosophy of religion. In his *De Providentia*, for example, he attempts to show how belief in divine providence can be maintained even in the face of the occurrence of such personal misfortunes as pain and various natural disasters, and Philo gives some of the standard replies, as when he argues (*Prov.* II.43) that some natural 'evils' in fact benefit mankind (as water and wind help to provide 'sustenance, growth and maturity to animals and plants'). 'If', he argues (in a way frequently met with in discussions of the problem), 'these sometimes harm persons who travel by sea out of season or tillers of the land there is nothing' surprising in that. 'They are but a small fraction and his care is for the whole human race' (*ibid.* 44). But, he argues, 'earthquakes, pestilence, thunderbolts and the like though said to be visitations from God are not really such. For nothing evil at all is caused by God, and these things are generated by changes in the elements' (*ibid.* 53), 'attendant circumstances' and not 'primary works of nature'. Philo also asserts that some 'evils' are therapeutic and disciplinary in character and some are sent by 'the Governor of this great city of the world' (*ibid.* 39) as punishments and as agencies by means of which wickedness is purged away. But Philo is hard pressed, as many have been since, to find an adequate explanation for the suffering of the innocent, such as (and this is his example) Socrates. His answer that those thought good by us are not necessarily deemed to be good by God will not do. He can, in the end (*Prov.* II.36), say only: 'Let us never then prefer our own tribunal to that of God and assert that it is more infallible and wiser in counsel, for that religion forbids.'

One other way Philo adopts to attempt to deal with the problem of the existence of evil is assigning its creation to other beings than God himself. In his comments on Gen. 1: 26 he explains that God employed 'the powers that are associated with him' in the creation of man because 'the soul of man was to be susceptible of conceptions of evil things and good things' and God 'deemed it necessary to assign the creation of evil things to other makers, reserving that of good things to himself alone' (*Fug.* 70). Elsewhere, in *Conf. Ling.* 179, having earlier (*ibid.* 175) said that God 'allowed his subject to have the fashioning of some things', Philo states that creation was shared by God and his lieutenants so that 'man's right actions might be attributable to God, but his sins to others'. It did not seem fitting, Philo concludes, 'that the road to wickedness within the reasonable soul should be of his making, and therefore he delegated the forming of this part to his inferiors'. Philo, in *Op. Mund.* 75, also interprets the words 'Let us make' in Gen. 1: 26 as implying the use by God of 'fellow-workers' in the act of creation. Again, Philo assigns the creation of the good possibilities in man to God himself and that of the evil to the 'others from the number of his subordinates', since 'it could not be that the Father should be the cause of an evil thing to his offspring'. What Philo says about the work of angels accords with this, for there are good, beneficial angels, employed by God to confer blessings on man (see, e.g., *Leg. All.* III.177), not the 'principal boons' bestowed by God himself but the 'secondary gifts . . . such as involve riddance from ills'. There are also, however, the punitive angels (see *Fug.* 66), who inflict punishments on those who deserve it, 'though not without his command given in virtue of his sovereignty' (*ibid.*). But in his account of the plagues suffered by the Egyptians Philo says that three of them were inflicted directly by God (*Vit. Mos.* I.97), 'without any human agent' (*ibid.* 130).

Philo, then, struggles very hard to achieve a coherent and consistent analysis such as has baffled believers and theologians of Judaism and Christianity alike, but it is doubtful if he succeeds in setting out anything like a full or final solution to the problem. He certainly wishes to assert that God is ultimately supreme as Creator of and in the universe and that, in the words of Isa. 45: 7, he is the Maker of good and evil, weal and woe; he assigns the ultimate responsibility for the whole of creation to God, since a dualism is unthinkable, either directly or indirectly, but he also wishes to avoid associating God, without detracting from his power, and because of his holiness and goodness, with the existence of evil or its creation.

God's 'properties'. As we have already seen, the fact that God's essence cannot be apprehended by man does not mean that he has no positive or definite character. Philo, however, does not speak of God's 'qualities'. He prefers instead to refer to God's 'properties'. It has been pointed out that in doing so he was probably thinking of Aristotle's definition of a 'property' as belonging uniquely to one being alone, unlike a 'quality', which could belong to other beings. Properties were also different from 'accidents', which are possessed by material objects and human beings. Some of God's 'properties' have already been discussed, and one or two others will be mentioned below, but one 'property' which is perhaps *the* property is that of 'activity'. In Philo's view, and he is here echoing philosophical ideas of a Greek kind, it is the property of God to act, which property we do not ascribe to any created being, for the property of the created is to suffer activity (*Cher.* 77). The word 'property' here translates the Greek expression *to idion*, which means 'that which is peculiarly its own' (that is, in this case, the 'property' of activity which belongs to God alone). Human activity is derivative and secondary. Indeed, all activity in the world has its source in God, 'inasmuch as he is to all besides the source of action' (*Leg. All.* I.5).

Unchangeableness is also, paradoxically, another of God's properties. In *Leg. All.* II.33 Philo explains: 'every created thing must necessarily undergo change, for this is its property, even as unchangeableness is the property of God'. Philo states emphatically that the man who, among other things, thinks 'that [God] is not incapable of change, wrongs himself not God' (*Leg. All.* I.51). God is, as well as being One and incorruptible, 'unchangeable'. Like heaven, which is always 'the same in itself' (*Quaest. in Gn.* IV.97), God is also 'without change' (*ibid.* I.93). There was a time when men were 'stable, constant, immobile, peaceful and eternal', and Philo adds: 'similarly and in the same way they believed God to be, just as he is in truth' (*ibid.* 42). Elsewhere (*ibid.* IV.1) Philo speaks of 'the unwearied and unchanging true being of God' (cf. *Quaest. in Ex.* II.37 and 46). Even though God, when he reveals himself to worshippers, conveys different impressions of himself (for example, 'giving himself the likeness of angels'), he does not actually alter his own nature, 'for he is unchangeable' (*Som.* I.232).

Another of God's 'properties' is his unity, and with that is associated his simplicity. God is sometimes called by Philo *to hen*, 'the One', as he is described in *Rer. Div. Her.* 216. In *Decal.* 65 Philo exhorts his readers 'to acknowledge and honour one God who is above all' (see above, p. 45). 'There is nothing equal or superior to God. And no lesser thing is resolved into him. If he do so assimilate any lesser thing, he also will be lessened. And if he can be made less, he will also be capable of corruption; and even to imagine this were blasphemous. The "one" and the "monad" are, therefore, the only standard for determining the category to which God belongs. Rather should we say, the One God is the sole standard for the "monad"' (*Leg. All.* II.3). It has been demonstrated that what Philo has done to arrive at his doctrine of God's simplicity of being is to deduce from God's unlikeness to man or anything corporeal God's incorporeality, and that this is then interpreted by him as implying that God's nature is uniquely simple and uncompounded. God, in other words, is pure Being. It is this conclusion that leads Philo to avoid the use of the word 'quality' with reference to God and to refer instead – something he finds useful and necessary – to God's 'properties'. But, for Philo, properties are not those accidents (in the philosophical sense of that word) which differentiate one thing from another. Ultimately, for Philo, God himself in the simplicity of his essence is not only incorporeal; he is indefinable and unknowable and indescribable. By saying this, it has been argued, Philo introduced a new idea into the history of philosophy, an idea which was to have a profound influence on all later thinkers concerned with the philosophical question of God (including, of course, Christian ones seeking to construct a doctrine of God for Christianity).

However, in addition to what he has to say about God's 'properties', Philo also introduces into what he says about God the notion of his 'powers'. The 'properties', really, put together, constitute the 'powers'. In *Som.* II.254, for example, Philo, having interpreted the name Jerusalem as meaning 'vision of peace' (*ibid.*

250), states that 'the Potencies of the Existent have many names, and of that company peace is not only a member but a leader'. Much of what Philo says about the 'powers' of God is, however, by way of comment on the two Septuagint names or titles by which God is identified: *theos* (God), corresponding to the Hebrew *Elohim*, and *kurios* (Lord), corresponding to the Hebrew *Yahweh*, the vocalised form of the Tetragrammaton (see above, pp. 40–1). In *Conf. Ling.* 137, Philo, after noting that the aspect of the Deity which 'transcends his Potencies cannot be conceived of at all in terms of place, but only as pure being', states that 'that Potency of his by which he made and ordered all things' is called 'God' in virtue of the derivation of the word (which Philo takes to be from the verb *tithēmi*, with the meaning 'to put', 'to place' and, therefore, 'to order' or 'to make'). The same understanding of the word is found in *Leg. All.* III.73, where Philo says that 'God' is 'the name of the goodness pertaining to the First Cause'; but here the term 'God' is distinguished from 'Lord', which it is clear from what he says is the term applied to the absolute 'power' of God employed by him as Ruler and Governor – his sovereignty, which is sometimes employed destructively. *Abr.* 121 also explains the meaning of both terms. The Deity, there referred to as 'the Father of the Universe', it is explained, Scripture calls 'he that IS . . . his proper name'; but, Philo goes on, 'on either side of him, are the senior potencies, the nearest to him the creative and the kingly'. 'The title of the former', he adds, 'is God, since it made and ordered the All; the title of the latter is Lord, since it is the fundamental right of the maker to rule and control what he has brought into being.'

The 'powers' of God. Philo sometimes speaks of the 'powers', which are divided by him into two groups associated with the two senior potencies, as 'properties' of God and sometimes as separate, created beings or Ideas. In *Fug.* 94–6 he refers to the 'powers' as distinct from God himself; he uses the same sort of language about them in *Cher.* 27–8, yet in the very next paragraph it is clear from his language that it is not merely the sovereignty and beneficence of God as 'powers' distinct from him, but the sovereignty and beneficence of God himself, that he has in mind. In *Leg. All.* III.174 Philo does not speak of the beneficent or propitious 'power' of God, but says: 'in reality . . . we have God propitious to us'. Here again we have an aspect of Philo's thinking about God which was of some importance to the makers of Christian doctrine: namely, the use of language which speaks of God's attributes or properties but which also appears to confer upon them an independent existence within his being or apart from him.

Within what Philo says about God's 'powers' there is one aspect of his thought that is of special interest to students of the Christian doctrine of God, especially of the doctrine of the Trinity. It is what he says about man's perception of God as a 'triad' (though it will be seen that there is no concept, such as did develop within Christianity, of God as triune or as a Trinity of Persons). In *Deus Imm.* 3 Philo states that, illuminated by 'the bright and pure rays of wisdom . . . the sage sees God and his potencies', and in *Migr. Abr.* 76 he refers to 'God and his most Holy powers'. In *Abr.* 121–2, however, he goes even further: there he states that 'the central place is held by the Father of the Universe' (that is, 'He is that IS'), while 'on either side of him are the senior potencies, the nearest to him, the creative and the kingly', who, he explains, have the names 'God' and 'Lord' (see above, p. 50). He continues: 'So the central Being with each of his potencies as his squire presents to the mind which has vision the appearance sometimes of one, sometimes of three: of one, when that mind is highly purified and, passing beyond not merely the multiplicity of other numbers, but even the dyad which is next to the unit, presses on to the ideal form which is free from mixture and complexity, and being self-contained needs nothing more; of three when, as yet uninitiated into the highest mysteries, it is still a votary only of the minor rites and unable to apprehend the Existent alone by Itself and apart from all else, but only through its actions, as either creative or ruling.' In *Quaest. in Gn.* IV.8 Philo indicates that the apprehension of God in this last way is a lesser form of knowledge, when he says: 'He in his oneness is likened to a triad because of the weakness of the beholders.' Earlier (*ibid.* 2) he had said: 'He cannot be seen in his oneness without something [else], the chief powers that exist immediately with him [namely] the creative, which is called God, and the kingly, which is called Lord.' The virtuous man, Philo continues, becomes 'altogether an eye' so that 'having become an eye, he begins to see the sovereign, holy and divine vision in such a way that the single appearance appears as a triad, and the triad as a unity'.

The problem of anthropomorphic language. Philo frequently quotes or alludes to the words of Num. 23: 19 in the course of his many attacks upon anthropomorphism. One element within Philo's doctrine of God which is the immediate consequence of his rejection of anthropomorphism is his belief in the impassibility of God. As he puts it in *Abr.* 202, 'the nature of God is without grief or fear and wholly exempt from passion of any kind, and alone partakes of perfect happiness and bliss'. The problem of the anthropomorphic language of Scripture is dealt with by Philo in many passages, but especially in *Deus Imm.* 56–9. Since God is uncreated, Philo asserts, he does not need any of the properties of created beings (see below, pp. 53–4 and 55–9).

Philo returns to the problem of biblical anthropomorphisms in *Som.* I.234ff. There again he explains that the Scriptures have spoken of God as like a man in order 'to provide instruction and teaching for the life of those who lack wisdom'. Philo has just referred (*ibid.* 233) to an old saying (an allusion to Homer's *Odyssey* XVII.485; cf. above, p. 42): 'that the deity goes the round of the cities in the likeness now of this man now of that man'. But the Bible never likens God to 'any particular man', though anthropomorphic descriptions are used for the benefit of those who would otherwise form no conception of God at all because of their inability to conceive of him incorporeally. But there is something worse than thinking of God anthropomorphically, in corporeal terms, and that is thinking of him as 'of human passions', an 'impious thought' accepted by many (*Sacr. AC* 95). For Philo it is absolutely without doubt that 'the nature of God is without grief or fear and wholly exempt from passion of any kind' (*Abr.* 202). Part of what is involved in Philo's revulsion from anthropomorphism is his recognition that 'if God has human forms and parts, he must needs also have human passions and experiences' (*Poster. C.* 4). 'We shun indeed . . . the monstrosity of saying that God is of human form', he writes in *Sacr. AC* 95, 'but in actual fact we accept the impious thought that he is of human passions'. At first sight *Som.* II.179 might seem to provide an example of anthropomorphism in Philo's own language about God, for he exclaims, 'how great an evil is the wrath of God' (and indeed refers to the 'gladness' of God). But for Philo 'wrath' is 'that passionless opposition to sin which we may reasonably ascribe to the Divine' (cf. the discussion of wrath in Dodd's commentary on Romans (1932)). Justification for such an interpretation is to be found in *Deus Imm.* 70–3, where

Philo is discussing the mention of the wrath of God in Gen. 6: 6–7. He makes the comment 'Now the passion of wrath, which is properly speaking an attribute of men, is here used in a more metaphorical sense' (the truth expressed being that 'all our actions' are 'worthy of blame and censure').

One of the occurrences of the words of Num. 23: 19 to be found in Philo's works occurs in *Deus Imm.* 62, where Philo joins to the words 'God is not as a man' the words 'nor yet is he as the heaven or the universe'. A more emphatic exclusion of anthropomorphism, anthropopathism, and indeed the likening of God to any other being, can hardly be imagined. Similar language is employed in *Leg. All.* 1.36, where, commenting on the words of Gen. 2: 7, Philo dismisses the idea of God's having organs such as a mouth or nostrils and adds: 'for God is not only not in the form of man, but belongs to no class or kind'. The idea of an incarnation of either God himself or his Logos, the idea of either God himself or his Logos becoming man, would seem to be ruled out altogether, both by statements already quoted and by those such as the one referring to Gen. 1: 26 in *Op. Mund.* 69: 'Let no one represent the likeness as one to a bodily form; for neither is God in human form, nor is the human body Godlike.' In *Vit. Cont.* 6 he writes: 'How could one and the same person be both mortal and immortal, to say nothing of the reproach attaching to the original source of their birth?', and continues by ridiculing the very idea of ascribing to the 'blissful and divine powers' the 'licentiousness of wanton youth' or implying that the 'thrice blessed and exempt from every passion' actually had intercourse with women. The least that would be required, if an incarnation were to take place, would be an Immaculate Conception and a Virgin Birth. But Philo believed that 'mortal and immortal may not share the same home' (*Rer. Div. Her.* 265). The Logos, he states categorically, never mixes 'with the medley of things that have come into being only to perish' (*ibid.* 234). In *Mut. Nom.* 181 Philo refers to the wish 'to make out the created to be uncreated, the mortal immortal, the perishable imperishable, and if it is not blasphemy to say it, man to be God'. Philo's form of words indicates his powerful disapproval of such tendencies. In *Gig.* 42 he says quite simply: 'God has no likeness even to what is noblest of things born.' It is interesting to note what Philo has to say in *Abr.* 107–18 about the three angels who visited Abraham. He makes it clear that 'even if we think of the strangers as men' they were in fact 'holy and divine beings' and that therefore 'it is a marvel indeed that though they neither ate nor drank they gave the appearance of both eating and drinking'. 'But', Philo continues, 'that is a secondary matter; the first and greatest wonder is that, though incorporeal, they assumed human form to do kindness to the man of worth.' In a passage already referred to (*Som.* I.238ff.) Philo, commenting on Gen. 31: 13, asks why readers of Scripture wonder at 'his assuming the likeness of angels, seeing that for the succour of those that are in need he assumes that of men?' Philo makes it clear, however, that God 'occupied the place of an angel only so far as appeared, without changing'. Here is an unashamedly docetic view of God's occupation of both angelic and human forms. There could be no real assumption by God of angelic, let alone human, form. The only solution for Philo, in situations where such a problem arose, was a thoroughgoing docetism.

Philo, then, never seriously deviates from what, in *Quaest. in Gn.* I.55, is said by him to be one of 'the highest principles' (which are two): namely, 'that God is not like man'. However, in the case of Moses, he comes very near to the view that God had manifested himself in the life of a man.

Moses and 'the heroes'. According to *Vit. Mos.* II.292, Moses was 'king, lawgiver, high priest, prophet' and 'in each function he won the highest place' (*ibid.* 3). Philo does insist that Moses was 'after all but a mortal creature' (*ibid.* 6), and at the beginning of his *De Vita Mosis* declares that his purpose is to write Moses' life and to tell his story, using both the information Scripture supplies and what he has learned from 'the elders of the nation' (*Vit. Mos.* I.1–4). The result is that he possesses a closer knowledge than others, he believes, of Moses' life-history.

In *Omn. Prob. Lib.* 105, referring to 'the heroes', Philo says that they possess 'a greatness above human nature' and are rightly called 'demigods'. But even human beings can achieve a life of virtue (*ibid.* 106ff.). Socrates, according to *Som.* I.58, 'was a human being'; Terah, by contrast, was a symbol (of self-knowledge). But Moses, like Socrates, was for Philo a real human being. Moses often appears in Philo's writings as a symbol of wisdom, but that is precisely because he is himself 'the wise' or 'the all-wise'. So Philo tells the story of Moses as he knew it from the Scriptures and from the traditions handed on to him by the Jewish elders. It is, at times, a highly idealised account of Moses' life, as when we are told that the boy Moses was soon able to advance beyond the capacities of the teachers who came to him from Greece and elsewhere, so much so that his education seemed to be 'a case rather of recollection than of learning' (*Vit. Mos.* I.21). Philo tells how Moses propounded riddles his teachers could not solve and amazed his contemporaries by the way he exercised self-control (cf. Luke 2: 46–7). So amazed were observers of his life that they even 'considered earnestly what the mind which dwelt in his body like an image in its shrine could be, whether it was human or divine or a mixture of both, so utterly unlike was it to the majority, soaring above them and exalted to a grander height' (*ibid.* I.27).

From birth Moses, Philo tells us, had 'an appearance of more than ordinary goodliness' (*ibid.* I.9), and frequent references are made to Moses' outstanding moral and religious qualities and his wisdom. He was a man loved by God as few others have been and a man of 'special holiness' (*Virt.* 201), even the holiest of men. He is described in one place as 'the most perfect of men' (*Ebr.* 94). Reference is made to his priestly piety (*Vit. Mos.* II.66) and his constant and unbroken nobility of life, and other virtues are described (see *ibid.* I.24, I.29, II.58). Philo is nowhere prepared to allow that there was in Moses any sin or imperfection. Even the murder of the Egyptian is treated as 'a righteous action' (*ibid.* I.44).

Much is said about Moses' wisdom and its divine source and inspiration (for example, in *Leg. All.* III.140; *Gig.* 47; *Spec. Leg.* IV.175; *Plant.* 27, etc.). Moses is designated, in *Vit. Mos.* II.2, the *philosophus rex* of Plato's *Republic*. According to *Op. Mund.* 8, he 'attained the very summit of philosophy', and he is credited with discoveries wrongly (according to Philo) attributed to others. It was Moses, for example, not Heraclitus, 'who long ago discovered the truth that opposites are formed from the same whole'.

Philo naturally thought that Moses was the supreme High Priest, exercising an incomparable priesthood (see, for example, *Rer. Div. Her.* 182; *Ebr.* 126) and bestowing a 'blessing which nothing in the world can surpass' (*Vit. Mos.* II.67). Other passages describe various aspects of Moses' priestly work (e.g. *Praem. Poen.* 56; *Vit. Mos* II.5; *Virt.* 79; *Deus Imm.* 156), stressing his office as intercessor.

So lofty is the estimate of Moses found in Philo's writings that one is led to ask if Philo thought of him as actually divine. Philo himself asked this question. In *Vit. Mos.* I.158 he asks: 'Was not the joy of his partnership with the Father and Maker of all magnified also by the honour of being deemed worthy to bear the same title?' He continues: 'For he was named god and king (*theos kai basileus*) of the whole nation and entered, we are told, into the darkness where God was.' In *Som.* II.189 the name 'God' is said to be 'a prerogative assigned to the chief prophet, Moses, while he was still in Egypt, where he is entitled the God of Pharaoh.' So, for Philo, the title *theos*, applicable to the Logos (the form *ho theos* being reserved for God alone: see *Som.* I.227–30), is applicable to Moses, since he was not a man – not merely a man, that is. It is said of Moses, that while he was not a god, he was not a man either but one contiguous with both extremes. To Aaron, then, the word 'god' cannot be applied, though to Moses it can, not merely because when the mind is ministering to God in its purity, as in the case of Moses, 'it is not human but divine' (*Rer. Div. Her.* 84), but because of the close association in Philo's mind, amounting at times to an identification, of Moses and the Logos. In *Mut. Nom.* 110ff. Philo interprets the Shepherd of Ps. 23: 1 as the Divine Word which guides men away from the material world. Since it is Moses who, for Philo, rescues mankind from the bondage of matter, the clear implication is, or appears to be, that, in a real sense, Moses is (or is an expression, an embodiment, of) the Logos. Philo does in fact, in *Migr. Abr.* 23, call Moses the Logos, the 'law-giving Word'. He can even say, in *Vit. Mos.* I.155, that God committed to Moses the entire cosmos as a possession fit for God's heir. One distinguished Philo specialist has decided that, in the case of the words of *Mut. Nom.* 110ff., Moses is 'the agent, if not the exact equivalent, of the saving Logos'. Another says that Moses is more than once represented as a type of the Logos, citing as one example *Congr.* 170.

For Philo Moses is at least associated with the role of the eternal Logos who is 'the form of forms' (*Quaest. in Ex.* II.124; cf. what is said within the passage in *ibid.* 117, which, though it has probably been revised by a Christian scribe, almost certainly contains genuinely Philonic material). Among many other passages of special interest to students of the New Testament, and in particular of the cosmological role assigned there to Christ, is the fact that for Philo the Logos, and therefore in some sense Moses, was involved in the creation of the universe and binds together all things.

Nor can it be ignored that when Philo is describing the 'prompting' of the human mind by the 'mystic Moses' (to use a description of him by one of Philo's most learned and enthusiastic devotees) he uses the same verb (*hupēcheo*) used also by him to describe the 'prompting' of the prophets by God. So, in *Som*. II.252 Philo uses this verb (*hupēchei*) to describe what 'the invisible spirit' of God says, as he does also earlier in the same treatise (*ibid*. II.2) when he affirms that God 'invisibly suggests' things to us, whereas in *Som* I.164 it is Moses who is asked to be man's 'prompter'.

Of special interest to those who study Philo's writings as the most important element in the body of thought which makes up what is usually referred to as hellenistic Judaism is what Philo says about the birth of Moses, since it bears some relation to what is said in the New Testament about the miraculous birth of Jesus. In *Quaest. in Ex*. II.46 Philo explains that Moses experienced a 'second birth better than the first'. In the case of the second birth, Philo says, Moses had no mother, 'but only a father, who is [the Father] of all'. In his new existence, we are told, Moses differed from ordinary men by having no body. It is also said that Moses' 'divine birth happened to come about for him in accordance with the ever-virginal nature of the hebdomad'.

When Philo describes Moses' death, he not only tells how Moses himself miraculously foretold it and of the great sorrow of the people (*Vit. Mos*. II.291), but also how, when he was ready to leave 'this mortal life for immortality', God 'resolved his twofold nature of soul and body into a single unity, transforming his whole being into mind, pure as sunlight', so enabling him to prophesy 'to each tribe in particular the things which were to be and hereafter must come to pass' (*Vit. Mos*. II.288). So Moses, at his death, becomes, like God, pure light. In *Virt*. 76 Philo tells how Moses 'began to pass over from mortal existence to life immortal' and how gradually his body was stripped away from his soul ready for his soul's 'natural removal hence' (see pp. 231 and 234).

There is also a most remarkable passage in *Som*. I.164ff. It consists of a prayer addressed *to* Moses. In it occurs the petition 'Do thou, thyself, O Sacred Guide, be our prompter and preside over our steps and never tire of anointing our eyes, until, conducting us to the hidden light of hallowed words, thou display to us the fast-locked lovelinesses invisible to the uninitiate.' It has been said, with some justification, that the words are not addressed to someone who is dead and gone, but to someone who is an active and present power, and that the prayer can be compared to those addressed by Christian mystics to Christ. It is interesting, as we have seen already, that the English word 'prompter' in the translation quoted is in fact part of the verb *hupēcheo* used by Philo of God's 'prompting' of man's mind and the 'suggestions' he makes to men. It is also certainly the case that Moses, whose death had occurred centuries before Philo wrote, is appealed to as one who, Philo believed, could play a part as revealer, guide and illuminator in the intellectual and spiritual pilgrimage of the believer and thinker and who did so from a position of access to the innermost secrets of God.

Clearly Moses was for Philo a *theios anēr*, a divine man, but at times, without infringing his Jewish monotheism and monolatry, Philo seems to go further and, while not interpreting Moses' human life as an incarnation of the divine Logos, comes near to views of Christ such as those put forward in John's Gospel, particularly its Prologue. Paul does not use the term *logos*, but in Col. 1. 15–17 Christ is described as 'the image of the invisible God' (cf. 2 Cor. 4: 4) and as the agent of creation. Again, Hebrews stresses most emphatically the total authenticity of Jesus' humanity and may (at 4: 13) apply the term *logos* to him.

Despite all that Philo says about the anthropomorphisms of Scripture and about the difference between the human and the divine, he says, referring to the 'grievous impiety' involved in the deification of a human being that 'sooner could God change into a man than a man into God' (*Leg. Gaj.* 118). He does not suggest that Moses was a case of God's changing *eis anthrōpon* (into a man), but there is nevertheless a tendency within Philo's thought for him to regard Moses as a unique human being with divine qualities. If ever a man was God it was surely in the case of Moses. Philo himself occasionally does what he accuses the Alexandrians of doing: mistakenly but incessantly, in the case of the Roman Emperor, using 'plainly and without any indirection terms which other people commonly employ when speaking of God'. The Emperor, according to Philo, was in the process at one stage of converting the Jerusalem Temple into a temple 'to bear the name of Gaius, "the new Zeus made manifest [*Dios Epiphanous*]"' (*Leg. Gaj.* 346; see above, p. 10). What Caligula wished to claim for himself, that he was a manifestation in bodily, human form of divine Zeus, Philo claimed, in a special, limited sense that differs from the nature of the claim made by Christianity for Jesus, that Moses' human life was a manifestation, an epiphany (*epiphaneia*), of God. And he does this without allowing Moses as a real, historical person to dissolve, as Hagar and Sarah do (see *Congr.* 180), into something merely symbolic. Philo frequently writes in a way that suggests that events which happen in time cannot have an eternal significance or a final value, yet what he says about the life-history of Moses – and other examples have been noted above – is in certain respects an exception to the general rule. It has been suggested that for Philo Judaism had no history or development, or any important literature, between the time of Moses and his own day, an astonishing fact in view of his liberal references to the history and literature of other nations. But it may be that this view was in part the consequence of what he believed to be the truth about the life-history of Moses. Indifferent to facts and interested primarily in ideas he may have been, but for Philo one fact to which he could not be indifferent was the *Vita Mosis*, since many of the most important lessons men needed were to be learned from the life of Moses and not merely from his teaching (see below, pp. 115–19).

How can God be known? If Moses was indeed in some sense a manifestation of God, and if important lessons about God which men can learn are to be learned from Moses, this leads on to the more general question of how God can be known, how Moses knew him, how Philo came to know him, and how Philo's readers could share such knowledge. We have seen how Philo affirms that the essence of the Deity is unknowable. On many occasions, however, Philo makes use of *a posteriori* arguments as proofs that God exists. A typical example of Philo's use of the *a posteriori* kind of argument for God's existence is to be found in *Quaest. in Gn.* II.34. There he says, among other things, that when the sense of sight (a special faculty) sees the movements of the sun and moon and the other heavenly bodies and 'the order which is above all description', it sees at the same time, and reports it to the mind, 'the one true certain Creator of the world'. He also asserts that 'it is necessary that there be some Creator and Father', for 'it would be impossible for harmony and order and measure and proportions of truth and such concord and real prosperity and happiness to come about by themselves'. At many points in his writings Philo is obviously trying to answer the objections of those who 'suppose that there is no invisible and conceptual cause outside what the senses perceive' (*Decal.* 59). Thus: 'Some distinctly deny that there is such a thing as the Godhead' (*Praem. Poen.* 40). He identifies one group of unbelievers as saying that 'nothing exists beyond this world' and that it is 'uncreated' (*Som.* II.283ff.). There are various kinds of agnosticism and atheism. There are those who have doubts about the eternal existence of God. Then there are those who deny God's existence, saying that it is 'a mere assertion of men obscuring the truth with myth and fiction' (*Op. Mund.* 170ff.). Then there are those who say that the world itself is eternal but uncreated. And, finally, there are those who, using words cleverly, say that nothing exists beyond the world and that it is uncreated. It is possible to identify, among these different kinds of agnostics and atheists, sceptics, Stoics and others.

To the views of all who reject the idea of God's existence Philo opposes the teaching of Moses, which, he believed, showed that rational reflection led inexorably to the conclusion that God does exist. 'Your reason will show you that, as there is mind in you, so is there in the universe' (*Migr. Abr.* 186). In *Praem. Poen.* 40 he insists, as he does elsewhere, 'to God alone it is permitted to apprehend God', but nevertheless he claims that the existence of the Deity, the Divine Mind, may be inferred by analogy from the human mind: 'The human mind evidently occupies a position in men precisely answering to that which the great Ruler occupies in all the world' (*Op. Mund.* 69).

Also, reflection on the nature of the world leads the rational man to conclude that God exists. There are those 'who have had the strength through knowledge to envisage the Maker and Ruler of all' (*Praem. Poen.* 41). He continues with an eloquent description of the orderliness in nature and in the universe as a whole which leads such men to conclude both that it cannot all have come into being automatically, but must be the work of 'an architect and world-maker', and that 'there must be a providence' (since a maker is bound to care for what he makes). At the end of this particular section (*Praem. Poen.* 43) he describes the thought processes of such 'truly admirable persons . . . superior to the other classes' as an advance 'from down to up by a sort of heavenly ladder' and concludes that 'by reason and reflection' they have 'happily inferred the Creator from his works'.

There are several places in Philo's works where he uses the argument to a First Cause. In *Poster. C.* 28 Philo infers the existence of an Unmoved Mover – that 'the Existent Being (*to on*) who moves and turns all else is himself exempt from movement and turning' – from the words of Deut. 5: 31 (see below, pp. 198–9). But in *Op. Mund.* 8–9 he refers to Moses' outstanding position in the realm of philosophical thought which meant that he 'could not fail to recognise that the universal must consist of two parts, one part active Cause and the other passive object; and that the active Cause is the perfectly pure and unsullied Mind of the universe . . . while the passive part is in itself incapable of life and motion, but, when set in motion and shaped and quickened by Mind, changes into the most perfect masterpiece, namely this world'. What Philo says here about the nature of matter, lacking efficiency and causality, shows why, apart from other considerations, he concludes that the 'Highest of Causes' (*Som.* I.190) had to be Mind. For Philo too, once a man has recognised causes at work in the world he is then logically obliged to confess 'that even the causes which come higher in the chain of causation owe their existence to the Cause which is highest and first of all' (*Conf. Ling.* 124). And that such a First Cause must be Mind Philo is convinced must be the case: 'It cannot be that while in yourself there is a mind appointed as your ruler which all the community of the body obeys and each of the senses follows, the world, the fairest, and greatest and most perfect work of all, of which everything else is a part, is without a king who holds it together and directs it with justice' (*Abr.* 74). It is clear from Philo's words in *Migr. Abr.* 186 that intellectual scrutiny of oneself, let alone the universe, leads to the conclusion that in a way that is comparable to the relationship in man's life between mind and body, so also in the universe Mind rules over the material.

For Philo the idea of a universe existing without a cause was unthinkable. So also was the idea of God's being anything less than the First Cause. He describes Enoch allegorically as representing those who do not look beyond effects for their causes and who think that God is 'either not the cause in any sense or not the first cause' (*Conf. Ling.* 123). Elsewhere he speaks of the action on men's minds of 'the Highest of Causes' (*Som.* I.190). Later God is described as 'the supreme Cause' (*ibid.* I.240). So, then, there exists for Philo the possibility of knowledge of God's existence. It is both direct and indirect, but it is always based upon rational and reverent contemplation of the world. In some instances, it is the result of a revelation, given to a prophet; in others, it is the conclusion of syllogistic or logical argumentation. Moses' knowledge was the result of his having been 'divinely instructed in the greater and most essential part of Nature's lore' (*Op. Mund.* 8).

Man's mind also is capable of being inspired, as Moses' was, to aspire to God. This is not surprising, perhaps, since 'nothing earth-born is more like God than man', especially in respect of his mind, which is 'in a fashion a god to him' (*Op. Mund.* 69). When the mind, 'on soaring wing', contemplates higher and yet higher realms of reality and has passed beyond the universe of material objects, it reaches out to the intelligible world and 'is seized by a sober intoxication, like those filled with Corybantic frenzy, and is inspired, possessed by a longing far other than theirs and a nobler desire'. But 'amid its longing to see him, pure and untempered rays of concentrated light stream forth like a torrent, so that by its gleams the eye of the understanding is dazzled'. So, in the end, Philo seems to be saying here, man is denied access, beyond 'the topmost arch of the things perceptible to mind', to the vision of God himself (*ibid.* 70–1).

However, elsewhere Philo seems to imply, or state, that what is true in the case of prophetic inspiration is applicable to man's knowledge of God. In *Leg. All.* 1.36–8 he interprets the words 'breathed into' of Gen. 2: 7, as meaning that God breathes his Spirit into man so that man may receive 'a conception of him'. Such a possibility could never have arisen if God had not acted as he did. Philo concludes: 'For the mind of man would never have ventured to soar so high as to grasp the nature of God, had not God himself drawn it up to himself, so far as it was possible that the mind of man should be drawn up, and stamped it with the impress of the powers that are within the scope of its understanding.' Here again, Philo at first seems to suggest that man's mind can grasp the nature of God, but his concluding words attach a significant qualification and limitation. It is also not quite clear whether by 'the spirit or breath' (*ibid.* 37) he means, as the form of words used above ('his Spirit') suggests, his own spirit, or the rational soul of man. *To de empneomenon to pneuma* may be not God's Spirit, but the rational spirit of man with which God's Spirit endows man and through which it bears witness. However, it is not impossible that Philo means both: that man's knowledge of God is possible because of the rational spirit he possesses, *and* because God communicates such knowledge to him.

The Oneness of God. Describing Abraham, Philo explains how he realised that 'the delusions of the polytheistic creed' would prevent him from discovering 'the One, who alone is eternal and the Father of all things'. Already he was acting under 'divine inspiration'.

Prompted by the fire of yearning, fanned by divine warnings, he set out to seek for the One. He did not pause 'until he received clearer visions, not of his essence, for that is impossible, but of his existence and providence'. There then follows a description of Abraham's state of possession when 'everything in him changed to something better, eyes, complexion, stature, carriage, movements, voice . . . For the divine spirit which was breathed upon him from on high made its lodging in his soul, and invested his body with singular beauty, his voice with persuasiveness, and his hearers with understanding' (*Virt.* 211ff.). What Philo goes on to say makes it clear that what happened to Abraham can happen to others also. Even more emphatic language is used of the divine ecstasy experienced by Abraham within the statements to be found in *Quaest. in Gn.* III.9. In such a state 'the mind is divinely possessed and becomes filled with God'. In *Quaest. in Gn.* IV.29 Philo describes how the soul of the God-possessed man leaves him during the period of possession but then returns and man resumes his ordinary life. Ecstasy is not a permanent state of the human mind. So, in *Gig.* 20, Philo can say, with reference to Gen. 6: 3: 'The spirit sometimes stays awhile, but it does not abide for ever among us, the mass of men.' But 'even over the reprobate hovers often of a sudden the vision of the excellent', though in such cases it is a momentary, fleeting experience. In *Cher.* 98ff. Philo speaks of the souls of men as 'a region open to his invisible entrance' and as capable of being made lodging-places 'fit for God'. The 'worthy house' for God to dwell in is 'the soul that is fitted to receive him'. 'Justly and rightly then shall we say that in the invisible soul the invisible God has his earthly dwelling-place.' Philo states that 'in the understandings of those who have been purified to the utmost the Ruler of the universe walks noiselessly, alone, invisibly' and that even in the understandings of 'those who are still undergoing cleansing and have not yet fully washed their life defiled and stained by the body's weight there walk angels, divine words, making them bright and clean with the doctrines of all that is good and beautiful' (*Som.* I.148). *Som.* II.250ff. returns to the theme of the mind of man as the house or temple of God. The Existent is not to be sought among the regions of earth, but rather in a soul, free from turmoil, 'whose sight is keen, which has set before it as its aim to live in contemplation and peace'. There could be no 'grander or holier house' for God in the whole range of existence, than 'the vision-seeking mind'. God, or God's Spirit, is here described by

Philo as 'the invisible spirit, the familiar secret tenant' whom he hears telling him that the great and precious matter of which man is ignorant he will ungrudgingly show, bestowing authentic peace, free from illusion, and from the warfare of created things. So Philo can elsewhere (*Praem. Poen.* 123) say: 'in truth the wise man's mind is a palace and house of God'. So, whatever may be said by Philo about the knowledge of God's essence, God himself, or one of his Potencies (peace) or his Spirit, can be said to dwell in the mind or soul of the rational man. Hence Philo can say, of himself and his knowledge of God, that there is a higher thought than the interpretation of the allegorical significance of the Cherubim offered by him in *Cher.* 25–6: 'It comes from a voice in my own soul, which oftentimes is God-possessed and divines where it does not know' (*ibid.* 27). There is, then, a kind of knowledge prompted by the Spirit within man, knowledge which comes when, as with the prophets, God himself, or the Spirit or one of the Potencies, takes up residence in the soul. Philo refers to the 'voice' which told him that while God is one, 'his highest and chiefest powers are two', and that they are united by a third, Reason (*logos*). It is the 'mind' (*dianoia*) that Philo urges to admit the image of the Cherubim which will teach the truth of God's sovereignty and beneficence.

God as light. One important aspect of Philo's teaching on the subject of man's knowledge of God is related to what he says about God as light. The most satisfactory metaphor that Philo could find to describe God's nature was the metaphor of light. Light was to him – an Alexandrian bathed in the light of the eastern Mediterranean – 'the most beautiful of existing things, and a ministrant of things divine' (*Quaest. in Gn.* II.34); and, not surprisingly, citing Ps. 27: 1 (cf. p. 107), he says 'God is light', and also 'He is not only light, but the archetype of every other light.' The Logos, which 'contained all his fullness', was also light. According to *Cher.* 96–7 God is 'himself his own light. For the eye of the Absolutely Existent needs no other light to effect perception, but he himself is the archetypal essence of which myriads of rays are the effluence, none visible to sense, all to the mind.' There is, then, that in the invisible order of mind the knowing of which corresponds to, is comparable to (though of course not identical with), physical light in the realm of sense-perception. To the physical sense of sight God is totally invisible, a fact which Philo explains as due to God's decision that it was not fitting for him to be apprehended 'by the eyes of the body, perhaps because it was contrary to holiness that the mortal should touch the eternal' (*Abr.* 76). He concludes: 'For our sight could not have borne the rays that pour from him that IS, since it is not even able to look upon the beams of the sun.' God, then, can be seen, but not by human eyes. It is clear that the light which is divine is not physical and that the seeing of it does not involve the bodily sense of sight, for 'when you hear that God was seen by man, you must think that this takes place without the light which the senses know, for what belongs to mind can be apprehended only by the mental powers' (*Mut. Nom.* 6). He says of God's light: 'God is the fountain of the purest radiance, and so when he reveals himself to a soul the rays he puts forth are free from all shadow and of intense brightness' (*ibid.*). If man cannot know, with the limited powers of his mind, the essence of the Existent, he can nevertheless experience a powerful awareness of the dazzling intellectual light of God. But, though the imagery of light was found to be indispensable for Philo when speaking about God, it is clear from many of the things he says that even intellectual light could not be said to be that which constituted his essence. God is light for Philo, but also more than light. At creation, 'God when he gave birth to all things, not only brought them into sight, but also made things which before were not, not just handling material as an artificer, but being himself its creator' (*Som.* 1.76). Yet light remained the most satisfactory metaphor available to Philo to use in relation to God in respect of his relationship to man and his presence in men's lives. 'For as when the sun has risen the darkness disappears, and all things are filled with light, so when God, the spiritual sun, rises and shines upon the soul, the gloomy night of passions and vices is scattered, and virtue reveals the peerless brightness of her form in all its purity and loveliness' (*Virt.* 164). Philo calls God 'the sun of the sun, in the realm of mind what that is in the realm of sense, and from invisible fountains he supplies the visible beams to the sun which our eyes behold' (*Spec. Leg.* 1.279). 'When the knowledge of the Existent shines, it wraps everything in light, and thus renders invisible even bodies which seemed brightest in themselves' (*Ebr.* 44). He implies that the most advanced knowledge of God is that possessed by those who 'have had the power to apprehend him through himself without the co-operation of any reasoning process to lead them to the sight' (*Praem. Poen.* 43). He calls such people 'holy and genuine worshippers and friends of God'. Among them is Israel, 'the God-seer who sees not his real nature, for that, as I said, is impossible – but that he IS' (*ibid.* 44). The knowledge of God such a man possesses comes 'at the summons of him alone who has willed to reveal his existence as a person to the suppliant'. He then uses again the analogy of the perception of light and enunciates the general principle, with relation to the physical universe, 'light seen by light'. Applied to God this means that 'God too is his own brightness and is discerned through himself alone, without anything co-operating or being able to co-operate in giving a perfect apprehension of his existence' (*ibid.* 45). Philo concludes that, despite the 'happy guess' made by those who find the Creator in his creation, 'The seekers for truth are those who envisage God through God, light through light' (*ibid.* 46). These words carry the plain implication that God can be known by man apart from inferences based upon the nature of the created order, but also that there is absolutely nothing comparable to God that can provide an analogy, except and even that is only an analogy, light. But, Philo seems to be saying, just as when we look up at the sun we have an intense, even blinding, awareness of its real presence, without being able to describe it in terms of its essential characteristics, so men can become aware, with that same intensity of awareness, only at an intellectual level, of the real presence of God. Philo would have assented, as a devout Jew, to the statement 'No man has seen God at any time' (John 1: 18; cf. 1 John 4: 12). But in the passage in the *De Praemiis* he seems to be insisting that God can be known by men as more than the final term in a logical *a posteriori* argument. His essence may be beyond man's knowledge, but there are those who enjoy or experience a vivid sense of the dazzling brightness of God's reality. The man who has 'made the excellent his own has for his crown the vision of God' (*Praem. Poen.* 27). 'Belief in God, life-long joy, the perpetual vision of the Existent – what can anyone conceive more profitable or more august than these?' (*ibid.*). What indeed! Not only does 'the Man of Practice' (Jacob) see 'the conceptual world' in the brilliant light of 'a beam purer than ether', but also God 'did not grudge to grant him the vision of himself in so far as it was possible for mortal and created nature to contain it', a vision which 'only showed that he IS, not what he is', since 'to God alone is it permitted to apprehend God' (*Praem. Poen.* 36–40). In the case of Moses, Philo explains, there is no need to be at a loss as to how he came to have a 'conception of the invisible God'. Moses 'learnt it by a divine communication', which the Creator, aware of the desirability of man's obtaining a conception of him, made possible by breathing into him 'of his own Deity. The invisible Deity stamped on the invisible soul the impress of Itself' (*Det. Pot. Ins.* 86). It is this presence within man of the invisible image of the invisible Deity that makes it possible for him to have a conception of God. When Philo states that God 'did not deem it right to be apprehended by the eyes of the body' (*Abr.* 76), he plainly implies, what he elsewhere states, that the 'eyes' of the soul can apprehend God.

If God's essence cannot be seen directly, he can be known by man through the action of his 'powers', to which reference has been made above (pp. 50–1). Moses received a 'divine communication' (Exod. 33: 23) which meant that 'all that follows in the wake of God is within the good man's apprehension, while he himself alone is beyond it'. God is 'brought within ken by the powers that follow and attend him' (*Poster. C.* 169). Earlier in the same treatise Philo had said that when Moses besought God to reveal his nature to him he embarked upon 'a quest of that which is beyond matter and beyond sight', but he does say that though God transcends all that he has made, 'he has caused his powers to extend themselves throughout the Universe to its utmost bounds' (*ibid.* 13–16). Though Philo states emphatically that no single created being is capable by his own efforts of attaining the knowledge of 'the God who verily exists', he does not suggest that the same impossibility exists in the case of human knowledge of the divine powers. Even the slight element of doubt present in the previous passage is absent from *Fug.* 165, where, having said of Moses that 'he did not succeed in finding anything by search respecting the essence of him that IS', he goes on to explain that the words of Exod. 33: 23, the 'divine communication', mean that it is sufficient for man 'to come to a knowledge of all that follows on after God and in his wake': namely, the divine powers (see pp. 47 and 50–1.).

It is only fair to point out that there is an important passage in which Philo seems to be asserting that not only the Deity in his essence but also the powers are unknowable. This is *Spec. Leg.* 1.41ff.: there, Philo begins by stating that, since light can only be known by light, Moses asked God to reveal himself to him. God, however, replied that, though willing to grant all the benefits man was capable of receiving, he could not bestow knowledge of himself, for 'the apprehension of me is something more than human nature, yea even the whole heaven and universe, will be able to contain'. Philo then describes how, in response to Moses' request to be allowed to apprehend 'the powers that keep guard around thee', God says: 'The powers which thou seekest to know are discerned not by sight but by mind even as I, whose they are, am discerned by mind and not by sight.' All that God can grant Moses, according to this passage, is, since the powers themselves are 'beyond your apprehension', 'a sort of impress and copy of their active working'. Since the powers are here said to be the Platonic Forms or Ideas (*ibid.* 48) – this being the only place where Philo explicitly equates the powers with the Platonic Ideas (see below, pp. 110–11; though cf. *Cher.* 51) – God is obliged to tell Moses: 'Do not, then, hope to be ever able to apprehend me or any of my powers in our essence' (*ibid.* 49). However, God grants to Moses 'a share of what is attainable' and urges him to contemplate the universe with the unsleeping eye of the mind and to long for wisdom which, he says, 'fills its scholars and disciples with verities glorious in their exceeding loveliness' (*ibid.* 50). According to Philo, when Moses heard this, he 'kept the yearning for the invisible aflame in his heart'. It has been suggested that Philo's words in these passages imply a view of a growing vision and knowledge of the essence of God, even though such knowledge can never be complete. God can at least be known by man in relation to the exercise of his creative and kingly powers and in terms of his many 'properties'. Since God is light, it is only as man partakes of the nature of light that a pure vision of him is attained, but that is precisely what can happen to man. For, as Philo puts it in *Quaest. in Gn.* IV.46, '[the mind] becoming light is elevated to higher things, and looking around observes what is in the air and in the ether and the whole heaven together'. This 'ascent' is figuratively called 'mountain', or more truly 'wisdom'. For God to be envisaged it must be by light, and for man such a vision of God is possible when the mind partakes of the divine light. That this does occur seems to be the plain implication of the words (in *Som.* I.113–14) 'while there is abiding in the soul that most God-like and incorporeal light' and 'While, then, God still pours upon you the rays of his sacred light'.

Man's relationship with God. That the relationship between man and God is not a purely intellectual one appears to be shown by the way in which Philo speaks of man as a 'house' inhabited by God. In *Som.* I.149 occurs the exhortation 'Be zealous, therefore, O soul, to become a house of God, a holy temple, a most beauteous abiding-place, for perchance the Master of the whole world's household shall be thine too and keep thee under his care as his special house, to preserve thee evermore strongly guarded and unharmed.' Elsewhere, in *Quaest. in Ex.* II.51, having already urged his reader to become an animate shrine of the Father, he writes: 'the beginning and end of happiness is to be able to see God'. The implication is that the man who does make his soul a shrine for God can, in some real sense, see him. Other passages in which Philo speaks of the soul as a shrine or temple of God are *Som.* I.215, where, of the 'two temples of God', one is said to be 'the rational soul, whose Priest is the real Man', and *Gig.* 45ff., where he says that, since God is everywhere, he is near us, and that the divine spirit of wisdom may abide with us as it did with Moses.

Also, that there is more to Philo's understanding of man's relationship with God than the intellectual, rational elements is shown by the many occasions on which he speaks of God as lovable. In *Det. Pot. Ins.* 56, having accepted, with qualifications, a definition of religion as 'a caring for God', he goes on to say that 'to God men can bring nothing except a disposition full of love to their Master'. In *Poster. C.* 69 Philo quotes Moses' definition of 'living in accordance with God' as 'consisting in loving him' (he cites part of Deut. 30: 19–20). What God asks of man, Philo says in *Spec. Leg.* I.299–300, is not something difficult: it is simply 'to love him as a benefactor . . . to serve him not half-heartedly but with thy whole soul filled with the determination to love him'. In *Abr.* 50 he speaks of 'affection for the true God' as 'returned by him'. In *Deus Imm.* 69 he says that the 'most suitable' attitude for those whose thoughts of God contain no anthropomorphic distortions is 'to love him'.

Associated with Philo's words on the theme of man's love of God is what he says about prayer (see above, p. 34). In *Plant.* 161 Philo observes that his Jewish forefathers never failed, before they inaugurated any 'noble business . . . to tarry to pray and offer sacrifices'.

Sacrifice. Philo, then, does not reject the idea of sacrifice to God. When he says, in *Spec. Leg.* I.271, that 'God does not rejoice in sacrifices even if one offer hecatombs, for all things are his possessions, yet though he possesses he needs none of them', he is probably doing no more than to echo the criticism of the abuse of sacrifice contained in such passages as Micah 6: 7 and Ps. 50: 12–13. He is attempting to stress, as Sirach did (Sir. 35: 1–11), that the mere external performance of the sacrificial rites unaccompanied by obedience to the Law and righteousness of life is unacceptable to God (cf. Aristeas 234, 170 and 172: see Bartlett 1985: pp. 11ff.). Philo himself tells us of at least one occasion in his life when he went up to Jerusalem 'to offer up prayers and sacrifices' (*Prov.* 64). He also wrote at great length, in *Spec. Leg.* I, about Jewish sacrificial rites. His allegorical exegesis, for example, in *Spec. Leg.* I.167, shows not that Philo rejected the idea of sacrifice, but that he wished his readers to understand that sacrifice must be offered 'with no infirmity or ailment or evil affection in the soul' and that as important as the sacrificial victim offered was the quality of life of the offerer and the 'prayers or thanks' accompanying the gift. Philo was, however, acutely aware of the inadequacy of temple and sacrifice, even of other less material elements in the ritual of earthly worship. 'It is not possible genuinely to express our gratitude to God by means of buildings and oblations and sacrifices, as is the custom of most people, for even the whole world were not a temple adequate to yield the honour due to him. Nay, it must be expressed by means of hymns of praise, and these not such as the audible voice shall sing, but strains raised and re-echoed by the mind too pure for eye to discern' (*Plant.* 126). It is noticeable how, whether he is writing as he does here or as he does in other places, that gratitude or thanksgiving is something to which Philo attaches great importance. Whatever else may be said about Philo's God, he is certainly a God who evoked in Philo the profoundest sense of gratitude, since 'the work most appropriate to God is conferring boons, that most fitting to creation giving thanks' (*ibid.* 130). Since man can give God nothing else, he should make thanksgiving his perpetual study: 'Let us never tire of composing eulogies in prose and poetry, to the end that, whether with or without musical accompaniment, whichever of its appointed functions the voice may exercise, be it eloquent speech or song, high honour may be given both to the world and to the Creator of the world; the former, as one has said, the most perfect of things produced, the latter the best of producers' (*ibid.* 131). God is for Philo a God who prompts his worshippers to be 'ceaselessly engaged in conning hymns of thanksgiving to him' (*ibid.* 135).

At one important point in his *De Plantatione* Philo approaches very close, as he does elsewhere in other respects, to the teaching of his Jewish contemporary, Jesus of Nazareth, and of other writers of the New Testament. Writing about sacrifice, which he describes as 'a plant most fair', he notes that there is sometimes a 'parasitic growth' which becomes attached to it, superstition. This should be excised, he advises, 'For some have imagined that it is piety to slaughter oxen and allot to the altars portions of what they have got by stealing, or by repudiating debts, or by defrauding creditors, or by seizing property and cattle-lifting, thinking, in their gross defilement, that impunity for their offences is a thing that can be bought. "Nay, nay", I would say to them, "no bribes, O foolish ones, can reach God's tribunal." He turns his face away from those who approach with guilty intent, even though they lead to his altar a hundred bullocks every day, and accepts the guiltless, although they sacrifice nothing at all. God delights in altars beset by a choir of Virtues, albeit no fire burn on them' (*ibid.* 107–8).

Philo's mysticism. Philo's religion has sometimes been characterised as mystical and Philo described as a mystic. This is not the place for a discussion of the propriety of the description of the Judaism expounded by Philo as a mystery or a mystery religion. But there can be little doubt that the language of mysticism is used by Philo very frequently. In *Quaest. in Gn.* IV.47 he states: 'There are three ways of life which are well known: the contemplative, the active and the pleasurable. Great and excellent is the contemplative.' He often speaks of 'initiation', as in *Cher.* 48, where he addresses his readers as 'you initiated' (*ō mustai*) and declares: 'I myself was initiated under Moses the God-beloved into his greater mysteries' (cf. *Leg. All.* III.219). A distinction has been drawn by a modern Jewish scholar between the goal of Rabbinic Judaism, understanding of the Torah and obedience to it, and the goal of Philo's Judaism, 'mystic communion with the Godhead'. The latter was certainly Philo's supreme goal, though it did not exclude or displace the former (any more than Rabbinic Judaism *per se* excludes the goal of mystical communion with God). If the belief that one enjoys the *visio Dei*, together with the reception of divine revelations, makes one a mystic, then not only was Moses a mystic, by Philo's reckoning, but so also was Philo himself. Philo often speaks of himself, as he does in *Spec. Leg.* III.1, as 'borne aloft into the heights with a soul possessed by some God-sent inspiration', of his sense of union with God or his powers, of the sense of being a dwelling-place for God, of his longing to participate in the divine and so to achieve wholeness, of the visions he experienced, and of the state of ecstasy into which his union with the divine introduced him. This would justify the description of him as a mystic, and to ignore the mystical element in Philo's thought is to omit something fundamental and essential to it. It may not be so absurd, as some have suggested, to see in Philo a process which, though not quite a transformation of Judaism into a mystery religion, yet involved a powerful influence on it by the language, rites and practices, but especially the thought-patterns and motifs, of the Greek mystery religions that flourished in the world of his day. In *Rer. Div. Her.* 249 Philo describes three different kinds of ecstasy, the third one, 'the best form of all', being 'the divine possession or frenzy to which the prophets as a class are subject'. It is 'what the inspired and God-possessed experience' (*ibid.* 258). He describes what happens when man experiences this ecstasy later (*ibid.* 264). He states that when the 'sun' of the human mind sets, the divine 'sun' rises. Then 'natural ecstasy and divine possession and madness fall upon us'. This rising of the divine 'sun' in men is equated with the arrival of the divine Spirit (*ibid.* 265). So, for Philo, there are occasions when the divine Spirit or 'sun' takes up its residence in us in place of human reason and man experiences an ecstatic kind of enthusiasm and madness, in which he is out of his mind because temporarily God's 'sun' or Spirit has taken it over. In this state man becomes not a Christopher but a God-bearer (the Greek word Philo uses is *theophorētos*).

Moses: the supreme theologian. It would be unsatisfactory to complete any account of Philo's doctrine of God without a word about his view of Moses as the supreme theologian. Much of what Philo knew of God – all that did not come to him from within his own communion with God – came from Moses. In *Poster. C.* 28 he calls Moses 'the all-wise', and in several passages he calls him simply the 'theologian', as, for example, in *Quaest. in Ex.* II.87. In a nearby passage (*ibid.* II.88) Moses is addressed *ō kurie ho theologos* ('O Master Theologian'), which is exactly what he was in Philo's eyes. In *Mut. Nom.* 7 (see below, pp. 86 and 88) Moses is described as 'the explorer of nature which lies beyond our vision', so that, far from being one of the 'simpletons' of *Leg. All.* I.91 'who inquire about God's substance' or limited, like other men, in having 'no organ' by means of which the Existent can be envisaged, Moses was, as one great Philonist has put it, the God–man. In *Sacr. AC* 9 Philo, describing Moses as what the same scholar calls a special type of incarnation, says that 'even when he sent him as a loan to the earthly sphere and suffered him to dwell therein, he gifted him with no ordinary excellence, such as that which kings and rulers have, wherewith to hold sway and sovereignty over the passions of the soul, but he appointed him as god (*eis theon*), placing all the bodily region and the mind which rules it in subjection and slavery to him'. It was as one who was, like the Logos, *theos*, that Moses constructed the theology which Philo seeks to interpret and commend in his writings. Moses, for Philo, stood above all other theologians, since he had 'undergone initiation into the great mysteries' (*Leg. All.* III.100) and had therefore obtained 'a clear vision of the increated One' (*ibid.*). 'Moses has God for his Instructor', he adds (*ibid.* 102). The divine spirit of wisdom took up its residence permanently in Moses (*Gig.* 47), as it may also do in us, if on our part there is a proper reverence and awe and receptivity.

When taken together with what Philo says about the allegorical interpretation of the Scriptures, his doctrine of God tends to create a two-tier Judaism: the Judaism of the Jews of simple faith and obedience, and the intellectual and mystical Judaism of those who could understand the subtleties of allegorical exegesis and who could share in the religious ecstasy of men like Philo. This is especially so in the philosophical content and the emphasis upon greater or higher mysteries which are only within the reach of the initiated. Developing Christian theology did much the same for Christianity. But it is a doctrine of God which deserves recognition as a profound contribution to the thought and piety of Judaism and which, as well as being an enormously important part of the background to Christianity in the New Testament period, proved to be a useful place of exploration for the Christian theologians, who were faced with the task of transforming the witness and *kērugma* of the New Testament into the doctrine and dogma of Patristic and later Christianity.

PHILO'S ATTACK ON ANTHROPOMORPHISM AND ANTHROPOPATHISM (*Deus Imm.* 51–68 (XI–XIV))

In this passage Philo, as he often does, attacks anthropomorphism and anthropopathism with his usual vigour. We also see further evidence of how he viewed and interpreted the Jewish Scriptures. In addition, other aspects of his doctrine of God – apart from his rejection of anthropomorphism and anthropopathism – are presented.

Anthropomorphism (*Deus Imm.* 51–9)

(51) Having explained with sufficient clarity these matters, let us
look at the next words, which are as follows, 'I will blot out
man whom I made from the face of the earth, from man to
beast, from creeping things to fowls of heaven, because I
(52) was wroth in that I made him' [Gen. 6: 7]. Now some
people, when they hear the words just quoted, imagine that
the Existent Being gives way to wrath and anger, whereas
he is not susceptible to passion in any form. It is the peculiar
characteristic of human weakness to be prone to feel
disquiet, but God experiences neither the irrational passions
of the soul, nor do the parts and limbs of the body belong in
the least measure to God. Nevertheless, the Lawgiver speaks
of such things in relation to God, but only in so far as they
serve as an elementary introduction for those who could not
(53) otherwise form correct opinions. For in all the laws which
are in the form of commands or prohibitions, and they
alone are laws in the proper meaning of the word, there are
two principal affirmations made with respect to the great
Cause of all things, one that 'God is not as a man' [Num. 23:
(54) 19]; the other that he is as a man. But though the first of
these assertions, on the one hand, is confirmed by the most
certain truth, the latter is, on the other hand, introduced for
the instruction of the many. Therefore also it is said
concerning him, 'like a man he shall train his son' [Deut. 8:
5]. So it is for the sake of instruction and admonition, not

because God is really such by nature, that these words are
(55) used. For among men some are soul lovers, some body
lovers. The companions of the soul, who are capable of
converse with incorporeal beings, do not compare the
living God, the Existent One, to any species of created
being. They have dissociated God from every distinct or
separate quality, for the thing that most contributes to his
blessedness and to his supreme felicity is the fact that his
being is comprehended as simple, naked being, without any
definite characteristic. They are content with the basic
conception of his existence and do not attempt to invest him
(56) with any form. But those who have entered into an
agreement and a compact with the body are unable to
throw off the garment of the flesh, the flesh's robes, and to
behold that existence which needs nothing in its unique
solitariness, and which is incomparable and simple, unmixed with anything else and unalloyed, uncompounded
with anything else. They therefore think of the Creator of
all things as they do of themselves, not realising that while a
being which is made up of a combination of many faculties
requires many parts in order to supply the needs of each,
God, because he is uncreated and the Being who has
brought into being all other things, stands in need of none of
those properties which belong to his creatures.

(57) For what can we say? Shall we say that if he possesses our
bodily parts and organs he has feet to use for walking from
one place to another? But where will he go or walk since he
fills all places with his presence? And to whom will he go,
since there is no-one equal in honour to him? And why
would he walk? It cannot be out of any concern for his
health as it is with us. Again, are we to say that he has hands
for the purpose of giving and receiving? Yet in fact he
receives nothing from anyone. Indeed he has no needs and
possesses everything. When he does give he employs as the
minister of his gifts the Reason by whose agency he also

(58) created the world. Furthermore God has no need of eyes, the organs which, without the light which is perceived by the senses, lack receptive power. But that light is a created light, whereas God saw before creation, using himself as
(59) light. Why do we need to mention the organs of eating anything? For if he has those organs, then he eats and is filled, and when he is satisfied he stops eating, only to resume after a rest when he feels the need to eat again. Upon the accompaniments and consequences of this I am not going to dwell, for they are mythical fictions of the impious, who represent God, in word, only as endued with human form, but, in fact and reality, as experiencing human passions.

(51) *I was wroth*: Philo states that, having made clear the point that God had made man capable of knowing good and evil, had imposed upon them the duty of choosing the better rather than the worse and had given them, in the shape of reason, an incorruptible faculty to discriminate between them, he intends now to go on to examine the words of Gen. 6: 7. The problem the verse creates for him is that it attributes the emotion of anger to God.

(52) *he is not susceptible to passion*: some readers of Gen. 6: 7, Philo suggests at this point, will mistakenly think that God does experience our human emotions. Disquiet, says Philo, is *the peculiar characteristic of human weakness* and neither any of the *irrational passions* of the human soul nor any parts or limbs of the human body *belong in the least measure to God*. God is wholly other and transcendent.

Moses, however, spoke about God in the way he does in Gen. 6: 7 in order to accommodate himself to human weakness. The language of the verse in question, and of verses like it, has a didactic purpose; it serves *as an elementary introduction for those who could not otherwise form correct opinions*. What Philo means is that the description of God as capable of being angry – though in reality the word 'angry' applies only to a human being experiencing a particular emotion – is likely to make men fear him and awaken in them a proper respect for him. There are those who need the simplification of anthropomorphic language to give them some conception of God, inadequate though it may be.

(53) *God is not as a man . . . he is as a man*: Moses, in the case of the laws which are properly so-called, laws which embrace commands and prohibitions, sets forth these two leading principles. One is a quotation from Num. 23: 19, the other occurs, for example, in the statement in Deut. 8: 5. The full text of the latter verse makes Moses' purpose clear. God is portrayed *as a man*, as if he experienced human emotions, for the purpose of educating man. It is not the case that God in fact is *as a man* in any respect at all. Moses does not use the words of Deut. 8: 5 because God's nature really is like human nature. There is no real similarity (*homoiousia*) between the two, let alone identity (*homoousia*). Neither word is applicable to the relationship between the divine and human natures.

(54) *the most certain truth*: Philo asserts that the statement of Num. 23: 19 is surely grounded in truth, whereas the statement in Deut. 8: 5 is there *for the instruction of the many*. The less intellectually minded readers of the Old Testament need the help of anthropomorphic language. It teaches them things about God which otherwise they would not learn, though it is itself profoundly untrue if taken literally.

(55) *some are soul lovers, some body lovers*: mankind it thus divided into two categories. Those who are *companions of the soul* are *capable of converse with* intelligible and *incorporeal beings* and make no comparisons of *the Existent* (*to on*) to any form of created being. For they realise that God is to be dissociated from any category or class or quality. One of the facts which contribute to the supreme blessedness and felicity of God is that *his being is comprehended as simple naked being, without any definite characteristc.* Here is a characteristically Philonic – and therefore philosophical – definition of God. Created beings have particular characteristics; a man, for example is this or that, tall or short, wise or foolish, and so on. God is simply God; he is Pure Being. The *companions of the soul* (those men, that is, who are of a philosophical bent) do not picture God's being as having a particular form (*morphē*) analogous to some form of created being, but conceive only of his existence. God is, for them, He Who IS.

To be able to know God beyond that point would involve the possession of knowledge equal to God's self-awareness, his omniscience. But even the knowledge of God's existence, which is all that can be apprehended by man's mind, is the result of 'clear intuition' rather than that of intellectual processes in the human mind.

(56) *the garment of the flesh*: worn by the other category of men, who have made a compact with the body: this prevents them from seeing that existence which needs nothing in its unique self-sufficiency and is in its absolute simplicity free from all admixture and composition. God, for Philo, is *simple* being in the sense that he is Pure Being. Like the One of Parmenides, he is the Pure Being which transcends all predicates. He is similar to the God of Aristotle and the God of Plotinus in being beyond the world and his derivatives, and also in being indefinable, a Being with regard to whom there is more truth for man in silence than in words. But those who are companions of the body, clothed inescapably in *the garments of the flesh* think of *the Creator of all things* (God) as like themselves, a union of soul and body. They do not appreciate that, while a composite being such as man needs several parts to minister to the needs of his several faculties, God, because he is uncreated and the Author of the creation of others, requires none of *the properties* which belong to his creatures. Philo states here that God possesses no *properties*. *Properties* here does not correspond to the word usually so translated, for, while Philo does not speak of God's 'qualities' (which could belong to other beings), he does speak (as in *Cher*. 77, where he says it is an attribute of God to act) of those 'qualities' which belong uniquely to him (see above, p. 48).

(57) *where will he go*?: Philo draws out the consequences of an anthropomorphic view of God. If God did have bodily parts and organs, he would possess feet with which to walk about. But there is nowhere to go for One whose presence *fills all places*. The omnipresence of God makes the idea of a God possessing feet, like a man, ludicrous. Philo also asks a number of rhetorical questions, the answers to which all show the absurdity of anthropomorphic conceptions of the Deity. He argues, by means of his questions, that there is no one to whom God can go, since he has no equal. There is also no reason for his taking a walk, since it could not be, as with men, for reasons of health (walking was recommended by Aristotle as health-giving). The possession of hands implies the actions of giving and receiving, yet God receives nothing from anyone, needing nothing and possessing everything. Also, when God gives he employs as *minister of his gifts* the Reason by which he made the world. God, therefore, does bestow gifts on mankind, but to do so employs his Logos, here described as his Agent in the creation of the world (see below, pp. 112–13).

(58) *God saw before creation*: just as God does not need feet or

hands, so also he does not need eyes to see with. Human eyes, Philo reminds his readers, can see only where there is light. But, he adds, that material light was created. Seeing for human beings became possible only after the creation of light, whereas *God saw before creation*, being himself his own light. As the psalmist sang, 'The Lord is my light' (Ps. 27: 1); or, as it is put in 1 John 1: 5, 'God is light and in him is no darkness at all.' But that divine light is not the light which meets our sense. It is pure intellectual light, the light of pure mind. In this connection, elsewhere, Philo speaks of those who seek for truth as those who form their ideas of God from God, light from light (*Praem. Poen.* 46). Though no analogy from creation is adequate or entirely satisfactory, the imagery of light – the physical light experienced by Philo being clear Mediterranean light – is the best that Philo could find to use about God. But God is not only able to see without sense-perceptible light, since, like Aristotle's First Mover, he is immaterial; his substance is imperceptible by sense; he is his own intellectual light. There are similarities too with Aristotle's conception of God as *noēsis noēseōs* (Thought of Thought), since Philo's God both is the light by which he sees and *is* Light.

(59) *mythical fictions of the impious*: that is how Philo characterises the descriptions of God as possessing parts and limbs such as, to mention the next example Philo gives, *the organs of eating anything*. If God did possess such organs, he argues, he would eat and be filled, rest and then feel hungry again, and, he adds, *Upon the accompaniments and consequences of this I am not going to dwell*. Such *mythical fictions* are the product of impiety on the part of those who *represent God, in word, only as endued with human form, but, in fact and reality, as experiencing human passions*. For Philo there is only one thing worse than anthropomorphism and that is anthropopathism. Philo regarded the body as the tomb of the soul and the good life as involving a struggle to subdue the passions of the flesh and indeed the whole life of the body. It is not surprising that he viewed anthropomorphic language about God with such hostility. It is also not surprising that nothing quite like the Christian concept of the Incarnation of the divine Logos appears in his pages.

Anthropopathism (*Deus Imm.* 60–8)

(60) Why, then, does Moses speak of the Uncreated as having feet and hands, and as coming up and going out? And why

does he speak of him as clothing himself in armour to repel his enemies? For he does speak of him as carrying a sword, and employing as his weapons arrows, and winds and destructive fire (the poets describe them, using other words, as thunderbolt and whirlwind, and say that they are the weapons of the Cause of all things). In addition, why does Moses speak of God's jealousy, his wrath, his fits of anger, and other feelings like these, speaking of them as similar to
(61) those felt by man? But to those who ask questions such as these Moses answers thus: 'Gentlemen, the lawgiver who wishes to establish the most excellent system of laws must have one goal constantly before his eyes, to do good to all who come within his sphere of influence. Those, therefore, who have received a generously gifted nature and an education faultless in all respects, and who also find that their subsequent path in life lies in a straight and even direction, take truth with them as their companion, and, being instructed by her in the mysteries of the Existent which admit of no falsehood, do not attribute any of the
(62) attributes of created being to him. Such men find that principal affirmation in the sacred Scriptures most pertinent, that 'God is not as a man', but neither is he as heaven nor the material universe. For these are species indued with distinctive attributes which are perceived by the outward senses. But he is not apprehensible even by the mind, except merely in respect of his essence, the fact that he *is*. For his existence, indeed, is a fact which we can comprehend concerning him, but beyond the fact of his existence we can understand nothing.

(63) But those who have a natural intelligence that is duller and more sluggish, and who have been badly educated in their childhood, who do not possess a clear power of vision, stand in need of physicians in the shape of admonishers or lawgivers, who can devise the necessary remedy ap-
(64) propriate to their present complaint. Thus ill-disciplined

slaves benefit from the attentions of a severe schoolmaster who frightens them, for they are afraid of the punishments he inflicts and the threats he utters and are, in spite of themselves, schooled by fear. Such men learn what is false, through which they will profit, even if they cannot be made
(65) wise by the truth. For also in the case of patients suffering from dangerous illnesses the most reputable doctors do not venture to tell them the whole truth, knowing that this would make them more despondent and would not effect a cure for the disease, whereas, however, as a result of being told the opposite of the truth they would endure more readily the condition afflicting them, and it is more likely
(66) that the illness would be relieved. For what physician in his right mind would say to a patient under his care, 'Sir, you need to have surgery, or cauterisation, or an amputation.'? No one would speak in that way. For if he did, the patient would become depressed before the treatment could be applied and so the existing illness would have added to it another, in his soul, more grievous than the first, and he would firmly reject the treatment. If, however, through the physician's deceit, the patient was led to expect the opposite outcome to his illness, he would gladly submit to everything the doctor did with patience, even though the methods employed to save his life proved to be most
(67) painful. Therefore the lawgiver, being the best of physicians of the passions and diseases of the soul, set before himself one task and one goal, to excise by the very roots the diseases of the mind, so that not a single root might be left behind
(68) capable of again putting forth shoots incapable of cure. In this way, then, he hoped to be able to eradicate the evil, by the method of representing the supreme Cause as sometimes indulging in threats and frequently displaying indignation and implacable anger, and moreover as employing offensive weapons in his onslaughts on the wicked. For only in this way can the fool be corrected. And therefore it

> appears to me that to the two principal assertions mentioned above, namely that God is as a man, and that God is not as a man, are connected two other principles, closely consequent upon them and associated with them, namely, that of fear and that of love. For I see that all the law's exhortations to piety refer either to the love or the fear of the Existent One. In the case of those who do not attribute to their conception of the Existent any share of parts or passions, but honour him for himself alone in a manner which is fitting in the case of God, to love him is the most natural response. But in the case of others it is more appropriate to fear him.

(60) *feet and hands*: this section comes in the midst of what Philo writes in an attempt to deal with the problem of the anthropomorphisms of Scripture, as we have already seen. The particular passage on which he is commenting, Gen. 6: 7, contains an example of such anthropomorphism: the attribution of anger to God. Having given his reasons for Moses' description of God in such terms, Philo now proceeds to ask why it was that, if God does not have or need bodily parts and organs, Moses spoke of such things in relation to the Deity, whom he here calls *the Uncreated*, a reminder that an uncreated Being cannot have those parts or qualities which belong to created beings. Why, Philo asks, did Moses speak of God's arming himself, using wind and fire as his weapons? Philo notes that the poets call *the weapons of the Cause, thunderbolt and whirlwind*, different words for the same thing. Philo clearly knew about the Greek god Zeus, 'the Cloud-compeller' as he is described in Homer's *Iliad*, the god whose most frightening weapon was his thunderbolt, the only piece missing unhappily from the magnificent statue of him in the National Museum, Athens. He also had in mind passages from the Old Testament in which God is either portrayed as a God of wind and fire or as a God who employs these and other natural forces as instruments of his wrath (see, e.g., Gen. 8: 1, Exod. 9: 27, 15: 10, Ps. 135: 7, Isa. 27: 8, 41: 16, 66: 16, and many others).

Why also, Philo asks, did Moses speak of God's jealousy, wrath, words of anger, and other emotions of a human kind? Philo cannot allow that God is ever angry in a human fashion, and he later repeats the explanation for the existence of Scriptural anthropomorphism given in the *Sacr. AC* 94–5 (see paras. 70ff. of the present treatise).

(61) *Moses answers thus*: the reply that Moses would give, according to Philo, is that a lawgiver who aims at the best must have only one aim. It must be his intention *to do good to all who come within his sphere of influence*. For a man like Moses, who possessed a gifted nature and whose training was faultless, and who thus pursued a straight course in life, with truth as a *companion*, and was admitted by her into the infallible mysteries of the Existent, does not *attribute any of the attributes of created being to him*. Anthropomorphism is for Philo wholly excluded from a true doctrine of God.

(62) *God is not as a man*: as he so often does, Philo quotes the words of Num. 23: 19, and extends the improper ways of speaking of God that are excluded from the proper conception of God by adding the words *neither is he as Heaven nor the material universe*. This addition may have been aimed at the Stoics, since Zeno, Chrysippus and Posidonius are all credited with having believed that the whole world and the heavens were the substance of God (or were the divine substance). From the Zeno fragments it certainly seems that he defined God as the fiery mind of the world and said that God was a bodily substance made up of the whole universe. Tertullian says that, according to Zeno, God permeates the material world as honey runs through a honeycomb. Heaven and earth are entities which are perceptible by the human senses. That is something which by definition God cannot be.

he is not apprehensible even by the mind: here we meet one of Philo's most distinctive and difficult conceptions. God is not perceived by any of the senses – he cannot be seen, touched, smelt, heard or tasted. But, more than that, he cannot be perceived by the mind, save in *the fact that he is*. One might have expected Philo, the philosopher–theologian, to define God in terms which allowed the apprehension of him by the human intellect, the highest faculty in man. But in fact that is not so. All that the human mind can achieve is to apprehend *that* he exists. *What* he is in his essence, his attributes and qualities or properties, cannot be directly apprehended, not even by the human mind (see pp. 38–9, 87, 89–90). Man apprehends only God's existence, and nothing of what lies outside that existence. Philo is not here alluding to supernatural existences other than God, but to knowledge about God than knowledge of the mere fact of his existence. Man can know that there is a God, but not, by reason, what kind of God he is.

(63) *physicians in the shape of admonishers*: some men lack natural

intelligence and have been *badly educated*. These weaker brethren, who have no *clear power of vision*, need the discipline of fear, the medicine of anthropomorphism appropriate to their condition to help them.

(64) *schooled by fear*: Philo continues the above line of argument. Fear is a necessary part of the education of the dense and dull, just as ill-disciplined and foolish slaves profit from a master who frightens them. The serious point of all this is that by reading the Scriptures with their (false) anthropomorphisms such men may nevertheless be brought to wisdom. If not *by the truth*, the goal may be attained by *what is false*, by means of the truths of Scripture expressed in the untrue forms of anthropomorphic language. It is interesting to find that Philo does not exclude the literalists, those who do not appreciate that the real truth of Scripture lies beneath its anthropomorphic level of language, from access to wisdom.

(65) *the illness would be relieved*: picking up the medical analogy used earlier, Philo now compares the presence of anthropomorphism in Scripture to the practice of doctors in not telling their patients the whole truth about their ailments, lest they should become disheartened and hindered from recovering, but instead encouraging them by medically ethical 'lies' to endure their troubles patiently and so get well. The anthropomorphisms of Scripture, then, are like the falsely optimistic words used by a doctor to promote the well-being of his patients.

(66) *the physician's deceit*: Philo here compares Moses' use of anthropomorphisms to the way in which a surgeon does not tell a patient in need of extensive surgery of the drastic nature of the operation he has in mind. To do that would be to add a malady of the soul to the existing malady of the body. Deceived by optimistic words on the part of the surgeon, the patient will gladly endure the treatment, no matter how painful it may prove to be. So, with Moses, the reader may in the end be enabled, even by the deceits of anthropomorphism, to see the truth which the Scriptures contain. All the analogies Philo has used imply that, though the method of attaining the end is painful, the literalist reader of Scripture may at last be brought to wisdom. His explanation of Scriptural anthropomorphism also implies that for many the ascent to a proper understanding of God is difficult and painful, but that, through Moses' use of anthropomorphic language about him, God graciously accommodates himself to human weakness and inadequacy.

(67) *the best of physicians*: Philo is, of course, referring to Moses, here also described as *the lawgiver*. The conditions Moses had to deal with were *the passions and diseases of the soul*. He therefore determined *to excise by the very roots the diseases of the mind* and to leave no trace of them which might spring to life again. This was essential because there is a malady of the soul, a soul-sickness, *incapable of cure*. So Philo sees the Scriptures as a kind of medicine of the soul, able to cure the fundamental ills of mankind, and Moses as the doctor and surgeon who both creates and administers. The 'drug' of anthropomorphic language is used by Dr Moses, but only as a preliminary part of the treatment required to achieve in the end a total excision of the whole anthropomorphic condition of mankind when thinking about God.

(68) *onslaughts on the wicked*: Philo explains that weapons of war, together with threats, indignation and implacable anger, are often said by Moses to be used by *the supreme Cause* in his campaign against the unrighteous. It is the only way to deal with fools. So it seems that the two maxims, *God is as a man* and *God is not as a man*, are closely linked with two other principles, fear and love. In the Law all exhortations to piety refer *either to the love or the fear of the Existent One*. For those who do not allow anthropomorphic ideas of God to enter their heads love for God is the more suitable, since they *honour him for himself alone*, whereas for the others fear is more fitting. God is for Philo, then, the supreme Being, to whom the proper and most natural response is one of love. But that is possible only in the case of the philosophical soul. God can, however, be found by those who are incapable of philosophical reflection, but their response is one of fear, activated by the anthropomorphic language of Scripture. There is always, however, the possibility of an ascent by man from anthropomorphic ways of thinking about God to a philosophical awareness of his existence as Pure Being, and from an attitude of fear towards him to one of love for him.

THE REVELATION OF GOD TO MAN (*Mut. Nom.* 7–30 (II–IV))

The treatise in which this passage occurs is an exposition of Gen. 17: 1–5 and 15–22. The main subject of the opening paragraphs is the appearance to Abraham of the Lord and God's words 'I am thy God' (LXX). Philo offers here some explanation of how it is that the 'Unknowable' can in fact be known by man – and to what extent. Philo has already explained (para. 3) that Abraham's vision did not involve 'the eyes of the body'. It is the eye of the soul 'which receives the impression of the divine appearance'. When the Old Testament says that 'God was seen by man' the reference to something that takes place 'without any reference to that light which is perceptible by the external senses' (para. 6) is invariably the case. What belongs to the realm of the mind, Philo's emphatic declaration makes clear, can only be apprehended by the intellect.

Another major theme of the passage is the namelessness of God, and Philo has something to say about the correct understanding of the title 'Lord God'.

God the Existent (Mut. Nom. 7–14)

(7) Do not, however, think that the Existent, which truly exists, is ever seen or apprehended by any human being; for in ourselves we have no organ by which we can conceive it, neither sense-perception – for it is not an object which can be discerned by sense – nor mind. Therefore Moses, the observer of the invisible regions of being, the man who really saw God, for the sacred Scriptures tell us that he entered 'into the darkness' [Exod. 20: 21], which is a figurative way of referring to existence invisible and incorporeal, when he had investigated everything everywhere, sought to see clearly him who is much desired and
(8) who is alone good. But when he found nothing, even remotely resembling what he had hoped to behold, Moses then gave up any hope of receiving instruction on the matter from others and flew for refuge to the very Being himself that he was seeking and prayed to him, saying, 'Reveal thyself to me that I may see with knowledge' [Exod. 33: 13]. Nevertheless he failed to achieve the objective he had set himself. A knowledge, however, of those bodies and things which are below the Existent is judged by God to be the most all-sufficient gift even for the
(9) most excellent members of the mortal race. For it is said to him, 'Thou shalt see what is behind me, but my face thou shalt not see' (Exod. 33: 23). It is as if he was intended to

receive the answer: as many bodies and things that are
beneath the Existent may be apprehended by him, even
though not all of them are as yet apprehended, but that one
(10) Being by his very nature cannot be seen by man. And why
should it be considered so remarkable a phenomenon that
the Existent cannot be apprehended by man, since even the
mind within each of us is also unknown by us? For who has
even seen the immortal nature of the soul, that obscure
entity which has given birth to an infinite number of
divisions among the sophists, who have brought forward
opposing opinions, some of which are contradictory of each
other or even wholly inconsistent with any kind of nature?

(11) It was, therefore, quite consistent with reason that no
personal name even can be properly assigned to the
Existent. Do you not see that to the prophet who truly
desires to know and who asks what answer he is to give to
those who question him concerning his name he says, 'I am
that I am' [Exod. 3: 14], which is equivalent to saying, 'It is
(12) my nature to be, not to be described by name.' But in order
that the human race may not be wholly devoid of any
appellation which they may give to the most excellent of
beings, he gives them permission to use by a licence of
language, as though it were his proper name, the word *Lord*
God, the Lord of the three natural orders, teaching,
perfection, and of the practice of virtue, of which Abraham,
Isaac and Jacob are the scriptural symbols. For this, he says,
is 'My age-long name', as if it had been discovered in the age
within which men now live, not in the period before all
time existed. It is also 'a memorial' not set beyond
recollection or knowledge, and, furthermore, it is addressed
to persons who have been born and not to unrevealed
(13) natures. For those who enter into a mortal existence stand in
need of an alternative for the divine name, so that if not the
reality itself they may approach the name of the supreme
excellence and be brought into a relationship with it on the

basis of that. And the oracle delivered as from the mouth of the Ruler of the whole universe declares that no proper name of God has been revealed to any human being. 'I was seen', he says, 'of Abraham, Isaac and Jacob, being their God, and my name of "Lord" I did not reveal to them' [Exod. 6: 3]. But when the words are correctly translated and placed in their proper order they will read 'My proper name I did not reveal to them', but only the substitute that is commonly, but with some inaccuracy, used, the reasons for
(14) which misuse are set out above. Indeed, so completely indescribable is the Existent that even those powers which minister to him do not tell us his proper name. Therefore, after the wrestling-match in which the Practiser engaged in his search for virtue, he says to the invisible Master, 'Announce to me thy name', but he said, 'Why dost thou ask this my name?' [Gen. 32: 29]. And he does not disclose his peculiar and proper name, 'For', he says, 'it is sufficient for you to benefit from my worship, but as for names, which are symbols of created things, do not seek for them among imperishable natures.'

(7) *we have no organ by which we can conceive it*: Philo is here affirming that, despite what is said in Gen. 17: 1, it must not be supposed that Abraham *apprehended* God, *the Existent*. There is no organ of sense-perception which can apprehend God, since God is not perceptible by sense at all. Nor is there any organ in *mind*, any mental faculty, by which God can be *seen*.

apprehended: the verb Philo uses here, *katalambano*, carries within it the suggestion of bringing down. There is no way in which man can bring God down to his own level. There is, however, a real sense in which God comes down and makes himself known to man.

the observer of the invisible regions of being: this is, of course, Moses, as Philo informs us. Moses entered, as the Old Testament tells in Exod. 20: 21, 'into the darkness' (cf. Philo's treatment of this text in *Poster. C.* 14ff., though there are differences between that passage (see below, pp. 185ff.) and this one)).

existence invisible and incorporeal: that is what the darkness of the

Exodus passage represents. In that darkness Moses searched everywhere, looking into everything, in his desire to see clearly and plainly the God who is *much desired*. The reason for the persistence of Moses' search is hinted at in the brief description of God as he who is alone good. Moses embodied for Philo man's quest for the Good.

(8) *he found nothing*: Philo interprets Moses' experience in the darkness where, Exod. 20: 21 says, 'God was' as one of disappointment and frustration. There was no hint that something might be discovered, and not even an approximation to what he had hoped to see. That is what the darkness signified to Philo. It stood for man's total failure to penetrate the secrets of God. However, even though Moses the all-wise could not succeed and had no hope of learning from others, he took refuge with *the very Being himself that he was seeking*, with God himself, and prayed, in the words of Exod. 33: 13 (a verse which forms part of the description of a later event in the Exodus narrative, when Moses went into the tent outside the camp), asking God to reveal himself. He wanted to see God *with knowledge* (*gnōstōs*). Even then Moses failed to achieve his objective. He did, however, receive something in answer to his prayer. God allowed him to know the realm *of those bodies and things which are below the Existent*. That, says Philo, is no mean privilege. It is *the most all-sufficient gift even for the most excellent members of the mortal race* (which is what Moses was).

(9) *my face thou shalt not see*: God judged that it was enough for Moses to see the things below himself, but not his countenance. Philo here quotes the words of Exod. 33: 23, which he takes as meaning that. Below the level of the Existent things material and immaterial are available to apprehension, though not necessarily yet apprehended. God, however, *by his very nature cannot be seen*. The vision of God in his essence is not granted to men. In *Poster. C.* 14ff., where Philo also expounds Exod. 33: 23, he concludes that Moses' search was not, however, altogether fruitless, since the discovery that the Existent One is incomprehensible is an important one (see above, p. 188).

(10) *the Existent cannot be apprehended by man*: Philo argues that the fact that this is so should not surprise us, since we cannot know even our own minds. 'The mind which is in each of us is able to comprehend all other things, but has not the capability of understanding itself' (*Leg. All.* 1.91). If the human mind is unknowable by the human mind, so runs the *a fortiori* argument,

how much more is it the case that God, who is pure Mind, is unknowable. Philo alludes in passing to the *infinite number of divisions among the sophists* about the nature of the soul. These sophists, he says, have propounded opinions contrary to one another or even diametrically opposed. So Philo finds another unknowable in his universe – the human mind or soul.

the sophists: these men were early Greek philosophers who made man himself the subject of their critical and empirical enquiries. They acquired a reputation, not always deserved, for hair-splitting and for refuting the truth and showing something false to be true by false but plausible reasonings. Plato disliked them, partly because they accepted payment for teaching and partly because they fell so far short of Socrates. Philo here reveals in the form of words he uses a tendency to react in a Platonic way to the sheer argumentativeness of the sophists.

(11) *no personal name even can be properly assigned to the Existent*: Philo cites as evidence for this conclusion Exod. 3: 14, where God says to Moses, 'I am he that IS'. Philo interprets the words of God as meaning *my nature* [*is*] *to be, not to be described by name*.

Philo interprets the incident recorded in Gen. 22: 3–4 as meaning that Abraham could not actually reach him who is 'the essence of God, but sees him afar off'. He adds that all Abraham in fact saw was 'that God is at a distance from every creature, and that any comprehension of him is removed to a great distance from all human intellect'. He also refers to him as 'God who may not be named nor spoken of and who is in every way incomprehensible' (*Som.* I.66–7). It is for this reason that Philo frequently designates God *ho ōn* (He who IS). He does, however, mention the Tetragrammaton, the four-letter word YHWH, known to English readers of the Old Testament as Jehovah or Yahweh (see Exod. 3: 15, where the word 'LORD' stands for the Hebrew YHWH) (cf. pp. 40–1). In *Vit Mos.* II.203 Philo cites Lev. 24: 15–16 (LXX) as a warning that *naming* God is worse than cursing his name. He asserts that the holy name of God is a name 'which may only be mentioned or heard by holy men having their ears and their tongues purified by wisdom, and by no-one else at all in any place whatever' (*ibid.* 114). For Philo, then, God, while possessing no proper name, does have a name that is above every name, a designation appropriate to his transcendent state of pure being (cf. *Som.* I.230).

(12) *by a licence of language*: thus, and thus only, according to

Philo, did Moses provide a title by which men may address *the most excellent of beings*.

as though it were his proper name: the title in question is not in fact the proper name of God, since he has no such name, unless it be the sacred Tetragrammaton, but the Greek title *Lord God*.

the three natural orders: Philo frequently applies the Aristotelian idea of the three aspects of education – teaching, perfection and practice – to Abraham, Isaac and Jacob (as he does, for example, in *Abr.* 52ff., though there the educational trinity is given as teaching, nature and practice, the more usual form). The main point of the present passage is to affirm that God provides the title *Lord God* as applicable to himself in relation to the *three natural orders* of which, in Scripture, the three patriarchs are symbols.

My age-long name: what God said, Philo tells us, was that this name he has given men to use is *age-long*, belonging to the era of human existence, not to the time prior to the human era. It is also, according to Philo's interpretation of Exod. 3: 15 (LXX), *a memorial* too, not beyond memory or apprehension, and, finally, it is a name given to generations (Exod. 3: 15, LXX), to living human beings, not to those never born.

Despite his eternal namelessness, and out of kindness for mankind, God has given men a name to use when they speak about him. And despite his utter incomprehensibility he has provided men with a name which they can both learn and remember.

(13) *an alternative for the divine name*: this is a necessity for mortal beings, if they are to approach *if not the reality itself* at least *the name of the supreme excellence and be brought into a relationship with it*. The namelessness of God does not mean, for Philo, that men cannot enter into a right relationship with God. It means only that they cannot fully comprehend the nature of the Existent One with whom they may have communion.

no proper name of God has been revealed to any: that God has revealed no proper name as belonging to himself is shown, Philo claims, by the fact that Scripture contains an *oracle* recorded as if spoken by God himself. The *oracle* is Exod. 6: 3, where God appears to say that he was seen *of Abraham, Isaac and Jacob, being their God, and my name of 'Lord' I did not reveal to them*, but in fact, when the correct meaning of the words is understood, what God actually said, was, *My proper name I did not reveal to them*. Philo obtains this meaning by a rather unusual interpretation of the word-order of Exod. 3: 14 (LXX), involving a transposition of the words so that the word which can mean 'Lord' is positioned to mean 'proper' (name). When this transposition has been effected, it makes Exod. 3: 14 into a clear and unambiguous statement that God did not reveal his proper name to the patriarchs, from which Philo deduces that he revealed only the substitute. The reasons for withholding his name are those already set out by Philo in earlier paragraphs.

(14) *even those powers which minister to him do not tell us his proper name*: at work in the service of God, and in particular mediating between him and his creation, are the Potencies or 'powers', but even they, exalted beings that they are, do not divulge God's proper name. When Jacob (the Man of Practice, *the Practiser*) wrestled with a man *in his search for virtue*, and was told that he had striven with God and had prevailed and that his name, which he was asked to give, would henceforth be Israel, and then asked *the invisible Master* to announce his name, there came the interrogative reply *Why dost thou ask this my name?* According to Philo God refused to tell *his peculiar and proper name*. Actually Gen. 32: 29 simply says that Jacob–Israel received a blessing. Philo took the conclusion to the incident as meaning that it was enough for Jacob to receive God's blessing, without being given a name for God, since names are *symbols of created things* and are not to be sought in the case of *imperishable natures*. It is noteworthy that Philo is quite sure that men may receive blessings from God even when they cannot name him. To be able to comprehend God's essence by naming him is one thing, to be the recipient of his blessings another.

God the indescribable (*Mut. Nom.* 15–22)

(15) Do not, therefore, think that it is a hard saying that the Highest and Most Ancient of all things should be indescribable when his Word has no name of its own which we can use. And indeed if he is indescribable he is also inconceivable and incomprehensible. We must therefore understand that the statement, 'The Lord was seen of Abraham' [Gen. 17: 1] must not to be taken to mean that the Cause of all had shone forth and become visible to him (for what human mind is capable of containing the vastness of such a vision?), but rather to refer to the appearance of

one of the Powers which surround him, the kingly Power,
(16) for the title Lord indicates authority and sovereignty. When our minds were occupied by the airy speculations of the Chaldaeans, they attributed to the world powers which they regarded as causes of what exists. But when the mind migrated from the Chaldaean doctrines, it then knew that the world moved, guided and directed by a ruler, of whose
(17) authority it received a vision. It is therefore said that 'The Lord (not "The Existent") was seen of him', as if the meaning were, The king has been manifested, he who was from the beginning but was not as yet recognised by the soul which, though late in receiving enlightenment, did not continue for ever in ignorance, but received a vision that there is an Authority which rules over all existing things.

(18) But the Ruler, when he has appeared, bestows a still higher gift on the one who sees and hears him. He says to him, 'I am thy God'. For of which of all things constituting creation, I might ask, art Thou not God? But his Word, which is his interpreter, will teach me that he is not in this instance speaking of the world, of which he is in every respect the Creator and God, but about the souls of men which he did not judge to be worthy to be cared for all in
(19) the same way. He thinks fit to be called the Lord and Master of the bad, the God of those who are making progress towards improvement, but of those who are the most excellent and the most perfect both Lord and God at the same time. For example, when he set Pharaoh before us as the extreme case of impiety he never once called himself (his Lord or) his God, but addresses the wise Moses thus, for he says to him, 'Behold, I give thee as god to Pharaoh' [Exod. 7: 1]. But he has in many passages of the sacred oracles
(20–1) which he has given called himself Lord. Such forms of speech as these are to be read, 'These things saith the Lord' [Exod. 7:17], and at the very beginning of what he has been saying we read, 'The Lord spake unto Moses, saying, "I am

the Lord, speak unto Pharaoh, the king of Egypt, all that I speak to thee''' [Exod. 6: 29]. And Moses says to him, Pharaoh, 'Whenever I go forth from the city I will spread out my hands to the Lord, and the sounds shall cease and the hail and the rain shall not be, that thou mayest know that to the Lord belongs the earth' (that is, everything that is made up of flesh or earth), 'and thou' (that is, the mind which the body carries about with it), 'and thy servants' (that is, the collection of thoughts which act as guardian of the mind), 'for I know that ye have not feared the Lord' [Exod. 9: 29–30], by which he means not the Lord as he is commonly referred to and in different senses, but him who is in truth
(22) the Lord. For no one who is created is truly a lord, not even a king though he extends his sovereignty from one end of the earth to the other. Only the Uncreated is indubitably the Ruler, and the man who reverences and fears his authority receives a reward of authentic value in the form of his admonitions, whereas the end of the man who despises him is to be totally and miserably destroyed.

(15) *his Word has no name of its own*: this fact should make it easier to accept that *the Highest . . . of all things*, God, remains nameless. The Logos, then, has no name *which we can use*. With that one may contrast the statement in the Christological hymn recorded by Paul in Philippians that God has bestowed on Jesus Christ 'the name which is above every name' (Phil. 2: 9). A name which is 'above every name' could, of course, be no name at all, rather than the highest imaginable name, in which case the writer of the early *carmen Christi* and Paul would be at one with Philo, and it might even be the case that Phil. 2: 9 becomes a passage where the deity of Christ is affirmed with less ambiguity than elsewhere in the New Testament, since it attributes to Christ the namelessness which belongs to God and Logos, or at least the unnameable 'name' of the Deity.

Philo deduces from the fact that God is essentially nameless that the words of Gen. 17: 1, which tells us the vision of God by Abraham, must not be understood to mean that *the Cause of all had shone forth and become visible to him*. No human mind could possibly contain *the vastness of such a vision*. What actually happened was that one of the Potencies or *Powers* which serve God made an appearance. The particular Potency in this case was the kingly (the other being the creative). The title 'Lord' indicates that it was the kingly Potency that appeared, since the creative Potency is designated by the word God.

(16) *the airy speculations of the Chaldaeans*: Philo thus describes the thoughts entertained by men before they arrived at a vision of the universe which included belief in God, and in particular he has in mind the astrological ideas of the Chaldaeans. They believed, according to him, that events on earth were influenced by the heavenly bodies, but even worse they said that created things were first causes, and even imagined that the visible world was the only thing that existed. In particular, the Chaldaeans, who are of course the Stoics (Philo frequently attacks them using that name for them), attributed to the world causal powers. But when the mind migrates from *the Chaldaean doctrines* it recognises that the world has for its charioteer and pilot a Ruler whose sovereignty was presented to it in *a vision*. So, in visions of his Potencies, God may be seen, though only thus indirectly.

(17) *The king has been manifested*: it is the king, *not 'The Existent'*, who has been seen. God has manifested his kingly rule through the appearance in a vision of his kingly Potency. God had always been sovereign over his universe, but up to that point his sovereignty had gone unrecognised by the human race. However, though long untutored, the souls of men could not remain permanently in ignorance of God. The vision described in Gen. 17: 1 was received. It is a vision which, incidentally, reveals that there is nothing outside the divine rule. God *rules over all existing things*.

(18) *a still higher gift*: this, *the Ruler*, when he manifests himself, bestows upon the man who sees and hears him. What God says to such a man is, '*I am thy God*' (Gen. 17: 1, LXX). This prompts Philo to ask if there is anything in the multitude of created things which does not have him as its *theos*. The Scriptures, here characterised as God's *interpreter*, the word that interprets God to men, makes clear to Philo that when God declares himself to be God, it is not of the world, but of men, that he is speaking. God is undoubtedly the Creator of the universe, but, even though they do not deserve *to be cared for all in the same way*, God is also the God of all human beings.

There is a definite form of universalism in Philo's writings, the ultimate consequences of which are worked out, though by no means fully, in *Praem. Poen.* 162–72.

(19) *Lord and God at the same time*: Philo explains that God wills to be called *Lord and Master* in the case of the bad, God in the case of those *who are making progress towards improvement*, but God and Lord in the case of *the most excellent and the most perfect*. This conclusion is forced on Philo by the fact that Scripture refers to God in at least these two ways: as God (in the case of Exod. 7: 1) and also as Lord. Men, then, are divided into those who recognise God as Creator, those who acknowledge him as Sovereign, and those who are distinguished from the rest because to them he is both Creator and Ruler of all things.

(20–1) *These things saith the Lord*: this is an example of Scripture's use of the title 'Lord' of God. It comes from Exod. 7: 17. The same usage is found at the beginning of the speech quoted in the previous section (in Exod. 6: 29). The words quoted by Philo are addressed to Moses. Moses' words from Exod. 9: 29 are also quoted, since they too refer to God as 'the Lord'. In his comment on the verse Philo suggests that the reference to *the sounds* and *the hail and the rain* means that *to the Lord belongs the earth*, which he interprets as indicating *everything that is made up of flesh or earth*, while the *thou* of the next part of God's speech denotes *the mind which the body carries about with it*, and finally the words *and thy servants* refer to the thoughts which form the mind's *guardian*. The last words of Exod. 9: 29, which show that Moses was aware that Pharaoh and his servants had not yet learned to fear the Lord, refer, Philo says, not to the Lord who is merely so-called, but to *him who is in truth the Lord*.

(22) *no one who is created is truly a lord*: here Philo states emphatically that, no matter how extensive the sovereignty of an earthly ruler, such sovereignty, even though it be *from one end of the earth to the other*, in no way matches the sovereignty of God, who alone *is indubitably the Ruler*. Philo also warns his readers that God is to be feared and reverenced and that those who do live in fear and awe of him soon realise that his admonitions are of great value to them, not least because they preserve them from the fate of those who despise him and consequently have nothing to look forward to but a miserable end.

Lord and God (*Mut. Nom.* 23–30)

(23) Therefore he is exhibited as the Lord of the foolish, holding over them the terrors appropriate to him as Ruler. But of those who are making progress he is described as God in the Scriptures, as in the present passage, 'I am thy God', or 'I am thy God, increase and multiply' [Gen. 35: 11]. And in the case of those who are perfect he is both Lord and God, as in the Decalogue, 'I am thy Lord God' [Exod. 20: 2], and in another passage, 'The Lord God of your fathers' [Deut. 4:
(24) 1], for he thinks it is right for the wicked man to be subject to him as his Lord, so that being in a state of awe and groaning he should be afraid of his Master; that the man who is making progress should receive benefits from him as God so that by means of these benefits he should arrive at perfection; that the perfect man should be guided by him as Lord and receive benefits from him as God. For by means of the one he endures without lapsing, and by means of the
(25) other he is wholly a man of God. This is shown best of all in Moses' case. 'This is the blessing', we read, 'which Moses, the man of God, gave' [Deut. 33: 1]. Oh! Of what an all-lovely and sacred exchange is he found worthy, to give
(26) himself in return for God's providential care. But do not suppose that God becomes man's in the same way that man becomes God's, for as a man he is God's as his possession, whereas God becomes man's to be his glory and helper, whom he boasts in and from whom he receives assistance. If, then, you wish to have God as the inheritance of your mind, work first of all to become an inheritance worthy of him to receive, and you will achieve that if you avoid all acts of folly which are your own handiwork and the result of free-will.

(27) But we should not forget either that the statement, 'I am thy God', is made by a certain figurative misuse of language rather than with strict propriety, for the nature of the

Existent, in so far as he is the Existent, is not relative to anything else. He is full of himself and is sufficient for himself, and it was so both before the creation of the world
(28) and will be after it. He cannot change or alter, having no need of any other thing or being whatever, so that while all things are his, he, properly speaking, does not belong to anyone or anything. But the Powers which he has extended into the created order to be of benefit to the world he has constructed are sometimes referred to as being in a certain sense relative: for instance his kingly and beneficial Powers, for as King he is the King of someone and as a benefactor he is the benefactor of someone, while the king's subject and
(29) the receiver of the benefit is wholly distinct from him. Akin to these Powers is the creative *Power* which is called God, because by means of this Power the Father, who is the begetter and Artificer of all things, made the whole universe, so that 'I am thy God' is equivalent in meaning to
(30) 'I am the Maker and Artificer'. And the greatest gift we can receive is to have him for our Architect, who is also the Architect of the whole world, for he did not make the soul of the wicked man, since wickedness involves hostility to God, and he was not acting on his own when he made the intermediate soul, since, according to Moses the sacred historian, such a soul was liable, like wax, to receive the divergent impressions of good and evil.

(23) *both Lord and God*: Philo regards the passage from Exodus which he has cited as proof that God is both the Lord of the foolish, of whom he is the awe-inspiring Sovereign, and God of those who are making progress in their lives, the earnest strivers. Gen. 35: 11, as well as the words *I am thy God*, supports this. But, for the perfect God is both Lord and God, and for proof of this Philo turns to the Decalogue (Exod. 20: 2) and Deut. 4: 1 in particular. God, then, is Lord and God of mankind, but especially is he the good man's God.

(24) *wholly a man of God*: this is what the perfect man can become, for while the wicked are subject to God as Lord and face

him with awe and fear, the man who is striving to make progress is helped by the kindnesses of God to reach perfection, while the perfect man, both guided by God as his Lord and helped by him as his God, remains, on the one hand, free from lapses, and, on the other, becomes *a man of God* (*anthrōpos theou*). Progress towards a state in which God is man's God is more rapidly made by him who perseveres in living as God's man.

(25) *Moses' case*: Philo claims that what he has been saying about God is best demonstrated in Moses' case, for Scripture (Deut. 33: 1) refers to a blessing given by Moses, the man of God (*anthrōpos theou*). Philo comments on the glorious and holy exchange which took place when, in return for God's protecting care, Moses gave himself to God. That is what it means to be a man of God. Philo means his readers to appreciate that anyone who dedicates his life to God can receive in return his protecting care (*theia pronoia*). God becomes a man's God when a man becomes God's man.

(26) *do not suppose that God becomes man's*: but care is needed in speaking about God as man's. Man may become God's possession; he may belong, like Moses, wholly to God. But it should not be supposed, Philo hastens to warn, that God can become man's possession in precisely the same way. Man can be possessed, owned by God. God is man's in the sense that he is *his glory and helper*. Men may glory in God and receive help from him.

Philo goes on to say that if a man desires to have God as *the inheritance of* [*his*] *mind* (*dianoias klēron*), he must first put right his own personal relationship with God. That means starting with his own life, making himself *an inheritance worthy of him to receive*. But that goal is attainable only if the faults in his life for which man is himself responsible by his own ignorance or malice are overcome and left behind, and if man turns to God of his own free-will. However, it is clear that for Philo God is a Being who, though transcendent and unknowable in his essence of Pure Being, is approachable and who cares for man and gives him his aid (see above, p. 37–8).

(27) *by a certain figurative misuse of language*: here Philo returns to the thought that the words '*I am thy God*' (Gen. 17: 1, LXX) are not used in their proper sense. That is because God as God, *the Existent, in so far as he is the Existent* is not relative (*pros ti*) to anything else. God is absolute, complete in himself, for he is full of himself, his whole Being being himself. It must not be concluded that Philo's language is meant to stress God's solitary independence to the

point where he is placed beyond the reach of every relation. Nothing can add to or complete God's perfect fulness and exhaustive completeness, and therefore there can be no relationship which might infringe his absolute independence. A relationship between him and man, for example, would involve the implication that God was not complete in himself and needed man in order to be complete. Pure being is complete in itself. God, therefore, is *sufficient for himself.* He is this eternally, so that he was self-sufficient before the creation of the world took place and equally after creation. Since the idea of creation implies the existence of a relationship between the Creator and his creation and his creatures, Philo felt obliged to find a way of avoiding the suggestion that *to on* could be *relative* (*pros ti*) to *anything*. In the Prologue to John's Gospel the Logos is said to be *pros ton theon.*

(28) *He cannot change or alter*: the unchangeable God, Philo says, needs nothing from outside himself. Everything is his, but he belongs to no one and nothing. God needs nothing that anyone else can supply and he needs no one else to fulfil his existence, though sometimes men speak by analogy from their own experience as if he did. However – and this is how Philo attempts to overcome the difficulty he has created by his emphatic statement of God's solitary completeness – certain aspects of his being, his *Powers* or Potencies, God has projected into creation, directed towards the world and man. He has done this for the benefit of the creation and his creatures, the existence of which is said to be due to him. *He has constructed* the universe. These divine Potencies, Philo explains, are *sometimes referred to as being in a certain sense relative* (*hōsanei pros ti*). There is clearly something about the expression *pros ti* by itself which required Philo to precede it by the word *hōsanei* (*quasi*). The relativity of the *Powers* of God which he has directed towards the world is a *quasi*-relativity. It has been suggested, correctly I think, that the word *hōsanei*, translatable as 'in a sense' or as *quasi*, was put there because the dependence implied by the words *pros ti* is one-sided, not mutual. Mutual dependence where on one side there is involved in the relationship a *Power* or Potency of God would be for Philo unthinkable. Such a relationship of interdependence would infringe the absolute independence of God. Philo seems to mean that the 'powers' of God can relate to other beings, or to the objects in the physical universe, without any alteration of their essential nature. Perhaps Philo was endeavouring to find a way of saying that objects and persons may relate to them, and so are

relative in their being, but at the same time seeking to avoid any words that would imply that they themselves were relative. This kind of struggle to avoid misunderstanding is necessary when it is believed of God that 'his nature is entirely perfect, or rather God is himself the perfection and completion and boundary of happiness, partaking of nothing else by which he can be rendered better' (*Cher.* 86).

Philo again describes the Potencies or divine *Powers* here as the *kingly* and the *beneficial*. They are involved in relationships, for kings rule subjects and the existence of benefactors implies the existence of beneficiaries. Two parties or sides are involved in the concepts of both kingship and benefaction.

(29) *the creative Power*: a third Power is God the Creator, the Agent through whom *the Father*, God himself, *made the whole universe*. There is an indication in Philo's Greek at this point that he regarded the word *theos* as derived from the verb *tithemi* (cf. *Conf. Ling.* 137), which means to place (cf. p. 50). God is called here *the begetter and Artificer* of the universe, but it is said that he created it *through* his Potency, so that in Gen. 17: 1 the words '*I am thy God*' are equivalent to '*I am the Maker and Artificer*'. There is in Philo, therefore, a doctrine of the creation of the world indirectly through the agency of his creative Potency or *Power*, though no non-Jewish idea of a subordinate Being existing independently of God should be introduced at this point. For Philo God is himself the Creator, though it was through one aspect of his being projected away from himself that the creation was effected. The creative Potency is not, however, a separate being (or Being). It should also be said that Philo never departs from the Jewish idea of creation *ex nihilo* (except perhaps in the *De Aeternitate Mundi*, where he seems to support the view that matter is uncreated and eternal). Creation is not the work of a 'lower' God, the *Demiourgos* (a workman, in the Platonic system, the Maker of the world) using formless matter, but a Creator of both form and matter.

When within Judaism God's transcendence began to be spoken of in the kind of language used in Isa. 40ff., it is not surprising to find that attempts were in due course made to understand creation and God's relationship to his creatures in terms of mediators, such as Sophia (in Proverbs, the Book of Wisdom, Ecclesiasticus, etc.) and the Logos. Philo represents such a tendency, reinforced by the combination of a native Jewish sense of God's transcendence with philosophical ideas drawn from the Greek world of thought.

(30) *the greatest gift*: that for Philo here is to have as *our Architect . . . the Architect of the whole world.* This then leads Philo into a discussion of the creation of various kinds of human beings, the wicked and those who are in the intermediate stage between good and evil as having taken place only through subordinates (as he will interpret the 'Let *us* make' of Gen. 1: 26 to mean in the following sections). He will also claim that only the good were created by God himself, the good being the ascetics who have transcended the bodily part of themselves, a rare breed of men, and also the gentle wise who serve God and man, men who are 'eminent in the practice of piety and do not despise human beings' (para. 39). Such men are not only well-pleasing 'to' but also 'before' God (para. 40). To be inspired with 'heaven-sent madness', like Enoch, is to be pleasing to God, but, according to Philo, the followers of 'a tame and gentle wisdom' which expresses itself in obedience to the commandments, the practice of kindness towards friends, a readiness to defend one's country, and the careful observance of one's duties to all men, are summoned by God to himself and approved with his special favour (*charis*). Philo, despite all that he says about God's absolute independence, and without in any way contradicting it, can speak of a God who graciously cares for his creatures (para. 45), using the word *charis* to describe God's unconditional mercy much as Paul does in his Epistle to the Romans.

2. Philo's Logos doctrine

The Logos doctrine of Philo – if indeed it can be said that he had a *single* Logos doctrine – is part of his doctrine of God. It was a logical requirement of that doctrine, especially in regard to its emphasis on the transcendence of God. If there had not been Logos doctrines already in existence for his use, Philo would almost certainly have created the concept with its associated vocabulary. The term Logos is used by him very frequently and, partly because the ideas it was used to express are difficult and complex ones, and partly because Philo's own thought is also profound and complex, it is difficult to give a clear and coherent statement of Philo's thought in this area. A chapter on his Logos doctrine could be as long as the one on his doctrine of God. Requirements of space, however, mean that a severe abbreviation of what Philo has to say must take place, with the inevitable distortion and misrepresentation of his ideas that this involves. There are, perhaps, inconsistencies and even contradictions within Philo's thought on the subject of the Logos. It is always, however, difficult for a modern mind to grasp wholly what it is that an ancient writer – especially one who is avidly devoted to both scriptural Judaism and Greek philosophy – had in mind, and one suspects more than once that what looks like an inconsistency or a contradiction does so because of the intellectual and religious viewpoint of the (usually non-Jewish) reader of his works.

The meaning and use of the term Logos. Part of the complexity of the subject of Philo's Logos doctrine is due to the extremely wide range of meanings which the word *logos* may have in Greek. Of these many meanings the one that it definitely should not have – despite the Vulgate's *verbum* and some English translations of the Prologue to John's Gospel – is the meaning 'word'. It is better for the student of Philo, and of the New Testament, to retain the word Logos itself, and always to remember, when *Verbum* or Word (even with capital V or W) is used in translations of John 1, that something much more than the Latin or English words indicate was in the original author's mind.

The primary meaning of Logos, as it was used in Philo's world and by Philo, is more than, to quote one definition, 'the spiritual Mind of the transcendent God'. Logos means, among other things, the rational thought of mind expressed in utterance or speech. It is something present within the total reality of God himself, within the natural order of the universe, within man himself, but it is primarily with the Logos of God, the Logos with a capital L, that we shall be concerned.

Philo was able to use the Logos concept – and did not have to invent it in order to retain both his belief in God's transcendence and his conviction that God was in touch with his world – because it was present in the thought, for example, of the Stoics. Stoicism, described as a system attractive to Philo because of its ethical teaching, made considerable use of the Logos concept. It did so in its account of the rational law – the word Logos was used to designate this – which holds together and governs the life of natural phenomena. For Philo the Stoic concept needed, of course, to be detached from the pantheism of Stoicism and united with the Jewish conception of divine transcendence. Philo was probably, as has been suggested, looking round for an appropriate term for the divine Mind. The more obvious term, *nous*, was already in use, within Stoicism and elsewhere, for the human mind, so, carrying with it some of its Stoic associations of meaning, but also given new contents, the term Logos came to be used by Philo for the divine Mind. Philo was probably encouraged to use the term and to use it in the way he did by the preparation for its employment in what the Old Testament said about 'the Word of God'. He had only to unite in his thinking the account of creation in Gen. 1 – creation by the 'word' of God – and passages such as Ps. 33: 6, 'The Lord's word made the heavens', or Ps. 147: 18 or Ps. 148: 8 – passages which link the ongoing life of the created order with the 'word' of God. He would no doubt have noticed that the LXX translation of the three psalms mentioned employs the word *logos*, which is also used in Wisd. 9: 1, a verse which affirms that everything was made by God's 'word'. Furthermore, Philo could easily apply to his own philosophical and religious purposes the statements, in Exod. 34 and Deut. 10, that the Word of God was revealed in the Law. He knew also that 'the word of the law' was what came to the prophets (see Isa. 2: 1; Jer. 1: 2 – a verse in which there is an interesting transition from *rhema* to *logos*; Ezek. 3: 16). Philo was no doubt particularly interested in the statement in Isa. 2: 1 that the 'word' was *seen* by the prophet.

In *Leg. All.* 1.65 Philo states, in his allegorical exposition of Gen. 2: 10–14, that 'River' denotes generic virtue, goodness. This issues forth, he explains, out of Eden, as the Wisdom of God, and this is the Reason (*logos*) of God. Here is a clear statement, such as is found elsewhere in Philo's writings, identifying Wisdom and the Logos, a process no doubt justified in Philo's mind by the fact that Scripture assigns to Wisdom attributes and functions also assigned to the Logos. This happens in the statement about creation in Ps. 104: 24 (cf. Prov. 3: 19; Jer. 10: 12), the statement about the 'wisdom' which comes out of the mouth of God (cf. what is said about Wisdom in Prov. 8: 1ff.). In Wisd. Sol. 9–12 Wisdom is equated with the Logos (cf. Ecclus. 24: 23ff.). So, there was already within Judaism language about Wisdom which was so close to what was said elsewhere about the Logos as to justify the virtual abandonment of the feminine term, Wisdom (*sophia*), and the adoption instead of the masculine noun, *logos*, much more useful because of its masculinity to both Jewish and Christian writers in the first century AD.

The Logos as mediator. Perhaps the thought that was uppermost in Philo's mind when he used the term Logos was that of mediation. God was never for him a transcendent Being whose thoughts were totally and utterly beyond man's reach. Even if God is transcendent, he is not, for Philo, silent. He speaks and communicates, and for Philo the term Logos denotes the Thought of God expressed in a form that is, at least indirectly, accessible to men and knowable by them. It has been suggested that, by the time Philo wrote, the problem of reconciling the transcendence and the immanence of God had become acute within Judaism. As we have seen earlier (pp. 42–3), Philo had much to say about the transcendence of God. He could even say, having just affirmed the omnipresence of God (though with the usual qualifying statement that 'To be everywhere and nowhere is his property and his alone'), that 'this divine nature which presents itself to us, as visible and comprehensible and everywhere, is in reality invisible, incomprehensible and nowhere' (*Conf. Ling.* 136–8). In *Op. Mund.* 69ff. Philo is discussing the possibilities open to man in view of the fact that, in a sense, his mind is 'a god to him'. He describes how the human mind lifts its gaze beyond the material world to reach out after 'the intelligible world', and sees therein the surpassingly lovely Ideas. It is then 'seized by a sober intoxication, like those filled with Corybantic frenzy, and is inspired, possessed by a longing far other than theirs and a nobler desire'. It seems to be on its way to 'the Great King himself', but 'amid its longing to see him, pure and untempered rays of concentrated light stream forth like a torrent, so that by its gleams the eye of the understanding is dazzled'. So the sight of 'the Great King himself' is denied to man.

The problem of the sheer transcendence of God created a situation within which, without finding a solution to the problem, Philo could have written nothing about God, since he could have known nothing about him. Whether the solution which Philo adopted did anything more than, as Bultmann suggests, substitute one version of transcendence, in terms of the opposition between matter and spirit, for others is a matter for discussion. But Philo certainly believed he had found a solution, and the student of his writings should read not only the *De Opificio Mundi* passage just referred to, but also, for example, *Quaest. in Ex.* II.51, where Philo, expounding Exod. 25: 7, states: 'For if, O mind, thou dost not prepare thyself of thyself, excising desires, pleasures, griefs, fears, follies, injustices and related evils, and dost [not] change and adapt thyself to the vision of holiness, thou wilt end thy life in blindness, unable to see the intelligible sun. If, however, thou art worthily initiated and canst be consecrated to God and in a certain sense become an animate shrine of the Father, [then] instead of having closed eyes, thou wilt see the First [Cause] and in wakefulness thou wilt cease from the deep sleep in which thou hast been held. Then will appear to thee that manifest One, who causes incorporeal rays to shine for thee, and grants visions of the unambiguous and indescribable things of nature and the abundant sources of other good things. For the beginning and end of happiness is to be able to see God.' But ascent to that ultimate *visio Dei* is possible for men only because God has expressed his inward thought in his Logos, which is, among other things, the sun of the transcendent world of Ideas. For it is the case, as Philo says of the Logos in the *Decal.* 105, that 'nothing so much assures its predominance as that through it is best given the revelation of the Father and Maker of all, for in it, as in a mirror (cf. 1 Cor. 13: 12), the mind has a vision of God'.

The Logos as light. The Logos for Philo is the uttered or expressed Thought of God. Not surprisingly, therefore, just as God is light and the archetypal source of every other light, so is the Logos. So, 'Wisdom is God's archetypal luminary and the sun is a copy and image of it' (*Migr. Abr.* 40), but also it is 'the supreme Divine Word' who is said to be 'the fountain of Wisdom' (*Fug.* 97). It will not be a surprise to readers of the Prologue to John's Gospel, where it is affirmed that 'the Word was God', to find that Philo, without intending to infringe his Jewish monotheism, and without in fact doing so (though some Jewish writers have accused Philo of introducing a conception utterly alien to it and one which damaged its absolute character), calls the Logos 'the second God', in whose image man has been made (*Quaest. in Gn.* II.62). He also, incidentally, calls the 'creative (power)' 'God', while the 'royal (power)' is called 'Lord'; or, rather, Philo notes that that is how these two powers are described in Scripture. The description of the Logos as 'the second God' Philo deduces from the statement 'in the image of god he made man' in Gen. 9: 6. In other words, Philo derives his usage here from Scripture. Lest one be tempted to see in Philo's language more than part of the conceptual background to the process of Christian theological development that began with the New Testament and instead see actual anticipations of Athanasian language, it is important also to note that in *Leg. All.* II.86 Philo states that 'the primal existence is God, and next to him is the Word of God'. The Logos is also here said to be 'the wisdom of God' which he 'marked off highest and chiefest from his powers'. In *Som.*I.229–30, as we saw in the previous chapter, only when the word *theos* denotes God himself is the article used. The title, *theos*, without the article, is, however, given to 'his chief Word' (see p. 56). In other words, though the Logos is neither God nor a god, it is the primary, secondary layer (as it were) of the effulgence or emanation of the divine light, the Thought of God – and therefore appropriately called either 'the second God' or allowed the title *theos* – expressed, for example, in the rational order of the universe intelligible to the human mind. It is doubtful if we should do justice to Philo's view of the Logos if we described it as an intermediary. To regard the Logos as an intermediary in the proper and fullest sense would perhaps involve a departure from the Jewish view of God as a living God, himself active in the world and history – a step not taken by Philo. It cannot be emphasised enough that the Logos for Philo is God's Logos, the incorporeal Word or Thought of God, not a distinct and separate being having its own divine ontological status, subordinate to God.

The Logos as the image of God. However, Philo frequently uses language which sounds as if he does treat the Logos as a divine hypostasis. He speaks of the Logos, for example, as the Image of God. In *Som.* II.45, speaking of creation, Philo tells how God 'stamped the entire universe with his image and an ideal form [he here calls the Logos an Idea], even his own Word'. In *Plant.* 18 the word *charaktēr* is used of the relationship, in the creative process, between the 'seal' of God and 'the eternal Word'. The 'Thought' of God is expressed primarily in the rational order visible in the universe. In that respect the Logos is the *eikon* of God. But the Logos is also the Thought of God expressed in such a way that man can apprehend and comprehend it. In *Conf. Ling.* 97 Philo says that it is fitting for those who desire to see the Existent at least to see 'his image, the most holy Word, and after the Word its most perfect work of all that our senses know, even this world'. Ths Logos is a bridge between God and mankind because it is the divine rationality impressed upon the natural order, in so far as it is capable of receiving it, and yet closely united to God as flowing from his essence (see pp. 120–1). It is perhaps only necessary to add that Philo's habit of personifying the Logos as, for example, a high-priest figure, must not be mistaken for full-blooded personalisation.

It is sometimes deduced from the fact that Philo speaks in some passages of the mediatorial role of the Logos and in others of the time when he existed alone that the Logos, and the powers, were intermediary beings. In *Leg. All.* II.1–2 Philo affirms that 'it is good that the Alone should be alone', and immediately adds: 'but God, being One, is alone and unique, and like God there is nothing' (cf. *Op Mund.* 23; see below, pp. 130 and 134–5). But the words of Gen. 2: 18 on which he is commenting yield a further meaning, namely 'that neither before creation was there anything with God, nor, when the universe had come into being, does anything take its place with him'. Nothing Philo says about the Logos involves a real contradiction of that statement. That to man he is apprehended through his Logos involves no statement of distinctions within God or of distinguishable persons within his Godhead, nor does it involve for Philo such beliefs about God or the Logos. The absolute solitude and loneliness of God in his essence are not fundamentally altered for Philo by the fact that God's Thought, his Logos, is expressed in the production of the ideal cosmos and, indirectly, the actual cosmos.

However, the Logos is the highest self-expression of God. In

Fug. 101 the 'Divine Word' is said to be 'high above' the divine powers, and has not been 'visibly portrayed, being like to no one of the objects of sense'. The Logos is 'the Image of God, chiefest of all Beings intellectually perceived, placed nearest, with no intervening distance, to the Alone truly Existent One'. So close is the relationship between God and his Logos that Philo here calls the latter 'the charioteer of the Powers' while God himself is said to be seated in the chariot 'giving directions to the charioteer for the right wielding of the reins of the Universe'. In his account of the creation of man Philo, following Genesis, states that 'man was made a likeness and imitation of the Word', and that the 'perfect beauty' of man (before the Fall) was due to the fact that 'the Word of God surpasses beauty itself, beauty that is, as it exists in Nature'. Incidentally this means that for Philo the Logos 'is not only adorned with beauty, but is himself in very truth beauty's fairest adornment' (*Op. Mund.* 139). The relationship between the Logos and the powers – after an emphatic statement that 'God is indeed one' – is made clear in *Cher.* 27–8. There Philo says that between the two powers, God's goodness and his sovereignty, there is 'a third which unites them, Reason, for it is through Reason [*logō(i)*] that God is both ruler and good'.

The eternity of the Logos. Connected with what Philo says about the superiority of the Logos is what he says about its eternity. According to *Plant.* 8 and other passages, the Logos is *ho aidios logos* (see *Conf. Ling.* 146; pp. 125–6). The Logos is not, like the Christian Son/Logos, unbegotten. In *Leg. All.* III. 175 Philo states that 'the word of God is above all the world, and is eldest and most all-embracing of created things'. The New Testament student's mind turns at once to John 1: 3, where the evangelist makes a statement, with reference to the Logos, that 'no single thing was created without him'. Philo's statement in the *Leg. All.* III passage seems to involve the idea of the definite inferiority of the Logos to God and to place it, or him, in the category of 'created things', a category which includes many other things besides the Logos. It also seems to represent a quite different viewpoint from that of the author of the Fourth Gospel, who seems, in his Prologue, to be insisting that nothing that has been made came into existence apart from the Logos. It is possible to see how Philo's thought and language influenced early Christian thinkers; impossible, if proper attention is paid to them, to confuse the two.

If it is asked how the Logos can be both eternal and yet not unbegotten, the answer is quite simply that, though not unbegotten, the Logos will now never cease to be. The Logos, which is between the unbegotten Father on the one hand, and the universe and man on the other, is neither made nor begotten. It is logically dependent on God and cannot be conceived of as self-existent, and it is this that makes Philo use language at times which comes close to affirming the begottenness of the Logos or that the Logos is among the body of created things. But, as the *eikōn* (image) passages show, God's Logos is an expression of his Thought, than which no better one could be available to man.

The term 'only-begotten' (*monogenēs*), used in the Christian creed, is not used by Philo of the Logos, but in so far as what Philo does have to say about the Logos and God is an aid to the understanding of that term (in, for example, John 1: 18), the conclusion might have to be to interpret the word as denoting uniqueness without excluding the idea of dependence on God.

The precise relationship of the Logos to God is not easy to define. The use of the expression the 'first'·God (*Leg. All.* III.207), implies the existence of 'the second God' (*Quaest. in Gn.* II.62) and the propriety of applying the term *theos* to the Logos. There is a sense in which the Logos is *theos*, more than *theios* (divine), without being 'God', for the Logos is God's Logos, not God. The Logos does not exhaust the being of God. However, as Philo puts it in *Conf. Ling.* 95–7, those who 'serve the Existent', led by Moses ('the nature beloved of God'), 'shall behold the place which in fact is the Word, where stands God, the never changing, never swerving' and also 'the world of our senses'. Seeing 'the most holy Word' and 'after the Word its most perfect work of all that our senses know, even this world' is what philosophy, as he understands it, is all about. It is interesting to note that Philo defines philosophy here as 'the earnest desire to see these things exactly as they are'. Philosophy, then, involves the *visio Verbi*, the vision of the Logos which is the place occupied by God. By that combination of the intellectualism and mysticism which made up Philo's outlook, it is possible to arrive at the awareness that there is a God, that there is a place in which he stands.

Inevitably, since the Logos is the expression of the Thought of God, is in fact God's Expressed Thought, there is for Philo a very close link between the Logos and the world of Ideas or Forms which he adopted – and adapted – from Plato (see below, p. 111). It is in fact Philo, not Plato himself, who appears to have been the first to use the phrase *kosmos noētos* (intelligible world) for the Platonic, or rather Mosaic, world of Ideas. The expression *kosmos noētos*, not found at all in Plato, occurs in Philo's *Gig.* 61, where he makes it quite clear that the *kosmos noētos* is the community in totality of the imperishable and incorporeal Ideas. Regarded as a totality, that community or commonwealth is the Logos (see below, p. 135).

In *Som.* 1.186, speaking again of the world which 'only intellect can perceive', Philo states that it was 'framed from the eternal forms in him who was appointed in accordance with Divine bounties'. The 'in him' most probably refers to the Logos, in which case Philo here seems to imply that the world of Ideas is within the Logos rather than being identical and coterminous with it. That the Logos embraces, rather than is to be equated with, the world of Ideas is also suggested by the words of *Conf. Ling.* 172, where Philo states: 'Through these Potencies the incorporeal and intelligible world was framed.' Philo goes on to explain that the *kosmos noētos* is 'a system of invisible ideal forms'.

But because the Ideas are Ideas, the infinite variety of ideal archetypes of the actual world, existing within the divine Logos or Mind, the Logos or Mind of God, Philo often refers to their creation by God (see *Op. Mund.* 16ff.; pp. 131–6); though, as has been noted, Philo avoids the use of the term *nous* for the divine Mind, and uses instead the word *Logos*, almost certainly because he wanted *Logos* reserved for the Mind of God and *nous* to denote, as in Aristotle, the human rational faculty, or mind (see above, p. 104).

It needs to be noted, of course, that the Logos, as the Mind or Reason in which the Ideas exist, acquires a certain independence of God's essence. And it is this, the world of Ideas in its totality, that was the model for the material universe which God has created. Philo's language frequently personifies the Logos in relation to the act of creation, so that the Logos appears as a kind of personal Agent performing the actual work of creating (see *Op. Mund.* 24; pp. 130 and 135). The instrumentality of the Logos in creation is clearly stated in *Spec. Leg.* 1.81: 'And the image of God is the Word through whom the whole universe was framed.' But it would appear wrong to interpret Philo's language about the Logos' role in creation as involving the idea of creation as an operation shared by a partner or co-worker with God. The Logos, it needs to be stressed over and over again – especially for Christian readers of Philo's works – is the Logos of God, God's Logos. It is *eikōn* in relation to God, *idea* (ideal form) in relation to the material world, but Philo's words in *Som.* II.45 should be recalled. There Philo states of the material universe that 'when it had no definite character God moulded it into definiteness, and, when he had perfected it, stamped the entire universe with his image and an ideal form, even his own Word'. The subject of the verb *etypōse* (formed), and of the other verbs used of creative process, is God. The Logos here is referred to as if it were an instrument in God's hands rather than an Agent through whom he performed the act of creation.

The Logos as the power of God in the world. At times Philo's Logos is a kind of cosmic power present in the world. It is that which binds all things together and causes them to cohere. This aspect of Philo's Logos doctrine has close affinities with Stoicism and the thought of Heraclitus in particular (see p. 104). As for Paul, it is the Son who is 'the image of the invisible God' in whom 'all things consist' (or cohere: Col. 1: 15–17), so Philo, using similar language, can speak of the Logos as the unbreakable bond (*desmos*) which holds the universe together in a coherent, unified whole. The Logos is also described as 'the ruler and steersman of all' (*Cher.* 36). Philo appears to mean by this and other passages that there is a rational plan which governs the life of the universe, and to be affirming that the Logos is 'simply the instrument through which the divine purpose is carried out'. God, he says, 'directs the affairs of men through the operation of that rational law which is bound up in the very constitution of the world' (Drummond 1888: II.200). In *Sacr AC* 51 Philo refers to 'the right reason which is our pilot and guide', a reference to the rule of 'right reason' in human life; though it is certainly the case for Philo that the 'right reason' (*orthos logos*) in man is a reflection of the divine Logos at work in the universe. Every participation within human experience in good or ill is due to the 'armed angel, the reason of God [*theou logon*]' (*Cher.* 35). The 'house of God' (Gen. 28: 17) is said to be the Logos, since it is not the visible world but the one that is 'withdrawn from sight, and apprehended only by soul as soul', i.e., that is purely spiritual or rational. He also adds that the Logos both is 'antecedent to all that has come into existence' and is 'the Word, which the Helmsman of the Universe grasps as a rudder to guide all things on their course'. To complete the important set of statements Philo makes in this passage about the Logos, he also says that God employed the Logos 'as his instrument, that the fabric of his handiwork might be without reproach' 'when he was fashioning the world' (*Migr. Abr.* 5–6). Philo uses the idea of the creation of the world by God using his Logos as his instrument (*organon*) to express his belief that the universe – except for the physical body and the irrational element in man – is a reflection of the ideal pattern in God's mind. That such an interpretation of Philo's use of the word 'instrument' is justified is based on the evidence of the description of the 'form' as 'instrument' and upon the parable of creation in, for example, *Op. Mund.* 16–20 (see pp. 131–3).

The statements of *Migr. Abr.* 6 and *Op. Mund.* 16–20 are in strict parallelism. The Logos, as Philo understood it, was God's 'instrument' (*organon*) in the sense that it was God's 'pattern' (*paradeigma*), just as one may say that perhaps the most important instrument possessed by a sculptor is not the chisel in his hand, but the idea of what he is about to carve that exists in his mind. There is no need, in the case of what Philo says about the cosmological agency or instrumentality of the Logos, to see evidence of belief in a being apart from God, though one may perhaps properly refer to an aspect of, or an element within, the totality of the Godhead. Having said that, however, it must be remembered that there are places, as we have seen, in which it appears that Philo speaks of the Logos as a created, or begotten, intermediary divine Being.

In *Rer. Div. Her.* 206 (see pp. 109–10) Philo describes the Logos as 'being neither uncreated as God, nor yet created as human beings'. This seems to be contradicted by the statements in *Leg. All.* III.175 and *Migr. Abr.* 6. In the former Philo states that the Logos is above all the world and is 'eldest and most all-embracing of created things'. In the latter it is said that the Logos is 'antecedent to all that has come into existence'. In *Conf. Ling.* 41 the Logos is said to be 'imperishable' compared with God, who is 'eternal', and, later in the same work (*ibid.* 147), the Logos is described as 'the eldest-born image of God'. In *Decal.* 134 the adjective *aidios* (eternal) is used of the Logos.

The Logos and man. An important aspect of what Philo says about the Logos concerns man's relationship with it. In *Rer. Div. Her.* 119 the Logos is called, among other things, the *spermatikos*, the divine Logos, which 'implants its seed' within men. All men, therefore, participate to some extent in the life of the Logos. 'Man was made a likeness and imitation of the Word, when the Divine Breath was breathed into his face' (*Op. Mund.* 139; cf. *ibid.* 146: 'Every man, in respect of his mind, is allied to the divine Reason, having come into being as a copy or fragment or ray of that blessed nature'). All men are, in one sense at least, God's sons, as the Logos can be called God's Son. This is connected with Philo's understanding, based on the Genesis narrative, of man as created in the image of God, for the Logos is, as we have seen, God's *eikōn*. However, men become sons in the fullest sense only by fellowship with the Logos, which means living the life of reason (and abandoning the life of the flesh, the body, since the body is in effect a tomb for the human soul: see *Spec. Leg.* IV.188). It is the Logos that brings man to repentance and salvation by entering the soul and making man aware of his sins and bidding them be cleared out in order that the Logos might be able to perform the necessary work of healing (*Deus Imm.* 134–5; cf. *Rer. Div. Her.* 63–4). According to *Leg. All.* III.173, the Logos is the heavenly bread (Philo is commenting on Exod. 16: 15) which God supplies to feed men (it is noticeable in this passage how Philo passes from the LXX's *rhēma* to the term *logos* – a point, together with many others, not to be overlooked in the exegesis of, for example, Heb. 11: 3). The mysterious bread of heaven referred to in Exodus is 'the Divine Word, from which all kinds of instruction and wisdom flow in perpetual stream'. He calls the Logos 'the heavenly nourishment' which is the 'ethereal wisdom' poured upon minds that delight in contemplation. The effects of feeding upon the Logos are ethical, as well as mystical and intellectual, for, as Philo goes on, 'This Divine ordinance fills the soul that has vision alike with light and sweetness, flashing forth the radiancy of truth and with the honied grace of persuasion imparting sweetness to those who hunger and thirst after nobility of character' (*Fug.* 137–9). This passage reinforces what is said elsewhere in Philo's works to emphasise the practical and active aspect of the life of the Jew who shared in Philo's mystical and intellectual form of Judaism. In *Congr.* 70 Philo stresses the importance of deeds and actions, this being only one of the many passages in which the ethical character of Philonic Judaism is exhibited.

And, of course, as we have already seen, men who desire to know God by seeing him are not permitted such a vision, but instead are allowed to see the *Imago Dei*, 'the most holy Word' (*Conf. Ling.* 97). In another passage (*Migr. Abr.* 173–5), Philo also states that as long as the man who 'follows God . . . falls short of perfection' he possesses as his Leader 'the Divine Word'. When such a man 'has arrived at full knowledge', he will run as fast as his Leader, and they will both become 'attendants on the All-leading God'. Men, who are akin to the divine Logos by virtue of their rationality, as the passages from the *De Opificio Mundi* quoted above show, will at least behold the Logos and even gaze on the Existent. More seems to be involved here, in the ultimate beatific vision, than in passages such as *Op. Mund.* 31, where Philo allows no more than that the 'invisible light perceptible only by mind has come into being, as an image of the Divine Word who brought it within our ken'.

The Logos and Moses. A special connection exists for Philo between the Logos and Moses, whose life he wrote (see above, pp. 56–9). It has been said that this is so, and indeed that Moses is a type of the Logos, because, among other things, Moses reports the words of the Lord. Alongside the eulogistic statements made about Moses in Philo's *De Vita Mosis* is the statement in *Gig.* 47 that 'the divine spirit of wisdom' abode a long time with 'Moses the wise'. Like the Logos, Moses is also described as a 'high priest' (*Rer. Div. Her.* 182; cf. *Ebr.* 126). Moses, as a priest, was given a 'blessing which nothing in the world can surpass' (*Vit. Mos.* II.67). So lofty is the estimate of Moses found in Philo's works that one is led to ask if Philo thought of him as actually divine, as an incarnation of the Logos, or as being a Logophany. Philo himself raises the question of Moses' divinity: 'Was not the joy of his partnership with the Father and Maker of all magnified also by the honour of being deemed worthy to bear the same title? For he was named god [*theos*] and king of the whole nation, and entered, we are told, into the darkness where God [*ho theos*] was' (*Vit. Mos.* I.158). Here God himself is designated *ho theos*, while Moses was named (*ōnomasthē*: i.e. bore the name) *theos*. This distinction, in the case of Moses and God, between the application of *theos* with and without the article, is similar to that which Philo says applies, as we have seen already (p. 107), in the case of God and his Logos. In *Som.* II.189 the name God is said to be 'a prerogative assigned to the chief prophet, Moses'. Philo also says that as *theos* Moses was 'not a man' (*oude anthrōpos*), but 'one contiguous with both extremes' (cf. *Rer. Div. Her.* 84).

Philo often speaks of Moses as divinely inspired, as in *Quaest. in Ex.* II.29, where his words include the statement that 'he who is resolved into the nature of unity, is said to come near God in a kind of family relation, for having given up and left behind all mortal kinds, he is changed into the divine, so that such men become kin to God and truly divine'.

Not surprisingly, there is a close association in Philo's thinking between Moses and the divine Logos. In *Mut. Nom.* 110ff., Philo interprets the 'Shepherd' of Ps. 23: 1 as 'the divine word' which guides men away from things material and earthly. Since it is Moses who rescues mankind from the bondage of matter, the clear implication is that, in a real sense, Moses is (or is an expression or manifestation of) the Logos. Philo does in fact call Moses the Logos, the 'Law-giving Word' (*Migr. Abr.* 23). He can even say what the New Testament writers say of the Son (e.g., John 1: 10) that God committed to Moses the entire cosmos as a possession fit for God's heir (*Vit. Mos.* 1.155). One distinguished Philonist has decided that in the case of *Mut. Nom.* 110–11. Moses is being described as 'the agent, if not the exact equivalent of the Saving Logos'. According to *Congr.* 170 Moses is 'the prophet-word' (*ho prophētēs logos*). It has also been concluded that the prayer in *Som.* 1.164ff. is a prayer, addressed to Moses as 'Sacred Guide', similar to those addressed by Christian mystics to Christ.

Strictly speaking, for Philo Moses was a man inspired by or inhabited by the Spirit of God or the Logos, but in some passages – for example, *Sacr. AC* 8–10 – Moses is one of those whom God advanced higher than others and 'stationed . . . beside himself'. So little part did his physical body play in his life, Philo tells us, that nothing is said in Scripture about his separation from it. If Moses was an incarnation, the process of occupation of a human life by the divine Logos went so far as to result in an almost total exclusion of the human flesh of Moses. However, though the 'bodily region' was placed in a position of subjection within Moses' life, it was by 'that Word by which also the whole universe was formed'. The result of such interaction between body and Logos was that in his case, according to Scripture, 'no man knows his grave' (Deut. 34: 6) (*Sacr. AC* 10). Philo adds the question 'who has powers such that he could perceive the passing of a perfect soul to him that "IS"?'. The soul of such a person at such a moment is, says Philo, 'filled with the spirit of God' (the Greek in fact being *epitheiazousan* – called upon as god).

One particular respect in which Moses and the Logos are alike in their unlikeness to God himself is that, contrasted with God, who is nameless, Moses, like the Logos, is many-named. The Logos is said to be the possessor of many names (*poluōnomon*: *Conf. Ling.* 146; see p. 124; so also in *Mut. Nom.* 125). This possession of many names is a characteristic of the Logos who is, for Philo, *theos*. Moses too is described as a 'truly God-inspired soul' and as being, because of his wisdom, *theos* (*ibid.* 128). Philo was at times forced to face precisely the same difficulties as confronted the early Christian theologians. He was a devout Jewish monotheist, and yet he was forced into contradictions of that absolute monotheism, especially in what he said about Moses. Even the lover of the divine becomes, according to *Omn. Prob. Lib.* 43–4, 'a god', though only 'a god to men' and not to the whole of the natural order. Moses, Philo argues, was 'not deemed worthy of divine rank in his own right', yet because 'he had God for a friend' he did possess 'absolute felicity'. It has been suggested that Philo did at times think of Moses as God's substitute in his relationships with men. Therefore, a passage in the *De Virtutibus* implies that, as a 'divine man', he was sinless. What he says is that absolutely not to sin is a property of God alone, or perhaps of a divine man (*ibid.* 177; see p. 45). When Philo goes on to say that Moses, earlier described as 'most holy Moses, who was a lover of virtue and goodness', recalled his fellow-Jews to monotheism (*monarchia*) instead of polytheism (*poluarchia*), it is clear that any beliefs he held about the divinity of Moses were held together with an unswerving belief in the unique and absolute sovereignty of God.

The question that has been raised of the possibility of an incarnation of the Logos within the human life-history of Moses raises also the question of whether or not the Logos of Philo was personal. Philo certainly speaks of the Logos in personal terms, as, for example, the Son of God (*Conf. Ling.* 146; see pp. 125–6). The same implication seems to lie behind such titles as a 'high-priest' in *Som.* I.215, but it is doubtful if personification proceeds to the point of personalisation. The Logos of Philo is never, as it was later in Christian theology, a 'person' within the one Godhead. There may well have been, to Philo's mind, some kind of incarnation of the divine Logos within the life-history of the human Moses – thus making Moses a divine–human being – but there is nothing in that Philonic conception that is precisely the same as the Christian concept of the Incarnation within a particular human life (that of Jesus of Nazareth), of the Person within a Triune Deity designated the Son or Logos. Philo did perhaps think in terms of the deification of Moses, but not of an incarnation within Moses' life of the divine Logos. Because of the diametrically opposed qualities of flesh and spirit, the deification process involved the gradual and finally total eradication of flesh from the life of Moses. That is nearer to the Docetic Christologies of early – and modern – Christianity, to that seen by some in John's Gospel, than to the doctrine of the Incarnation subscribed to, in theory at least, by orthodox Christianity. Philo states that 'nothing mortal can be made in the likeness of the most high One and Father of the universe but [only] in that of the second God, who is his Logos' (*Quaest. in Gn.* II.62). Christianity, however, made the claim that a particular mortal man, Jesus the Jew, was made in the likeness of the High One and Father. It also claims that the Logos made man was the likeness of God within the life of a man, not merely of a 'second God' but of a second Person within the one God. Unless in *Praem. Poen.* 165, one of the rare passages of Philonic eschatology, the 'vision divine and superhuman' is, as it could be, a reference to the Logos in a Messianic role, there is no connection in Philo's thought between the Logos and the Messiah of Judaism. For John the Logos made flesh is the Son, as in Philo, and the agent of creation, but he is also the Son of God, the Messiah. Philo makes no mention of the Jewish Messiah and, therefore, no suggestion that the Logos became incarnate and was the Messiah. When Paul came to write 1 Corinthians he interpreted the 'spiritual rock' which followed the Israelites at the time of Exodus as Christ: 'and the rock was Christ' (1 Cor. 10: 4). When Philo described the incident of the Burning Bush he said that in the midst of the flame was 'a form of the fairest beauty' which was 'an image supremely divine in appearance, refulgent with a light brighter than the light of fire' (*Vit. Mos.* I.66). It might be supposed, he says, that such an image was an image of him that IS; but he prefers to say that it was an angel or herald, using visible events, the burning of a weak bramble bush, to offer hope to the persecuted. Describing the Exodus, he alludes to the cloud which went behind the Israelites to guide them, stating that within it was 'the vision of the Godhead flashing rays of fire' (*Vit. Mos.* II.254). The Burning Bush passage seems to require no reference to the Messiah, or even perhaps to the Logos, though there is reference to an angelic image.

Philo's ideas on the subject of the Logos are extremely interesting and important, as part of the history of Logos thinking in general and of the development of Jewish Logos thinking in particular. They illustrate what can happen when a devout Jew with philosophical interests and expertise seeks to give expression to his essentially Jewish faith by using Greek philosophical concepts and the Logos concept in particular. Philo's works are an enormously important part of the background to the New Testament and need therefore to be studied carefully by all New Testament students and students of the later development of the Christian Logos doctrine. His Logos doctrine shows how it is possible for a monotheist to embrace the belief in a Logos, a divine Logos, without modifying his doctrine of God into one involving a Godhead of more than one Person. It also shows how a Jew, in the New Testament era, could speak of an association between the Logos and a particular man in a way that at times sounds like incarnational language and at other times maintains absolutely the separate identity of the Logos and the particular man in question. But it is perhaps wise, when reading Philo's works as part of the background, for example, to John's Gospel, not to be misled into attributing to Philo Judaeus, Philo the Jew, ideas which became part of the development of Logos thinking only in the minds of some of the writers who contributed to the Christian New Testament. Even Philo's Logos doctrine, however interesting to the student of Christian literature, is part of the history of Jewish thinking.

THE LOGOS AS LINK BETWEEN CREATOR AND CREATED
(*Rer. Div. Her.* 205–6 (XLII))

(205) To his Logos, his chief messenger, senior in rank, the Father who created all things has given as a pre-eminent gift the privilege of standing on the frontier of being to separate what has been created from the Creator. The same Word is a continual suppliant to the immortal God on behalf of mortal man, who is exposed to affliction, and
(206) is also the ambassador of the ruler to the subject race. The Word rejoices in this gift and exulting in it describes it in these words, 'I stood between the Lord and you' [Deut. 5: 5], that is, being neither uncreated like God, nor yet created like you, but midway between the two extremes, a pledge to both sides; to the Creator a guarantee that the

> whole race would never revolt entirely and choose disorder rather than order; to the creature, to reinforce its hopes that the merciful God would never overlook his own handiwork. For I am the proclaimer of the knowledge of peaceful tidings to creation from the God who has determined to destroy wars, who is ever the guardian of peace.

In this short passage Philo describes the mediatorial role of the Logos, midway between God on the one hand and the created world and mankind on the other. The Logos, as here presented, is both the representative of man to God, a kind of High Priest, and of God to man.

(205) *his chief messenger*: here Philo describes the divine Logos as God's archangel, who is pre-eminent in both age and honour. To his Logos, Philo says, God has assigned a special function, *of standing on the frontier of being to separate what has been created from the Creator*. But, as well as being a kind of boundary and barrier separating God from the created order, the Logos also pleads with God on behalf of mankind and acts as *ambassador of the ruler to the subject race*. Here, as elsewhere, Philo personifies the Logos as a kind of High Priest figure, but it is perhaps a mistake to take this for a full-blooded personalisation.

Philo's doctrine of the transcendence of God required him to develop the idea of mediation by the Logos between God and his creation; otherwise there would have been no kind of communication or relationship. The mediatory role of the Jewish high-priest provided Philo with the perfect material from which to extract, by allegorical exegesis, the concept of the High Priest Logos, as he describes him in *Migr. Abr.* 102. In *Som.* 1.215 Philo says that God has two temples, one of which is 'this world, in which the high-priest is the divine Word'. *Cher.* 17 describes the Logos as 'the priest and prophet', while *Gig.* 52 simply speaks of the high-priest as Reason. One other passage which is interesting and of importance in this connection is *Spec. Leg.* 1.80ff., where the Logos is said to be the Image of God 'by which all the world was made', and the garments worn by the Jewish high-priest symbolise the universe worn by the Logos. The significance of this is indicated by Philo in the closing words of the section: 'For the signs of every thing on earth are engraved and firmly fixed in heaven.' The Logos, that is, represents or presents the universe to God.

(206) *midway between the two extremes*: this is Philo's phrase to describe the position of the Logos, a position in which the Logos glories, proudly describing it in the words of Deut. 5: 5. This leads Philo to state that the Logos is neither *uncreated like God*, nor created like man. It is midway between the two extremities and is therefore, Philo says, *a pledge to both sides*. It assures God that the creature will never altogether rebel against his sovereignty and choose disorder rather than order. It also assures man that God is merciful and will never forget his own work. What the Logos does is, therefore, in effect, to convey to mankind the message that God is a God of peace whose desire it is that there should be perpetual peace, and who is the permanent guardian of peace.

God himself utterly transcends his creation, yet he is never totally silent. His transcendence does not mean that he is utterly beyond man's reach; nor is his Thought. He speaks and communicates, and for Philo the term Logos denotes the Thought of God expressed in a form that is, at least indirectly, accessible to man and knowable by him. The Logos also expresses, on behalf of man, what he cannot adequately express for himself. The Logos is both the divine ambassador to man and man's representative before God. Since the Logos is not for Philo a distinct and separate being, having its own ontological status, subordinate to God, but is God's Logos, the incorporeal Word or Thought of God, Philo's statements in the present passage mean that within the totality of the divine Being there is an acknowledgement by the merciful Creator of the plight and needs of the creature. The picture of the Logos as clothed in the garments of the universe also implies a close and intimate relationship between the Creator and his creation. The expressed Thought or Word of God runs throughout every part of the created order, and, from a different point of view, the whole creation, including mankind, is represented within the Thought of God. The Thought or Logos of God can indeed be said to be a kind of High Priest representing mankind to God.

'I AM THE GOD WHO APPEARED TO THEE' (*Som.* I.227–30 (XXXIX))

(227) For, according to Scripture, he says 'I have seen all that Laban doeth unto thee' [Gen. 31: 12], namely, the opposite of the blessings which I bestowed upon you,

things which are inexorably impure, rejected as spurious, belonging altogether to the realm of darkness.

But this does not mean that the man who relies on the hope of divine comradeship needs to cower and be afraid, for to him God addresses the words, 'I am the God who appeared to thee in the place of God' (Gen. 31: 13, LXX).
(228) It is surely a considerable justification for boasting for the soul that God should think fit to appear to it and to converse with it. And do not fail to note carefully what is said here, but examine the words thoroughly and ask if there really are two gods. For it is said, 'I am the God who appeared to thee' not 'in my place' but 'in the place of God', as though the reference were to that of some other
(229) God. What then ought we to say? He that is truly God is One, but those who are called gods by an abuse of language are numerous. Therefore the sacred scripture in the present passage has indicated that it is the true God that is meant by the use of the article in the statement, 'I am *the* God' (*ho theos*), but when the word is used incorrectly there is no article, as in the words, 'Who appeared to thee in the place' not 'of *the* God' (*tou theou*), but simply 'of God' (*theou*).
(230) Here he gives the title 'God' to his chief Word, not from any superstitious attitude to the application of names, but with one goal before him, to fit the words to the facts. For in another passage the sacred historian, having enquired if he who IS has any name, came to know with certainty that he has no proper name, and that whatever name anyone may use of him will involve an abuse of language; for it is not the nature of him that IS to be described by name, but only to be.

In this very important short section Philo discusses the propriety of applying the term 'God' to the Logos. Philo distinguishes between superstition and true religion and indicates how he understood the relationship between God and the Logos.

(227) *the hope of divine comradeship*: in the first part of this

paragraph Philo is commenting on the words of Gen. 31: 12, which, allegorically expounded, describe what the evil-designing character does to the man initiated into the secrets of true philosophy. The man who relies on the hope of God's friendship should not, however, says Philo, be afraid, for God, as the words of Gen. 31: 13 show, has assured him of his presence.

(228) *a considerable justification for boasting*: the fact that God condescends to reveal himself to and converse with man is what constitutes a sound basis for self-congratulation. But Philo has not failed, inveterate allegorist as he is, to notice that in the Septuagint translation of Gen. 31: 13 the Hebrew word 'Bethel' is rendered 'place of God'. He may have failed to understand that the word 'Bethel' had in fact been translated. But what struck him was that the language of the verse raised the question of whether or not there were 'two Gods', since God says, 'I am the God who appeared to thee in the place of God' (Bethel). God does not, Philo notes, say, *'in my place'*, but *'in the place of God'*, giving the impression that there is another God in whose Place he appeared.

(229) *He that is truly God is One*: this is Philo's emphatic answer to his own question *What then ought we to say?* Of the oneness of God there can, for Philo, be no doubt. He calls God *to hen* ('the One') (*Rer. Div. Her.* 216) and has much to say along the lines of the statement in *Leg. All.* II.1 that 'God is alone and by himself, being One' (cf. *Decal.* 65). It is only, in Philo's view, the gods of pagan polytheism, who are many, who are improperly so called – a subject to which Philo often turns, believing, as he did, that polytheism and idolatry were the worst of all sins. In one place Philo, describing what goes on in 'the contest of wickedness', says that alongside atheists who deny the existence of God, there are those who have introduced a 'multitude of [deities] male and female, older and younger' (*Spec. Leg.* I.330–1).

Because such false beliefs are held, and statements made which imply that there is more than one God, Scripture in Gen. 31: 13 emphasises that he is truly God by placing the definite article before the word God (*ho theos*, which is equivalent to *the* God in English). In the Greek New Testament it is usual to find the article so placed before the word *theos*. In the LXX Gen. 31: 13, however, there are no articles in the phrase *the place of God*, despite the English translation. So Philo prepares to make an important deduction from the difference between the form '*the* God' (in English God) and the later 'of God' (without a *the*).

(230) *his chief Word*: it is to the Logos, the chief Word of God, that the title God (*theos*, not *ho theos*: that is, God, but not the God) applies. This is not done, Philo says, out of *any superstitious attitude* or out of an excess of scrupulousness in the use of words, but in order to use words correctly to express facts, to express the truth by accommodating language to the needs of the truth to be expressed. Nor does Philo wish it to be thought that by assigning the name God to the Logos he is himself guilty of *deisidaimonia*, in the sense of superstition.

Philo's application here of the term God to the Logos is part of his general practice. In *Leg. All.* III.206 he speaks of God as the First Cause, an expression which implies the existence of a second God, who is in fact referred to in *Quaest. in Gn.* II.62, in the statement 'no mortal thing' could have been made in the likeness of 'the supreme Father of the Universe', but only in that of the second God, who is his Logos. In that passage, it is also to be noted, Philo speaks of God's first Logos. Even though Philo does speak of 'the eternal Word' (*Plant.* 18) and in many places refers to the 'eldership among the angels' enjoyed by the Logos (*Conf. Ling.* 146; see p. 125–6), it is clear that absolute priority and superiority belong to God.

he has no proper name: here Philo repeats his view that God is essentially nameless, a view stated in the passage (*Mut. Nom.* 11ff.) commented on above (see pp. 39–40). Any name used of God is used, Philo asserts, by *an abuse of language*. In *Decal.* 94 Philo refers to the many variations of the divine name, but he makes it abundantly clear there and elsewhere that the essentially nameless God is named in Scripture only as a concession to human weakness. The names of God are all part of the anthropomorphic language of the Old Testament used in order to awake in its less philosophical readers an awareness of God and reverence for him (see above, pp. 84 and 91).

God possesses *no proper name* because there is no particular thing that he is. God is pure Being, *to on*. It is his nature to be, not to be spoken of, and certainly not to be spoken of as possessing particular qualities, for that would be to place limits to his being. But the Logos, unlike God, does have 'many names' (*Conf. Ling.* 146). To the Logos the word God can properly be applied, in the sense indicated above, but the difference between God and his Logos is made clear by the fact that God is nameless while the Logos has many names, and also by the fact that, though the Logos is their 'ruler', he is placed 'among the angels'. As one might have expected to find, Philo remains quite clear about the relative positions of God and the Logos. The Logos is the Logos *of God*. There is never, therefore, any question of the Logos being equal or superior to God. How could his Logos be equal or superior to himself? The difference between the Deity and his Logos is that the Deity is in essence nameless, whereas the extension of his Thought into an expression which man can comprehend can be named, indeed has of necessity many names.

'SONS OF GOD' (*Conf. Ling.* 145–6 (XXVIII))

(145) But those who have real knowledge of the One are properly called 'Sons of God', as Moses also describes them when he says, 'Ye are sons of the Lord God' [Deut. 14: 1], and 'God who begat thee' [*ibid.* 32: 18], and 'Is he not himself thy father?' [*ibid.* 6]. Accordingly, it is a natural consequence that those who have this disposition of soul reckon only the good to be beautiful, an attitude which is a kind of fortification constructed by experienced fighters against the view which makes pleasure the end with the
(146) aim of overturning and demolishing it. But even if as yet there is no-one who is worthy to be called a Son of God, nevertheless let him strive intensely to be assigned to a place under God's First-born, the Logos, who holds the eldership among the angels, the archangel, as it were, who possesses many names. For the names by which he is called include the Beginning, and the Name of God, and his Word, and the man answering to God's image, and he that sees, that is Israel.

(145) *Sons of God*: this designation rightly applies, according to Philo's interpretation of Moses' words in Deut. 14: 1 and 32: 6 and 18, to *those who have real knowledge of the One*. Such men hold moral beauty to be the only good, and this helps to counteract and overcome the influence of those who serve the cause which makes pleasure the supreme end in life. Philo is probably referring to the Stoics and Epicureans, as usual a little unfairly.

(146) *the eldership among the angels*: this is the position occupied

by the Logos, here described also as *God's First-born.* To become a *Son of God* a man must order his life in accordance with the rule of the Logos, here called an *angel* (on angels, see above, p. 125). The Logos, to whom man must submit himself if he wishes to be a child of God, is also said to be the ruler of the angels. Unlike God, who is nameless, the Logos, we are told, *possesses many names.* It is interesting to observe that Moses too is said by Philo to have many names (*Mut. Nom.* 125ff.), a fact which, with others, suggests the possibility that there was in Philo's mind a special relationship between Moses and the Logos, even perhaps that Moses was an incarnation of the Logos. Among the names of Moses mentioned by Philo in the *De Mutatione Nominum* passage are Man of God and god (*theos*) of Pharaoh (this last because of the mercy he showed to Pharaoh, for mercy is the peculiar prerogative of a god). The names here assigned to the Logos by Philo are five, as follows:

the Beginning: the Logos is not, as we have seen, eternal in the absolute sense that God is eternal. It does, however, pre-exist the created order. It was there in the beginning, the Agent or Instrument of creation. It is sometimes viewed by Philo as the archetypal Idea. In speaking of the creation of man, at one point Philo states that the soul of man is a creation of the divine Spirit, 'stamped and impressed with the seal of God, the impression of which is the Eternal Word' (*Plant.* 18). It is because the Logos is 'the archetypal Word of the First Cause' (*ibid.* 20) that he can be named the Beginning. Philo refers to the creation of the world by God as having taken place *ex archēs* (*Spec. Leg.* 1.300), and while God himself is called the beginning and goal of all things (*Plant.* 77), the Logos, because it was that through which God effected the creation of the world, the first principle, and because of the sovereignty it exercises over the universe, is also called the *Archē* (Beginning) (cf. *Cher.* 7 and *Rer. Div. Her.* 62). For Philo the word 'beginning' denotes more than chronological priority (cf. *Op. Mund.* 27), pointing to a qualitative superiority which is an attribute appropriate to the divine Logos.

the Name of God: God himself is nameless, whereas the Logos has many names, one of which is God. Knowledge of a name for Philo implies knowledge of the essence of the thing or person named. Man cannot know God's essence directly, but indirect knowledge of God is possible through his Logos, his Name. The nearest man can get to knowledge of God's essence, in fact, is knowledge of the Logos. The Logos is, therefore, in a real sense *the Name of God*. The

Logos plays a mediatorial role in creation and in epistemology, in the realm of man's knowledge of God.

his Word: the Logos is the uttered Thought of God, as contrasted with the Thought which God keeps to himself. Philo elaborated his Logos doctrine in an attempt to overcome the problem created by belief in the utter transcendence of God for someone who wanted to maintain that God could be known and seen. For Philo 'the beginning and end of happiness is to see God' (*Quaest. in Ex.* II.51). But, for him, ascent to the ultimate *visio Dei* is possible only because God has expressed his inward Thought (*logos endiathetos*) in his Logos. Of that Logos, Philo says nothing 'has received its precedence so completely . . . because it is by its means that the Creator and Father of the Universe is most especially made manifest; for the mind beholds God in this as in a mirror' (*Decal.* 105; cf. 1 Cor. 13: 12).

the man answering to God's image: in his interpretation of the account of the creation in Scripture, Philo describes the Logos, in many places, as God's image and the ideal form which he stamped upon the world (see, e.g., *Som.* II.45). In *Op. Mund.* 25 Philo uses similar language of the creation of man, alluding to Gen. 1: 27 (see p. 109). But in *Leg. All.* II.4 Philo distinguishes between two kinds of men: one made in accordance with the divine image and the other 'made out of the earth'. The image of God is a pattern from which copies are made. He calls this man *the man answering to God's image*. That would seem to imply that the Ideal Man is made after the divine image, whereas ordinary men are copies of the Ideal Man. But in the present passage it is the Logos who is the Man after the divine image, which makes good sense if it is remembered that for Philo the Logos *is* the world of Ideas, the *kosmos noētos* (see below, pp. 129, 132–3). In *Gig.* 61 the parallelism between 'the world which is perceptible only by the intellect' and the phrase 'the commonwealth of Ideas' shows that the *kosmos noētos* is the total community of the imperishable and incorporeal Ideas. As a totality, that commonwealth of Ideas is the Logos (cf. *Conf. Ling.* 172). What God created first, according to Philo's treatise on creation, was the intelligible world, for which Philo chose to use the word Logos rather than the word *nous*, so that he could retain *nous* for the human mind and Logos for the Mind or Thought of God.

he that sees, that is Israel: Israel means, according to Philo, 'seeing God' (see p. 66). Israel is, of course, a symbol for the mind or soul which enjoys the vision of God. The vision involved transcends perception and represents the highest kind of seeing possible, the sight of the Existent. It is, therefore, intellectual or mystical vision. Usually it is attributed to men such as Moses and those who engage in philosophical meditation, but in the present passage it is the sight of God enjoyed by the Logos, by sharing in which those who are frustrated in their desire to be God's sons at least attain to sonship of the Logos and so, indirectly, do enjoy a vision of God. The kind of intellectual seeing involved, the seeing of the understanding, which constitutes such sonship of the Logos is described in *Abr.* 57–8; it involves a stretching of 'the eye of the soul'.

THE ELEMENTS OF CREATION (*Op. Mund.* 16–25 (IV–VI))

(16) We must enumerate as many as we can of the elements embraced in his account (of creation), since to refer to them all would be impossible. Its pre-eminent element is the intelligible world, as the account of the 'One' demonstrates. For God, being God, knew beforehand that a beautiful copy could never exist apart from a beautiful model, and that no objects of perception would be faultless which were not fashioned in the likeness of an archetype conceived only by the intellect. When, therefore, he determined to create the visible world, he first formed that one which is perceptible only by the intellect, in order that, being able to use a pattern wholly God-like and incorporeal, he might make the material world, a younger creation, the precise image of the earlier, older one, to contain in itself as many different kinds of objects perceptible to the senses as the other world contains of those which are visible to the
(17) intellect only. To attempt to describe or even to imagine that world which consists of ideas as being in some place is not permissible, but how it is made up we can understand if we pay close attention to some image drawn from things around us. When a city is being founded, in order to satisfy the overweening ambition of some king or ruler who is

claiming totalitarian power, and is at the same time a man of brilliant ideas who is eager to embellish his prosperity, there comes on the scene sometimes a man who by his training has become an expert architect and who, when he sees the favourable climatic conditions of the site and its convenient situation, first of all sketches in his mind more or less all the parts of the city which is to be constructed – the temples, the gymnasia, the presidential assembly halls, the market-places, the harbour, the docks, the streets, the lay-out of the city-walls, the dwelling-houses and the public and other
(18) buildings. Then, having received in his own mind, graven, as it were, on wax, the shape of each of the buildings, he thenceforth carries about in his mind the image of a city, although it is as yet perceptible only to mind. But, by the power of the memory which is innate in him, he calls to mind the mental image and fixes their imprints even more distinctly upon it; finally, like a good workman, keeping his eyes fixed on his mental model, he begins to create the city of stones and timber, making material objects resemble each
(19) of the incorporeal ideas. Now we must think of God in a similar way, who, when he had decided to found the one great city, the macro-city, first of all conceived in his mind images of its components, on the basis of which he established a world perceptible only by the mind, and then, using that as a pattern, completed the sense-perceptible one.
(20) As, therefore, the city which was prefigured in the mind of the architect has no external place, but was stamped solely in the mind of the workman as on a seal, so also the universe which consisted of ideas could have had no other location than the divine Reason, which had made them, for what other place could there be capable of receiving and containing, I do not say all of them, but any single one of
(21) them whatsoever in its pure mental form? Now the power likewise which was capable of creating the world is just such a one, having as its source that goodness which is grounded

in truth. For if anyone wanted to search for the cause, on account of which this whole was created, it seems to me that he would not be mistaken if he concluded, as one of the ancients did, that the Father and Creator is good, because of which he did not grudge a share of his own excellent nature to an existence which of itself has nothing good or beautiful,
(22) but was capable of becoming everything. For of itself existence was destitute of order, without quality, without soul, of no distinctive character, and full of disorder, confusion and disharmony; but it underwent a change in the opposite direction, the best, to order, quality, animation, likeness, perfect arrangement, harmony, and to everything that is characteristic of the more excellent
(23) model. And God, with no counsellor to help him – for who else was there? – but acting on his own initiative alone, decided that it was fitting to shower rich and abundant favours upon that nature which, without the divine gift, was incapable of gaining possession of any good things. But God does not bestow his favours according to the greatness of his own graces – for they are illimitable and eternal – but according to the capacity of the recipients. For the capacity of creation to receive benefits does not match the natural power of God to bestow them, for the powers of God are infinitely vast, but the creation, too weak to cope with their abundance, would have collapsed under it if God had not appropriately measured his bounty, allocating to each its
(24) due portion. If, however, anyone should wish to use words in a less disguised way, he would have to say nothing other than that the world discerned by the intellect is nothing other than the Word of God when he was already occupied in the act of creation. For (using the illustration employed above) a city while still perceptible only by the mind is nothing else but the reason of the architect while he is
(25) engaged in the process of planning the city-to-be. It is Moses who lays this down, not I. Accordingly, when he

> records the creation of man in the words which follow (in the Genesis narrative), he affirms expressly that he was made in the image of God. And if the part is an image of an image, it is clear that so also is the whole, and if the whole world of sense-perception, which is greater than any human image, is a copy of the divine image, it is obvious that the archetypal seal, which we affirm to be the intelligible world, must be the pattern, the archetypal idea of ideas, the Word or Logos of God.

This section includes part of Philo's discussion of the creation stories in Gen. 1 and 2.

(16) *Its pre-eminent element*: Philo, in the preceding section, has noted that Moses did not in fact call the first of the days of creation by the term 'first'. He is alluding to the statement in Gen. 1: 5: 'And there was evening and there was morning, one day.' Philo was fascinated by numbers in general, by the number one and the concept of 'the One', by the idea of the monad, unity. He decides, therefore, that he must give an account of everything embraced by the 'one', the first, day, though he realises that it will be an impossible undertaking. Supreme among the elements embraced by the 'one' is *the intelligible world* (*ho kosmos noētos*). That is *the pre-eminent element*. He has demonstrated this, he claims, in a treatise, lost to us, dealing with the whole subject of 'the One'. God, being God, he says, assumed that *a beautiful copy* would never be produced without *a beautiful model* (*paradeigma*). He also knew that no object in the world of sense-perception would be faultless which was not a copy of *an archetype conceived only by the intellect*. God, therefore, when he decided to create the visible world *first formed that one which is perceptible only by the intellect*. He did this so that he might have available *a pattern wholly God-like and incorporeal*. This he would use later in his creation of the material universe. That material world would then be the image of the immaterial one and would include as many objects of sense-perception as the other contained objects of intelligence. Here is a thoroughly Platonic view of creation, such as is found in Plato's *Timaeus* (see also p. 142). A simplified version of Plato's *Timaeus* creation-doctrine would present the *Demiurge* as God and would place the Ideas beyond the material world and outside of God. The *Demiurge* becomes, for Philo, the God of the Old Testament, but

the relationship between God and the Ideas is not exactly the same in Philo's thought as in Plato.

(17–18) *that world which consists of ideas*: to think or speak of the world of Ideas as if it existed in space somewhere is, Philo thought, improper. But the world of space and time around us does supply us with an analogy for thinking and speaking about the world of Ideas. Then Philo describes how, when a city is being built for a despotic king or ruler who wants to add to the grandeur of his possessions, he makes use of a trained architect, who, having made the necessary inspection of the proposed site, pictures in his own mind what the city will look like when completed, with all its buildings and streets. This imaginative pre-construction of the city is, Philo says, like having an impression of the things which will be in the city-complex made in wax. The architect can thus carry about the image of the city which is the creation of his mind.

his eyes fixed on his mental model: once he has formed a clear and distinct impression in his mind of the city as it will be when built, the architect, using his powers of memory, can recall the individual images of the various parts of the city, particular images which can go to make up the whole *image of a city*. The more he thinks about the picture he has of the projected city, the sharper do the mental images become. The actual building of the city is a matter of his translating the mental picture into structures of stone and timber, all the time making reference to the mental images in his mind. The aim of the construction process is to make the physical shapes and structures of the city correspond as closely as possible to the ideas in the architect's mind, *the incorporeal ideas*.

(19) *the one great city*: the analogy between the creation of the world and the design and building of a city leads Philo to speak of the universe as a city, a metaphor which emphasises the unity of the created world. The phrase Philo uses here to describe the universe makes it clear that, in his view, there is nothing in the material realm which is the equal of the universe which God has made. When God decided to make the world (and it was an act of will, a decision on his part), like the architect in Philo's parable, he first *conceived in his mind images of its components*. Out of these he created a world anterior to the physical world, a world *perceptible only by the mind*. Using that world, the intelligible world, as the universe's pattern, he then created the world perceptible by the senses, the world we can see, whose sounds we can hear, with things in it capable of being touched or tasted or smelled.

(20) *the universe which consisted of ideas*: the plan of the city which the architect constructed in his mind did not exist, at first, outside his mind, in the outer world.

as on a seal: rather it had been imprinted on his mind as a shape can be imprinted upon wax by a signet ring. The picture which Philo has in mind in the passages where he speaks about a *seal* or something being sealed is of an image being clearly and indelibly imprinted upon wax, to which the more common modern equivalent is the use of stamps to cancel postal-orders or to record our entry into a country upon our passport.

There is a parallel between mundane matters of that kind and the process of creation, in Philo's view, for just as the imagined city was at first located only in the architect's mind, when it was still only a dream, so *the universe which consisted of ideas* has no other location – and this means no location at all, strictly speaking, no position in space – than *the divine Reason* (*ho theios logos*).

which had made them: with the identification of the *place* of the Ideas as the Logos, and this description of the creative role of the Logos, we have come at last to what Philo has to say about the Logos in the present treatise.

The Logos, then, is the *place* (of the Ideas), an unavoidable metaphor from the world to which the Logos does not really belong used to describe the non-spatial domain which is alone able to contain even one of God's powers in its pure state. Philo here also assigns to the Logos the work of ordering and arranging the universe. The idea of the forms as the pattern for the created world is Platonic, the idea of the mind as a place of forms is from Aristotle, and these two ideas Philo has attempted to weld on to a Jewish doctrine of creation.

(21) *that goodness which is grounded in truth*: the particular power of which Philo is thinking in the present section is the creative power by which the universe was made. Its source is the perfect goodness of the Deity. Philo more than once, as he does here, says that the cause for the sake of which the world was created, the final cause, was God's goodness. He notes that the men of old affirmed that the Father and Maker of all is good. Chief among these men of old, the fathers of the Jewish race, was Moses, who, according to Philo, taught that 'the cause of the creation of the world' was 'the goodness of the living God, which was the most important of his graces' and 'itself the cause' (*Deus Imm.* 108). The creation of the world was, for Philo, an expression of God's love and goodness. In

the present passage Philo adds the further thought that God's goodness led him to give a share in his own perfect nature to that which is itself neither fair nor lovely but is capable of becoming all things: that is, matter. This aspect of Philo's view of creation should not be overlooked. Despite his dualistic view of reality, a view which leads him to despise the physical at times, Philo's outlook is basically optimistic and hopeful. Anything is possible, especially for a creation upon which God bestows part of himself.

(22) *it underwent a change*: in itself matter is disordered, without qualitative differences or similarities; it has no soul. It is what the philosophers called formless matter, an amorphous mass, its parts ill-adjusted to one another and the whole in a state of disharmony. Matter is described by Philo here in a series of technical terms which are like those in Plato, Aristotle and the Stoic writers (see below, p. 142). In other treaties Philo repeats some of these descriptions and adds other terms. In *Spec. Leg.* I.328 he calls matter 'misshapen and confused'. In *Rer. Div. Her.* 140 it is said that to be 'destitute of form . . . and all distinctive qualities' is a characteristic of matter (cf. *Mut. Nom.* 135). *Som.* II.45 describes matter as 'previously devoid of shape'.

But the material substratum of the universe was capable of being transformed and given the qualities it had hitherto lacked, qualities which Philo lists. It was given these when creation took place, and it was made to resemble *the more excellent model* ('Idea' is the word actually used by Philo). Relevant to what Philo says at this point is what he says in more than one place about the Logos as the 'Cutter' (see, for example, *Rer. Div. Her.* 140, where it is stated that God employed his 'own Word, the divider of all things' to divide 'the essence of the universe', previously 'without form or qualities', and to shape animals and plants from the four elements which were segregated from the original formal matter). So, for Philo, the actual creation of particular species of animals and plants, as well as the separation off from matter of the four elements, was the work of the divine Logos.

(23) *with no counsellor to help him*: in *Leg. All.* II.1–2 and elsewhere Philo interprets Gen. 2: 18 to mean that God, unlike man, is alone, solitary. Therefore, unaided – since there was no one beside him to help – God decided to confer *rich and abundant favours* upon formless matter, since of itself it was powerless to obtain anything good. Philo is trying to explain how a material universe, which plainly contains much that is good, came to obtain such

things. The good things in the universe came from God, and the number of them which he bestowed is in proportion not to the vastness of what God has to give, but to the capacities of the recipients. God's powers are overwhelmingly vast. There is far more to God than can be measured by what the creation has received, for God is infinite in his being. Creation could not absorb all that God could give and would have disintegrated if it had had to do so. God therefore conferred his benefits upon the world in proportion to its capacity to receive them, ensuring a perfect correlation between gift and recipient.

(24) *the world discerned by the intellect*: that world, the *kosmos noētos*, Philo here affirms, is the Logos of God *when he was already occupied in the act of creation*. In *Sacr. AC* 83 Philo speaks of the Logos as completed in 'innumerable varieties of ideas'. Sometimes it is said that the Logos as God's Thought enters upon a second phase of its existence as the divine Thought expressed and having an existence outside God's essence. It is not certain that this is how Philo intended his words to be understood. He does speak of the Logos as the totality of Ideas and as the place, metaphorically speaking, of Ideas (see above, para. 20; and cf. *Som.* 1.66). In *Som.* 1.62 Philo states that God has 'filled' his own Logos 'wholly and entirely with incorporeal powers'. But divine Thought expressed does not necessarily involve the idea of an incorporeal Mind 'outside of God's essence' (to quote a phrase that has been used in this connection). Even when Philo speaks of the 'pre-Logos God' (see above, p. 107), he is not speaking of priority in time. God is greater than his thoughts, greater than his Logos, but his Logos is his, is part of him. In the case of God essence involves Thought, Logos.

in the act of creation: for Philo the Jew, God is the Creator. He is called Maker and Father (para. 7), the Creator (*Cher.* 46), and in many passages the same and other terms are used to affirm belief in God's creativity. Whatever agents or methods he employed, God is himself the sole source of creative causality, who acted at creation on his own initiative (see above, para. 23). Philo then reverts to his own parabolic illustration of the architect and the city. The city which can be discerned only by the intellect is the reasoning faculty of the architect engaged in the planning of the city. The Logos, then, is the Mind of God engaged in the rational process of designing the world that was to come into being.

(25) *It is Moses who lays this down, not I*: Philo may have been

profoundly influenced by Greek philosophers, Plato, Aristotle, the Stoics and others, but he attributes his interpretation of the creation narrative in Genesis, and his explanation that the Logos is the Mind of God in which reside the incorporeal Ideas, to Moses. Moses is the supreme authority for Philo. It may seem at times that Philo tries to claim for Judaism whatever appealed to him in the writings of the philosophers, simply by appearing to extract it from the Jewish Scriptures by employing the allegorical method of exegesis. Sometimes, we may suspect, that *is* what he does, though with the best of intentions. Sometimes he does it because the philosophical ideas he has met in his study seem to him so sound and good that he feels he must associate his Judaism with them. Sometimes, no doubt, he saw hints of them in Scripture where another would not have done. And sometimes he recognised that what Plato or Aristotle had expressed in one way, the Old Testament, or rather Moses, had expressed in another way. All he was doing was to make the overlapping and similarities obvious and explicit.

We should not be surprised that Philo made use of language and ideas which he encountered in the writings of Greek philosophers in presenting his own original and individual interpretation of Judaism, for this kind of borrowing is always taking place in the history of ideas. Philo's own language and ideas made a powerful appeal to theologians of the Christian Church, and his influence upon some of his Christian contemporaries and successors was perhaps considerable. The process by which his ideas, his method of scriptural exegesis and his lexicographical thesaurus exerted their influence upon Christianity may have begun as early as the period of some of the first New Testament authors, or at least it may be said that his language, and the ideas it was used to express, belonged to a vast hellenistic pool of conceptual tools from which both he and some early Christian writers drew. If Philo borrowed words and concepts from Plato and Aristotle, those words and concepts as used by Philo, or at least some of them, entered into the cultural background against which documents such as the Fourth Gospel must be studied if they are to be understood.

THE HIGH PRIEST AS THE DIVINE WORD (*Fug.* 106–12 (xx))

(106) The fourth and last of the points we proposed to discuss is the subject of the time appointed for the return of the

fugitives, namely at the time of the death of the High Priest. Great difficulty is created by this if it is taken literally. For the penalties imposed by the law in this matter are totally unequal even though identical offences have been committed, since some will be banished for a longer time
(107) and others for a shorter time. For some of the High Priests live to a ripe old age, while others die very young; some are appointed in their youth, others not until they are very old. And, furthermore, some of those found guilty of unintentional homicide were banished at the beginning of the High Priest's term of office, some at a time when the High Priest was near to the point of death. So that some are deprived of life in their homeland for an extremely long period, others only for a day, perhaps, after which they will return, heads held high, exulting and laughing in the presence of the nearest relatives of those who have
(108) been killed by them. We shall escape from this difficulty with this unmanageable passage, which is almost inexplicable, and be able to render it reasonably, if we adopt the scientific method of interpretation which seeks the meaning beneath the surface of the literal words. For *we* say that the High Priest was not a man, but a Divine Word having no part in intentional or even unintentional errors.
(109) For Moses says that he cannot be defiled in respect of his father, the mind, or his mother, sense-perception [Lev. 21: 1], since, I imagine, he received incorruptible and wholly pure parents, his father being God and Wisdom his mother, through whom all things came into existence;
(110) because, moreover, he has been anointed with oil, by which I mean that the principal part of him is illumined by a brilliant light, so that he is thought to be worthy 'to put on the garments'. Now the supreme Word of him that IS puts on as garments the world, for he arrays himself with earth, air, water, fire, and all that issues from these. But the clothing of the soul is, in part, the body, while the mind of

(111) the wise man is clothed in virtues. And it is also said that he will never take the mitre from off his head; he will never, that is, lay aside the kingly diadem, the symbol of an authority which is not indeed absolute, but that of a viceroy, but nevertheless an object of admiration; 'nor' in
(112) addition 'will he rend his clothes' [Lev. 21: 10]. For the Word of him that IS is the bond of all that exists, as has been stated, and holds all things together and binds them into a whole, preventing them from being loosened or separated. And up to a point the soul, as far as it has received power, does not permit any parts of the body to be cut off or separated contrary to their nature, but, so far as it is its responsibility, it keeps all the parts complete and conducts them in their relationships with one another in an unbroken harmony and unity. And, likewise, the thoroughly purified mind of the wise man preserved the virtues in undamaged and unimpaired condition, reinforcing in an even more solid good that kinship and fellowship which belong to them by nature.

Here Philo explains what he means by calling the High Priest the Lôgos, and *vice versa*, as he does elsewhere (cf. *Migr. Abr.* 102). This passage also lets us see Philo the allegorical exegete at work again.

(106) *the death of the High Priest*: this is an allusion to the passage in Num. 35: 9–34 which states that refugees must remain in the 'cities of refuge' until the death of the High Priest in office at the time of their offence. Other aspects of the passage have already been dealt with. We notice that Philo selects passages for exegesis either because they suit his purposes or because they are part of the text expounded to an academic audience or to a synagogue of liberal Jews in Alexandria.

if it is taken literally: a statement about the time prescribed for the return of refugees, a time pinpointed as the moment of the High Priest's death, would, taken literally, present *great difficulty*, at least for someone like Philo. He notes some of the more obvious difficulties of such passages as Num. 35: 28. Unequal penalties are imposed for equal crimes, since the length of exile varies according to the life-span of the High Priest.

(107) *only for a day*: so absurd are the regulations laid down in Num. 35 that a single day is all the exile endured by some of those guilty of unintentional homicide, manslaughter, while others are condemned to spend a long period in banishment. This is because some offences were committed early in the life of a long-serving High Priest appointed in his youth, while others were committed just before a High Priest's death. Justice is mocked, for the latter category of offenders can return arrogantly, laughing insolently even at the close relatives of their victims.

(108) *the scientific method of interpretation*: this means, of course, the allegorical method. It is, as we have seen above, a method which involves looking for the hidden meaning of the literal words. The adoption of such a method of exegesis, however, enables the reader to avoid the difficulties of the literal meaning of the text.

By allegorical exegesis Philo arrives at the conclusion that the *High Priest* is not a human being at all, but is *a Divine Word*. As such it has no part in unrighteousness, whether intentional or unintentional. The text of Scripture, then, refers not to a human being, but to a perfectly sinless divine Being, the Logos. Just how divine the Logos is has been made clear already in an earlier passage. There it was said that the Logos has not been visibly portrayed and is the Image of God – 'the most ancient of all the objects of intellect . . . placed in the closest proximity to the only truly existing God without any partition or distance . . . between them' (para. 101) – who speaks to his Logos, as it were, with the intimacy of the occupant of the chariot of the universe speaking to the charioteer.

(109) *incorruptible and wholly pure parents*: Philo here describes, as it were, the genealogy of the Logos, but first states that the Logos cannot be defiled, as other men (even High Priests) can, by mind, here called father, or by sense-perception, here called mother. Philo probably had in mind, since he regards the High Priest as a symbol of the Logos, the words of Lev. 21: 11, a verse which says that the Jewish High Priest should not touch either the corpse of his father or that of his mother, or indeed any corpse, because of the risk of defilement. The reason why no defilement can take place in the case of the Logos is that, unlike an earthly High Priest, there are no human parents and no parents in the form of mind and sense-perception. The Logos is the spotless child of spotless parents. His Father is God, the Father of all; his Mother is Wisdom, *through whom all things came into existence*. Here the role of God's Agent at

creation is assigned, as in Prov. 8: 27–31 and Wisd. Sol. 9: 9, to Wisdom rather than to the Logos – an apparent separation of the two. But that there is no real division between the Logos and Wisdom is shown by the fact that in *Spec. Leg.* I.81 Philo states that 'the image of God is the Word through whom the whole universe was made', and similarly in *Sacr. AC* 8 he says: 'that Word by whom the whole universe was made'. Why, then, does Philo appear in the present passage to differentiate between the Logos and Wisdom? It would appear that, when he is thinking of the Logos as immanent in the world, he uses the word Logos, but that *sometimes* when he is thinking of the incorporeal Logos of the intelligible world he uses the term Wisdom, though it is clear from what he says that the High Priest is a symbol of the Logos in both its aspects.

It should not be forgotten that Philo did not, of course, mean that the Logos was begotten, though in *Leg. All.* III.175 he does say that 'the word of God is over all the world, and is the most ancient and the most universal of all things that are created'. This seems to place the Logos firmly in the class of created things, a view to be contrasted perhaps with John 1: 8 (see above, pp. 109–10). It should, in this connection, be noted that when Philo says that the Logos has Wisdom for its Mother, he simply means that the immanent Logos has its source in the intelligible Logos.

(110) *illumined by a brilliant light*: continuing his allegorical interpretation of the High Priest as the divine Logos, Philo alludes to the anointing of the earthly High Priest, stating that the *principal part* is filled with *a brilliant light*. God himself is Light, and the Logos' guiding faculty is encircled by a brilliant light. So brilliant is the light which illuminates the Logos' faculty of leading or ruling that, in some words from Lev. 21: 10, he is reckoned worthy 'to put on the garments'.

the garments: Philo explains here that, like garments, the Logos has 'put on' the world and its contents. Philo comments elsewhere on the symbolism of the High Priest's garments (see, e.g., *Migr. Abr.* 102–5). In *Vit. Mos.* II.117 Philo states that the vesture of the High Priest represents 'the world and its parts', including the four elements, the heavenly bodies and the zodiacal powers. Elsewhere it is said that the garments symbolise the hemispheres and the signs of the Zodiac, and that in fact the 'sacred dress' is 'a representation of the universe' (*Spec. Leg.* I.85–96). In the present passage what Philo does is to suggest that the High Priest symbolises the Logos immanent in the visible world. This is Philo's way of finding in Scripture an affirmation of the fact that the divine Logos is at work in the universe, in its fabric and its life. It is this that gives it order and harmony and keeps it in being and on its course. A similar role is attributed to the Son in New Testament theology, as, for example, in Heb. 1: 3 and Col. 1: 17.

the clothing of the soul is, in part, the body: here Philo offers an analogy from human existence to the presence of the divine Logos within the life of the universe. The relationship between the Logos and the world is likened to the relationship between the body and the soul, the former being a kind of garment for the latter. Likewise the virtues clothe the understanding of the wise man. Philo regards the Logos in this way, as the mode of entry of the divine Mind or Thought into the life of the world, because his view of God's transcendence prevents him from thinking or speaking of direct contact between God and the material universe. Contact between God and the world is made through the medium of the Logos.

(111) *the kingly diadem*: part of the description of the High Priest in Lev. 21 is that he 'shall not let the hair of his head go loose'. Philo quotes some of these words, from the Septuagint translation, but interpolates a reference to a *diadem*, changes the verb and produces a statement that *he will never take the mitre from off his head*. He explains this as meaning that the High Priest is not to *lay aside the kingly diadem*. This for him is the symbol of more than absolute sovereignty. It is the symbol of an admirable viceroyalty, a marvellous supremacy: that is, a supremacy at which one can only marvel. To the Logos belongs such power. If in the New Testament it can be said that the Son upholds all things 'by the word of his power' (Heb. 1: 3), Philo attributes the same kind of power to the Logos immanent in the world, the kind of power attributed to Christ in Col. 1: 17: 'in him all things consist' (see also below, on para. 112).

The final statement from Lev. 21 upon which Philo comments is the one in which it is said that the High Priest shall nor tear his garments.

(112) *the bond of all that exists*: what binds the diverse elements which go to make up the varied life of the universe into a coherent and ordered and harmonious whole is *the Word of him that IS*. This repeats what Philo says elsewhere: e.g., in *Plant*. 9, where what he says is that God made his Word 'the indissoluble bond of the

universe', and in *Rer. Div. Her.* 188, where the Logos is said to be 'glue and a chain'. Other passages where there are similar statements include *Deus Imm.* 35 and *Vit. Mos.* II.133, with which one may compare Wisd. Sol. 7: 17.

Philo's statement confirms the view that in this passage he is thinking of the immanent Logos, not the pre-mundane Logos of the incorporeal (or the Logos in its pre-mundane phase).

Philo is using here a term, *bond*, which Plato uses in the *Timaeus* of the world-soul which binds the universe together. Plato's terminology almost certainly helped Philo to spell out his cosmology and provided him with the term *desmos* (bond) to describe the Logos. But it should also be noted that Philo speaks of God himself as *the bond* which unites the diverse parts of the universe. God is *the bond of all that exists*, one who *holds all things together* indissolubly and binds fast 'what portions are dissoluble' (*Rer. Div. Her.* 23). Behind the immanent Logos binding the universe into a unified whole, ultimately there is the cohesive power of God himself. It is finally God who holds the universe 'so that it may last for ever' (*Sacr. AC* 40). It is he who administers the affairs of the universe (*Conf. Ling.* 170) and who is Ruler of the universe (*Spec. Leg.* IV.200). He too can be described as the steersman of the cosmos (*Decal.* 53), a description applied both to the the Logos and to God. In *Aet. Mund.* 83, as well as in *Spec. Leg.* IV.200, it is applied to God, whereas in *Deus Imm.* 129 and *Sacr. AC* 51 it is applied to the Logos. It can be said that one must guard against the danger of regarding Philo's Logos as a god, since beyond the Logos is God. But it can also be said that one must perhaps guard against separating God and his Logos so that the latter appears to be a being separate and distinct from God rather than the Logos of God – his Mind, if we are thinking of the rational order and coherence of the universe, expressed in Thought and permeating all things.

the soul: Philo offers another analogy, this time between the role of the immanent Logos in the world and the life-principle or soul in man's body. The soul holds the parts of the body together and keeps it alive, as far as that lies in its power. It holds the limbs and organs together in a coherent, unified whole. So also the purified mind of the wise man keeps his virtues intact, uniting them even more closely together than they would otherwise be. That unifying role is the Logos' role in the universe. As the soul is to the body, as the purified mind to the life of the wise man, so is the Logos to the universe. Without its presence the universe would disintegrate into its constituent parts; only by virtue of the presence of the Logos does the universe cohere and abide as a unity.

3. Philo's allegorical exegesis of Scripture

Almost everything Philo wrote about the Jewish Scriptures, and almost everything in those Scriptures, he interpreted allegorically. He regarded the Old Testament as the inspired Word of God – especially the Pentateuch, which could 'never be convicted of false witness' (*Abr.* 258) – and as 'speaking to every man' (*Mut. Nom.* 215). But Scripture, he believed, required careful interpretation. With a few exceptions, as we have already seen, his treatises are expositions of sections of the Pentateuch. Philo was a devout Jew (see above, pp. 2–5) and he took the Jewish Scriptures very seriously, but that did not mean that he took them literally at every point. In Philo's view, the Hebrew Scriptures were composed by their author(s) in a state comparable to that of the philosopher when inspired to recall intelligible Ideas beyond the world of sense and matter, and the Septuagint translators, filled with a similar kind of inspiration, produced an infallibly accurate rendering of the Hebrew into Greek. The Jewish prophet, when writing what was to become Scripture, was a man to whom 'nothing is unknown', since he possessed 'a spiritual sun and unclouded rays to give him a full and clear apprehension of things unseen by sense but apprehended by the understanding [*dianoia*]' (*Spec. Leg.* IV.192). They trained themselves with 'the laws of their fathers, which could not possibly have been conceived by the human soul without divine inspiration' (*Omn. Prob. Lib.* 80). Such an elevated view of the character of the Scriptures placed upon the Jewish scholar a heavy responsibility to seek a correct interpretation of them. But Philo was an unusual kind of Jewish intellectual in that he had become interested in philosophy to the extent of becoming something of a philosopher himself – the first Jew whom one can call a philosopher in anything like the modern sense of the word. The philosophy he had embraced, with enthusiasm, was largely a mixture of Platonism and Stoicism, with Platonism and in particular the Platonic Theory of Ideas contributing the most to his way of thinking (see above, pp. 2–3, and p. 228). He was therefore confronted with the necessity of reconciling the Greek philosophical ideas and ideals he had accepted with the scriptural religion and morality he had, as a Jew, inherited from his ancestors. In addition, he was faced with the problem of dealing, in a way that satisfied the philosopher in him without denying the beliefs he shared with his fellow-Jews, with statements and passages in the text of the Scriptures which were, in various ways and for various reasons, offensive and unacceptable. It was fortunate for him that the allegorical method of exegesis lay to hand for his use, for it presented him with the perfect tool, handled by him with extreme skill, for deriving philosophical ideas from even the most unlikely sections of the Pentateuch.

The difference between an allegory and allegorical exegesis. It is important to understand the difference between the creation of an allegory and the interpretation of a text, not necessarily created by its author as an allegory, by the allegorical method of exegesis. A writer, a novelist for example, may decide to give expression to his views, about life or the future of man or anything else, indirectly by means of an allegory, usually a narrative in which characters and objects in the fictional sequence of events are symbols for the realities which make up the truth or truths which the author wishes to communicate to his readers. Such an allegorical narrative, to be understood properly, must be decoded either laboriously item by item or, with more subtle allegories, by a growing recognition and awareness as it is read that beneath the surface meaning lies a less obvious but more profound meaning. Bunyan's *Pilgrim's Progress* is an example of allegory, though not necessarily the best or even a very good one (it is hardly subtle in its indirection; in fact the names of the characters clearly indicate the meaning of the real story that is being told). An example of poetic allegory is Dante's *Divine Comedy*. Some, or all, of Jesus' parables may be allegories: stories about, for example, sowing and harvesting and shepherds seeking and finding lost sheep, which indirectly speak about aspects of the Kingdom of God. Allegories, then, by their very nature need to be understood as such and interpreted by means of the allegorical method of exegesis, a method which recognises that in an allegory all is not what it seems and that a story about one subject may in fact be about something else, but that it is told as it is because its creator intended it to stimulate its readers into fresh ways of thinking about something else in a wholly different dimension of reality. It is possible, however, to apply the method appropriate to and intended for allegories to texts which are not allegories. This involves treating the non-allegorical as if it were an allegory. So skilful was his manipulation of the allegorical method of interpretation that Philo could surely have extracted a statement of Plato's Theory of Ideas from a railway timetable! Because the literal meaning of much of the Pentateuch was either unacceptable to him (for reasons discussed below) or was not particularly inspiring or elevating in what it had to say, Philo turned with alacrity and, we may suspect, relief to the allegorical method of exegesis because it enabled him to remain a loyal and devoted student of his people's Scripture, without feeling committed to the literal meaning of its every statement, and to retain his attachment to the philosophical understanding of reality he had derived from, among others, Plato and the Stoics.

The allegory of Pleasure and Virtue. Philo, however, was devoid of that particular kind of literary creativity which enables an author to produce allegories of high quality. One of the most interesting, though not inspiring, examples of his allegorical exegesis is to be found in *Sacr. AC* 19ff. It is an exposition of Deut. 21: 15–17, the Mosaic law regarding a man who has two wives, one loved by him and one hated. Philo at once explains – turning immediately to allegorical interpretation – that 'each of us is mated with two wives': one, hated, being Pleasure, the other, loved by us, being Virtue. Then Philo carries on the allegorical exposition of Scripture he has begun into a kind of allegory or parable of his own in which Pleasure is depicted as a harlot or courtesan, whom Philo describes in great detail. It is not pure allegory, refined allegory, since we are told by Philo that it is about pleasure, and not a harlot, that he is really writing. In the narrative of the encounter between Pleasure and Virtue, Virtue is provoked by Pleasure's alluring and tempting words to come forward and make her own speech to man. She reveals the truth about Pleasure, adding to Pleasure's self-description a list, the like of which is found nowhere else in Philo's works, of the 150 vices to which man will succumb if he yields to the wiles of Pleasure. Then Virtue offers to men something, toil, which is apparently painful but which leads to all that is good. Like light, Philo explains, toil is indispensable. Philo's allegory is based upon the fable of Xenophon, ascribed by him to Prodicus, in which Vice and Virtue plead with Hercules when he stands at the crossroads of life. The Philonic version of the allegorical fable has been described as poor stuff and Philo himself as entirely devoid of creative genius. Perhaps it would be fairer to say that such genius as Philo possessed was not of the literary, poetic kind which creates great allegory. It was as an allegorical exegete that Philo excelled, turning what others had written – narratives, genealogies, numbers, people, place-names, and almost everything else in Scripture – into allegories which he interpreted in such a way as to yield truths, moral, spiritual and metaphysical, of a most elevated kind.

The origins of allegory. The allegorical method of exegesis was one that had existed long before Philo employed it so comprehensively and effectively. The first occurrence of the word allegory, with reference to a statement which appears to say one thing but really means another, is in the writing of the Stoic Cleanthes in the third century BC. Other Greek thinkers had applied the allegorical method of interpretation to Homer's poems, treating Homer's gods as symbols of ethical and unethical behaviour. It has been noted, too, that allegorical exegesis existed in Alexandria before Philo's time. The Septuagint itself exhibits allegorising tendencies, as when it paraphrases some of the Hebrew Bible's anthropomorphisms. The Book of Wisdom contains allegorical interpretations – the pillar of Exod. 17: 19 is equated with Wisdom in Wisd. Sol. 10: 17 and the 'destroyer' of Exod. 12: 23 is equated with the Word of God in Wisd. Sol. 18: 15. Aristobulus apparently wrote commentaries on the Mosaic laws in the second century BC, in which he sought to prove that the Greek philosophers and poets had access to a proto-Septuagint. Such fragments of his work as we possess show that the allegorical method was employed in order to soften or remove the anthropomorphisms of the Old Testament. The *Letter of Aristeas*, probably to be dated *c.* 150–100 BC, represents that tendency within Diaspora Judaism to feel uneasy about the apparently mythological elements in the Old Testament. Eleazar is praised for his defence of the Pentateuch by demonstration that some of the Mosaic laws need to be interpreted spiritually. The law forbidding the eating of birds of prey really teaches men not to rob or oppress their fellows (see Bartlett 1985: 11ff.).

Care is needed when parallels are being drawn between allegorical exegesis of the Jewish Scriptures as practised by Philo and the interpretation of those same Scriptures by the rabbinic teachers. Philo was certainly able to indulge in his allegorising of Scripture only because Judaism allowed a generous degree of freedom to the exegete to depart from the strictly literal meaning of the text of Scripture. The Talmudic literature does contain allegorical interpretations similar to those in Philo. In one place, for example, the tree of Exod. 15: 25 is said to be a symbol of the Law. There is none of the extended philosophical allegorising, however, of the Philonic corpus. Nevertheless, the principle is exactly the same: one thing in Scripture is interpreted by something else. In the case of the rabbis, the latter, as well as the former, is scriptural in wording or meaning, whereas in the case of Philo the word of Scripture is frequently interpreted in terms of Greek philosophical ideas. Like Philo, the rabbis were concerned about the anthropomorphisms of Scripture, explaining them as permitted by God in order to aid human understanding. But the methods employed by the rabbis to deal with passages the literal meaning of which presented difficulties were different from those of Philo. In the case of a passage regarded by Philo as paradoxical and by the Palestinian rabbis as obscure (Lev. 13: 11–13), Philo insisted that it must be interpreted allegorically, while the rabbis modestly affirmed that only God knows what it means. It is not so much a difference of exegetical techniques – even though there is a difference at that level – that separates Philo from rabbinic Judaism. The basic and fundamental difference is in attitudes to what was regarded by both Philo and the rabbis as sacred Scripture. The rabbis regarded the text of the Scriptures with greater awe than Philo. He was prepared, aided by his allegorical techniques of exegesis, to supply what the text appeared to lack and to do it from sources far removed from the Jewish Scriptures in origin and character.

In *Plant.* 127–9 Philo gives a version of the Greek story in Hesiod about how Zeus slept with Mnemosyne, who subsequently gave birth to the Nine Muses. Philo calls it 'an old story', and the form of it which he gives is de-anthropomorphised. The Greek myth, described by Philo as 'the invention of wise men', was understood by him, as he suggests it had already been understood, as embodying the truth that the God who created the universe perfect in every detail also created 'the family of the Muses and hymnody', thus enabling men to praise the Creator and his perfect creation. In this passage Philo says that his ears were 'for ever greedy for teaching' and that this led him to accept and use the story as one which, understood as an allegory, or as a myth to be interpreted allegorically, expressed an important truth. That Philo's greedy ears were dependent on other teachers and exegetes, some within Judaism and some without, is made clear by his use of such formulas as 'I have also heard some natural philosophers who took the passage allegorically' (*Abr.* 99). In some contexts the phrase 'natural philosophers' is more or less equivalent to our term theologian, good theologians for Philo being allegorising exegetes. The equation of 'natural philosophers' with theologians is almost certainly required in *Vit. Mos.* II.216, where 'the study of the truths of nature' to which the Jews are said to dedicate themselves every seventh day is what we would call the study of theology.

So, clearly, Philo inherited a tradition of expounding the Scriptures allegorically which had already been practised for some time outside and inside Judaism. It is interesting also to note that Philo states that it was 'not without good reason' that the 'natural philosophers' took part of the story of Abraham, the account of the marriage of his wife to a king of Egypt (Gen. 12: 10–20), allegorically, for the obvious reason that, taken literally, it contained things that were unpalatable and unacceptable to Philo and any devout and enlightened reader of Scripture. In *Jos.* 151 Philo states: 'I have heard, however, some scholars give an allegorical exposition of this part of the story in a different form.' He was able, therefore, to justify his own use of the allegorical method by citing the works of his predecessors, and contemporaries, within Judaism. In this particular case an interpretation which might have been expected to appeal to Philo, since it is one which treats the story in question as being really about the superiority of the mind over the body, is presented by him and then abandoned, with the words 'So much for this' (*Jos.* 157), and without the lengthy kind of elaboration common in his works. The richness of the allegorical tradition of scriptural exegesis within Alexandrian Judaism is shown by the fact that the teachings of those whom he calls 'the interpreters of the holy Scriptures' (*Spec. Leg.* II.159), the exegetes, provided him with suggestions some of which he accepts, as in *Mut. Nom.* 141, and some of which he rejects, as in the case of what he regards as the mistaken interpretation of the Tree of Life referred to in *Leg. All.* I.59. In *Vit. Mos.* II.98 Philo states 'Some hold . . .', but immediately in the next paragraph expresses his own different opinion, introducing his interpretation of the text of Scripture with the words, 'I should myself say . . .' In one instance, in *Rer. Div. Her.* 280, his words, 'but possibly, as some say', indicate a hesitation on the part of Philo about a view held by some exegetes.

There was, then, an existing tradition of allegorical exegesis, at least in Alexandria, though no prohibition of freedom for debate and difference of opinion. It is likely that the number of allegorical exegetes was considerable, since Philo, in some of the passages already referred to, and, for example, in *Plant.* 52, introduces his discussion with the statement 'Some have maintained'. It sounds as if he is here, and elsewhere, referring to a body of exegetes, a school or schools, rather than to isolated individuals whom he could, or felt he had to, name. The statement in *Spec. Leg.* II.147, 'But to those who are accustomed to turn literal facts into allegory', tells us both that there were probably considerable numbers of allegorical exegetes in Alexandria and that their motive in turning to allegory was to avoid the difficulties and banalities of the literal meaning of Scripture and to discover in it exciting moral and philosophical ideas to do with, for example, 'the purification of the soul'.

Allegorical exegesis as a mystery. Philo describes allegorical exegesis as a 'mystery' into which one must be initiated, and he designates non-allegorical exegetes as 'those who are unversed in allegory and the nature-truth which loves to conceal its meaning' (*Fug.* 179). So Philo's allegorical technique of exegesis is related to the mystical side of his personality and to the mystical element in his thought, though the connection made by him between initiation into the mystery of allegorisation and allegorical exegesis itself is further evidence also of his desire to incorporate into his interpretation of his Jewish faith as many of the good things he saw in the world of secular thought and civilisation around him as he could manage.

Philo could even go so far, at one point in his description of allegorical exegesis as a divine mystery, as to say that those who do not follow him and his co-allegorists have in effect corrupted Judaism into superstition. Those who have done this are those who are not willing to receive the lesson of the 'divine mystery', since they refuse to be 'initiated' and to receive 'the holiest secret'. Non-allegorical exegesis is no more than 'barren words and phrases' uttered under the spell of 'the deadly curse of vanity' and accompanied by 'silly usages and ritual' (*Cher.* 42). It seems that, for Philo, Judaism was much more than the observance of religious ritual and the acceptance of the literal meaning of the text of Scripture. That he describes it as 'the holiest secret' suggests that, while there were other practitioners of it within Judaism, it was not the way of the majority, and the passage just referred to seems to imply that it was the intellectually and spiritually superior Jews who were capable of practising it, though Philo's words also make it clear that he did not wish to exclude from the ranks of the allegorists 'those who in simplicity of heart practise the piety which is true and genuine'. He also wished, probably because he was aware that he and his co-allegorists might be charged with pride, to level that charge against the literalists who rejected allegory.

Allegorical exegesis of Scripture, then, required an intellectual power possessed by the few but denied to the many, though both the few and the many may equally possess genuine piety. Allegory, Philo says, is 'the method dear to men with their eyes opened' (*Plant.* 36), a company evidently small in number. The smallness of the number was no doubt due to the fact that allegorical exegesis required its exponents to be 'natural philosophers' (*Abr.* 99; see also *Poster. C.* 7; pp. 177 and 183).

Philo's use of Greek terminology. In the course of his own allegorical expositions of Scripture Philo uses several of the technical terms employed in relation to allegory in the Greek schools of philosophy and rhetoric. For example, he uses the word *ainigma* (enigma) in *Som.* II.3 and 4 and in *Leg. All.* III.226 and 231. He also employs the technical term *ainissesthai* (to have a figurative meaning). In *Som.* II.3–4 he says of 'the Vision that appeared on the heavenly stairway' (a dream of Joseph as a boy) that it was 'indeed enigmatic [*ainigmatodes*]', though 'the riddle [*ainigma*]' was 'not in very high degree concealed from the quick-sighted'. Philo had clearly read widely, was familiar with the technical terms of allegory used in rhetoric, and drew them into the formidable literary armoury which he used to expound, commend and defend Judaism. He also came, as a result of the acquisition of the hermeneutical tool of allegorical exegesis, to regard the Jewish Scriptures, and in particular the Pentateuch, 'owing to the deep and impenetrable nature of the riddle involved in them', as demanding 'scientific skill' for their interpretation. Only by the exercise of this 'scientific skill' in interpreting the scriptural allegories could Philo succeed in retaining a biblically based philosophy while at the same time incorporating into his system of thought a substantial amount of Platonism and Stoicism, together with other philosophical ideas from (mainly) Greek sources. The verb 'to mean figuratively' or 'to have a figurative meaning' is used, for example, in *Poster. C.* 18 (see p. 186). In *Det. Pot. Ins.* 155 Philo warns the reader of Scripture 'Let him carefully note the sense which it conveys in a figure [*ainittetai*] through deeper meanings underlying the expressions employed' (cf. *ibid.*, 178). The words *deigma* and *hypodeigma* (sign, example), which formed part of the technical vocabulary of the secular Greek allegorists, are also used by Philo (e.g., in *Poster. C.* 122; *Conf. Ling.* 163; *Sacr. AC* 120, 139). In *Op. Mund.* 157 he refuses to accept that the early stories of Genesis are 'mythical fictions'. They are, in reality, he believed, *deigmata*: that is, 'modes of making ideas visible'. In the course of his comments on the story of the temptation in the Garden of Eden he says that 'the serpent spoken of is a fit symbol of pleasure'; so he uses the language of symbolism. The language of Scripture is the language of symbolism.

Philo and the literalists. Not surprisingly, Philo's adoption, defence and comprehensive application of the allegorical method of exegesis led him into conflict with those within Alexandrian Judaism who took the Scriptures literally as a matter of principle. Much of what Philo writes implies the existence of a majority of teachers, and readers, of Scripture who disliked and rejected the allegorical method, partly no doubt because of the, to them, alien ideas it enabled scholars such as Philo himself to introduce into Judaism, displacing in the process what they regarded as the authentic voice of Judaism. Philo engages in a running debate with the literalists, whose interpretations of Scripture he does not wish to reject wholesale, but rather to prune and supplement. To Philo those who could see only what was written on the surface and failed to look for and therefore to find the deeper meaning which he was convinced was there were unintelligent and stubbornly conservative. To be 'unversed in allegory' (*Fug.* 179) is, for Philo, to be insensitive to the meaning hidden below the surface of Scripture, to be unaware that the words of Scripture are, literally, *hypodeigmata*. In *Som.* 1.39 Philo labels the literalists or fundamentalists 'men of narrow citizenship' and contrasts them with those who are citizens of a greater country, 'men of higher thought and feeling'. In *Det. Pot. Ins.* 22 he characterises his opponents, who point out that allegorical exegesis offers things not present in the text, as men who 'are themselves, too, in some sort astray [like the man in Gen. 37: 15 who wandered on the plain], owing to their inability to see clearly the right way in matters generally'. They have been struck by 'partial blindness of the soul's eye'. The kind of thing levelled by the literalists at Philo and his colleagues can be inferred from his retorts. It is apparent that the literalists regarded Philo and his allegorising friends as possessed of a false sense of superiority and as rather patronising in their attitude, as intellectual snobs, but also, more dangerously, as betrayers of the true sense of Scripture. Allegorical exegesis of the Scriptures, especially when it resulted in philosophical ideas from a variety of non-Jewish sources being foisted on the sacred texts, required a vigorous defence and met with a fierce resistance. The modern battle between those who feel compelled to deal with myths by a process of demythologising and those for whom the alleged myths tell of what really happened is not a new one. When in the process of his allegorical expositions of Scripture Philo removed the myths he believed to be there and treated them as *deigmata* or *hypodeigmata*, symbolical of a higher or deeper meaning, he took sides in the same battle as still rages today in the post-Bultmann era of New Testament interpretation. Philo's polemic against the Alexandrian literalists was created in part by the fact that his opponents believed that by simply taking the statements of Scripture literally they had full access to its truth. Those holding such a view regarded Philo as a dangerous foe because he, finding the merely literal meaning inadequate or unsatisfying, claimed that it was necessary, in order to reach the full meaning of the text, to dig beneath the surface with the techniques and tools of allegorical hermeneutics. In fact the so-called literalists did not restrict themselves to an absolutely literalistic interpretation of the Old Testament text, but there is an enormous gap between their near-literalism and Philo's much freer allegorical interpretation.

When Philo deals, in his *De Agricultura*, with the passage in Gen. 9: 20–1 which describes how Noah began to be 'an husbandman' he cannot accept that the passage merely describes the agricultural pursuits of Noah. What the literalists miss, he believes, is something revealed by the fact that Scripture indicated Moses as a 'shepherd' (Exod. 3: 1) and that others were designated by the same term (Jacob, for example, in Gen. 30: 36). There is much, much more to the meaning of passages such as these than the literalists saw. Far from being descriptions of two different kinds of farming activity on the part of various Old Testament characters, the terms relate to a philosophical understanding of life as involving various elements, the body and its organs, and the mind, which may, or may not, properly control the body and its impulses. For Noah to be 'an husbandman', as Philo interprets Gen. 9: 20, is for him to be a righteous man exercising 'soul-husbandry' (see *Agric.* 20). The unrighteous man, symbolised by Cain (Gen. 4: 2), is described as a tiller of the ground. Those whom Scripture calls 'cattle-rearers' are people who permit 'the organs of sexual lust . . . to gorge themselves wholesale with all that they crave after' (*ibid.* 38–9). The title of 'shepherd' is applied, Philo says, to those who restrict the impulses of the lower nature and cut off 'all excessive and hurtful luxuriance' (*ibid.* 39). Like a shepherd ruling over his flock, 'the wise' rule over 'the irrational tendency common to all mankind' (*ibid.* 41). So, on Philo's view of Scripture, the passages about husbandmen, cattle-rearers, tillers of the ground and shepherds are really about the life of mind and body and the relation of the one to the other. For Philo, of course, Scripture invites the reader to aspire above all to the life of the 'shepherd': that is, to the life of the wise man who can control the body and its lusts. It is not surprising that the literalists, even if they would not have dissented from Philo's general view of the proper relationship between mind and body in human life, regarded Philo's exegesis as intruding additional meanings into Scripture rather than drawing out its true meaning. It is just possible that behind the conflict between Philo and the literalists lies a fundamental difference of opinion on the subject of body and mind. The literalists may have regarded Philo's somewhat negative view of the body as un-Jewish, like his excessive intellectualism.

Philo and the apostate Jews – allegorical and literal interpretations. It has also been noted that in Alexandria there was a third group of people who rejected the allegorical method of scriptural exegesis espoused so enthusiastically by Philo. This consisted of those apostate Jews for whom the literal meaning of the Old Testament was unacceptable and for whom no amount of allegorical exegesis could provide a convincing interpretation of it. Philo may be referring to apostate Jews in *Conf. Ling.* 2, speaking of them as people 'who cherish a dislike of the institutions of our fathers and make it their constant study to denounce and decry the Laws'. A particular individual, who not merely abandoned Judaism but spent his time subsequently ridiculing it is mentioned by name in *Leg. Gaj.* 168–70. He is called Helicon, and is said to be quick-witted, prone to scoff and jest, and to be possessed of 'the gift of the gab', but mixing jests with malice – jests apparently directed against 'the Jews and their customs' even though he had been trained in Judaism 'right from the cradle'. Helicon certainly appears to have been a renegade Jew who became a critic of his former faith, but whether he was a critic of the scriptural exegesis practised by Philo and his co-allegorists as well as of the exponents of literalism is not, as has been claimed, absolutely certain. But there clearly were those whom Philo could describe as 'malicious' critics who used their 'inventive talent' to attack even 'the letter', the literal meaning, let alone 'the inner meaning' (*Agric.* 157) of the Old Testament. More explicitly and fully, in *Mut. Nom.* 61–2 Philo tells of how he had heard 'the scoffing and railing of a godless and impious fellow' who 'in a sneering way' mocked the interpretation of the difference between the names Abram and Abraham, Sarai and Sarah, as containing a meaning that goes far beyond the mere addition or subtraction of letters of the alphabet. It is possible that such a scoffer was an apostate Jew making fun of both the literalist and the allegorical handling of Scripture (especially as extremely strong language is used about him in the description 'the unclean miscreant'). But it is equally possible that the person involved was a non-Jewish sceptic poking fun at what would seem to him the fanciful and incredible conclusions of biblical exegesis as practised by both Philo and the literalists, but especially at Philo's allegorical method. The reference in *Ebr.* 65 to those who mock the practitioners of allegorical exegesis is almost certainly not to apostates, but rather to Jewish devotees of scripture who are satisfied with its surface meaning and are 'deceived by the semblances that lie ready before their eyes but do not descry the values which are unseen and wrapt in shadow'.

It is important to note also that Philo criticised those who accepted only the allegorical meaning of Scripture. He himself frequently both expounds the literal and obvious meaning of an Old Testament passage and indicates that he regards this literal meaning as important and valuable. In *Som.* I.120 Philo states: 'Our admiration is extorted not only by the lawgiver's allegorical and philosophical teaching, but by the way in which the literal narrative inculcates the practice of toil and endurance.' In *Det. Pot.*

Ins. 22 Philo's condemnation of the literalists involves a charge of 'partial blindness of the soul's eye', the implication being that they are at fault not in what they extract from Scripture at the literal level, but in what they fail to extract from it by allegorical exegesis. In *Migr. Abr.* 91 Philo makes it quite clear that, while what is said in Genesis about the Sabbath is meant 'to teach the power of the Unoriginate and the non-action of created beings' (that is, to yield to the allegorical exegete a truth about God's nature and human nature), it also urges: 'let us not for this reason abrogate the laws laid down for its observance'. With reference to 'the Feast' (or the keeping of festivals in general), Philo states that this is 'a symbol (*symbolon*) of gladness of soul and of thankfulness to God' but also a set of regulations to be observed for 'the general gatherings of the year's seasons' (*ibid.* 92). He makes a similar statement with regard to the law about circumcision (*ibid.*), and he concludes the paragraph in question with the words, 'Why, we shall be ignoring the sanctity of the Temple and a thousand other things, if we are going to pay heed to nothing except what is shown us by the inner meaning of things.' The final stage in the argument about the literal and the allegorical in this important section of Philo's works is his affirmation that, just as body and soul are each important, so also as well as seeking the allegorical meaning of Scripture 'we must pay heed to the letter of the laws' (*ibid.* 93). Indeed Philo argues that it is only by keeping and observing the laws of Scripture in their literal sense that the reader can 'gain a clearer conception of those things of which these are the symbols'. An element of self-protecting defensiveness enters into Philo's argument in the final words of the paragraph: 'and besides that we shall not incur the censure of the many and the charges they are sure to bring against us' (*ibid.*).

It looks as if Philo had already met criticism for appearing to neglect the literal meaning of the text of Scripture by stressing the deeper level of truth allegorical exegesis revealed and as if he accepted that the minimum price he had to pay for the luxury of associating Greek philosophical ideas with the Jewish Scriptures at their hidden, deeper level of meaning was a genuine or assumed regard for and observance of their literal force. In *Sacr. AC* 78 Philo concedes that 'if not for the acquisition of perfect virtue, at any rate for the life of civic virtue', it is valuable to feed one's mind on 'ancient and time-honoured thoughts' contained in Scripture, 'to trace the venerable tradition of noble deeds, which historians and all the family of poets have handed down to the memory of their own and future generations'. There is, however, a higher wisdom and a higher virtue attainable by man. So, according to Philo, man should not 'reject any learning that has grown grey through time'; indeed he should make it his aim 'to read the writings of the sages and listen to proverbs and old-world stories from the lips of those who know antiquity, and ever seek for knowledge about the men and deeds of old' (*ibid.* 79). But, though 'it is sweet to leave nothing unknown', there is a superior, 'self-inspired wisdom' that God can cause to grow in the soul and this surpasses all else, for it is the wisdom of God rather than 'the guidance of men'. In *Conf. Ling.* 190, Philo, having in the previous paragraphs (*ibid.* 183–9) offered his own allegorical explanation of Gen. 11: 7 (that God employed his lieutenants or angels to bring the punishment of 'confusion' upon the impious), refers to the conclusion of those who merely follow 'the outward and obvious' that the passage in question has to do with 'the origin of the Greek and barbarian languages'. Philo adds the interesting remark, 'I would not censure such persons, for perhaps the truth is with them also.' However, he cannot resist also saying that he would exhort the literalists to 'press on to allegorical interpretations and to recognise that the letter is to the oracle but as the shadow to the substance'. So it would be quite false to say that Philo had no time for the literal meaning of Scripture, though he himself indubitably preferred to 'press on to allegorical interpretations'.

Now why was this so? What were Philo's reasons for adopting this particular method of biblical exegesis known to us as the allegorical method? The first thing that must be said is that Philo was driven to the allegorical method of exegesis – if it had not already existed, he would have had to invent it (see p. 147) – because of his lofty view of God and Scripture. For him, Scripture (what Christians call the Old Testament) was the inspired Word of God. In particular, for him, this was true of the Pentateuch, the Torah. Scripture could 'never be convicted of false witness' (*Abr.* 258). As an intelligent, educated, cultured reader, he saw, however, that, taken literally, Scripture could be found guilty of being and doing what as God's own Word it could neither be nor do. Allegorical exegesis enabled Philo to remain true to his no doubt totally sincere conviction as a Jew of the inspired character of Scripture and to the insights into truth gained from his study of the philosophers of the Graeco-Roman world. Scripture, he believed, speaks as God's Word to every man (*Mut. Nom.* 215), but it requires careful interpretation before its universal message can be understood; and the careful interpretation accorded to both what was said and what was meant was the allegorical interpretation. Philo believed that Scripture contained nothing unworthy at all. In *Som.* 1.92–4 he discusses Exod. 22: 26–7 and demonstrates the absurdity which a literal interpretation of the injunction contained therein involves. To be content with such an interpretation is 'a mark of men who have utterly failed to see the greatness of the excellence of the infinitely great God'. In a sense, therefore, it is Philo's doctrine of God that is the ultimate cause of his adoption of the allegorical mode of exegesis. In *Det. Pot. Ins.* 13 he affirms: 'If, O my understanding, thou searchest on this wise into the oracles which are both words of God and laws given by men whom God loves, thou shalt not be compelled to admit anything base or unworthy of their dignity.' Because the Scriptures are God's words as well as his Word, nothing unworthy of him can be found in them. That it appears at first sight in certain passages that it is otherwise is because the true meaning of the text has not been grasped. To grasp it the reader needs to be an allegorist or to hear or read what the allegorical expositor has to say. Philo made sure that at least for his public this last need was met.

Philo's view of Scripture. The view of Scripture held by Philo led him inevitably to ask, as he does in the passage just cited (*Det. Pot. Ins.* 13), 'How could any sensible person admit the very narrative of which we are now speaking?' The narrative in question merely tells how Jacob sent his son, and not a servant, to bring news of his other children (see Gen. 37: 14). If Philo could not bring himself to 'admit' the story of the sending of Joseph by Jacob, how much more did he feel compelled to decline to admit other things contained in Scripture. The pressure of this powerful disinclination led him to develop what has been described as 'The Two-level View of Scripture'. Rejecting the view that the literal meaning of the entire body of Scripture was valueless, he nevertheless concluded that 'All or most of the law-book is an allegory' (*Jos.* 28). His reaction to most of the Scripture passages he handles is to see in them two levels of meaning, one below the other, or two meanings side by side. It has been noted that this view of Scripture, while evident throughout his writings, is most apparent in the *Quaestiones et Solutiones in Genesin* and the *Quaestiones et Solutiones in Exodum*, perhaps because these two treatises were addressed to a less sophisticated audience than that addressed in his other works, and one less ready, therefore, to discard the literal meaning. At any rate, in these two treatises Philo regularly expounds the two meanings, usually dealing with the literal meaning first and then with the allegorical, though sometimes in the reverse order. A variety of expressions is used by him to mark the transition from one to the other. A typical example of the kind of thing Philo says occurs in the *Quaest. in Gn.* I.94, where, commenting on Gen. 6: 7, he says 'The literal meaning is this . . .', and then a little later, 'But as for the allegorical meaning . . .'. Sometimes he does not give the literal meaning, but passes immediately to the allegorical, and sometimes he says: 'so far as the literal meaning is concerned, there is no need to give an explicit interpretation' (*Quaest. in Gn.* I.6).

Two expressions which Philo uses frequently in the two *Quaestiones* volumes shed important light on his understanding of the task of the exegete. When he refers to the 'literal meaning' of a text, the expression he often uses is *to rhēton* (what the text actually says). When he refers to the 'deeper meanings' he often uses the phrase *to pros dianoian* (the meaning addressed to the mind) denoting the meaning which it requires intellectual perception to penetrate and absorb. Even he sometimes admits that, while the literal meaning of a passage is clear, the most he can say about the allegorical meaning is that it 'must be somewhat as follows'. Such is the distance between the surface meaning of the written words and their deeper, symbolical meaning that Philo himself occasionally claims to have succeeded only in getting near to it (see *Quaest. in Gn.* II.25).

In *Leg. All.* II.14 Philo praises Moses with reference to what he says in the story in Gen. 2 of the creation of Adam and Eve: 'Here his literal statement and his symbolic interpretation alike claim our admiration.' The implication of this statement is that Moses, as author of Scripture, was responsible both for the literal meaning and also for the allegorical truth it contained. The task of the allegorical exegete such as Philo was simply that of uncovering what Moses had said beneath the surface of his words (as well as expounding, where necessary, the meaning of 'the literal statement'). In *Ebr.* 130, after a typical piece of allegorical exegesis of a passage he is expounding, he says 'In a literal sense too, this command deserves our admiration', and in *Som.* I.120, with reference to Gen. 28: 11, 'Our admiration is extorted not only by the lawgiver's allegorical and philosophical teaching, but by the way in which the literal narrative inculcates the practice of toil and endurance.'

Philo has a large number of phrases for introducing the second, allegorical, meaning in those places where he first expounds the literal. In *Abr.* 217, having referred to the 'actual words of the story', he then proceeds to discuss the meaning of the story for those who pass 'from the literal to the spiritual' ('the spiritual' here being *ta noēta*, that which is perceptible only by the intellect). Later (*ibid.* 236) he contrasts the content of the Scriptures 'read literally' with the meaning they have when contemplated as 'facts stripped of the body and in naked reality'. Such a deeper meaning is accessible only to those who 'live with the soul rather than with the body'. The outer level of meaning, the literal, quickly and easily understood (though not without value), needs to be peeled off, stripped away, if the inner, hidden meaning is to be comprehended. That inner, deeper meaning is to be evaluated in relation to the literal meaning, according to Philo, in the same way as the soul is valued by him in relation to the body (its tomb, or prison). One of the most common ways Philo adopts of introducing the two levels of scriptural meaning is, as in *Jos.* 28, where he refers first to the 'literal account of the story' he has given, and then to 'the underlying meaning' he needs to spell out. The underlying meaning is *ta en hyponoiais* (that which can be detected underneath (the surface)). Later in *Jos.* 125, Philo explains that it is his purpose 'to examine the more allegorical meaning after the literal', using a similar phrase about the allegorical meaning to that which he uses in the *Leg. All.* II.14 passage referred to above. In *Abr.* 88 the word he uses for 'exposition', a word which frequently occurs, is *apodosis*. It is used of both the literal and the allegorical interpretations, but the allegorical exposition is contrasted with the literal as that which is applicable 'to the soul' rather than 'to the man'. In *Abr.* 131 Philo argues that the exposition he has been giving of a particular feature of the text is supported both by 'the principles of allegory' and by 'the literal text'. What Philo says later in the same treatise (*ibid.* 147) is interesting not only because again we meet in his words the common distinction between the literal meaning and the allegorical meaning, but because the former is characterised as 'the natural and obvious rendering of the story as suited for the multitude', and the latter as 'the hidden and inward meaning which appeals to the few who study soul characteristics rather than bodily forms'. He also uses the adverb 'symbolically' to introduce the allegorical exegesis. In *Decal.* 1 Philo makes a promise, abundantly fulfilled by him in his writings: 'if some allegorical interpretation should appear to underlie them [i.e. the written laws of Scripture], I shall not fail to state it'.

The importance for Philo of allegorical exegesis. There is good reason for believing that Philo contributed enormously to the development of the practice of allegorical exegesis as the means of uncovering the second and deeper of the two levels of meaning and truth in Scripture, but not for crediting him, as has been sometimes done, with its invention or discovery. What is undoubtedly true of Philo is that, no matter what he may say, with absolute sincerity, about the importance of the literal meaning of Scripture, it is the allegorical meaning that is for him without question the more important. It is what Scripture has to say to man – and that means for him what God has to say – at its profoundest level. In his discussion of Samuel in the *De Ebrietate* he concedes that 'probably there was an actual man called Samuel' (*Ebr.* 144), but his main interest as an exegete is in Samuel as a Symbol of 'a mind which rejoices in the service and the worship of God'. Philo does not deny the existence of the historical Samuel, but, perhaps because he was 'the greatest of kings and prophets' (the hero of 1 Kings (LXX) and the first king-maker), he finds the ingredients of Samuel's life as told in the Old Testament to be appropriate symbols of ideas and attitudes which as a theologian–philosopher he finds acceptable and desirable and commendable. Also, although the 'probably' he uses with reference to the existence of the historical Samuel is the word of a cautious historian, Philo was not really a historian interested in reconstructing Israel's history. The transition from the historical Samuel to the symbolical Samuel, a transition he desired to make as speedily as possible, was made easy for him by the fact that the historical Samuel was 'probably' the kind of man, devoted to the worship and service of God, who aptly symbolises therefore the intellectual worship and service of God. Historians who note the transition from a historical Jesus to a theological Christ should note the similarity, though there is a great deal more to that latter transition than one from historical man to symbol (the Johannine symbolism, be it noted, is symbolism which, there is no good reason to doubt, was prompted and fed by knowledge of the historical Jesus). In the case of Samuel, Philo was nudged in the direction of treating him as a symbol rather than as a historical character whose life and deeds Scripture recorded because, as he says, 'his name by interpretation means "appointed or ordered to God"' (*ibid.* 144). There is not always, however, this kind of indication in the literal level of meaning of the hidden, deeper level. But, whether that is so or not, the two levels of meaning are related to each other as body to soul (*Migr. Abr.* 93). That means that each must be taken seriously (just as men must care for the body, since it is the dwelling-place of the soul). Attention paid to the 'body' of Scripture, its literal meaning, will be repaid by greater understanding of the truths which it symbolises; also, as Philo adds in a practical and realistic comment, 'we shall not incur the censure of the many and the charges they are sure to bring against us'. However, although Philo more than once urges that careful attention should be paid to the letter of Scripture, he also makes quite clear his view that those who remain content with the outer level of meaning are lacking in self-criticism – 'careless inquirers' (*Deus Imm.* 21). Philo uses here the same verb (*ainittesthai*) of the false interpretation of Scripture by such readers as he uses of its allegorical exegesis (see pp. 151–2). Even the restriction of one's interests to the letter of Scripture can lead one to suppose, incorrectly, 'that the lawgiver is hinting that the Creator repented of the creation of men'. Philo seems to be implying that a supposedly literal interpretation of Scripture involves spelling out explicitly things only hinted at. The allegorical exegete is one who seeks to find out what it really is that the Scriptures hint at as their true meaning. All exegesis, in other words, involves going beyond the mere letter of Scripture, whatever the reader's intention may be. In that case, Philo argues it is important to interpret Scripture's hints accurately.

The method of allegorical exegesis employed by him is, he claims, the way from the letter to the essential truth of Scripture beyond, though unfortunately Philo neither seeks nor gives any convincing reasons for arriving at the conclusions he reaches. He does, however, have a variety of reasons for adopting the method. To those who challenge the kind of interpretation of Scripture he offers, Philo answers by asking his critics not to censure the claims of allegorists to knowledge in such things, and by suggesting that uncritical restriction of the meaning of Scripture to its literal sense reveals an unwillingness to search deeply and a confinement of one's attention to 'the mere surface' and the superficial. To find the underlying truth of Scripture requires, furthermore, 'a great and celestial understanding which has ceased to be ensnared by aught of the things that surround us' (*Rer. Div. Her.* 91–3). That can be said of Abraham; it is not something Philo claims to have attained himself. But it is the ideal, the goal, of the allegorical expositor of Scripture. Because, then, of the relationship between the literal and the spiritual meaning of Scripture, a relationship described by Philo in *Abr.* 131ff. and 147, he urges his readers not to halt at 'the natural and obvious', but 'to press on to allegorical interpretations and to recognise that the letter is to the oracle but as the shadow to the substance and that the higher values therein revealed are what really and truly exist' (*Conf. Ling.* 190).

Philo's Platonic epistemology. Philo next reveals one of the major sources of his allegorical method, his Platonic epistemology. In *Op. Mund.* 16 (see above. pp. 128–31 and 131–6) he explains, along thoroughly Platonic lines, that 'this visible world' was made only after God had first 'fully formed the intelligible world' (the adjective is *noētos*, and the noun *kosmos*; earlier the verb used of the making of the visible world is that associated with the noun *dēmiourgos*, *dēmiourgeō*), so that the one could serve as the incorporeal pattern for the other. The *kosmos noētos,* the world of Ideas knowable only by mind (see above, pp. 128, 135), is what Moses saw on the top of Mount Sinai. Philo, in *Quaest. in Ex.* II.90, states that Moses was shown 'the paradeigmatic essences', wholly incorporeal. One of the best examples of Philo's version is in *Som.* I. 185–7: there he distinguishes between 'this world discerned by sense' and the world 'which only intellect can perceive', a world which was 'framed from the eternal forms'. The latter world of Ideas can be apprehended only by passing on to it from this world. No idea can be obtained of incorporeal existences 'except by making material objects our starting-point'. It is this Platonic theory that Philo applies to the Scriptures of his nation. Their text comes to be for him, at the literal level of meaning, the visible world of sense beyond which the reader must proceed if he is to reach the incorporeal world of real existence. As far as the authorship of Scripture is concerned, his view is that Moses wrote down, using the language of allegory to do it, what he had seen of the incorporeal world of real essences. Philo was perhaps driven to this view of Scripture because, having tasted and enjoyed – indeed become obsessed by – the delights of Greek philosophy, he regarded Moses as the philosophical predecessor and inspiration of Plato and Platonism. Confronted with the text of the Pentateuch and holding that view, Philo must have turned with relief and satisfaction to the allegorical method of interpretation. When he says, in *Rer. Div. Her.* 111, that the soul is what man uses 'to study the higher verities of mental things and real existences' and that 'the organ of his voice' is to hymn the world and its Creator, he means by the intellectual study of 'mental things and real existences' the allegorical study of Scripture. What Moses learned of 'the secrets of the most holy mysteries' he imparts, as 'the hierophant and teacher of divine rites', to 'those whose ears are purified' (*Gig.* 54): that is, to those who have been instructed in the art of allegorical interpretation.

But it must not be thought that the allegorical method of exegesis was for Philo merely a method of studying and interpreting Scripture. It further involved the application to the text of Scripture of the same mental faculty employed when God (or heavenly things such as the invisible Forms) is known. In *Abr.* 119 Philo explains: 'Spoken words contain symbols of things apprehended by the understanding only.' The truth about reality recorded in Scripture can be apprehended only by those who read the holy Scriptures with their understanding rather than with their eyes. An important aspect of Philo's view of scriptural exegesis is his belief that the understanding which enables man to know the incorporeal and invisible Forms of ideal reality is the faculty which also enables man to encounter the truth about those Forms as he reads Scripture. The literal meaning of Scripture, accessible to the superficial reader, corresponds to the world of sense-perception; the truth accessible to allegorical interpretation is truth related to the timeless world of Ideas.

Examples of Philo's method. An example of how Philo deals with a passage of the Old Testament is his treatment of Abraham's migration from Chaldaea to Canaan. He simply alludes in passing to the migrations 'set forth by the literal text of the scriptures' as 'made by a man of wisdom', but then proceeds to interpret them 'according to the laws of allegory' (*Abr.* 68). What those laws are involves the application of the text to 'the soul' (*ibid.* 88), with the result that the conclusion is reached that the real migration being described is seen to be that of the man who refuses to remain 'rooted in the realm of sense' and to believe that the 'visible world' is God, but who, using reason, turns his gaze upon the intelligible order which is superior to the visible and towards the divine Maker and Ruler. The same intellectual pilgrimage Philo sees described in the Scripture as Abraham's migration from Chaldaea to Canaan is possible for the reader of Scripture who understands them as allegories and leaves behind the literal Chaldaea and presses on to the invisible Canaan. Also, Philo believed that what the Greeks gained from the teaching of their 'most approved philosophy' the Jews gain from their customs and laws, 'the knowledge of the highest and most ancient Cause of all things, having rejected all the errors about created gods' (*Virt.* 65; see pp. 223 and 228). But that gain is made only when the laws of Scripture are interpreted allegorically.

The biblical story (or stories) describes not just the actual experiences of the characters involved, but also the experience open to all men. God can lead all men out of the Egypt, away from the Chaldaea of sense-perception, into the promised land of incorporeal Ideas. It has been said, correctly: 'Through Philo's hermeneutics the people of Israel's experiences are made contemporary with our own.' So, in *Praem. Poen.* 61–5 he discusses the 'houses' of Abraham, Isaac and Jacob, seeing in what is said about them descriptions of the qualities possessed by three types of soul and their different kinds of behaviour. These descriptions can be appreciated only when the 'literal story' is seen as being 'symbolical of a hidden meaning which demands examination'. For Philo, only Jacob's children were qualified to be the foundation of the twelve tribes which expanded into the nation of Israel. It was this 'household' that, 'kept safe from harm, perfect, and united both in the literal history and in the allegorical interpretation', was rewarded with the 'chieftaincy' of the tribes of the nation. The perfection of the house of Jacob, at the allegorical level, was that it embraced 'the plenitude of virtues', leaving no room in itself for anything else and bestowing blessings on those around it comparable to the influence in the upper realms of the universe of the Zodiac.

For Philo the true meaning of the Exodus story (*Poster. C.* 155–7) is that God leads us 'out of our bodily passions', the various passions being symbolised in the narrative by the barren track, waterless Marah, and so on; Egypt, the place of departure still desired by us, being 'the refuge of a desolate and licentious life'; the 'syrup' of Exod. 15: 25, produced by the tree cast into the water, symbolising the 'sweetening tree' cast into our souls by God, 'producing love of labour instead of hatred of labour'. Allegorical understanding of the Scripture both enables us to know that the Creator empowers us to rise 'superior to anything whatever' and also is that by means of which we so rise.

What has frequently been observed – and it is the inevitable consequence of the fact that, though Philo speaks of the 'laws of allegory' he never actually spells them out (unsuccessful attempts have been made to reconstruct them) – is that he is able to interpret a narrative from Scripture allegorically in more than one sense. Joseph in his coat of many colours, for example, is a symbol of the many-sided pride of worldly life. This is most unfair to the biblical Joseph, but was probably due to the fact that Joseph's life was lived out for the most part in Egypt (the symbol of the body and its passions). But Joseph's coat also symbolises political pragmatism (*Jos.* 32) and 'the good that is, which is given by the senses, the last and latest in the scale of goods' (*Conf. Ling.* 72).

The words of God in Gen. 3: 15 are taken by Philo as having two different meanings (*Leg. All.* III.188–9); they state that a good mind will watch out for pleasure in order to destroy it and that a foolish mind will watch out for pleasure in order to enjoy it. Esau is interpreted as a symbol of 'the worse part of the soul' which makes war on the better (*Fug.* 24, 43) and as the irrational nature of man (*Leg. All.* III.88–9). In another passage (*ibid.* 193) Esau symbolises folly (cf. *Sacr. AC* 17), and in yet another he is the symbol of passion (*Rer. Div. Her.* 251–4). The language of the story of Esau in Gen. 25 and 26 is the source for a number of details of the allegorical interpretation of him offered by Philo.

The several layers of symbolism that Philo finds in the story of Esau, and the different meanings he gives to Joseph, are discovered by him because in his view that is what Scripture is like – a multi-layered allegory which retains a literal meaning too. Sometimes, as in the case of the double account of the creation of animals, the text of Scripture itself invites the skilled exegete to find at least two meanings. This Philo does here, and he expounds them in *Leg. All.* II.12–13, explaining that the first passage (Gen. 1: 24) refers to the creation of the *genera* and the second (Gen. 2: 19) to the creation of the *species*. But to Philo the *genera* and *species* concerned are 'the originals of the passions' and the various species of passion. It is not to animals that Genesis refers, but to animal passions in man. In *Som.* I.133–56 Philo offers a fourfold interpretation of Jacob's ladder. It is, first of all, 'a figurative name for the air', the 'abode of incorporeal souls'. It is, secondly, 'in human beings', soul, whose foot is sense-perception and whose head is 'the heavenly' element, and throughout which the 'words' of God move up and down incessantly. It is, thirdly, the life of the 'practisers' who are drawn both upwards and downwards, 'a life of alternate days' (a Philonic quotation from the *Odyssey*), a life oscillating between the worse and the better. And it is, fourthly, the life of the ordinary man which moves on an 'uneven course' from good fortune to bad fortune, from one condition to its opposite, its 'uneven tenor manifestly laid bare by time's unerring test'.

Several different interpretations of the cherubim are offered. Together with the turning sword of flame, they symbolise 'the revolution of the whole heaven' (*Cher.* 21). But there are other possible meanings, as Philo indicates: 'This then is one interpretation of the allegory of the Cherubim' (*ibid.* 25). One of the other interpretations is that 'the two Cherubim represent the two hemispheres' (*ibid.*). They also, however – and this is the meaning revealed to Philo by a voice in his soul, which, he says, 'oftentimes is god-possessed and divines where it does not know' – represent the one God's two 'highest and chiefest powers', goodness and sovereignty (*ibid.* 27). In this case the fiery sword is the symbol of reason. In *Vit. Mos.* II.85–100 he also interprets the Cherubim, while mentioning other possibilities, as 'allegorical representations of the two most august and highest potencies of him that IS, the creative and kingly'.

In the same passage Philo states, with reference to the Ark of the Covenant, that it 'appears to be a symbol in a theological sense of the gracious power of God' (*ibid.* II.96). He regards the same, 'in the human sense', as symbolic of a mind which is gracious to itself and suppresses its proneness to pride.

A particularly interesting and compact set of allegorical interpretations of the Tree of Life is given by Philo in *Quaest. in Gn.* I.10. Five meanings are attributed to the Tree. Philo quotes some exegetes who say that the Tree is the earth, since it causes growth; others say that the Tree is a symbol of the seven circles of heaven; some say the Tree is the sun, yet others that it is the government of the soul, on the grounds that the soul strengthens sense-perception. The interpretation that presumably Philo favours, since he attributes it to 'worthy and excellent men', is the one that sees in the Tree a symbol of the best of the human virtues: namely, piety, 'through which pre-eminently the mind becomes immortal'. Philo is led to this wide-ranging assembly of allegorical interpretations because of a belief held by some that some plants are mortal and some immortal. This prompts him to ask the rhetorical question, 'And may it not be that this [i.e., the statement of Gen. 2: 9] is said allegorically?'.

The Septuagint as the inspired Word of God. It has been noted above (see p. 144) how Philo regarded the Scriptures he interpreted allegorically as the inspired Word of God. This inspired character belonged as much, in his view, to the Greek text of the Septuagint as to the Hebrew original. The Septuagint translators, like the inspired prophetic writers of the Hebrew Scriptures, when they began to compose 'became as it were possessed, and, under inspiration, wrote, not each several scribe something different, but the same word for word, as though dictated to each by an invisible prompter' (*Vit. Mos.* II.37). This was achieved despite the richness of Greek in synonyms and alternatives. Also, the Greek words selected 'coresponded literally' to the Hebrew. Original and translation are in fact, Philo affirms, 'sisters', to be regarded with reverence and awe, and the authors not merely translators but rather 'prophets and priests of the mysteries, whose sincerity and singleness of thought has enabled them to go hand in hand with the purest of spirits, the spirit of Moses' (*ibid.* II.40). In other words, the translators were 'hierophants', priests of the sacred mystery, which is, supremely, what Moses was (see *Leg. All.* III.123; *Sacr. AC* 94; *Poster. C.* 16; and see pp. 186 and 189). As has been observed, such a view of the Septuagint would have made the Hebrew Bible superfluous to the needs of a Greek. That Philo held it seems to prove that, despite the affirmations to the contrary by distinguished Philo scholars, Philo could not, or did not, check the Septuagint against the Hebrew. However, Philo was capable of maintaining the absolute fidelity of the Septuagint to the original Hebrew, even if he was fully conversant with biblical Hebrew, for the same reason that he could discover philosophical truths, at a great remove from the literal meaning of the text, in the narratives of the Old Testament, which were to him, of course, allegories. Because the Septuagint text enabled him, indeed required him, to read off from it the philosophical truths which for him constituted the true Judaism of the greatest philosopher, Moses, it must have been a perfect rendering of the Hebrew. Only a perfect text could yield a perfect philosophy such as Philo extracted from his Septuagint.

The inspiration of the allegorical exegete. Just as the writing of Scripture, and its translation into Greek, took place under the inspiration of God, so also the work of finding the allegorical meaning of it was a work of inspiration, the disclosure of the meaning of the text being given to the allegorical exegete, as one scholar puts it, as grace from God. Philo describes the process at work in himself in *Migr. Abr.* 34–5. He tells there how sometimes, when he sat down to write, nothing would come, but how on other occasions ideas fell in a shower from above and 'under the influence of Divine possession' he was filled with 'corybantic frenzy' and left unconscious of anything else. He obtained, he says, 'language, ideas, an enjoyment of light, keenest vision, pellucid distinctness of objects'. Philo is here claiming for himself what elsewhere, as we have seen, he claims for all true allegorical exegetes: the same kind of inspiration enjoyed by the prophets and, in particular, by the greatest of them, Moses. Philo explains (*Cher.* 49) how he was not slow to become a disciple of Jeremiah, a worthy hierophant. What happens when a man acts like Jeremiah and the other prophets, as a hierophant, and 'natural ecstasy and divine possession and madness fall upon us', is that the 'human light sets' while the 'divine light' dawns and rises (*Rer. Div. Her.* 264). That is what regularly befalls 'the fellowship of the prophets' (*ibid.* 265). So, finding the hidden meaning of Scripture is a matter not of human ingenuity, but of receptivity to the divine Spirit which possesses the prophetic interpreter. Such inspiration and possession were so total in the case of the canonical prophets that, when they were writing, they were ignorant of what they were saying (*Spec. Leg.* IV.49). Similarly, Philo and his co-allegorists, though to a lesser extent perhaps, were not aware of their own words and ideas, filled as they were, in moments of such corybantic frenzy, with ideas and words supplied from above. In *Cher.* 27 Philo describes how the true significance of the cherubim in Gen. 3: 24 was made known to him. He was told the meaning they had by a voice within his own soul. His soul, he adds, 'oftentimes is god-possessed and divines where it does not know'. The soul of the allegorical exegete is taken over by God. In *Som.* I.164 he suggests that the lessons learned from a study of the symbolic meaning of the different names of God in the Old Testament ought to prompt the 'blind' literalists to grow keen-sighted and to receive the gift of sight from the Scriptures, which would enable them to see the 'real nature of things' and not just the 'literal sense'. In other words, the elevating thoughts extracted from Scripture by allegorical exegesis ought to persuade those sceptical about its efficacy to seek similar illumination. He then offers a prayer to God, on behalf of himself and his readers, as to the great Hierophant himself, asking him to be their prompter and to preside over their steps and never tire of anointing their eyes until they reach the hidden light of the hallowed words of Scripture and see revealed 'the fast-locked loveliness invisible to the uninitiate'. Here, then, it is God who is the inspirer of the student of Scripture – not merely the prophets or Moses, but God himself who speaks to men as 'a still, small voice' within. It is God, called the Hierophant in *Som.* II.3 also, who prepares what the initiated see and hear and who reveals them within man's soul, invisibly suggesting 'things obscure to us but patent to himself' (*Som.* II.2). In the *Mut. Nom.* 139 Philo explains that, when he was reading Hos. 14: 9, 10 (LXX), he 'recognised the voice of the invisible master whose invisible hand plays on the instrument of human speech'. The same 'invisible hand' leads the reader of Scripture, if he is prepared to be passive and receptive before it, to see the underlying meaning of the text before him.

Philo did, however, concede that the allegorical meaning of Scripture accessible, under conditions of divine possession, to the exegete like himself, was 'obscure to the many' (*Abr.* 200; cf. *ibid.* 236). Only those 'who prefer the mental to the sensible and have the power to see it' can appreciate 'the elements of a further suggestion' going beyond the literal sense of, for example, the story of the Binding of Isaac in Gen. 22. Earlier (*Abr.* 147), he had contrasted 'the multitude' satisfied with the 'natural and obvious rendering of the story' with 'the few who study soul characteristics rather than bodily forms', who alone are capable of understanding 'the hidden and inward meaning' – a meaning which depends upon the reader's seeing the five cities as symbols (Gen. 18).

The allegorical exegetes, to whose company he belonged, Philo calls 'men with their eyes opened' to whom the allegorical method is dear (*Plant.* 36). In *Gig.* 54 Philo describes those who read the Scriptures allegorically as men (the few as opposed to the literalist many) who have stripped themselves of all created things and of 'mere opinion', which he likens to a veil or wrapping, and, with naked minds, approach God. Then, like Moses before him, such a man enters 'the invisible region' where he learns the secrets of the holy mysteries and becomes 'not only one of the congregation of the initiated, but also the hierophant and teacher of divine rites, which he will impart to those whose ears are purified'. The mention of the 'initiated' and those who have gone a stage further than others and become teachers of the initiated implies that there was in Alexandria a school – or schools – of allegorical exegesis, to which Philo belonged, over which perhaps he presided as the arch-hierophant. Philo elsewhere (*Cher.* 48) speaks of the initiated as those whose ears are 'purified': as those who can hear the inward, divine voice communicating to them the true, pure meaning of Scripture. He warns them, with regard to the mysteries, to 'babble not of them to any of the profane' (*ibid.*), but to keep knowledge of them to themselves and to associate with others who have been initiated, gleaning further enlightenment from them. In *Cher.* 42 Philo explains that it is pointless for the initiated to talk about the mysteries to the uninitiated because the latter 'have no other standards for measuring what is pure and holy but their barren words and phrases and their silly usages and ritual'. This is a warning to the recipients not themselves to undertake the instruction of the uninitiated, not a prohibition placed upon the enlightened teachers. There could be congregations of initiates, or congregations containing them, synagogues of philosophical Jews or embracing groups of such Jews, only if teachers such as Philo himself opened up Scripture in such a way that hitherto uninitiated Jews began to perceive behind the words and phrases of the text of the divine Scriptures the mysterious meaning hidden there. However, Philo does, on other occasions, point out to his readers the dangers of blabbing or babbling thoughtlessly about what has been revealed to them. Since every 'comer' cannot guard aright 'the sacred story' behind a passage of Scripture, the rule for the initiated must be 'secrecy and silence' (*Sacr. AC* 60). Philo's warnings, such as that contained in *Sacr. AC* 62, are for those who have passed through only the 'lesser' mysteries – the escape of the soul from the passions and the beginning of the life of philosophical reflection – but also for those who have proceeded to the 'greater' mysteries – the ascent to the perception of God (described in *ibid.* 59–60), which is said to involve admission into the 'inmost' mysteries (*ibid.* 60). What is revealed to the soul when it ascends to the inmost mysteries of God's being is too sacred a subject to be permitted in conversation between initiates and the uninitiated.

Only the experienced teacher can safely undertake the task of helping to open the minds of the latter.

Philo's opposition to anthropomorphism and myth-making. The most powerful of the reasons which led Philo to adopt the allegorical method of exegesis, apart from his desire to relate the Greek philosophical ideas which attracted him to the Jewish Scriptures, was his antipathy to anything which smacked of anthropomorphism (see above, pp. 52–4). Philo frequently quoted the words of Num. 23: 19, as he does in *Deus Imm.* 62 (see pp. 74 and 77), understanding them to mean that God is not to be likened to anything perceptible by the senses. God's essential incorporeality means that 'in reality God is not like man nor yet like the sun nor like heaven nor like the sense-perceptible world but [only] like God, if it is right to say even this' (*Quaest. in Gn.* II.54). God 'does not admit any likeness or comparison or parable' (*ibid.*). The assistance given to Philo, when he was faced with the embarrassment of the anthropomorphic character of the literal meaning of the Old Testament, can be gauged from his treatment of Gen. 4: 16 in *Poster. C.* 1–4 (see pp. 172–82).

Philo's refusal to accept the anthropomorphisms of the literal meaning of the text of the Old Testament, and his escape from the embarrassment of them through allegorical exegesis, resulted in an extremely restricted use of the literal meaning of many Old Testament passages, since, especially in the Pentateuch, there are many cases of anthropomorphic language. More than once he quotes Num. 23: 19, 'God is not a man' – a statement which in the Septuagint is translated as 'God is not like a man', and one which he took to mean that God should not be compared to any object or being in the realm of sense-perception (see above, pp. 77–8, 83).

Philo also found in the allegorical method of exegesis a means whereby the mythical elements of the Old Testament could be dealt with in a way which rendered them acceptable and tolerable, though in some instances he characterises the narratives as examples, if taken literally, of 'myth-making' (*muthopoia*). The word Philo uses here implies that he regards those who interpret the Scriptures purely in terms of their superficial, literal meaning as guilty of turning into myth what is not really myth but rather allegory. This involves more than the accusation that they are content with a literal interpretation; it carries with it the charge that they falsify Scripture by turning allegories into myths like the fables of Greek literature and so distorting its true nature. According to Philo the so-called 'mythical' stories of the Old Testament possess an inner meaning, whereas pagan myths do not. The narrative of Num. 21: 4–9, about fiery serpents and a brass serpent, is, understood literally, a story of 'prodigies and marvels', with one serpent speaking in a human voice and 'using quibbling arguments to an utterly guileless character' and another 'proving the author of complete deliverance to those who beheld it'; but the same story, when interpreted 'by the meanings that lie beneath the surface', reveals its true meanings as to do with life directed towards pleasure and life of a quite contrary kind, a life of self-control and patient endurance which obtains true health and safety (*Agric.* 96–101). Philo is quite sure that Moses did not introduce myths into what he wrote, since 'myth-making is a thing most alien to him' (*Gig.* 58).

So also Moses banished painting and sculpture from his commonwealth, as Plato did from his ideal republic, 'because their crafts belie the nature of truth and work deception and illusions through the eyes to souls that are ready to be seduced' (*ibid.* 59). Philo then proceeds to explain, with reference to Gen. 6: 4: 'So, then, it is no myth at all of giants that he sets before us; rather he wishes to show you that some men are earth-born, some heaven-born, and some God-born' (*ibid.* 60). The reference to 'the myths of the poets about the giants' which he makes (*ibid.* 58) may be an allusion to Homer, who did record myths. That these too may be interpreted allegorically does not alter the fact that Moses' narratives are quite different from them in being allegories and not myths at all. When Moses tells the story of Lot's wife, he is not 'inventing a fable', according to Philo, 'but indicating precisely a real fact', the real fact being the inner meaning, which is to do with the intellectual blindness which results from failure to use the mind (see *Fug.* 121). The lazy student disregards his teacher's efforts to train his mind and turns backwards to the hidden and dark side of life and 'so he turns into a pillar and becomes like a deaf and lifeless stone'.

The word *muthopoia* is used in *Leg. All.* I.43 to describe what those do who take literally the words of Gen. 2: 8. But to imagine that God actually planted a garden is a 'great impiety'. Elsewhere (in *Plant.* 32) Philo states that to believe that God really planted a garden in Eden would be an act of 'serious folly'. In this particular case the foolishness of the literal meaning of Scripture invites the reader to 'turn to allegory' (*ibid.* 36). In *Leg. All.* II.19 he explains that the words of Gen. 2: 21, at the literal level, are 'of the nature of a myth'. The Old Testament references are not, according to Philo, stories about 'prodigies and marvels' (*Agric.* 96). They need to have 'all that is mythical' stripped away so that the 'real sense' can be seen. Here Philo does seem to concede that there is a 'mythical' element within some of the Old Testament stories. Philo himself sometimes accepts statements in their literal sense. He offers a straightforward exposition of the account of God's placing of Adam in the Garden (Gen. 2: 15) in *Quaest. in Gn.* I. 14 and of the naming of the animals by Adam (*ibid.* 20–2). What is perhaps surprising is that in *Quaest. in Gn.* I. 32 he can argue, with reference to Gen. 3: 1ff. (the statement that the serpent spoke), that 'it is likely that not even in the beginning of the world's creation were the other animals without a share in speech', and that 'when some miraculous deed is prepared, God changes the inner nature'. So Philo is inconsistent. Sometimes he rejects the idea of a serpent capable of speaking as mythical and sometimes he accepts it as what happened at a very early stage in the history of the world. In connection with the making of clothes for Adam and Eve, he gives two interpretations, neither of which is purely literal but by both of which Scripture is said to indicate something 'symbolically' (*Quaest. in Gn.* I.40). Philo frequently, in the *Quaestiones et Solutiones in Genesin*, gives both the literal and the symbolical meaning, but occasionally, as in the case of the statement in Gen. 3: 8 that 'the sound was heard of the Lord God walking', he cannot bring himself to admit the literal meaning, since God is 'stable and immobile'. All he will concede is that 'as he is heard without speaking, so also he gives the impression of walking without actually walking, indeed without moving at all' (*Quaest. in Gn.* I.42). Philo's personal preference, in the matter of scriptural exegesis, is expressed in *Agric.* 97: 'when we interpret words by the meanings that lie beneath the surface, all that is mythical is removed out of our way, and the real sense becomes as clear as daylight' – in this case that the serpent is a symbol of pleasure and Eve of life.

There was in Jewish rabbinical exegesis of Scripture enough that was allegorical, or quasi-allegorical, to encourage Philo to proceed to a more thoroughgoing use of such hermeneutical tools, though it is likely that there were other, non-Jewish sources for his allegorical method of interpretation. Rabbinic exegesis could, for example, take both the word 'water' in Exod. 15: 22 and the word 'tree' in Exod. 15: 25 to refer to the Torah. The lover and the beloved in the Song of Songs could refer to both God and Israel. If allegorical exegesis means essentially the interpretation of a text in terms of something other than its obvious, literal meaning, then the examples of rabbinic exegesis referred to – and there are many others – are allegorical. Philo applied the method to many more passages of Scripture, especially in the Pentateuch, and his acceptance of Greek philosophical ideas led him to extract from the Old Testament texts some ideas which the rabbis of the Palestinian community would and could never have found there; but basically he and they were employing the same method in at least some areas. The only essential differences were the extent of the application of the method and the ideas it derived from Scripture. Both Philo and the rabbinic exegete accepted that not every verse of the Old Testament had to be taken literally. In the case both of the rabbis and of Philo this allowed an escape to be found from the embarrassment of the anthropomorphic language used by Scripture about God.

With reference to the anthropomorphic description of God in Ezek. 1: 26, a rabbi exclaims (*Genesis Rabbah* 27: 1): 'Great is the boldness of the prophets who describe God by the likeness of the creature.' A general rule of rabbinic exegesis, with reference to scriptural anthropomorphism, is 'The Torah speaks according to the language of man' (*Berakoth* 31b). The rabbis explained this element in the language of the Old Testament by saying: 'we describe God by terms borrowed from his creations in order to cause them to sink into the ear'. Philo also speaks of God's accommodating himself to the capacities of man's understanding as a reason for the anthropomorphism of Scripture, but he is driven, both by his Jewishness and by what he has learned from Plato and the Greek philosophers, to seek urgently to escape from the anthropomorphic level of language employed by the Old Testament authors.

THE NEED FOR FIGURATIVE INTERPRETATIONS (*Poster. C.* 1–32 (I–X))

In the first section of the *De Posteritate Caini*, Philo both denounces anthropomorphism and defends the allegorical method of exegesis. Because of the nature of that method, which allows the exegete to find in the words of Scripture meanings which do not appear to reside in them, much of what Philo has to say has nothing to do with 'the posterity of Cain'. In fact Philo expounds an aspect of his doctrine of God, that of his unknowability. He also reveals his attitude towards Epicureanism and towards Egyptian religious beliefs and practices as he understood them. His view of the physical universe is also woven into his exegesis, showing how wide a variety of ideas can be extracted from the Old Testament by the allegorical method.

God's presence (*Poster. C.* 1–12)

(1) 'And Cain went out from the face of God, and dwelt in the
land of Naid over against Eden' [Gen. 4: 16]. Now let us
raise the question whether in the books in which Moses acts
as God's interpreter we should take what he says figuratively, since the impressions derived from a literal interpre-
(2) tation are considerably in conflict with the truth. For if the
Existent Being has a face, and he who wants to get away
from it can with perfect ease depart to another place,
why do we reject the impiety of Epicureans or the atheism
of the Egyptians, or the mythical suppositions of which life
(3) is full? For a face is part of an animal, but God is a whole not
a part, so that we shall have to invent for him other parts
also, a neck, chest, hands, feet, and moreover a stomach and
genitalia, and all the rest of the innumerable internal and
(4) external organs. And if God has a human face it follows
necessarily that he must experience human passions. For in
the case of all these organs, as in the case of others, Nature
has not made idle superfluities but aids to the weakness of
those who possess them. And she has adapted them to their
different needs and in a manner appropriate to their peculiar
(5) natural necessities and services. And from whence does Cain
'go out'? From the palace of the Ruler of all? But what
house of God perceptible to the senses can exist except this
world, which it is impossible to devise a means of leaving?
For all created things are enclosed within it by a circle of the

sky. Indeed the particles of the deceased are dissolved into
their original elements and are again distributed among the
various powers of the universe out of which they were
made and the loan which was made to each man, as it were,
is restored, at different intervals of time, to Nature his
(6) creditor, whenever she chooses to recall her debts. Again, if
anyone goes away from someone he is then in a different
place from the person he left behind. But if this is true and
Cain goes out from God, it follows that there are some
portions of the universe deprived of God. Yet God has left
nothing empty or destitute of himself, but continually fills
(7) up everything completely. Now, if God has not a face, since
he exceeds the peculiarities that are characteristic of all
created things, and if he does not consist of parts, since he
encompasses all things and is encompassed by none, it is
impossible for anything in this world to depart from it as
from a city, seeing that nothing has been left over outside it.
What remains for us to do is to recognise that none of the
preceding things was spoken of in a strictly literal sense and
to embark upon the path of allegorical interpretation which
is dear to those versed in philosophy and to make that the
(8) starting-point of our exposition. If it is a difficult thing to
escape from the presence of a mortal king, must it not be
extremely difficult to leave behind the vision of God and
depart, determined never to see him again, that is, to
become incapable of receiving a mental picture of him
(9) through having lost the use of the eyes of the soul? As many
as have suffered the loss through necessity, overcome by the
might of an inexorable force, deserve pity rather than
hatred. But those who have voluntarily and of their own
choice turned aside from and abandoned the Existent
Being, going beyond the furthest limit of wickedness itself
– for what evil could one find equal to that? – such men
should not suffer the usual punishment of evil-doers, but
must be subjected to penalties which are most extraor-

dinary. And certainly no one could devise a newer or greater penalty than exile and banishment from the
(10) Sovereign of the Universe. Adam, then, is driven out by God, but Cain went out voluntarily. Moses demonstrates here for us each kind of departure, the one voluntary, the other involuntary. But the involuntary action which does not occur because of our intention will subsequently have applied to it such remedy as the circumstances render appropriate, 'for God shall raise up another seed in place of Abel whom Cain slew' [Gen. 4: 25]. There will be a male offspring, Seth, the 'Watering', created for the soul which
(11) did not turn aside deliberately. The voluntary act, since it took place with deliberate purpose and intention, must incur injuries for ever beyond healing. For, even as good deeds committed with forethought and intention are better than unintentional ones, so also among offences those that are unintentional are less weighty than those which are
(12) premeditated. Cain, then, has left the face of God, and will be the victim of the punishment which takes vengeance on sinners. But Moses gives to his disciples a most excellent commandment, 'to love God and hearken to and cleave to him' [Deut. 30: 20]. For this is the life which leads to true prosperity and length of days. In an extremely vivid manner he invites them to render homage to the Being who is the object of threefold yearning and a worthy object of love by saying that they should 'cleave to him', thereby indicating the continuous, constant and unbroken nature of the harmony and union that is founded upon an intimate relationship with God.

(1) *from the face of God*: the feature of the words in Gen. 4: 16 that prompted Philo to refuse to take them literally is that they speak of Cain's departure from God's presence. To refer thus to a departure from *the face of God* is blatantly anthropomorphic, and the words cannot therefore be literally true. Here is a case of scriptural anthropomorphism compelling Philo to allegorise. He then lays

down the general principle that no anthropomorphic statement about God is to be accepted as literally true. Why, then, does Scripture contain such statements as that in Gen. 4: 16? This question Philo answers elsewhere by saying that they appear 'for the instruction of the many' (*Deus Imm.* 54 (see above, pp. 74–5, 77); cf. *Som.* I.237).

Naid: see below, on para. 32.

Moses acts as God's interpreter: Philo eulogises Moses as 'a king and a lawgiver and a high priest and a prophet' and 'interpreter of the sacred laws' (*Vit. Mos.* II.3 and I.1). He also calls him 'the interpreter of the writings of nature' (*Rer. Div. Her.* 213), 'the steward and guardian of the sacred mysteries of the living God' (*Plant.* 26) and says he was 'always handling divine things' (*Mut. Nom.* 126). In his Life of Moses Philo says that Moses' associates could even ask, of his mind, 'whether it was a human mind or a divine intellect or something combined of the two' (*Vit. Mos.* I.27). Words attributed to God in Scripture are treated by Philo as Moses' words (*Conf. Ling.* 192), and Moses is addressed in prayer as the Sacred Guide who can conduct the reader of Scripture into the realms of hidden light beyond its pages and reveal 'the hidden things therein contained . . . invisible to those who are uninitiated' (*Som.* I.164).

figuratively (*tropikōteron*): Philo quotes the words of Gen. 4: 16 and then asks, his words indicating that in Scripture Moses acts as *God's interpreter*, whether Moses' statements ought to be taken literally or *figuratively*. The word used is a common one in passages where Philo is describing his method of interpreting a biblical text and is drawing attention to a deeper meaning beneath the literal surface. He gives as his reason for regarding the language of Scripture as figurative the fact that, in this instance, its literal sense gives an impression that is *considerably in conflict with the truth*.

In *Jos.* 125 he explains that he usually examines the allegorical meaning after looking at the literal. The literal meaning was not entirely obliterated by the deeper, allegorical sense. In general Philo does accept the two levels of meaning confronting him in the Old Testament text, though in the case of Gen. 4: 16 he admits only the figurative level (cf. *Som.* I.120–1). For Philo the words of the text of Scripture are the shadows cast by the allegorical substance beneath and behind them (cf. *Conf. Ling.* 190). Only rarely does Philo concede that both the literal and the allegorical meaning claim the reader's admiration, as he does in *Leg. All.* II.14.

(2) *if the Existent Being has a face*: here Philo insists that to take literally statements in Scripture about God's *face* makes it impossible to reject what he calls *the impiety of Epicureans*, the chief of their doctrines being that God has a human form. Philo is not perhaps wholly fair to Epicurus, since the Epicurean Cicero, for example, distinguishes between the body possessed by man and the 'body' possessed by God. Philo, it has to be admitted, treats Epicureanism somewhat superficially. For Epicurus, always referred to unfavourably by Philo, the gods do exist, though they do not intervene in human affairs, living in the *intermundia* (spaces between the worlds), beautiful and happy, with no thought of men's activities, eating and drinking and, of course, speaking in Greek! This kind of view, which attributes sexual differences and relationships, eating and breathing, a constitution of atoms, and other physical features, probably led to Philo's unfavourable reaction.

A literal interpretation of Scripture also leads, in Philo's view, to *the atheism of the Egyptians*. Statements of this kind in Philo were no doubt prompted by Egyptian animal worship, no better than sheer atheism to someone like Philo. Philo did not think it any better to attribute a face to God than to treat animals as gods. Philo never appears to have understood Egyptian religion and took a view of it similar to that found in Wisd. Sol. 15: 18. Philo always speaks scathingly of the religious beliefs of the Egyptians, as he does when he refers to 'the foolishness of the Egyptians' (*Spec. Leg.* 1.79), an expression reflecting the words of Lev. 18: 3 and Ezek. 20: 7, 8. One of his most critical comments on Egyptian impiety, which only shallow minds, he says, cannot see through, is in a passage in which he states that the Alexandrians have allowed the name of God to be shared by ibises, snakes and many other wild beasts (*Leg. Gaj.* 163; see also *Decal.* 76–9).

Not only, however, may literalism lead to Epicurean impiety and Egyptian atheism; it may also lead to mythology of the kind found in Greek literature (cf. *Decal.* 76; *Spec. Leg.* 1.79; *Migr. Abr.* 76). For Philo, myths such as those found in Homer are man-made and therefore false. Scripture as understood by Philo contains 'no mythical invention' (*Det. Pot. Ins.* 125). Philo thus associates himself with the Jewish and philosophical denunciation of myth in religion. Myths to him are the work of the 'impious' (*Deus Imm.* 59). They are properly called 'mythical fictions' which falsely attribute 'human passions' to God, whereas in reality God's nature is 'not susceptible to passion in any form' (*ibid.* 52; see above, pp. 79–85).

(3) *God is a whole not a part*: Philo's belief in the absolute unity and indivisibility of God also led him to reject literalism. Man cannot, in his view, apprehend anything of God except his existence (*Deus Imm.* 62; see above, pp. 80 and 83). A face, however, is a part of a living creature and, since *God is a whole*, if he has a face he must have other parts too, which, Philo believes, is patently absurd. God is an indivisible whole, complete in himself, not a composite being made up of many parts. *God is a whole* is a fundamental tenet of Philo's theology. As in Aristotle's philosophy, so in Philo's theology, God is *to hen*, the One, one and without parts. God is 'a single being: not a combination'. He has 'no mixture with anything else'. 'Oneness exists according to the one God' (*Leg. All.* II.2–3). One of the fears about literalism felt by Philo was to do with this powerful conviction of the oneness of God; he feared what he saw as the disastrous consequences of any weakening of it. Philo felt that to attribute *parts* to God would lead to anthropomorphism and this in turn inevitably to anthropopathism, something even worse (see *Sacr. AC* 94ff., where he is once more basing what he says on Num. 23: 19). To Philo the idea of God's having limbs and organs was a wholly unacceptable and impossible concept.

(4) *Nature has not made idle superfluities*: in this section Philo states with stark brutality what seemed to him the unavoidable consequence of anthropomorphism, anthropopathism. He supports his contention with the argument that in the world of nature there are no *idle superfluities*. Organs supplied by Nature to meet specific needs and particular wants and to fulfil necessary functions do not remain unused. If God did have organs and limbs – hands, feet, etc. – they would be there because he needed them and they would be used by him. Also, the organs supplied by Nature are *aids to the weakness of those who possess them*. The word *weakness* is one which is properly applicable to man and the created order, but not to God, the Creator. To possess organs of different kinds, therefore, would be a sign of weakness on God's part; it would make God like man by attributing to him human *astheneia*. Men possess organs because, in their weakness, they need them and the special services and ministries which together they can render to them.

But God, whom Philo calls *to on*, needs nothing. He is wholly self-sufficient, complete and perfect in every respect (cf. *Leg. All.*

II.2; *Op. Mund.* 23; see p. 43). In *Cher.* 123 Philo says that 'God distributes his good things, not like a seller vending his wares at a high price, but he is inclined to make presents of everything, pouring forth the inexhaustible fountains of his graces, and never desiring any return; for he has no need of anything nor is there any created being competent to give him a suitable gift in return.'

(5) *whence does Cain 'go out'?*: Cain symbolises for Philo the self-loving principle (*Sacr. AC* 3) which dwells in man's soul. He is here contrasted with the wise man who desires to see the Existent. Cain represents those self-lovers who ascribe all things to mind and self rather than to God and who honour the creation rather than the Creator (*Sacr. AC* 72).

To Philo the words of Gen. 4: 16, then, describe the going-out of the kind of person Cain stands for. So Philo first asks his question *whence does Cain 'go out'?* He cannot, Philo argues, go out from *the palace of the Ruler of all*, since that is the universe. There is no escape from the universe for man and in it God is omnipresent.

the circle of the sky: this is what, on Philo's view of the physical universe, is the furthermost boundary of creation. The universe, then, is a self-contained whole.

the particles of the deceased: these are broken down into their original elements and re-distributed. Not even death allows man to escape from the confines of the material universe.

the loan which was made to each man: this is an echo of some words in one of Plato's dialogues (the *Timaeus* 42E: see p. 73). There it is used of the four elements which make up man's physical body, which are bestowed upon him by the gods who created him but intended to be given back at the end of his life. For Philo, too, the constituent elements which make up man's body are returned into the common stock of the material universe to be re-cycled and re-used.

Nature his creditor: man is indebted to Nature, according to Philo, for the loan of a physical body, the consequence of which is that it is for Nature to choose when the debt is to be repaid. There is no hint here, or anywhere in Philo's works, of a hope for a bodily resurrection of the dead at some time in the future, nor indeed of a hope for any kind of resurrection.

The force of the argument of this section is that the statement about Cain's outgoing cannot be a statement about his exit from the world.

(6) *in a different place*: Philo reinforces the conclusion he has just

reached. If someone leaves a place, he takes up a new position, so that if Cain went out from God, he must have taken up a new position somewhere away from God. This would mean that there is some corner of the universe beyond God, *deprived of God*. However, for Philo that is impossible, since *God has left nothing empty or destitute of himself, but continually fills up everything completely*. God as the filler of all things is a common and familiar theme in Philo (see p. 43). In *Leg. All.* 1.44 Philo writes, 'God is full of himself and . . . sufficient for himself, filling up and surrounding everything else', while in *Conf. Ling.* 136 he states simply: 'God fills all things'. For Philo God is both transcendent, immanent and omnipresent, the last meaning that with him there is no place, no 'here' and 'there', since that would involve a limitation of him and the relation of parts to one another. Philo can say that God is both nowhere and everywhere: nowhere because he made space as well as bodies in space and, as space's Maker he is not within it; everywhere because he has extended his powers throughout the universe and thus left no place without his presence. To God in his essence, therefore, all terms of motion involving change of place are inapplicable. God's divine nature presents itself to man as 'visible, comprehensible and everywhere' yet is in reality 'invisible, incomprehensible and nowhere' (*Conf. Ling.* 134–9). God for Philo is everywhere in the corporeal world, exercising his providence in it, but he is no part of it and is unlike anything in it (see below, on para. 14).

(7) *if God has not a face*: this Philo takes for granted as true. The view that requires the total rejection of any possibility that God could have a human face, or any kind of face, is the view that God is a transcendent Being who is above and beyond *the peculiarities that are characteristic of all created things*, and also that he is not to be found in particular places, since he encompasses all things and *is encompassed by none*. Philo then argues that, if all this is true of God, if it *is* impossible for any part of the world to be removed from him as from a city, since there is nowhere outside the world to remove to, the only thing left for the reader of Gen. 4: 16 to do is to make up his mind that *none of the preceding things was spoken of in a strictly literal sense and to embark upon the path of allegorical interpretation which is dear to those versed in philosophy*. By *those versed in philosophy* he means those who discard mythical and popular notions of God and seek the reality and truth underlying them.

the starting-point of our exposition: Philo's discussion at this point has as its starting-point a simple *a fortiori* argument, which reveals one of his reasons for adopting the allegorical method of exegesis.

(8) *a difficult thing*: if it is difficult, Philo argues, for a subject to escape from his earthly king, it must be a thousand times more difficult *to leave behind him the vision of God and depart, determined never to see him again*. Philo interprets this allegorically, as the attempt *to become incapable of receiving a mental picture* of God *through having lost the use of the eyes of the soul*.

(9) *pity rather than hatred*: this would be the appropriate reaction, Philo says, when the loss of soul-vision happens to a man under compulsion, *overcome by the might of an inexorable force*. But those who *voluntarily* commit the supreme sin of departing from the Existent have, in Philo's view, perpetrated an act that transcends the utmost limits of wickedness. No evil is equal to it. Such a sin deserves the supreme penalty, a penalty far more severe than the penalties imposed on men, and there is no greater one than *exile and banishment from the sovereign of the Universe*.

But only by using allegorical exegesis can Philo escape from discussions of the meaning of the emigration of Cain to the land of Naid into the more rarefied atmosphere of thoughts about the possession, or loss, of the vision of God.

(10) *Adam, then, is driven out by God*: the Old Testament makes it plain that, whereas Cain departed voluntarily, Adam was driven out by God (Gen. 3: 24: 'he drove out the man'). In the passage before us Philo makes use of and applies to his own purposes the Old Testament distinction between voluntary sins and involuntary ones and the view expressed there that voluntary sins are far more serious in nature than involuntary ones (see Num. 15: 22–31). This is shown, according to Philo, by what is said about Abel, as contrasted with Cain, for God, in Abel's case, allowed a degree of 'healing' to take place. In Gen. 4: 25 God promised 'another seed' to replace Abel. This was Seth, whose name, according to Philo, symbolically means 'Watering', the man in whom the mind waters the senses, giving them the power they require (cf. *Poster. C.* 124–70). His birth was a partial remedy for Adam's involuntary departure from Eden.

(11) *The voluntary act . . . must incur injuries forever beyond healing*: just as right actions deliberately performed are of greater moral worth than right actions that are involuntary, so, in the case of sins, the involuntary ones are less serious than the voluntary ones. That Philo, however, is thinking of something far more

significant than Cain's emigration to Naid is shown by his statement that the act he had in mind is one that is *for ever beyond healing*.

(12) *Cain, then, has left the face of God*: Cain, the deliberate sinner, contrasted, as one who turns from God, with the wise man, who wants to see God, falls into the hands of the divine Judge who *takes vengeance on sinners*. What God wants for man, Philo explains, is set down by Moses in Deut. 30: 20, where he exhorts him 'to love God and hearken to and cleave to him'. It is this that brings the reward of true prosperity and length of days.

cleave to him: Philo notes that Scripture uses this anthropomorphic expression because it is vivid and expressive and serves to draw attention dramatically to the constant and continuous concord that results from making God our own.

the object of threefold yearning and a worthy object of love: it is, of course, God about whom this is said.

Seeing God (*Poster. C.* 13–21)

(13) These and other exhortations like them Moses addresses to others. But he himself desires so insatiably to see God and to be seen by him that he beseeches him to reveal as to an intimate acquaintance his own nature, which is so difficult to imagine [Exod. 33: 13], so that he will receive a view free of falsehood and will exchange doubt full of uncertainty for a well-grounded faith. And he will not allow his desire to weaken, but even though he loves an object which is difficult to attain, or rather is wholly unattainable, he still presses on, in no way relaxing his intense ardour, but brings to bear without hesitation and without vacillation all the
(14) means within his power to achieve success. At all events he will now penetrate into the thick darkness where God was [Exod. 20: 21]: that is, into those conceptions regarding the Existent Being which are unapproachable and which are without visible, material forms. For the Cause of all things is not situated in the darkness or, in general terms, in any place at all, but he transcends both place and time. For he has subjected all creation to his control and is surpassed by

nothing, but exceeds everything. But though he transcends and stands outside what he has made, it is nevertheless true that he fills the whole universe with his presence; for he has caused his Powers to extend to the limits of the universe, and in accordance with the laws of harmony has united each
(15) part with each. When, therefore, the God-loving soul seeks to find out what the Existent Being is in his essence he embarks upon a quest of that which is without form and invisible. The greatest boon which arises from this is the recognition that God, as far as his essence is concerned, is incomprehensible to every creature, and to see precisely
(16) this, that he is invisible. But the holy guide, it seems to me, even before he begins his investigation, appreciated its uselessness. That he did so is shown by the fact that he beseeches the Existent One himself to become his own informant and revealer of his own nature. For he says 'Manifest thyself to me' [Exod. 33: 13, LXX], indicating quite clearly thereby that there is not a single created being competent by himself to acquire knowledge of God in
(17) respect of his essence. Therefore Abraham also, when he came to the place of which God had spoken to him, looked up on the third day and 'seeth the place from afar' [Gen. 22: 3–4]. But what sort of place? The one at which he had already arrived? And how can it be distant if he had already
(18) come to it? But perhaps what is told under a figure here is this: the wise man is always longing to know the Ruler of the universe, and when proceeding along the path that leads through knowledge and wisdom, he first meets with divine words, and among these he takes a preliminary rest, and though he had meant to change direction and go by some other route, he now comes to a stop. For the eyes of his understanding have been opened and he sees with clear vision that he had prepared himself to take the athletic pursuit of an object difficult to capture, which constantly retreated before him, and retired to a distance, leaving its

pursuers behind by putting an immeasurable distance
(19) between itself and them. Rightly does he reflect that all the objects under the sky which travel fastest would be, as it were, standing still by comparison with the rapid movement of the sun, and the moon and the other stars. However, the entire heaven took its birth, and that which makes precedes that which is made. So, of necessity not only the other beings in the world around us, but also that which has the most rapid movement of all, the mind, would fall short by an indescribable distance of a proper comprehension of the First Cause. But the most incredible thing of all is that though the stars, which overtake all things that move, are themselves in motion, God, paradoxically, who outdist-
(20) ances them all, is motionless. And it is said of him that he, being identical with himself, is very near to us and yet very far from us, in contact with us through his creative and punitive powers, which are close to each individual; and yet at the same time he has driven created nature far away from his essential being, so that it is impossible for us to touch it,
(21) even with the immaterial efforts of pure mind. Therefore, with the lovers of God who engage in the quest for God, even if they never find him, we rejoice, for that done, the quest of the Good and the Beautiful, even if the goal be missed, is sufficient to provide a joyful foretaste. But, in the case of the self-loving, suffering Cain, we commiserate, for he has left his soul with no conception of the Existent One, having deliberately blunted that organ by which alone he might have seen him.

(13) *These and other exhortations . . .*: here, leaving for a moment what Moses urged others to do, a section begins on the subject of Moses' own desire to *see* (*horan*) God and *be seen by him*. So great was this desire on Moses' part that he implored God to reveal himself – *to reveal as to an intimate acquaintance his own nature*. Philo adds that God's nature is *so difficult to imagine*, but that Moses wanted a view *free of falsehood* and to exchange *doubt full of*

uncertainty for a well-grounded faith. Philo then states that Moses resolved not to slacken his efforts to reach his desired goal, even though he realised that it entailed a hard quest, indeed that to *see* God is in fact out of reach.

What Philo is doing in this section is both to describe Moses, who is contrasted sharply with both Adam and Cain, in his quest for God, and to describe also the God whom Moses desired to see and comprehend.

(14) *the thick darkness where God was*: according to Exod. 20: 21, Moses entered into the *thick darkness* where God resides. The darkness is interpreted as referring to *those conceptions regarding the Existent Being* (*peri tou ontos*) that are *unapproachable and which are without visible, material forms*. Here again Philo makes a statement which shows that for him the Old Testament was not to be taken literally: namely, that *the Cause of all things is not situated in the darkness, or, in general terms, in any place at all, but he transcends both place and time*. The relationship between God and the created order is that of controller and controlled, and Philo repeats his view that God is *surpassed by nothing, but exceeds everything*. However, though he is transcendent and beyond the created order, none the less *he fills the whole universe with his presence*. These words show Philo's concern to affirm both the transcendence of God and his immanence, both that he is above the world and that he is involved in it.

his Powers: to safeguard the transcendence of God without denying his presence in the world Philo, here as at many points in his works, affirms that God is present in the universe in and through *his Powers*. They reach to the utmost limits of creation and they consist of *those conceptions regarding the Existent Being which are unapproachable and which are without visible, material forms*. The idea of divine *Powers* which God caused to penetrate into every corner of the universe helped Philo to overcome the problem in any suggestion of contact between God himself and the material universe. So here again allegorical exegesis has enabled Philo to find in Scripture, beneath the obvious meaning, a meaning which was in harmony with his view, influenced both in its form and its content by philosophical ideas, of God. Allegorical exegesis also enabled him to avoid the inadequate conception of God which a literal interpretation of Scripture produced.

(15) *the God-loving soul*: such a soul inevitably *embarks upon a quest of that which is without form and invisible*, for that is precisely

what probing the question of the essence of the Existent Being involves. Nevertheless, Philo explains, although the quest is an impossible one, *the greatest boon* accrues to the seeker, namely *the recognition that God, as far as his essence is concerned, is incomprehensible to every creature. He is invisible*, says Philo. Not only is it the case that 'No man has seen God at any time' (John 1: 18), for never in past, present or future time does the possibility of God's being 'seen' exist.

(16) *the holy guide*: this refers to Moses, who is actually called a *hierophant*, a revealer of the sacred truth about God. Even he was aware, even before he began his search, that it was a futile undertaking. It was because of this that he implored God to be *his own informant* and to reveal *his own nature*. Moses realised that of God only that could be known which God himself chose to reveal and disclose. Philo quotes Moses' words in Exod. 33: 13 and adds an explanatory comment that they show clearly that there is no created being, not even Moses himself, who is *competent by himself to acquire knowledge of God in respect of his essence*.

(17) *what sort of place?*: when the reader of the Old Testament meets statements about Abraham such as the one in Gen. 22: 4, which, in an apparently contradictory fashion, says that, on reaching the place of which God had told him, Abraham 'seeth the place from afar', there is an apparent contradiction, since one does not normally see from afar a place already reached!

(18) *under a figure*: from the passage in Genesis which he is expounding Philo's mind turns to another, the one relating to Abraham, because he wants his readers to be aware that, though what is said appears to involve a contradiction, there is no contradiction if the statement in question is interpreted allegorically. So he proceeds to show how the Abraham passage is to be understood. The difficulty is removed if the reader recognises that something in Gen. 22: 4 is being told *under a figure* (*ainittetai*), the technical term used by Philo for the language of Scripture which has a meaning below the surface level hidden, until it is appropriately decoded, by the figures which make up the literal meaning. What is disclosed figuratively, according to Philo, is that the wise man is perpetually longing to discern the Ruler of the Universe. His pilgrimage takes him *via* wisdom and knowledge, the first contact involved being with *divine words* (*logois . . . theiois*), at which point a preliminary halt is made. Though he had intended to go further, the man stops there, doing so because he

sees, once the eyes of his understanding have been opened, that he has been in chase of an elusive quarry difficult to capture and always leaving its pursuers far behind. So utterly other and transcendent is God that even the wise man seeking to see him *comes to a stop*.

(19) *Rightly does he reflect . . .*: the wise man realises that, just as many things under the sky are motionless relative to the motion of the heavenly bodies, so even mind, which is swifter than other things in apprehension, comes short of the apprehension of the First Cause by an immeasurable distance.

that which has the most rapid movement of all: here Philo exhibits his unashamed intellectualism, for the swiftest of earthly things is, for him, undoubtedly the mind. Philo is a rationalist, a believer in the superiority of reason. But he is aware of reason's limitations in the search for knowledge of God. All that even the wisest mind can know of God in fact is that he exists (see above, pp. 38–42).

the most incredible thing of all: the supreme paradox in the universe is that the heavenly bodies, when they pass other moving bodies, are themselves in motion, while God, *who outdistances them all, is motionless*. It is perhaps not easy to recall that Philo is still, in theory, expounding Gen. 4: 16. In fact, as so often happens, the literal interpretation of Scripture was so inadequate and unsatisfying, and even the allegorical exegesis of one verse far from limitless in its possibilities for Philo, that he has gone off into a digression on the nature of God and the impossibility of man's quest for knowledge of God ever being successful.

(20) *he is very near to us and yet very far from us*: this is the conclusion Philo draws from his meditations and philosophisings on the nature of God. His closeness to men is due to the presence of *his creative and punitive powers*, for these are *close to each individual*. At the same time, however, God *has driven created nature far away from his essential being*. For Philo there was an enormous chasm between the material and the spiritual, between the corporeal and the intellectual, between created being and its Creator. So great is the gap that exists that Philo can say of God's *essential being*: *it is impossible for us to touch it even with the immaterial efforts of pure mind*.

(21) *the quest of the Good and the Beautiful*: this quest is one in which even *the lovers of God* who undertake the fruitless quest of *the Existent One* find joy, despite their lack of success in finding him. They rejoice because the quest itself, *even if the goal be missed, is sufficient to provide a joyful foretaste*. This expression, *joyful foretaste*,

implies that one day in the future, somehow, *the lovers of God* will find *the Good and the Beautiful*, but perhaps the ascent to Absolute Goodness and Beauty will be possible only when the soul or mind of man is no longer encumbered by a body.

we rejoice: the first person plural pronoun indicates that Philo identifies himself with the company of *the lovers of God*.

the self-loving Cain: here Philo returns to Gen. 4: 16 and the story of Cain's departure from Eden to the land of Naid (Nod). Cain, for Philo, is the scriptural symbol of the man who deserves to be pitied because he has left his own soul behind *with no conception of the Existent One*. He has *deliberately blunted that organ by which alone he might have seen him*. The deliberate sin of Cain was to extinguish in himself the capacity to see God. Gen. 4: 16 is, for Philo, primarily a warning to its readers of the danger of repeating the folly of the *self-loving Cain*. To do that is to depart from the presence of the Lord by taking his place for themselves, and by attributing to themselves and their own minds what is really God's.

The country called 'Tossing' (*Poster. C.* 22–32)

(22) It is worthwhile to look at the country into which he betakes himself when he is once far from the presence of God. It is called 'Tossing'. By this name the lawgiver indicates that the foolish man, under the blow of impulses devoid of stability and firmness, is subject to tossing and tumult, like the sea driven by contrary winds in the winter season, and has never even a single glimpse of calm or tranquillity. And as when a ship is tossed about at the mercy of the sea, it is no longer capable of being steered or of lowering its anchor but, being thrown about this way and that, it rolls to starboard and then to port and moves uncertainly, swaying to and fro; even so the worthless man, under the influence of a vacillating and tormented mind, powerless to direct the ship of life with any steadiness, is
(23) always tossing, ready to overturn his life. The perfect sequence of cause and effect at work here impresses me in more than a mediocre way. It happens that being near to a stable object produces a longing for stability by wanting to

be like it. Now that which is unwaveringly stable is God, and that which is in motion is the creation. He therefore who approaches God desires stability, but he who departs from him in so far as he is approaching the restless creation
(24) will in all likelihood be tossed about. Therefore it stands written in the Curses 'He shall not cause thee to rest, and there shall be no standing for the sole of thy feet', and a little further on 'thy life shall be hanging before thine eyes' [Deut. 28: 65, 66]. For it is of the foolish man to be for ever moving about in a manner contrary to right reason and to be hostile to calm and rest and not to fix himself firmly on
(25) any doctrine or to take a firm stand. Accordingly he judges matters differently at different times, and even about the same matters he will contradict himself even when no new factor has become involved – he can become in a moment of time great and small, enemy and friend, and, so to say, everything that is most inconsistent. And, as the lawgiver has said, his whole life is suspended, having no firm foothold, but is constantly being tossed about by circum-
(26) stances which drag and pull him in opposite directions. That is why the lawgiver says in another place 'he that hangeth on a tree is cursed of God' [Deut. 21: 23], for whereas we ought to hang upon God, the man of whom we are thinking fastens himself to his body, which is a tree-like burden in us. By so doing he exchanges hope for desire, the greatest of evils for the supreme good. For hope, on the one hand, being an expectation of good things, causes the mind to depend upon God who gives generously; desire, on the other hand, which creates irrational cravings, causes it to depend on the body, which nature has created to be a
(27) receptacle and realm of pleasures. Let these men, then, be hung on desire as from a halter. But the wise Abraham, since he is one who stands firm, draws near to God, the stable One, for Scripture says that 'he was standing before the Lord and he drew near and said' [Gen. 18: 22–3]. For

only a truly unchanging soul is able to gain a means of access to the unchanging God, and the soul that is really of such a disposition does truly stand very close to the divine power.
(28) Therefore the oracle vouchsafed to the all-wise Moses shows most clearly the extremely firm stability in which the virtuous man lives. The oracle is as follows: 'But as for thee stand thou here by me' [Deut. 5: 31]. This oracle is evidence for two things: first, that the Existent who moves and makes everything else to revolve is himself immobile and immutable; and, secondly, that he makes the virtuous man a participant in his nature, which is rest. For, in my view, just as things which are crooked are made straight by a straight ruler, so moving things are brought to a halt and made to
(29) stand still by the force of him who stands. In this passage he commands another to stand with him, but elsewhere he says: 'I will go down with thee into Egypt, and will bring thee up at last' [Gen. 46: 4]. He does not say 'thou with me'. Why not? Because calmness and stability are properties of God, but properties of creation are change of position and
(30) all movement which tends towards such change. When, therefore, he calls a man to the good peculiar to himself, he says 'Do thou stand with me', not 'I with thee'; for it is not the case that he will not become immobile, for he is always in that state. But when he comes to that which is the peculiar attribute of creation, he will quite rightly say 'I will go down with thee', for to thee change of place is fitting. So with me no-one will go down – for with me there is no changing – but one will remain immobile, because repose pleases me. But with those who go down by changing their place – for change of place is like a brother or a close parent – I will go down in all pervading presence without any change of locality, since I have filled the
(31) universe with myself. And this, also, I do through the pity I have for the rational nature, in order that it may be raised from the hell of the passions into the Olympian regions of

virtue, with me as Guide, who have laid down the road which leads to heaven and have marked it out as a highway for all suppliant souls, so that they may not grow weary as
(32) they walk on it. We have succeeded, therefore, in showing each side of the picture, the calm of the virtuous man, the agitated state of the foolish one. Let us now examine the consequences. For the lawgiver says that Naid, 'the tumult', to which the soul emigrated is opposite to Eden. 'Eden' is symbolic for right and divine, and it therefore has the meaning 'luxury'. For right reason enjoys and luxuriates, before all things, in good things which are pure and uncontaminated, which in addition are complete and full, while God, generous source of all wealth, pours down his virgin and immortal blessings. But evil by nature attacks the good, unjust the just, wise the foolish and every form of virtue every form of vice. Such is the meaning of the statement that Naid is opposite Eden.

(22) *the country into which he betakes himself*: Philo calls this country into which Cain went after his departure from the presence of God by a strange name, '*Tossing*'. There is sufficient similarity between the Hebrew word 'Nod', the land named in Gen. 4: 16 as Cain's destination, and the verb to toss to justify Philo, in his view, in interpreting the land of Nod as the country called '*Tossing*'.

subject to tossing and tumult: the kind of allegorical exegesis Philo practises results from time to time in the interpretation of one word in terms of another similar to it in spelling, even though they are not from the same family. The attractiveness of the similarity between the word 'Nod' and the verb 'to toss' for Philo resided in the fact that it enabled him to interpret *the foolish man*, the man who, like Cain, departs from God's presence, *as subject to tossing and tumult*, living in the land of Nod, which is the land of Tumult. Philo compares the unstable state of such a man to a stormy sea, on the grounds that the foolish man, like the one in the psalm who says, 'There is no God' (Ps. 14: 1), is *under the blow of impulses devoid of stability and firmness*. Like a storm-tossed ship at the mercy of the waves and rolling from side to side, the worthless man, of whom

Cain is the symbol, whose mind reels and is storm-driven, is powerless to make any steady progress in a particular direction but *is always tossing, ready to overturn his life*. That is the meaning of the second part of Gen. 4: 16 for Philo: the man who departs from God's presence embarks upon a life totally lacking in stability.

(23) *the perfect sequence of cause and effect*: Philo affirms that it is always the case that *being near to a stable object produces a longing for stability by wanting to be like it*. He goes on to say that *that which is unwaveringly stable is God* (creation being subject to movement). For Philo God is unswervingly stable and changeless. He is 'the Unchangeable', whereas creation is changeable. As he puts it in *Leg. All.* II.33, 'It is necessary, therefore, that every created thing should at times be changed. For this is a property of every created thing, just as it is an attribute of God to be unchangeable' (cf. *Deus Imm.* 22). He also, on several occasions, affirms that the man who draws near to God acquires a share in the divine stability (see, e.g., *Cher.* 19). There is, therefore, an opportunity for escape from the changeableness of created being. It comes through a study of philosophy in guilelessness and purity. From this, the chief object of which is God himself, comes a degree of freedom from the change which is characteristic of all around in the created order (see *Deus Imm.* 22).

He therefore who approaches God desires stability: since unchangeableness is the attribute of God (*Leg. All.* II.33) and he has none of the fickleness or instability of man, the wise man, who desires to escape from it all and seeks tranquillity (*Deus Imm.* 23), approaches God in order to come under the influence of the divine quiescence. But, says Philo, the man who forsakes God, as Cain did, becomes more deeply enmeshed in *the restless creation* and is, understandably, *tossed about*. The real lesson of the statement in Gen. 4: 16 about Cain's departure to Nod is, then, a warning about the loss of stability in life which forsaking God produces.

(24) *in the Curses*: Philo here supports his exegesis of Gen. 4: 16 by a reference to 'the Curses' (see Deut. 28: 15–68) in Deut. 28: 65, 66. The words of the verse quoted by Philo refer, according to his exegesis, to the *foolish man* and the life *contrary to right reason*, with no *calm and rest* and with no firm adherence to any particular principle in his life which is the consequence of his foolishness. That is what is meant by the words, addressed to the foolish, about, in the one case, there being no rest and standing for the soles of the feet, and, in the other, about the prospect of '*life . . . hanging before*

thine eyes'. The changelessness of God meant that for Philo the goal of religion was to escape from the restlessness and change of creation in quiet contemplation and calm.

'*thy life shall be hanging before thine eyes*': these words are quoted from Deut. 28: 66. In the original context the words refer to the fact that the man who forsakes God will be perpetually in doubt about his life. Philo is thinking of the motion of something that hangs suspended, say, from the branch of a tree. Such a suspended object is always in motion. The life of the man who has forsaken God is equally restless.

(25) *he judges matters differently at different times*: Philo is again describing the instability of the foolish man, by whom he means the man who does not take God seriously in his life. Such a man holds conflicting opinions. He becomes *great and small, enemy and friend*, and nearly every other pair of opposites in a moment of time. It was this that Moses had in mind in Deut. 28: 65, 66, the verses from the 'Curses' just quoted by Philo. The foolish, Cain-like man is dragged this way and that way by conflicting interests. Then the occurrence of the word *hanging* in the passage from the 'Curses' leads Philo's restless intellect – whatever may have been his spiritual state, his mind was for ever on the move – to yet another passage in the Old Testament from which he proceeds to quote.

(26) *we ought to hang upon God*: Philo introduces this statement by a reference to *another place* (actually Deut. 21: 23, though references to Scripture are usually without any precise indication of the book, chapter or verse) where *the lawgiver* has something to say which he considers relevant. What is said is a curse upon the criminal who is hanged upon a tree. Men who committed sins worthy of death were to be executed and then hung up on a tree, but the corpse was not to be left on the tree overnight. It was to be buried on the day of execution, since 'he that is hanged is accursed of God' (see Deut. 21: 22–3). This is the passage alluded to by Paul in Gal. 3: 13 (where Paul affirms that man has been redeemed from 'the curse of the law' by Christ's death upon the 'tree' of the Cross). Philo takes the words of Deut. 21: 23 as referring to the need for the thinking man *to hang upon God*, instead of being like the foolish man who *fastens himself to his body*. Philo's disparaging view of the body and a glimpse of his dualism between mind and body are present in his description of the body here as a *tree-like burden in us*. Philo elsewhere several times calls the body 'a dead thing' as he

does in *Leg. All.* III.69 (cf. *Migr. Abr.* 7; *Spec. Leg.* IV.188; *Quaest. in Gn.* IV.74, etc.). To live a life dominated by the body – and now Cain has become the symbol of such a life for Philo (cf. *Poster. C.* 38; *Det. Pot. Ins.* 119; *Conf. Ling.* 122) – is to abandon hope and to put *desire* in its place, *the greatest of evils for the supreme good.*

For hope . . . being an expectation of good things: Philo's definition of hope has some formal similarities with the definition of faith in Heb. 11: 1 (although the content of the ideas of faith and hope in Philo is quite different from the understanding of these two virtues in Hebrews). For Philo hope is *an expectation of good things*, and for that reason *causes the mind to depend upon God, who gives generously.* In contrast, *desire* (for pleasure) creates *irrational cravings* in man and focusses his attention on the body, *which nature has created to be a receptacle and realm of pleasures.* If that is so, it is not difficult to understand why Philo regarded the body as the tomb of the soul and why, for him, the man who desired to live a life of rational reflection needed to escape from the body, 'the polluted prison-house' (*Migr. Abr.* 9) and embark upon a life-long pilgrimage away from it and the senses.

(27) *Let these men, then, be hung on desire as from a halter*: the foolish man is condemned, in Philo's mind, to be hanged, suspended from desire in the way that a halter restrains a horse. The fool who denies God's existence is controlled and subjugated by desire. But Abraham, who is here introduced as representing wisdom, since he is one who *stands firm*, draws near to God *the stable One* (another Philonic phrase to describe God as unchanging and unwavering). Philo has in mind the words of Exod. 17: 6, 'I stand before thee there upon the rock in Horeb', spoken by God to Moses, through which the Old Testament teaches, according to Philo, that God is permanently immovable. Philo bases his description of God as 'the standing' or *stable One* (*ho hestōs theos*) upon the text of the Exod. 17: 6 (LXX). He reproduces the LXX *hestēka* of Exod. 17: 6 as 'stand' (cf. *Leg. All.* III.4; *Som.* II.221), though the English translations render the Hebrew as a future, 'I will stand'. Once again, Philo affirms that the stability of Abraham was due to his nearness to God, or, as he puts it, *only a truly unchanging soul is able to gain a means of access to the unchanging God, and the soul that is really of such a disposition does truly stand very close to the divine power.* Among many other things that he symbolises, Abraham symbolises law-abiding man and stability. In *Som.* II.219–23 Philo says 'that unchangeableness and steadiness belong

to God alone and to those who are the friends of God'. Having spoken of the unchangeableness of God, he goes on to say that some may share in God's immutability. Only God is absolutely immutable, but he can and does communicate to men, with other gifts, a share in this particular attribute. But those who receive such a gift must be men like Abraham. For Cain there is no participation in the divine immutability.

(28) *the extremely firm stability in which the virtuous man lives*: the phrase *virtuous man* is a common Philonic description of Abraham, used, for example in *Abr.* 85, since Abraham 'acquired piety, the most excellent of all possessions' (*Mut. Nom.* 76). That Abraham was truly steadfast is proved, Philo argues, by the oracle spoken by God to the all-wise Moses. God said to Moses: 'But as for thee, stand thou here by me' (Deut. 5: 31). These words are interpreted as meaning two things. They mean, first, that God is the unmoved Mover of all that moves, an Aristotelian way of describing the First Cause (see pp. 60–1), and, secondly, that *he makes the virtuous man a participant in his nature, which is rest.* The force of *him who stands* brings things and persons near to it to a stop. If Abraham is *the virtuous man*, Moses, we note, is the all-wise (cf. *Leg. All.* II.87, 93).

(29) *he commands another to stand with him*: in the case of Deut. 5: 31. Philo goes on, God commands someone else, Moses, to stand beside him, participating thereby in his immutability. In Gen. 46: 4, the passage which Philo refers to next, God states that he will accompany Jacob to Egypt and bring him back *at last*. Philo is struck by the fact that Scripture does not say *thou with me*, which would imply a journey to Egypt by God. The reason for this is that *calmness and stability are properties of God, but properties of creation are change of position and all movement which tends towards such change.*

(30) *the good peculiar to himself*: so God, when he invites a man to share his stability, does not speak of his moving towards the man, but invites the man to draw near to him. In the case of God there can be no movement followed by rest, for *he will not become immobile, for he is always in that state*. The good which belongs to him alone and which he alone therefore can bestow can be conferred on men without any movement on his part. However, when the thought is of creation, or a creature, the terminology used is appropriate, '*I will go down with thee*'. Expressing God's thought about himself in his own words Philo wrote: *so with me no one will go down – for with me there is no changing – but one will remain immobile, because repose pleases me.* Jas. 1: 17 also affirms that God is a

Being 'with whom can be no variation'. With men, however, to whom change is normal, when they go down God goes down, but he does so *without any change of locality, since I have filled the universe with myself.* The words *in all-pervading presence* render the Greek word *tonikōs*, the conjecture of one of the editors of the text of Philo. The verb from which the adverb comes means 'to extend oneself' and Philo, if the conjecture is correct, was thinking of God's self-extension into the whole universe. But care must be taken not to interpret *tonikōs* in too spatial a sense, even though Philo is using a word which has associations with the Stoic concept of 'tension', involving both expansion and condensation. Philo, seeking to express the idea of God's immovable omnipresence, uses Stoic terms, but with at least the intention of avoiding Stoic materialism.

without any change of locality: for Philo, there is no change of locality in the case of God, as it does not involve local movement, since God has already *filled the universe* with himself. Every theology which affirms the omnipresence of God and his immateriality is obliged to use spatial metaphors to speak of the former and thereby appear to contradict the latter.

(31) *a highway for all*: the action of God in going down, metaphorically speaking, with those who change their place, was prompted by *pity for the rational nature*. God desires to help reasoning beings to *be raised from the hell of the passions into the Olympian regions of virtue*. This he does as himself the guide along the road that leads to heaven, a phrase which suggests that God, for all his transcendence, is also 'a very present help' and that there is no sudden transformation of man, but rather steady progress. God himself has prepared the way that leads to heaven and made it *a highway for all suppliant souls* so that they may not tire as they pass along it. Here Philo pictures God as taking pity on the philosophical soul, the thoughtful believer, and guiding and helping it upwards. The idea of God as One who prepares for suppliants a highway that does not tire them is one of many in Philo's works which make it clear that for him God is a merciful Father.

(32) *each side of the picture*: what Philo has said so far involves a comparison of the calm state of the good man and the restlessness of the foolish. There is a sequel, to which Philo now turns. Moses, in Gen. 4: 16, says that the soul migrated to Naid (LXX), '*tumult*', which is opposite *Eden*. Naid or Nod, explained earlier as meaning *Tossing* (*salos*; see above, on para. 22), is symbolic for Philo of the

vice that creates *tumult* (*klonos*) in the soul of the foolish man (cf. *Cher.* 12; and see above, on paras. 1 and 22). It can also refer to *tumult*, the destination of Cain (here and above, para. 1).

In *Cher.* 12 Philo, also commenting on Gen. 4: 16, explains that Nod (Naid) is 'tossing' and that Eden is 'delight'; the former is 'a symbol of wickedness agitating the soul', the latter of 'virtue which creates for the soul a state of tranquillity and happiness'. In the present passage Philo says that Eden is a symbolic name for *right and divine* reason and so is literally rendered *luxury*. Right reason finds its pleasure in the enjoyment of *good things which are pure and uncontaminated . . . while God, generous source of all wealth, pours down his virgin and immortal blessings*. Evil, however, is by nature in conflict with the good. The meaning of Naid being opposite Eden is that there is perpetual conflict between unjust and just, wise and foolish, and all forms of virtue and all forms of vice. Cain, then, represents the man who, by departing from God, departs also from the life of right reason and pursues a life of vice.

Philo thus brings to an end this section of the *De Posteritate Caini*, though there are 150 more paragraphs devoted to the allegorical exposition of the scriptural statements about the offspring of Cain or the description of the Cain-like soul. It is interesting to note that, right at the end of the treatise, Philo observes that 'the origin of all wars' is the disorder within man himself, 'which is so formidable and unceasing'. Hence, for him, the importance of the lesson to be learned from the opening passages, that nearness to God in his stability confers at least relative stability on man. For Philo the war within the soul, the *tossing* and *tumult* chosen by Cain, is the most serious human conflict, for from souls disordered like Cain's, from those divided souls of whom Cain is the symbol, come all wars between nations. Surprisingly perhaps, Philo's allegorical exposition of the theme of 'The Posterity and Exile of Cain' arrives in the end at a conclusion that is as relevant to the present as to Philo's own day. Therefore, although Philo's chosen method of exegesis provides us with little help as to the meaning Gen. 4: 16 had for its original author, we may allow ourselves to be grateful that Philo found in the verse what he did – teaching which, in a profounder sense than he perhaps realised, is an important word about and for the descendants of Cain in their exile.

4. The ethical teaching of Philo

Inevitably within a religious philosophy taking the Old Testament as its basic text ethics plays an important part, and since the Old Testament was believed by Philo to be inspired by the one true God its ethics and those derived from it were believed to be superior to all others.

For one who was a subtle philosophical thinker and whose religion contained a profound and extensive element of mysticism – or at least possessed distinct mystical traits – Philo's attitude, because it was so thoroughly Jewish, was intensely practical and firmly incorporated the belief that its adherents must be actively involved in the life of mankind and society. As Philo himself asks, 'what use is the flute-player, however fine a performer he may be, if he remains quiet . . . or the harpist if he does not use his harp or in general any craftsman if he does not exercise his craft?' So 'motion . . . is the proper condition for the good . . . No knowledge is profitable to the possessors through the mere theory if it is not combined with practice' (*Congr.* 45–6). Philo, then, was not a religious thinker concerned only with theoretical matters. One of the most important means of acquiring the Good is 'through practice and not through teaching', for 'the practiser must be the imitator of a life'. Virtue may be achieved through teaching by the learner who 'listens to a voice and to words' (*ibid.* 69–70), but all true virtue is 'perfected through practice' (*ibid.* 35). Philo could write (*Cher.* 102) of the 'virtues and the good actions that follow them'.

The importance of the Jewish Law as the body of ethical material upon which Philo drew meant that he felt obliged to discuss the notions of law in the Greek philosophical system of his day. For him the Law of Moses was the only truly natural law, since it alone had been divinely revealed in a sense that he could accept. This conviction is related to his other conviction that the 'natural law', or the law 'in accordance with nature' sought by the Greek philosophers, could not possess the universality and eternity possessed by the Law of Moses, revealed by God, the sole Creator of nature. But Philo nevertheless made use of ideas he found in the writings of the philosophers, especially those of Aristotle and the Stoics. He distinguished between enacted laws, which need not remain unaltered, and the unalterable laws of nature, which are discovered when life is lived according to reason, contemplative reason. Philo also refers to enacted laws – unwritten in pre-Mosaic times – and the existence of obedience to Natural Law in pre-Mosaic times – in the lives of Enos, Enoch, Noah, Abraham, Isaac and Jacob. He even affirms that Noah acquired all the virtues ('Noah's perfection in virtues' (*Deus Imm.* 122; cf. *ibid.* 117)), 'the virtues of just Noah' (*ibid.*, 140, etc.). 'Noah', he says, 'became perfect, thereby shewing that he acquired not one virtue but all' (*Abr.* 34). He also states that Abraham, even before Moses, 'did all my Law' (Gen. 26: 5; *Migr. Abr.* 130). Philo even permits himself to say that Abraham obeyed the Law, or rather was 'himself a law and an unwritten statute' (*Abr.* 275–6). Abraham's attainment of perfect obedience to the Law is reflected, according to his change of name (*Mut. Nom.* 70ff.: 'Cease then to suppose that the Deity's gift was a change of name, instead of a betterment of character symbolised thereby'). These statements about the perfection of Noah and Abraham are related to the subject of the sinlessness of a select group of Old Testament characters which is to be discussed below.

But, to return to the question of the use of philosophical ideas about natural law which he found already in existence: Philo interpreted the Law of Nature as the incarnation within the natural order at the time of Creation of the pre-cosmic Logos. At Creation the incorporeal Logos was implanted in nature to act as its Law. Philo does not mean, therefore, when he writes about Abraham and other pre-Mosaic patriarchs, that they were following the unwritten statutes in the sense of following a natural impulse, but rather that they followed the Law, the Logos, implanted in nature as a whole. It was in that sense that they 'gladly accepted conformity with nature, holding that nature itself was, as indeed it is, the most venerable of statutes, and thus their whole life was one of happy obedience to law' (*Abr.* 5–6). This is how Philo takes a philosophical concept, natural law, and re-interprets and re-uses it, in the light of his reading of the Old Testament, in the service of his philosophical ethics.

It is only one of the ways in which Philo borrows from the Greek ethical systems of his day. He also borrows Aristotle's famous doctrine of the mean. Before Philo there were two main definitions of virtue: that of Aristotle and that of the Stoics. For Aristotle, a virtue is a mean between the two extremes of an excess or a deficiency. A man needs practical wisdom in order to judge what in any particular set of circumstances the true mean is, since it is not merely the arithmetical mean. Only the enlightened conscience of the prudent man sees that, with regard to the feeling of confidence, rashness is the excess and cowardice the deficiency, while courage is the mean, the virtue. Philo uses Exod. 20: 17 to support his use of the concept of the mean. He urges man to follow God 'with alert and unfailing steps', but also to keep on 'the straight course'. 'Let it [the mind] not incline', he says in commenting on the verse, 'either to what is on the right hand or to what is on the left', thus avoiding 'excesses and extravagances . . . shortcomings and deficiencies'. The best path for man is the 'central road', the road prepared by God for men of virtue (*Migr. Abr.* 146). In another passage he urges that 'deviations in either direction, whether of excess or of deficiency, whether they tend to strain or to laxity, are in fault, for in this matter the right is no less blameworthy than the left' (*Deus Imm.* 162). Moral advance is made along 'the midmost line'. Among numerous other examples that could be cited is the comment on Exod. 16: 4 (the manna passage): the Israelite is to gather 'what is adequate of itself and suitable, and neither more than sufficient so as to be excessive, nor on the other hand less so as to fall short' (*Leg. All.* III.165). With the application to his ethical teaching of Aristotle's doctrine of the mean one may compare the words of another Jewish writer, which describe 'the middle course' as 'the best course to pursue' (*Letter of Aristeas* 122: see Bartlett 1985: pp. 11ff.).

Philo and his fellow-philosophers. Philo frequently in his ethical teaching found himself compelled to disagree with his fellow-philosophers. In particular, he could not accept the Stoic view of emotions. The Stoic view was that virtue excludes emotion. The Stoic ideal for man is *apatheia* – absence of feeling or emotion. The early Stoic philosophers argued that all emotions – anger, pain, pity, etc. – are irrational and that the wise man should therefore attempt to excise them from his life. Unlike the Peripatetic, who believed in seeking after moderation, in attempting to achieve the mean between excess and deficiency, the Stoic tried to subdue and obliterate all feelings and emotions. This Philo could not accept, for to him some feelings and emotions were good and virtuous. Some emotions, mercy and compassion, are urged on men in numerous places in the Old Testament (e.g., Zech. 7: 9). Philo adopted the view put forward elsewhere by another Jewish writer: 'Moses governed his anger by his reason' (4 Macc. 2: 17; cf. 3: 3). The real need was for the good man to control and curb his emotions, not to annihilate them.

Philo also disagreed with the Stoics over their contention that all the emotions are equal. To Philo, since some laws are weightier than others and some lighter (to use rabbinic terms), some sins, involving emotions or feelings, are less grave. Piety and holiness are great virtues; piety, faith, holiness and justice are all in turn equally designated queen (or leader or chief) of the virtues. In the light of traditional Jewish teachings, Philo allied himself with the Peripatetics against the Stoics in regarding some emotions as virtuous and useful. He believed in the biblical virtue of 'righteous anger'. He even speaks, prompted by what an Old Testament narrative said (Exod. 32: 27), of 'the impulse of righteous anger' as 'accompanied by an inspiration from above and a God-sent possession' (*Fug.* 90). Elsewhere he speaks of appeasing the 'just wrath of the convicting wielder of the lash' by repenting of sins committed, yet he describes the recipient and requiter of man's repentance as gracious (*Som.* I.91). The man inspired with a zeal for virtue, he believed, is 'severe of temper and absolutely implacable against menstealers' (*Spec. Leg.* IV.14). Pity is a virtue he approves of, and also hatred of evil. In one place (*Spec. Leg.* I.55) he joins together 'hatred of evil and love of God' (cf. *Vit. Mos.* II.9, 'love of humanity, of justice, of goodness, and hatred of evil', qualities to which together Moses alone attained). The Stoic teacher Chrysippus rejected hatred of evil as inappropriate for the wise man (on the basis of Stoic arguments about the nature of evil, that no act is evil and reprehensible in itself and that a bad action may be performed with a sincerely good intention in a state of non-culpable ignorance). But for Philo hatred of evil was something Scripture taught men to feel.

The Stoics took the view that men are either good or bad, virtuous or vicious. Philo, conscious of the Jewish tradition that certain individuals, by the grace of God, are virtuous from birth, tended to accept that Stoic view that vice could be wholly annihilated – at least in the lives of a few special individuals who had received merciful assistance from God. Of Moses he says that, far from having to toil for virtue, he 'received it easily and without toil from the hands of God' (*Leg. All.* III.135). According to the *Leg. All.* III.140 Moses was 'the wise man in his perfection' (cf. *ibid.* 134: 'he being perfect'). He was 'Moses the most perfect of men' (*Ebr.* 94). He could even be given the title 'god' (*Vit. Mos.* I.158; *Som.* II.189). Elsewhere he is called divine and holy. In *Quaest. in Ex.* II.27 Moses is described as 'the most pure and god-loving mind' (cf. *ibid.* 29). Others who shared in this perfection of being included Melchizedek, 'the righteous king' whose life begins as that of 'a king peaceable and worthy of his own priesthood' (*Leg. All.* III.79). Of Isaac it is said that before his birth God determined that he should have 'a most excellent portion' (*ibid.* 85). Of Jacob Philo says, on the basis of Gen. 25: 23, that before his birth God had prepared his character and knew therefore that he would be 'of fine character and endowed with reason and better' and therefore 'princely and free' (*ibid.* 88–9). Noah also was perfect from birth (*ibid.* 77). His name, according to Philo, means 'rest' or 'righteous' and he could be said to be sinless even before he had performed a single deed because he was 'of an excellent nature from his birth' (*ibid.*). The reader of the New Testament should not fail to study carefully what Philo says about Noah's righteousness and indeed 'all things in the world and the world itself' as 'a free gift' of God (*ibid.* 78). What the righteous man discovers is what Noah discovered, that 'all things are a *grace* (*charin*) of God' (*ibid.*). So, for Philo, the goals of ethics can be reached by man, though only by the grace of God.

However, Philo worked out a compromise between Aristotelian and Stoic views, realising that those who achieved perfect virtue were only a privileged few. He stages a debate between Aaron and Moses, Aaron representing Aristotle and the view that emotions need to be controlled. In the case of the 'spirited element' in man, which may become unmanageable, he curbs and controls it by reason and other virtues. Moses, in the imaginary debate, represents the Stoic view that anger must be cut out completely, 'for no moderation of passion can satisfy him'. Moses is satisfied with nothing but 'complete absence of passion' (*apatheia* : *Leg. All.* III.128–9). Philo himself thinks that complete absence of passion is possible by the grace of God only for exceptional men. They receive 'a share of surpassing excellence, even the power to cut out the passions' (*ibid.* 131). For the majority of men who, like Aaron, progress gradually towards perfection, virtue consists in moderation of emotion (*metriopatheia*: *ibid.* 132). To this argument Philo adds the conclusion that an emotion controlled by reason becomes a virtue – *eupatheia* (a good feeling), a Stoic term used by Philo in his own way here and elsewhere. For the Stoics some emotions have the term applied to them since they are not emotions but equable states. They cannot be called virtues, as far as the Stoics are concerned, for virtue is *apatheia*. To the Stoics such states are somewhere between emotions and virtues; for Philo emotion ruled by reason so as to produce an equable state is a virtue, even though it is not *apatheia*. The way of God, which the virtuous may tread, is along a route which 'good feelings and virtue' can both walk (*Abr.* 204). Elsewhere Philo lists various virtues and then concludes with 'the other virtues and good emotions' (*Praem. Poen.* 160) (cf. *Migr. Abr.* 219; *Leg. All.* III.132). So *eupatheia* is closely linked to virtue. The Aristotelian virtue of *enkrateia*, self-control, is therefore part of virtue, in some cases. In particular, self-control is necessary to combat desire (*Decal.* 142); indeed, as we shall see later (pp. 260–2), the tenth commandment is a command to control desire. In one place, reflecting Aristotle's differentiation of virtue from emotion (the former involves choice, the latter is involuntary), Philo says that the Passover is celebrated 'when the soul studies to unlearn irrational passion and of its own free will experiences the higher form of passion which reason sanctions [*eulogon eupatheian*]' (*Rer. Div. Her.* 192).

So, for Philo, virtue does not mean the absence of emotion and feeling, but their moderate control, moderation. The majority of mankind is not sinless – and certainly not without feelings, good and bad – for 'absolutely not to sin is a property of God alone or perhaps of a divine man' (*Virt.* 177; see above, p. 117). Between the perfectly good man, however, and the wicked is the multitude which is neither perfectly good nor utterly bad. In *Leg. All.* I.93 Philo calls the inhabitant of this intermediate moral zone *ho mesos*. It is because most men are *mesos* that God addresses his commandments to them (*ibid.* 95). Those on the boundaries between the two moral extremities he elsewhere (*Som.* I.151–2) calls 'the practisers'. They live their lives on a kind of moral escalator, sometimes being taken up by the good and sometimes down by the bad. In the passage referring to the giving of the commandments to mankind Philo says: 'Quite naturally, then, does God give the commandments and exhortations before us to the earthly man who is neither bad nor good but midway between these' (*Leg. All.* I.95). Within Philo's ethical system, which is based upon the Pentateuch, with borrowings from Plato, Aristotle and the Stoics, the man who cannot achieve the highest virtues but only the middle ones is still able to receive God's reward (*Agric.* 121).

The Ten Commandments and other laws. Naturally the Ten Commandments are at the heart and centre of Philo's ethical thinking. The Law of Moses is the ideal, divinely inspired Law, the perfect natural law sought by the philosophers, and the Ten Commandments (to which a whole treatise of exposition is devoted) are the supreme catalogue of virtues. The commandments are classified in different ways. Philo speaks of positive and negative commands, commands and prohibitions, and divides the laws which relate to duties to God from those which relate to duties to one's fellow-men. This is an expression of the Jewish concept of the commandments as between man and God and man and man. Philo also includes the other laws in the Pentateuch as special, linked with the Ten Commandments (hence the title of one of his longer treatises – in four volumes – the *De Specialibus Legibus*). The Ten Commandments are the heads under which the special laws are grouped, the roots, sources or fountains to which the special laws are related. So Philo expounded the Ten Commandments in the *De Decalogo*, and then the associated laws in the *De Specialibus Legibus*.

For example, in the discussion of the special laws connected with the ninth commandment (*Spec. Leg.* IV.41–77), Philo interprets the words of Exod. 23: 3 in relation to the multitude of injunctions in Scripture to show pity and kindness, and argues that 'in no other action does man so much resemble God as in showing kindness', adding that there can be no greater good than to imitate God. He then proceeds to exhort the wealthy to make use of his stores of silver and gold 'for general use that he may soften the hard lot of the needy with the unction of his cheerfully given liberality (*ibid.* 73–4). The high are to help those of low estate and the strong the weak, and all who 'have drawn water from wisdom's wells' are to share their wisdom, especially with the gifted young, aiding their intellectual development. Philo concludes at this point: 'Such gems of varied beauty are interwoven in the laws, bidding us give wealth to the poor (it is only on the judgement seat that we are forbidden to show them compassion).' Not all the ethical teaching which Philo finds interwoven in the laws is of the order of that in the present passage – one which also seems to echo Ps. 112 (LXX Ps. 111), especially verses 3 and 9 – but there are many other 'gems of varied beauty' that he extracts from the Old Testament.

Since for Philo the Law of Moses is the ideal law, those who obey its commandments are exempt from passion and vice 'in a higher degree than those who are governed by other laws' (*Spec. Leg.* IV.55). The laws can therefore be classified in accordance with the virtues they help to implant in man, since all the virtues in man are implanted (a Platonic idea) by them. Following Plato, Philo divides the virtues into the earthly and the heavenly, the former being a copy or imitation of the latter. The heavenly virtues, or virtues of the soul, consist of virtues such as 'prudence, temperance and each of the others' (*Sobr.* 61), while the bodily virtues comprise 'health, efficiency of the senses, dexterity of limb and strength of muscle and such as are akin to these' (*ibid.*). In addition to virtues there are, of course, external advantages such as wealth, but these do not properly belong to a discussion of Philo's ethics, though in one place Philo calls the virtues and advantages in question 'three goods' (*Quaest. in Gn.* III.16). Elsewhere Philo divides the virtues into divine (of the soul) and human (bodily), or into the divine intellectual virtues and the human moral ones.

Categories of virtues. The basic distinction made by Philo, however, is between intellectual, moral and bodily virtues. He also makes an important distinction, following Aristotle, between virtue and action, stressing, with a variety of Aristotelian and Stoic expressions, the importance of the virtuous act, of right actions. Again following the Stoics and Aristotle, Philo distinguishes between contemplative virtues and practical virtues, intellectual virtues on the one hand and practical, moral ones on the other. Intellectual virtues have God as their object – they embrace right opinions and beliefs about him, his nature, his activity as Creator. Such a virtue is to believe that God exists; another is to believe that he exercises providential care over what he has created. The first four of the Ten Commandments were intended by Moses to teach the intellectual virtues. To possess all the intellectual virtues is, in Philo's view, to possess wisdom, which is knowledge of all the teachings contained in the Law (including revealed doctrines and ethical laws). Wisdom is also defined by Philo in terms of its four constituent virtues: piety, godliness, holiness and faith. Of these four virtues piety, wisdom in the service of God, is the queen (in *Decal.* 52 he calls piety the 'source' of virtue as God is the source of being), though elsewhere (*Leg. All.* I.70–1) Philo tries to show that 'prudence' (*phronēsis*) is 'first' among the four Cardinal Virtues. Philo was clearly influenced at many points by the Greek philosophers, but in what he says about wisdom he was probably influenced more than anything else by Prov. 1: 7.

In respect of what is for him one of the key virtues, faith, Philo differs from the philosophers, for to them faith was not a virtue. Influenced by Scripture, however, and especially by Gen. 15: 6, Philo regarded faith as an outstanding virtue for man to possess. He defines it in various ways, primarily as commitment to the belief that God is One and above all and that he provides for his world (*Virt.* 216). It is also defined by him as involving belief that there is one God, the God of Scripture, and no other (*Rer. Div. Her.* 92). When he is writing about faith in these and similar terms, she too is the queen of the virtues (like piety). Faith also, for Philo, involves belief in revealed truths (*Leg. All.* III.228) and, as in Gen. 15: 6, trust in God's promises (*Rer. Div. Her.* 100–1). 'It is not enough for the lover of wisdom to have high hopes and vast expectations through the oracular promises' (*ibid.* 100); that he will possess wisdom 'is a fact that he has completely and firmly grasped in virtue of the divine promises' (*ibid.* 101).

But basically faith is 'to put in God alone a trust which is pure and unalloyed' (*ibid.* 94) and 'to rest on the Existent only, firmly and without wavering' (*ibid.* 95). As such it is contrasted by Philo with trust in high office, fame and other external goods (*Abr.* 263). Philo frequently speaks of faith as trusting 'in God alone', something which is difficult because of our 'mortality', which attracts us to 'riches and repute and office and friends and health and strength, and many other things' (*Rer. Div. Her.* 92). In one of his most important statements about faith he says: 'Faith in God, then, is the one sure and infallible good, consolation of life, fulfilment of bright hopes, dearth of ills, harvest of goods, inacquaintance with misery, acquaintance with piety, heritage of happiness, all-round betterment of the soul which is firmly stayed on him who is the cause of all things and can do all things yet only wills the best' (*Abr.* 268). But there is not in the Philo passage anything closely approaching the definition of faith in Hebrews as that which is capable of giving substantial reality to things hitherto only hoped for and of constituting evidence of future events still unseen because they have not yet occurred. There is a parallel to the definition of faith in Heb. 11: 1 and 9 in the passage in which Philo is commenting on Gen. 15: 6 and suggests that what seems marvellous to most men is 'deemed no marvel at the judgement-bar of truth, but just an act of justice and nothing more' (*Rer. Div. Her.* 95). The similarity between the Philo passage and the one in Hebrews is the link between the description of the words of Gen. 15: 7 as 'a promise' (indeed 'the confirmation of an old promise') and the passage on Abraham in Heb. 11: 8–12, 17–22, with their reference to the relationship between faith and 'promise' (or the 'promises'). Other New Testament writers too speak about faith and promise in language similar to that of Philo and Hebrews. Unlike his Greek predecessors, then, Philo accorded to the attitude of faith, the attitude which trusts in God rather than in its own reasonings, the status of a lofty virtue. Similarly Paul in 1 Cor. 13: 13 gave love the distinction of being the 'greatest' of the virtues but nevertheless placed faith, with hope, close beside it.

Virtues to which Philo also gave a very important place are justice and humanity, two virtues which he often couples together (for example, in *Decal.* 164: see pp. 272, 275), as when he lists 'love of humanity', 'justice', along with 'goodness' and 'hatred of evil' (*Vit. Mos.* II.9). He can even affirm that these two virtues are the chief virtues in the sphere of man's relationships with his fellow-men. Philo's emphasis upon the importance of justice and humanity is linked with the point made earlier, that 'Moses does not allow any of those who use his sacred instruction to remain inactive at any season'. Justice and humanity are also the 'two main heads' of all the particular lessons and doctrines relating to the tasks of body and soul (*Spec. Leg.* II.63–4). When he concedes that men may find it too difficult for our nature's course to be directed 'amid the collected body of the many virtues' (*Mut. Nom.* 225), he suggests, as an alternative, that we should be contented, whenever it be granted, to 'consort with one of the specific virtues, with temperance, or courage, or justice or humanity' (*ibid.*). Even to bring to birth in the soul's womb one of these would be better than nothing.

Humanity, which for Philo meant giving help to those in need, was the virtue 'nearest in nature to piety, (*Virt.* 51: see pp. 219, 223). He says that Moses possessed humanity and fellow-feeling through a 'happy gift of natural goodness' (*ibid.* 80; see pp. 235, 241). The pious man, according to Philo's ethics, is the humane man.

Acknowledgement of the holiness of God and just dealings with one's fellow-man go hand in hand. Clustered around humanity are its fellow-virtues: concord, equality, grace and mercy. Likewise, Greek philanthropy (*philanthropia*) linked various virtues with justice, though humanity does not appear to be one of them (although in Latin philosophy *humanitas* does). Philo, however, ranks philanthropy as one of the leaders of the virtues, while justice is *the* leader. If, as Aristotle claimed, justice was the greatest of the virtues, and since Philo has coupled justice and humanity, this would explain the subsidiary leadership assigned to *philanthropia*. But the powerful influence exerted upon Philo by Jewish ethical tradition may be another, more important reason. Philo's elevation of *humanitas*, as well as the lofty place he gives to justice, is an expression of his fundamentally unchanged Jewishness. It has been pointed out that Philo takes *dikaiosunē* and *eleēmosunē* and treats them as variant descriptions of *philanthropia* (Deut. 6: 25, 24: 13; Isa. 1: 27; Dan. 4: 27 (=LXX 24)). *Tsedeqah* in Judaism came to be reckoned as of equality in weight to all other commandments (*Mishnah, Baba Bathra* 9a: see Maccoby 1988). Aristeas (131) says that *dikaiosunē* is one of the two principles which 'our lawgiver first of all [*prōton*] laid down', the other being 'piety' (*ibid.*).

Prayer. For Philo, as a devout Jew, one important virtue, not given any place by non-religious philosophers, is prayer. It is to one aspect of prayer, thanksgiving, that Philo draws attention when he states that 'each of the virtues is a holy matter, but thanksgiving is pre-eminently so' (*Plant.* 126). It is here that Philo observes that thanksgiving cannot be expressed by means of buildings and oblations and sacrifices, not even if the whole world were a temple. What must be used are the inaudible 'hymns of praise' of the mind. Philo also describes the mind that blesses God and is 'ceaselessly engaged in conning hymns of thanksgiving to him' as 'a rational and virtuous nature' (*ibid.* 135). Elsewhere he takes the word in Deut. 10: 20–1, 'He is thy praise' (LXX: 'He is thy boast'), to mean that of God alone is man to boast or be proud (*Spec. Leg.* 1.311), following this with the exhortation 'Let us follow after the good that is stable, unswerving, unchangeable and hold fast to our service [*hikesias*] as his suppliants and worshippers' (*ibid.* 312). Prayer and worship are for Philo important virtues because they involve the individual's attachment to the unchangeableness and immutability of God. In place of the material temple and its sacrifices, the house worthy of God must have its foundations laid in 'natural excellence and good teaching' and upon it should be reared 'virtues and noble actions' (*Cher.* 101). And, in teaching similar to that of Jesus in the Sermon on the Mount (Matt. 7: 17–18), Philo says that teaching and readiness to learn are 'like the roots of the tree that will bring forth good fruit'. Prayer is also for Philo superior to the virtuous act of sacrifice – though it does not necessarily replace it – since the genuine expression of gratitude is not possible with buildings, oblations and sacrifices (*Plant.* 126). Passages such as these perhaps reflect the teaching found in the Old Testament in passages such as Ps. 51: 15–19 and Mic. 6: 6–8.

Body and soul. Control of desire plays an important part in Philo's thinking about virtue. This aspect of his teaching needs to be seen in the context of his dualism, which amounts to a complete divorce at times between body and soul. Influenced by the Orphic views of Plato's *Phaedo*, Philo regarded the body as a severe hindrance to the soul in its striving for virtue, as dragging it down from its true functions and aspirations into the world of sense and passion. The body is for him at times thought of as the tomb of the soul (*Leg. All.* I.108; *Spec. Leg.* IV.188). He describes the soul as 'imprisoned in that dwelling-place of endless calamities – the body' (*Conf. Ling.* 177). In one passage he calls the body 'the grave of the soul' (*Quaest. in Gn.* IV.75). The soul, he says, is buried in the body 'as if in a grave' (*ibid.*). So he speaks of the need for man to escape from 'the foul prison-house' (*Migr. Abr.* 9). Philo has thus thoroughly absorbed and used the Orphic conception of the body as the tomb of the soul (*sōma–sēma*, literally 'body–grave'). He can even say that the body is 'wicked and a plotter against the soul, and is even a corpse and a dead thing' (*Leg. All.* III.69). Man walks about during his life 'always carrying a corpse' (*Quaest. in Gn.* IV.77). Yet, although Philo was aware of the adverse effects bodily life could have on a life of virtue, chiefly because of bodily passions, which are so powerful, and although he spoke time and time again about the need to despise the flesh and escape from the influence of the passions of the body and urged his readers to 'live with the soul rather than with the body' (*Abr.* 236), he had to accept that 'we consist of body and soul' (*Spec. Leg.* II.64) and that the life of virtue has to be achieved on earth within the human frame. For Philo men could not but be *in* the body, though to achieve virtue it was imperative that they should not be *of* it. His repeated exhortations to his readers to leave the body and its passions mean, he explains, 'Make thyself a stranger to them in judgement and purpose; let none of them cling to thee; rise superior to them all' (*Migr. Abr.* 7). It must not be forgotten, however, that Philo disagreed with the Stoic view that all (bodily) emotions are immoral and bad.

Philo made it clear in the ethical sections of his writings that one must not only act virtuously, but must also be in a state of virtue, a condition which involves subduing the body and the emotions. But he also stressed the importance of intention. Only a right intention makes an act virtuous (*Poster. C.* 10: see pp. 178, 184). To be virtuous an action, in its wholeness – from its inception in the mind to its consequences outside the person performing it – has to produce good fruit, good consequences, and also to be preceded by a good intention. The motive of an action determines its fundamental character. All virtue begins with hope – the beginning of good things is hope (*Abr.* 7). Human virtue is the product of hope; it is what men hope for. But, between hope and the final happiness the performance of a good action brings, there must be an intention on the part of man to live virtuously. Hope, good intention, good deed, happiness – that is the ethical sequence which Philo sketches.

The rewards for virtuous living lie, some of them, beyond this life, especially in the case of those who live righteously on earth but are subjected to suffering. There is, however, one reward that the virtuous man can receive here and now – the great reward of joy. The performance of the Law confers joy upon man as a present experience. 'After faith comes the reward set aside for the victorious champion who gained his virtue through nature and without a struggle. That reward is joy' (*Praem. Poen.* 31). Elsewhere Philo writes: 'there is no sweeter delight than that the soul should be charged through and through with justice, exercising itself in her eternal principles and doctrines and leaving no vacant place into which injustice can make its way' (*Spec. Leg.* IV.141). Philo speaks of the servant of God feeling more joy in that position than if he had been made king over all the world (*Rer. Div. Her.* 7).

There is also a rigorist note in Philo's teaching, but the stress, found also in the teaching of the rabbis, on the joy experienced by man in the performance of the commandments should not be overlooked. There are, however, numerous passages in Philo which are intensely rigorist. He states, for example, that the man who blames God for his sins should be punished by being deprived of access to 'the altar' (*Fug.* 80) and that 'the soul that has once been dismissed from hearth and home as irreconcilable, has been expelled for all eternity, and can never return to its ancient abode' (*Det. Pot. Ins.* 149). In *Leg. All.* III.213, he says: 'many souls have desired to repent and not been permitted by God to do so, but have gone away backward as though drawn by a change of current' (cf. *Cher.* 10).

The imitation of God. But at the same time there is within Philo's writings what can properly be called a Doctrine of Ethicisation by Grace, apart from Works. An important element in Philo's ethical teaching is the idea of the imitation of God. Philo states, at one point (*Migr. Abr.* 132), that the virtues of piety and faith 'adjust and unite the intent of the heart to the incorruptible Being: as Abraham when he believed is said to "come near to God" [Gen. 18: 23]'. But Philo goes further than this. He disagrees with both Aristotle and the Stoics about how virtue is acquired, insisting that it is by nature, practice and learning – and that all these come as a result of a divine dispensation. Philo sometimes uses the word 'works' in the bad sense it has in Paul's Romans and Galatians (or as in some Christian exegesis of those epistles), but there are a number of passages in which he insists that all three, nature, practice and learning, are necessary (*Som.* I.167; *Abr.* 53; *Praem. Poen.* 64–5). It is clear from these passages that by nature he means a divine dispensation, something brought about as a result of the free-will of God. So also practice or learning has a special meaning: it is the practice or learning of the laws of God. But it is important to notice that Philo states clearly, although it is with reference to Moses' utterances, that they are 'absolutely and entirely signs of the divine excellences, graciousness and beneficence, *by which he incites all men to noble conduct* [my italics], and particularly the nation of his worshippers, for whom he opens up the road which leads to happiness' (*Vit. Mos.* II.189). God is also described by Philo as 'the husband of Wisdom, dropping the seed of happiness for the race of mortals into good and virgin soil' (*Cher.* 49). He goes on to explain how God removes from human life 'degenerate and emasculate passions which unmanned it and plants instead the native growth of unpolluted virtues' (*ibid.* 50). Man can live with 'high hopes' of the descent of the divine potencies which will descend with laws and ordinances – but laws and ordinances accompanied by the divine power to live by them (*ibid.* 106). Philo contrasts haste to fulfil a promise to a fellow man and delay in fulfilling a promise to God, 'who lacks and needs nothing' (*Spec. Leg.* II.38). Man's good intention must precede a virtuous act, but there is no question of man's supplying God by it with something he needs. Rather, it is a case of God's grace supplying what man needs to perform the good deed. All this implies, of course, a choice on man's part, and Philo's ethical system embraces the idea of free-will. He accepts the traditional Jewish view that in man there are two impulses, an evil impulse and a good impulse (sometimes referring to the evil impulse as emotion or pleasure, though he states too that desire alone originates within ourselves and is voluntary). The tenth commandment is, according to Philo, a commandment to curb and control one's desire (*Decal.* 142: see pp. 260, 267), the corresponding virtue being *enkrateia* (an Aristotelian term meaning self-control). And according to Philo man is free either to control his desires and to subdue pleasure and emotion or to refuse to do so.

There are, however, exceptional individuals in the human race who do not need to exercise free-will in order to be virtuous, since they were virtuous from birth, though the majority of men are not sinless (see above, p. 116). Philo did not regard the divine sinlessness, however, as incommunicable to mortal men. A divine man could conceivably exist in whom God's sinlessness dwelt. All men may repent and receive God's mercy (*Virt.* 177: see p. 37), but a few, including Moses, have been made perfect, excising all passion (*Leg. All.* III.134: see above, pp. 116–17 However, the general rule is that 'sin is congenital to every created being, even the best, just because they are created' (*Vit. Mos.* II.147). Of special interest to students of what Philo says about the sinlessness of exceptional men is what is said about the sinlessness of Jesus in Hebrews in the New Testament (see especially Heb. 4: 15). Of similar value to students of Romans, in particular the argument in chapters 9–11 and the statement of 11: 26–9, is Philo's view that the special grace of the patriarchs was communicable to their descendants with the result that Israel would be saved despite the sins of most of its members. This view, that all Israel would be saved because of the 'merit of the Fathers', is based in part upon Deut. 10: 15 (cf. 4: 37 and 7: 6–8). Philo's interpretation of the doctrine (related by him to Exod. 12: 23) is offered in the words of

Leg. All. II.33–4, where the language he uses suggests that, while God lets evil ('destruction') into the life of Israel, he will not allow the total destruction of 'the seeing Israel', but will 'force him to rise and emerge as though from deep water and recover'. Philo, of course, took the view that all sinners may repent and 'desert, without looking back, to the ranks of virtue and abandon vice, that wicked mistress' (*Virt.* 181: see pp. 249, 254). But more will be said about repentance, another instance of Philo's disagreeing with the Greek philosophers, in the commentary which follows (see below pp. 248–55).

The problem of the period before Moses. One special subject with which Philo had to deal, in view of his belief that the Law of Moses was the supreme embodiment on earth of ethical truth, was that of the situation of mankind before Moses. The problem was solved by Philo by reference to the Logos. The pre-Creation Logos became at Creation the Law of Nature. When the material universe had no definite character God moulded it into definiteness and saw that it was perfect. He 'stamped the entire universe with his image and an ideal form, even his own Word' (*Som.* II.45). The pre-Mosaic patriarchs are said by Philo to have obeyed not the Law of Moses, since it did not exist, but the Law of Nature: that is, the Logos embodied in nature but not yet uttered in the Law of Moses. With reference to Abraham, Philo quotes Gen. 26: 5 and adds: 'He did them [the commandments], not taught by written words, but unwritten nature gave him the zeal to follow where wholesome and untainted impulse led him' (*Abr.* 275). Of Enos, Enoch and Noah he states that they followed 'the unwritten law' (*ibid.* 5). Such men 'gladly accepted conformity with nature, holding that nature itself was, as indeed it is, the most venerable of statutes, and thus their whole life was one of happy obedience to law' (*ibid.* 6; cf. *ibid.* 16). The identification of the Law of Nature with the Logos in nature is clearly expressed by Philo in the words 'So in another place he says, "Abraham did all my Law" [Gen. 26: 5]: "Law" being evidently nothing else than the divine Word enjoining what we ought to do and forbidding what we should not do' (*Migr. Abr.* 130). The Law of Moses, later to be promulgated, is 'the divine Word'. Then, in accordance with Jewish tradition, Philo singles out Noah for special mention as the man, before Moses, who came nearest to knowing and obeying the whole of the Law later embodied in the Ten Commandments. Hence the description within Judaism of the Noachian or Noachic laws, the laws later revealed in words which Noah discovered in nature. Of Noah Philo could even say that he 'became "perfect"' (*Abr.* 34). According to one passage (*Deus Imm.* 74), Noah found grace with God (Gen. 6: 8) 'so that he might mingle his saving mercy with the judgement pronounced on sinners'. He is later described as 'just', 'perfect', and 'well pleasing to God' (*ibid.* 118). Much else is said about Noah, but the passages referred to show that the Law (of Moses) could be obeyed and obeyed perfectly even before Moses had delivered it in its well-known form.

The Cardinal Virtues. Philo's ethical system also included his own personal version of the list of Cardinal Virtues. By the time of Philo these virtues as listed by philosophical writers embraced prudence, courage, justice and temperance. Philo indicates the difference between his own view of the Cardinal Virtues and that of the philosophers by asking, with reference to the Jewish places of prayer throughout the cities, what are they but 'schools of prudence and courage and temperance and justice, and also of piety, holiness and every virtue by which duties to God and men are discerned and rightly performed?' (*Vit. Mos.* II.216). In his list here Philo includes four of the intellectual virtues and two of the moral virtues. This arises from the fact that Philo considered that there were two sets of Cardinal Virtues. Those of the intellectual type, all of which are included under wisdom – piety, godliness, holiness and faith – are all virtues of man in relation to God. There are also Cardinal Virtues of the moral type – prudence, courage, temperance and justice (see also *Leg. All.* II.18). Unlike Plato and Aristotle, who thought that the State had a duty to teach both the intellectual and the moral virtues, Philo believed that the intellectual virtues are produced in us by teaching, whereas the moral virtues are acquired by habit only after they have been put into practice in our daily lives.

Philo attempts to add to the list of virtues by claiming that the study and teaching of the Law are virtuous acts. The teacher of the good laws of virtue 'must be placed on record as a perfect man' (*Spec. Leg.* IV.140). The result of the teacher's efforts is that learners everywhere and at all times are 'gladdened by visions of the just. For there is no sweeter delight than that the soul should be charged through and through with justice, exercising itself in her eternal principles and doctrines and leaving no vacant place into which injustice can make its way' (*ibid.* 141). So ethical teaching and the study of ethics, especially as they concern justice, are themselves virtues. Philo works with the assumption that there are those who love the body and the passions and so are deprived of the capacity to receive the divine message and are debarred 'from the holy congregation [Deut. 23: 1] in which the talk and study is always virtue' (*Deus Imm.* 111).

However, Philo is quite clear in his own mind that the commandments must never remain merely on our lips, since then we do not really accept them. We must add to lip-service 'deeds shown in the whole conduct of our lives' (*Praem. Poen.* 82). The divine ordinances are to be kept in obedience and God's precepts accepted – not merely heard, but carried out in life and conduct (*ibid.* 79). Philo states categorically that men must get some exercise and practice in the business of life and by the practice of virtue progress towards the good life, for 'the practical comes before the contemplative life' (*Fug.* 36). In *Quaest. in Gn.* IV.47 Philo states: 'There are three ways of life which are well known: the contemplative, the active, and the pleasurable. Great and excellent is the contemplative; slight and unbeautiful is the pleasurable; small and not small is the middle one, which touches on, and adheres to, both of them. It is small by reason of the fact that it is a close neighbour to pleasure; but it is great because of its nearness and also its kinship to contemplation.' Philo undoubtedly approved of – and engaged in – contemplation (*Abr.* 22–3; *Spec. Leg.* II.44–5, etc.); but his ineradicable Jewishness also means that in his ethical teaching there is a powerful emphasis on the practical aspects of religion and morality – the practice of religion and the practice of morality in life. The sacred Passover meant for him the passage from the life of passions to the practice of virtue with one's loins girded for the life of service. In *Leg. All.* III.165 he refers to the need 'when making it thy study to cross over from the passions . . . to take the forward step'. And an important part of the practice of virtue, for Philo, is the literal observance of the laws of the Sabbath, those relating to festivals, the Temple services, circumcision – even though all of these laws can be interpreted allegorically. Provided it is in accordance with the Law, the active life is to be as much praised as the contemplative life. The two belong together, and the one, the contemplative, must issue in the other, action. According to *Leg. All.* I.58, 'virtue involves theory and practice' and is 'of surpassing excellence in each respect; for indeed the theory of virtue is perfect in beauty, and the practice and exercise of it a prize to be striven for'. Elsewhere he writes: 'happiness results from the practice of perfect excellence' (*Agric.* 157). Philo borrowed much from the philosophers he studied, but his diligent perusal of the Jewish Scriptures meant that he could never forget that the Good is something to be practised as well as contemplated.

CONCERNING HUMANITY (*Virt.* 51–101 (IX–XIX))

In this treatise Philo deals with four major virtues: courage or manliness, humanity, repentance and nobility. In the first section he argues that true courage consists in knowledge, especially in the knowledge of those who exercise their minds for the benefit of others. Courage does, however, also embrace bravery in war, a bravery which brings success when it is due to the support of God and obedience to the Law.

The second section deals with *philanthropia* (humanity). It is followed by sections on repentance and nobility. Here we shall examine part of the section 'On Humanity' and subsequently the short section 'On Repentance' (see below, pp. 248–55). These serve as samples of Philo's teaching in what, because of its title, is his most obviously ethical treatise.

Humanity shown in Moses' choice of a successor (*Virt.* 51–65)

(51) Humanity, the next virtue to be considered, is nearest in nature to piety, being its sister and twin. The prophetic lawgiver who loved her as I have known no other man do – for he knew that she was a highway leading to holiness – used to train and instruct all the people who were his subjects in fellowship, presenting to them, like a designer's
(52) model, his own life as a fine and beautiful example. Now, the deeds which he performed from his early life until his old age for the care and protection of each and every man have been described in the two preceding works which I have devoted to the life of Moses. But there are two things which occurred at the end of his life which are worthy of mention as proofs of the continual and unbroken virtue

which, unmixed, he impressed as a final seal, clear and distinct, upon his soul, which had been shaped by the divine
(53) Image. For when the appointed limit of his human existence was on the point of being reached, and he knew by unmistakable hints that he must depart from this world to the next, he did not imitate other people, either kings or commoners, whose one eager ambition and prayer is to leave behind them sons as heirs; on the contrary, although he was the father of two sons, he did not bequeath the leadership of the nation to either, nor did he allow himself to be influenced by his family feelings and his affection for those near to him, though even if he had some suspicion of the worth of his own children, he had nephews of sound moral calibre who held the highest priestly office as a
(54) reward for their virtue. Perhaps, however, he decided that it would not be a good thing to withdraw them from the service of God or, as is very likely, considered that it would be impossible for the same persons to undertake successfully both offices, the priesthood and the kingship, the one professing devotion to the service of God, the other devoted to watching over men. Equally, perhaps, he did not think it a good idea to set himself up as the arbiter of such a great issue, and it is a very important matter to assess the person best fitted by nature for a position of ruling power, a role which almost requires the divine power which alone can
(55) with ease see the character of a man. Here is the clearest proof I can give of this statement. He had a friend whom he had known well almost from infancy, called Joshua. This friendship had been forged in none of the usual ways which in the case of others result in friendship, but by the impulse of a heavenly love, pure and authentically divine, from which all virtue is habitually derived. This Joshua lived with him under the same roof except when Moses had to observe solitude on occasions when he was under God's influence and receiving the divine oracles. He assisted Moses

in all his other duties, always in a different way from the multitude; he was almost his second-in-command and
(56) participated in the exercise of his leadership. But although Moses had over a long period put his fine goodness into word and deed, and – the most essential thing – his goodwill towards the people, it did not seem to him to be fitting to leave the succession even to him. He was afraid he might be deceived into thinking him a good man when in truth he was not, since the criteria of human judgement are by
(57) nature uncertain and unstable. And therefore he did not put his trust in his own judgement but implored and earnestly entreated God, who surveys the invisible soul and to whom alone it is given to be able to scrutinise thoroughly the human mind, to designate on the basis of his merits the man most capable of taking over the leadership, who would look after his subjects like a father. And, stretching up to heaven his pure and, if one may speak metaphorically, his virgin
(58) hands, he said, 'Let the God of spirits and all flesh look to find a man to set over the multitude to guard and protect it, a shepherd who shall lead it blamelessly that the nation may not decay like a flock scattered about without one to guide
(59) it.' And yet who would not have been struck with astonishment if they had heard such a prayer? 'What are you saying, Master?', he would ask. 'Have you not legitimate sons, have you not nephews? Leave the leadership most of all to your sons first, for they are natural heirs, but if you
(60) reject them as unworthy, at least to your brother's sons. But if you judge them also to be unsuitable and put the interests of the people at large before those of your nearest and dearest relations, you have at least a blameless friend who has given to you proof of perfect virtue – to you, the all-wise. Why, if choice is not to rest on birth but on moral quality, do you not acknowledge him as capable of
(61) receiving the power?.' But he will reply, 'It is right to take God as our judge in all things, especially in very important

issues, where a choice of good or ill brings happiness or, on the contrary, misery, for millions. Nothing is more important than the leadership of the nation, to which belong all the affairs of cities and countries both in war and peace. For, just as it is necessary for sound navigation to have a pilot of good judgement and knowledge, in the same way a governor of all-round wisdom is needed to obtain for
(62) his subjects in every place good government. Now wisdom is older not only than my generation but even the whole world, and it is not right that anyone should judge her except God himself and those who love her with a love that
(63) is sincere, pure and genuine. I have learned from my personal experience not to select anyone else and approve him for the office of government even from among those who seem to be suitable candidates. Indeed I did not of my own free-will choose the task of exercising care and presiding over the public affairs of the nation, nor did I receive my appointment from the hand of any human being, but it was God himself who revealed his will to me by clear oracles and distinct commandments and ordered me to assume the role of ruler; but at first I hesitated, pleading and praying, for I realised the greatness of the task, until, after he had issued his command many times, I finally
(64) obeyed him fearfully. How, then, could it be anything but absurd for me not to follow in the same steps, and, having had God's approval when I was about to assume the position of ruler, again give to God the election of a successor, without the intervention of human judgement, which has a closer affinity with appearances than with truth, especially as it was a case of the person being appointed to assume the presidency not over any ordinary nation, but one which is the most populous among all nations everywhere, one that has made the greatest profession of faith, the worship of him who truly exists and is Creator and Father

(65) of all? For whatever benefits are derived by its students from the most approved philosophy's teaching, the Jews gain from their ancient customs and laws the knowledge of the highest and most ancient Cause of all things, and have rejected all the errors about created gods. For no created being is in truth God, but only in man's opinion, lacking that most essential of divine attributes, eternity.'

(51) *the virtue . . . nearest in nature to piety*: this indicates how highly Philo placed humanity in his hierarchy of virtues, since piety is described by him as a 'queen' among the virtues (*Spec. Leg.* IV.147; *Praem. Poen.* 53, etc.). Later in the present treatise (para. 95) piety and humanity are both called the 'chief virtues'. Humanity is also said to be the *sister and twin* of piety. Philo's meaning is indicated by he quotation (*Decal.* 52, where it is implied that piety is the *archē* (beginning) of the virtues) of Prov. 1: 7, where, in the Septuagint, *eusebeia eis theon* (piety towards God) is said to be the *beginning* of discernment. Humanity itself is perhaps best defined by Philo as generous and brotherly treatment of others, Jews, strangers, and non-Jews alike, and as giving help to those in need. In relationships with slaves, for example, it must be remembered that a man may be a slave, but is a hired person, himself too a man, ultimately a kinsman. So he is to be given food and clothing and his other needs taken care of.

Philo claims that Moses *loved* humanity perhaps more than anyone else. The reader of the New Testament will recall the way in which, by Jesus, love of God and love of man were linked (e.g., Mark 12: 28–31). The linking of the two commandments, to love God and to love one's neighbour, goes back, of course, to the Old Testament (Lev. 19: 18, followed by 'I am the Lord'; cf. Deut. 6: 4; Exod. 20: 1ff.). In the case of Paul, a sequence of theological indicatives, statements of what God has done, is followed, both in Romans and Galatians, by exhortations to love (and to pursue other virtues). The relevant sections of the two epistles are Rom. 12–15 and Gal. 5–6.

a highway leading to holiness: because humanity constituted such an upward-leading high road Moses, we are told, used to incite and train all his subjects to embrace *fellowship* (*koinōnia*). Humanity, then, involves fellowship, the partnership of man with man and the sharing of one's possessions with those in need. This, according to Philo, is the *highway leading to holiness*. In the case of Abraham, both *eusebes* and *philanthrōpos*, piety was combined with kindness (*Abr.* 208).

fine and beautiful example: Philo also offers to his readers a model of the virtue he is describing – Moses. Moses' own life, as Philo presents it, is a kind of archetypal model of what true humanity consists of, not surprisingly since he was 'the greatest and most perfect man' (*Vit. Mos.* I.1; cf. I.27).

As well as associating humanity with piety, Philo also associates it with other virtues: in *Spec. Leg.* I.295 with fellowship, concord and equality, in *Vit. Mos.* II.242 with grace (or charity), and in *Som.* I.147 with mercy. In other words, humanity, as Philo understood it, embraces a number of connected virtues, all of which involve human relationships. If piety is the great Godward virtue, humanity is the great manward virtue.

(52) *the life of Moses*: here Philo refers his readers for proof of Moses' humanity to the two volumes of the *De Vita Mosis*. In fact not all the actions of Moses described do testify to Moses' humanity, though in general terms, supplemented by particular incidents, they do present him as a perfect, divine man, especially as his death approached (*Vit. Mos.* II.290–2). Earlier (*ibid.* 163) Philo had spoken of Moses' dilemma, as he heard on Sinai the sounds of the people carousing by the golden calf, 'between God's love for him and his own friendship for mankind' (*philanthrōpos*). One of Moses' laws, he says, is full of kindness and humanity (Deut. 15: 12–18). Philo can also refer to Moses' kindness (*philanthrōpia*), shown, for example, when he proclaimed a sabbatical year for the land (see paras. 97–8 of the present treatise). There are other references to Moses' *philanthrōpia* in later sections of the *De Virtutibus* – as we shall see.

at the end of his life: Philo has remembered one or two achievements of Moses which he feels deserve mention since they prove *the continual and unbroken virtue which, unmixed, he impressed as a final seal*. They were impressed clearly and distinctly on his soul, a soul which *had been shaped by the divine Image*. Such was Moses' self-control, according to Philo, that men who saw him wondered 'what kind of mind it was which dwelt in his body like an image in its shrine, whether it was a human mind or a divine intellect or something combined of the two . . . he had nothing resembling the majority but had gone beyond them all and was exalted to a sublimer height' (*Vit. Mos.* I.27). Even Moses' murder of the cruel Egyptian slavemaster is reckoned to be a 'pious action' since 'it was a pious action to destroy one who only lived for the destruction of others' (*ibid.* 44). At the time of his approaching death God 'changed his twofold nature of soul and body into the nature of a single body, transforming his whole being into mind, pure like the sun' (*ibid.* II.288). He also received the divine spirit and prophesied his own death and how he was to be buried, and Philo notes that the whole nation mourned his death for a month in memory of 'his unspeakable benevolence' and 'wisdom' in his care for each individual and for the whole nation (*ibid.* 291).

(53) *he did not imitate other people, either kings or commoners*: Philo here records the fact that Moses did not, as others do, bequeath the powers he had held to either of his two sons. The normal favouritism shown in such circumstances to members of one's own family was not shown by Moses, either to his sons or to his eligible nephews *who held the highest priestly office as a reward for their virtue.*

(54) *the arbiter of such a great issue*: Philo states that Moses did not feel that it was right to choose his own successor, either by withdrawing one from the priesthood or by asking one man to exercise both priesthood and sovereignty, nor did he think that he was the right judge of so important an issue, that of selecting the person best fitted for leadership. This is both evidence of Moses' humanity and a description which Philo felt was a necessary supplement to his *De Vita Mosis* volumes.

the divine power which alone can . . . see the character: Philo gives us a glimpse of his conception of God as omniscient (cf. 1 Sam. 16: 7). 'Could you, a man, or any other created thing hide yourself from God?' (*Det. Pot. Ins.* 153). God 'sees all things with an eye that never sleeps' (*Mut. Nom.* 40). It is a further sign of Moses' humanity, therefore, that he did not presume to judge as God does. On Philo's doctrine of God, see above, pp. 28–102.

(55) *pure and authentically divine*: these words describe the character of Moses' friendship with Joshua, a friendship not forged as other human friendships are. The friendship between Moses and Joshua was to Philo the *clearest proof* he could offer of the statement just made in the previous paragraph about Moses' modest unwillingness to be the one to decide who should be his successor. Joshua was at Moses' side all the time, except when Moses was *under God's influence and receiving the divine oracles*, and he stood by Moses as his lieutenant and co-governor.

(56) *He was afraid he might be deceived*: Moses was well aware of the excellence of Joshua in *word and deed* and of his loyalty to the nation. Yet he did not think he should leave the succession to him, since he was afraid that he might have misjudged him, thinking him a good man when he was not really so. Such misjudgements are easy to make *since the criteria of human judgement are by nature uncertain and unstable*.

(57) *did not put his trust in his own judgement*: the reluctance of Moses to trust in his own judgement is further evidence of his *humanitas*. Instead, in order to be sure that the nation received the best possible leader to succeed him, he sought God's guidance. Only God, he knew, can *scrutinise thoroughly the human mind*. Man, he was sure, can 'never escape the notice of him who looks into the recesses of the mind and walks in its most secret places' (*Deus Imm.* 9). Moses therefore prayed to God, stretching up his pure and, as it were, *virgin hands*, uttering the words, as recorded in Scripture, of Num. 27: 16–17.

(58) *a man to set over the multitude*: Philo's prayer, which draws upon the form of words found in the Septuagint, but which also paraphrases them somewhat, is for a man who will guard and protect the nation, *a shepherd who shall lead it blamelessly that the nation may not decay like a flock scattered about without one to guide it*. Here again is evidence, as Philo saw it, of Moses' humanity, his desire to secure a faultless leader to watch over the people.

(59–60) *for they are natural heirs*: Philo comments that anyone hearing Moses' prayer would have advised him to choose either one of his sons or one of his nephews as his successor, and Moses' failure to do so, far from impressing them with his humanity, would have astonished them, since sons and nephews take precedence over all others in the matter of succession. And even if he should reject his sons and nephews he had, among *the people at large*, his intimate friend, Joshua, whose unspotted virtue had been amply demonstrated to Moses' unerring wisdom. It might seem logical to make the choice of a successor on the basis of *moral quality*, which Joshua certainly possessed, if it was not to be made on the basis of relationship and descent.

(61) *It is right to take God as our judge*: it is because Moses, *in very important issues*, wanted to rely on God as arbiter that he chose neither his sons nor Joshua. The government of the people involves responsibility for their happiness, but can cause great misery to multitudes, and, in one sense, there is no matter greater

than sovereignty. A ship needs a good navigator, a state needs a leader of all-round wisdom in order to secure good order and a happy life for the people.

(62) *Now wisdom is older*: here Philo alludes to Prov. 8: 22–30: 'The Lord possessed me in the beginning of his way, before his works of old. I was set up from everlasting, from the beginning, or ever the earth was' (Prov. 8: 22–3, RV). Part of this speech of Wisdom personified is also quoted in *Ebr.* 31. The last verse of the section in Proverbs reads: 'Then I was by him, as a master workman; and I was daily his delight, rejoicing always before him' (Prov. 8: 30, RV). This (and indeed the whole passage) describes the cosmological role of wisdom, but in so doing also emphasises the fact that wisdom was for Philo a pre-existent, divine Being whom only God was capable of exercising, together with those whose love for her was *sincere, pure and genuine*.

On Wisdom in Jewish writings, see Job 28; Ecclus. 24; Baruch 3: 9–4: 4; Wisd. Sol. 8: 4–6; Prov. 3: 19, etc. In the New Testament, see Col. 1: 16, where Wisdom's creative role is assigned to Christ (cf. Heb. 1: 2–3, where a word *apaugasma* (reflection), used in Wisd. Sol. 7: 26 to describe Wisdom, is applied to the Son).

(63) *from my personal experience*: we are given here a brief comment by Philo on Moses' call. Philo informs us that, since Moses did not choose himself for his office and was not chosen by any other human being, he should not choose another for his work. The clear implication is that the work he refers to – to superintend and preside over public affairs – is work Philo was also engaged in (cf. *Flacc.* and *Leg. Gaj.*). Moses' work as leader of the nation was God-given (indicated by *clear oracles and distinct commandments*: see, e.g., Exod. 3: 1ff.). Reluctantly holding back, *pleading and praying*, Moses finally yielded to God's repeated command, though trembling with nervousness (Exod. 3: 6). In the biblical narrative, while nervousness is displayed, Moses does not seem to have been reluctant to undertake the task of national leadership.

(64) *again give to God*: Moses defended his decision not to choose his successor by saying that, with the example of his own experience before him, and having been approved by God himself, he should allow only God to do the choosing of his successor *without the intervention of human judgement*, since the latter *has a closer affinity with appearances than with truth*. Human judgement can discern what *appears* to be right but does not necessarily arrive at

the truth. Only to God, and to him alone, is it granted always to make a judgement that is sound and true.

A special reason Moses gives for leaving the choice of a leader to God is that Israel is not *any ordinary nation*, but *the most populous among all the nations everywhere* (a description not supported by the actual statistics). However, the great thing about Israel is that it ranks as the greatest of all nations since it is the *one that made the greatest profession of faith, the worship of him who truly exists*. It is in that, and not in its numerical size, that Israel's greatness really consists. Belief in God as Creator and belief that he is one are the central and most important beliefs of Israel. And its adherence to these beliefs is what made it so important for Moses to make the right decision – a decision characterised by humanity – about the choice of the person who was to succeed him.

(65) *their ancient customs and laws*: Philo compares what Jews gain from the customs of their nation, such as Temple worship and circumcision, and the laws and commandments enshrined in their Scriptures, with the benefits derived by its disciples from the teaching of *the most approved philosophy*. Philo is here almost certainly thinking of Platonism and Platonists. He may, however, have had in mind as well those Greek philosophers in general of whose teaching he approved, especially the Stoics, who defined their philosophy as the practice of wisdom (see above, pp. 203ff.).

What the Jews gain from their religion is the knowledge that God alone is uncreated (see *Leg. All.* II.1–3; *Op. Mund.* 23, where he refers to its teaching that from eternity God was alone and unaccompanied) and is the highest, most ancient Cause of all things, and that belief in created gods is a delusion. Only in men's fancies, Moses is made to say, are created gods real. Their unreality is shown, however, by their total lack of the divine attribute *eternity*.

Humanity shown in the installation of his successor and Moses' preparation for death (*Virt.* 66–79)

(66) This, then, is the first and most conspicuous proof of his great humanity and affection towards his whole race, but there is another which is not inferior to it. For when Joshua, who ranked as his most excellent pupil, who imitated his

moral qualities with the love worthy of them, had been approved of as the ruler of the people by the judgement of God, far from being depressed as others might have been at
(67) the fact that his own sons had not been chosen, he was in fact filled with unrestrained joy because there had been secured for the Hebrew people a ruler perfect in every respect (for he knew that the man chosen by God must be a man of noble virtue). Therefore he took Joshua by the right hand and brought him before the assembled multitude. He was unafraid of his own approaching death, but had rather added other new joys to his former ones, for he not only had the memory of his previous happiness, contributed to by a life containing every kind of virtue which had filled his life with delight, but also the hope that he was about to become immortal, as he exchanged the corruptible life for the incorruptible. So, with a visage made radiant by the joy of
(68) his soul, he spoke with cheerful exultation: 'For me the moment has already arrived to depart from the life of the body, but this man is a successor chosen by God to take care of you.' He then proceeded to repeat the words of the oracles which he had received as proof of God's appoint-
(69) ment of his successor, which were accepted. Then, looking towards Joshua, he urged him to prove himself a virtuous man and to pursue firmly wise policies, to inaugurate good plans of action, and to accomplish all his purposes with unyielding and vigorous determination. For though the one to whom he addressed these exhortations did not need them, Moses could not conceal the mutual affection they had for each other and for the people as a whole, by which he was, as it were, spurred on to lay bare what he thought
(70) would be advantageous. Also a divine command had been received by him telling him to encourage his successor to undertake charge of the nation with great courage and not to be apprehensive about the burden of leadership, so that all future leaders would find a standard and a law to guide

them by looking to Moses as their model and archetype, and none of them would be unwilling to give good advice to their successors, but they would all train and anoint their souls for exercise and discipline them in counsels and pieces
(71) of advice. For the exhortations of the good man are capable of lifting up the spirits of the dejected and raising them to the heights, establishing them above circumstances and events, and implanting in them a manner of thinking which
(72) is noble and resolute. Accordingly, when he had set out the duties of his subjects and of the heir to his authority, he went on to hymn the praises of God in a canticle, in which he rendered the last thanksgiving of his bodily life for the extraordinary and unprecedented graces he had been
(73) blessed with from his birth to his old age. He gathered together in a divine assembly the elements of the universe and the parts which are adapted for holding everything together, both earth and heaven, one of which is the dwelling-place of mortals, the other the home of the immortals. In the midst of all these he sang his canticles with all the kinds of harmony and symphony possible, in order that both men and ministering angels might lend an ear;
(74) men, as disciples, to learn to display thankfulness in a similar way, but the angels, vigilant observers of them, and from their own skill in music able to detect if a hymn was out of tune, and also as in some doubt as to whether any man thus imprisoned in a corruptible body could, like the sun and the moon and the holy choir of the rest of the stars, attune his soul to the divine instrument, the heaven and the entire
(75) universe. Thus, in his position among beings who form the choir of heaven, the great Revealer mingled with his grateful hymns of gratitude towards God his own genuine feelings of affection and good-will towards the nation, in which there were also reproofs for their past sins, warnings and invitations to wisdom for the present time, and

exhortations for the future couched in words of favourable hopes, the inevitable climax to which would be a happy
(76) conclusion. When he had finished his anthems, a mixture, as it were, of religion and humanity, he began to pass over from mortal life to life immortal and gradually began to be aware of the separate parts of which he was composed. His body, which encased him like a shell, was stripped off and his soul laid bare, longing according to its nature for its
(77) departure hence. Then, having prepared all things for his departure, he did not actually undertake his migration until he had honoured all the tribes of his nation by twelve harmonious prayers corresponding to the names of each of the tribal chiefs. All of these prayers, we must believe, will be fulfilled, for the one who offered them up was beloved of God, who is filled with love for man (the true philanthropist). They for whom the prayers were made were men of noble birth and had been placed in the highest rank under
(78) the supreme leader, the Maker and Father of all. [The prayers were requests for true goods, that they might possess them not only during this mortal life, but much more when the soul is freed from the bondage of the flesh.]
(79) For, it seems, Moses alone had seen from the beginning and had realised that the whole people enjoyed the closest of all possible affinities with things divine, an affinity far more genuine than that of blood, and, therefore, he pronounced it to be the heir of all good things which human nature is capable of receiving. What he himself possessed he gave them immediately, while what he did not have he interceded with God to supply to them, knowing that from the fountains of grace the supplies are inexhaustible, but are not showered upon all, but only upon those who are suppliants. Now suppliants are those who love a life of virtue, to whom it is permitted to draw water from the sacred fountains since they thirst for wisdom.

(66–7) *filled with unrestrained joy*: having given one proof of Moses' kindness and faithfulness, Philo refers to a second, *not inferior to it*. It is that when Joshua, whose life was a copy of Moses' own, had been chosen by God, Moses, far from being depressed because God had not chosen one of his sons, was intensely joyful.

a ruler perfect in every respect: the joy of Moses was occasioned by the recognition that the nation would be in the care of such a person. It was an axiom for Moses – and Philo – that *the man chosen by God must be a man of noble virtue*. So Moses presented Joshua to the people (see Num. 27: 22, 23). Unafraid of his own impending death, for him new joys were in fact added to the old ones, since he could not only remember earlier happy moments, which he owed to his virtuous life and which filled him with delight, but he also experienced *the hope that he was about to become immortal as he exchanged the corruptible life for the incorruptible*. Philo shared in the Jewish hope of immortality as expressed in Dan. 12: 2 and elsewhere, the homegoing of the spirit or soul of man to a further stage in the development of its relationship with God. But he does at times adopt a dualistic view of body and soul, and there is no doubt that the hope he here attributes to Moses – passage from the corruptible life of the body to the incorruptible life of the eternal soul – he also shared. So he greeted the prospect gladly and cheerfully.

(68) *the moment has already arrived*: here Philo nears the end of his supplement to the account given elsewhere (in *Vit. Mos.* II) of the final moments of Moses' earthly life. He describes the journey Moses is about to make as a departure from the life of the body. No longer would he be 'imprisoned in a corruptible body' (*ibid.* 74) or 'buried in the mortal body which may very properly be called its tomb' (*Spec. Leg.* IV.188). The many powers which the soul loses when it is clothed in a body, which it still had 'while unclothed and free from the entanglement of the body' (words which imply the pre-existence of the soul), it will regain after death (*Leg. All.* II.22). The mind, after the separation of body and soul, will see that the objects of sense have no true existence and that the body represents a domain whose judgements are spurious and corrupted and full of false opinions (*Rer. Div. Her.* 71). The process by which the mind is gnawed at and eaten by the senses will come to an end, and a life of the wholly intelligible and incorporeal will begin.

Moses, contemplating all this, then recited to the people God's message declaring his approval of Joshua.

(69) *what he thought would be advantageous*: Moses then addressed Joshua (see Deut. 31: 7, 23), giving him advice (which elaborates on the biblical words) on how to carry out his new responsibilities, for, although Joshua perhaps did not need the exhortations, Moses could not hide his personal friendship for Joshua and was also driven by his patriotism to *lay bare what he thought would be advantageous*.

(70) *a divine command had been received*: according to Philo, though not Deut. 31: 7, 23, Moses had received a divine command to exhort his successor and create in him the spirit required for his new task. Also, all future rulers, by looking to Moses as their archetype and model, would find what they needed to guide them when it came to their turn to advise their successors and address them with exhortations and words of encouragement.

(71) *the exhortations of the good man*: these, when offered by a good man, always encourage the nervous and uplift them so that they rise superior to themselves and are inspired to perform outstanding deeds.

(72) *the last thanksgiving*: Moses then, Philo tells us, proceeded to sing to God a final hymn of thanksgiving for *the extraordinary and unprecedented graces he had been blessed with from his birth to his old age*. One of these was, of course, humanity, for in these sections of the *De Virtutibus* Moses is being portrayed as a model of that virtue.

(73) *all the kinds of harmony and symphony*: surrounded by representative elements of the whole universe, earthly and heavenly, Moses sang his canticles which were pleasing to the ear of *both men and ministering angels* (cf. Heb. 1: 7, 14).

(74) *men, as disciples . . . angels, vigilant observers*: listening to the Mosaic canticles men were intended to learn, as disciples of Moses, thankfulness of heart, while the angels, as choral observers, were intended to note the perfection of the hymns sung by Moses even though he was *imprisoned in a corruptible body*. They were to observe that Moses, like the heavenly bodies, the sun and moon and the choir formed by other heavenly bodies, could *attune his soul to the divine instrument, the heaven and the entire universe*.

(75) *his own genuine feelings of affection and good-will towards the nation*: as the singers rendered their thanks to God, Moses, for his part, blended with the music his own feelings of love for his people. Philo's philosophical Deity is also, this passage makes clear, a God who could move men to feelings of affection for him. Moses, then, rebuked the people for past sins, admonished them in

a way appropriate to the present occasion and exhorted them with hopeful words of comfort for the future – hopeful words which, since the great Revealer spoke them, could not but be fulfilled.

The Song, in Deut. 31: 28–9, contains more of rebuke than of anything else, and it is difficult to find the 'keynote of mercy and hope' detected by Adam Smith (and by Philo).

(76) *a mixture of religion and humanity*: Philo describes Moses' hymns to God as a blend of religion and humanity, a blend of reverence for God and care for his fellow-Israelites. After he had sung them, Moses began to pass over *from mortal life to life immortal*. This is how death was viewed by Philo. One may compare it with Paul's view in 1 Cor. 15 (the exchange of the terrestrial, natural body for the spiritual body; cf. 2 Cor. 5: 1ff.). For Philo the process is one that involves the gradual disuniting of the elements which make up human nature. The body, *which encased him like a shell*, is stripped away and the soul laid bare, yearning for its removal hence (cf. 2 Cor. 5: 4). For Philo the bare soul is translated to the incorruptible regions; for Paul the soul is given a new, spiritual body or clothed in a 'habitation from heaven' (see 1 Cor. 15: 44; 2 Cor. 5: 2).

(77) *beloved of God who is filled with love for men*: before departing this life Moses, the beloved of God, addressed to God, the lover of men, benedictions upon the founders of Israel's tribes (see Deut. 33), benedictions which were bound to be fulfilled because of the nature of their offerer and those for whom they were offered, noble men in the army of the Father. Elsewhere, Philo says that these blessings, partially fulfilled already, will one day be fulfilled completely. Some of the blessings have already been experienced; others are still awaited, since 'the clearest testimony to the future is assured by what has been fulfilled in the past' (*Vit. Mos.* II.288).

(78) *requests for true goods*: this is Philo's description of the content of the prayers offered by Moses. He suggests that Moses asked for these *true goods* during the *mortal life* of Israel, but also, more importantly, *when the soul is freed from the bondage of the flesh*. Here we meet another example of Philo's dualistic way of referring to body and soul.

The enclosing square brackets to this paragraph indicate that some scholars see it as an interpolation not from the hand of Philo, especially since they cannot imagine his describing a request by Moses for *true goods* for the people in the life when the soul is free from the mortal body; since the life beyond death is wholly mind, 'pure like the sun' (*Vit. Mos.* II.288). Philo also interprets Gen. 15: 15 as meaning that the good man departs (he does not die); his soul 'completely purified cannot be extinguished and cannot die' (*Rer. Div. Her.* 276). Moses is said, after death, to have been advanced beyond species and types and placed beside God. In death, or beyond it, 'he is not connected with adding or taking away' (*Sacr. AC* 8). In these cases at least the idea of real goods in the life beyond death as something to be prayed for seems perhaps unthinkable. However, Philo may have been thinking of Moses as praying for something which he knew already existed in the life beyond death.

(79) *affinities with things divine*: Moses alone had realised, as his hymns and prayers showed, that the whole nation was related not just by ties of blood but by *an affinity far more genuine* which united it to God. For this reason, and this is an example of his humanity, his human caring for his fellow-men, he declared Israel to be *the heir of all good things*. His own possessions he gave them, and asked God to supply what was still lacking, knowing that *from the fountains of grace the supplies are inexhaustible, but are not showered upon all, but only upon those who are suppliants*. They are all lovers of virtue who are allowed to *draw water from the sacred fountains since they thirst for wisdom*. Holiness and wisdom cannot be separated; the one leads to the other.

Moses' *philanthrōpia* consists, in large measure, in his gift to his countrymen of the good things and his use of his position to seek from God whatever else they needed. And the primary gift he sought for them, as a lover of virtue, was wisdom.

Humanity shown in the laws (*Virt.* 80–101)

(80) We have now completed our statement of the proofs of the legislator's humanity and fellowship, which he possessed thanks to the happy gift of natural goodness, and also as a consequence of the lessons given in the divine commandments. But it is necessary also to speak of the precepts he left behind him, commanding subsequent ages to obey them. It is impossible to enumerate all of them, for that would be difficult, so we must at least mention those
(81) related to his intentions and closest to them. He did not

establish gentleness and humanity as fundamental in the society of human beings only, but with an incomparable generosity poured it out and extended it to the various species of animals and the various kinds of cultivated trees. We must speak about the ordinances he established with respect to each of these in turn, starting with those relating
(82) to man. He forbids anyone to lend money at interest to a brother, and he means by brother not only one who is of the same parents but also anyone who is a fellow-citizen or a fellow-countryman. For he does not think it is right to extract offspring from money, as a farmer does from his
(83) cattle. And he urges his subjects not to hang back on that account and to be unwilling to contribute, but rather with open hands and willing hearts to give to those who are in need, with the thought that a free gift is in a way a debt that will be repaid by the recipient in better times, but without constraint and with free-will. That is the best course of action, but if they do not want to give, apart from being forced, they should at least give with good-will and alacrity, with no intention of receiving back
(84) anything more than the capital. For thus the poor would not become more helpless by being compelled to give back more than they received, nor would the lenders be wronged though they recovered only what they gave. And yet not 'only'! For with the principle in place of the interest which they are willing not to accept, they will gain the best and most honourable things among men, kindness, sympathy, goodness, magnanimity, a good name and a good reputation. And what acquisition can
(85) there be equal to these? Even the mighty king himself will appear as the poorest of men if he is compared with a single virtue. For his wealth is inanimate, buried deep in storehouses or recesses in the ground, but the wealth of virtue is the ruling part of the soul; and the purest part of reality, heaven, and God, the Creator of all things, all lay

claim to it. Therefore must we designate the wealth of money-changers and usurers as in fact poverty, though they have the appearance of mighty kings with vast quantities of gold, but they have never seen, even in a
(86) dream, the wealth endowed with sight. And there are some who have reached such depths of depravity that if they have no money they lend food at interest, supplying it on condition that they receive back more than they provided. It would be a long time before such men would make a contribution to beggars, if they prepare famine and scarcity at a time of plenty and abundance, and make a profit out of the hunger of miserable men, and place on the scales meat and food only so that they do not give
(87) overweight. Therefore he unequivocally commands those who shall be members of his holy community to avoid every sort of profit of this kind, for such practices display the marks of an enslaved soul altogether unworthy of a free man, and of a soul which has been converted to
(88) savagery and a bestial nature. This is another of the commandments which prescribe humanity. The wages of the poor are to be paid on the same day as the work is done, not only because it is just that once a man has completed the work for which he has been engaged he should receive his payment immediately for his labour, but also because, as some say, the manual worker, or porter, who suffers hardships with his whole body like a beast of burden, should have his hopes rest upon his payment. If he receives it immediately, he is glad and is given strength to work the next day with redoubled zeal; but if he does not receive it, apart from the great trouble this causes him, he loses heart because of the distress he feels and his sinews are exhausted so that he is unable to face the routine duties of his work.
(89) He says further: let no money-lender enter into the home of his debtors to take back by force any guarantee or pledge for his loan; he is to stand outside in the porch and

quietly request them to bring it. And they, if they have it, must not withhold it, since it is fitting that the creditor should not misuse his power to behave arrogantly so as to insult those who have borrowed from him, and that the debtor should provide a proper guarantee as a reminder
(90) that he must repay the borrowed money. Who, furthermore, can fail to admire the commandment about reapers and grape-pickers? For he commands men at harvest-time not to gather the corn which falls from the sheaves, nor to cut down the whole crop, but to leave some part of the field unreaped. Thus, on the one hand, he makes the rich magnanimous and liberal with their wealth, by being compelled to sacrifice something of their property instead of eyeing it all greedily, not to collect it all together and bring it home like a treasure. On the other hand, he creates fresh confidence among the poor, for since they themselves have no personal resources, he allows them to go into the fields of their fellow-countrymen to gather a har-
(91) vest from what is left as if it were their own. Again, in the autumn he forbids the proprietors of the vineyards conducting the harvest to collect the grapes which fall on the ground and to glean the vines. He gave the same orders to the olive-pickers, as a very loving and just father of children who have not all enjoyed the same good fortune, some living in abundance, others reduced to the very existence of poverty. The latter he calls, in his great mercy and pity, and summons them to partake of the possessions of their brethren, using what belongs to others as if it were their own, not feeling any shame, but, to remedy their deprivations, permitting them to share not only in the fruit
(92) but also in the estates, at least in appearance. But there are some whose minds are so sordid and who have devoted themselves to money-making and driven themselves to death for every kind of profit, giving no thought to what its source might be, that they glean the olive-groves and

vineyards a second time and reap the whole of the barley-field and the wheat-fields, displaying openly their slavish
(93) niggardliness and also exhibiting their impiety. For they themselves have contributed little to the cultivation of their lands. The most numerous and most necessary things that make for a harvest and fertility come from nature: seasonable rains, the right air-temperature, constant nursing of the growing plants, the gentle dews, the life-giving breezes, the arrival without harm of the seasons of the year, so that in summer it is not too hot and in winter it is not too cold, and so that during the change from spring to
(94) autumn no injury is caused to the growing plants. And although they know these things and see that it is nature that is continually thus accomplishing her work and bestowing her rich gifts on them prodigally, they nevertheless boldly usurp her benefactions and, as though they themselves were the causes of everything, they give nothing to anyone. Their behaviour displays inhumanity and impiety as well, since they have not freely laboured to obtain virtue, and so he chastens them against their will with admonitions and holy laws which the good obey
(95) voluntarily, the wicked with bad grace. The laws decree that we give to the officiating priests as first-fruits a tithe of the corn and wine and oil and domestic animals and wool, but from the harvest fruits and fruits of other trees on a scale in proportion to the size of the harvest to be brought in full baskets, with hymns composed in honour of God. These hymns are preserved in writing in the sacred Scriptures. In addition, the first-born of oxen, sheep and goats are not to be classed as personal property, but are to be considered as first-fruits, so that men accustomed partly to honour God and partly not to take everything as gain for themselves, may be adorned with those chiefs virtues,
(96) piety and humanity. Again, he says, if you see an animal of one of your relations or friends, or anyone you know,

straying in the desert, lead it back and restore it; and if the owner is a long way away, guard it carefully with your own until, on his return, the owner can come and receive it as a deposit which he did not give, but which you, the one who found it, can restore to him because of your
(97) natural feelings of neighbourliness. And there are the laws enacted concerning the seventh year, according to which all land should be left fallow during that twelve months, and the poor allowed to enter with impunity upon the estates of the rich to gather the fruits which grow spontaneously, gifts of nature. Is that law not humane and
(98) merciful? For six years, he says, the owners should enjoy the land because they have purchased it and worked on it. But for one year, the seventh, let the poor and needy enjoy it as no agricultural work has been done in that year, and the enjoyment goes to those who have neither property nor money. For it was felt to be unjust that the one should have all the hard work and the other all the benefits. This law was given in order that the land, being left in a sense without any owners, with no cultivation contributing to its fertility, the produce might then be seen to proceed wholly from the generosity of God, offering itself, equal
(99) and abundant, to relieve the needy. Again, in all the laws laid down for the fiftieth year, do we not find the same excess of humanity? And who would not agree to this if he had not merely sipped with his lips the contents of the Law, but had feasted abundantly and revelled in its most
(100) sweet and beautiful doctrines? For in the fiftieth year all the measures enacted in relation to the seventh year are repeated, but he adds others which are even greater, the recovery by each of his own property which circumstances beyond his control had forced him to cede to someone else. He does not permit purchasers to retain absolute possession of the property of others, thus blockading and stopping up the road to covetousness, in order

to curb that treacherous passion, the source of all evils, desire. And he also did not think it right that owners should be deprived for ever of their goods, as that would be punishing them for their poverty, which it is unjust to punish, but which ought undoubtedly to meet with pity.

(101) There are also thousands of other ordinances relating to one's fellow-countrymen, good and humane, but as I have already dealt with them sufficiently in my previous works, I will content myself with those already discussed, which I have appended as a suitable sample.

(80) *the happy gift of natural goodness*: Philo himself feels that he has by now demonstrated Moses' possession of humanity and fellow-feeling (*philanthrōpia kai koinōnia*). These were part of Moses' natural disposition, but also the outcome of what he had learned from *the divine commandments*. Part of his humanity also, however, was his gift to posterity of the *precepts* – a subject too long, Philo concedes, to be dealt with fully in the present context. But, he adds, at least those laws and commandments *related to his intentions and closest to them* could be mentioned.

(81) *gentleness and humanity*: these two qualities were taken by Moses as essential to the relationships of men not only with one another, but also towards *the various species of animals and the various kinds of cultivated trees*. (Philo was an early 'green' or conservationist.) He announces his intention of referring to each of these in turn, starting with those affecting man.

Random examples from Moses' Law are the law about fallen fruit in the vineyard which is to be left for the poor (Lev. 19: 10), the commandment 'Thou shalt not muzzle the ox when he treadeth out the corn' (Deut. 25: 4), and the rule about not destroying trees when attacking a city (Deut. 20: 19–20), though there are many more.

(82) *offspring from money*: this is something, lending money on interest, or usury, which Moses strictly forbids. The law applies to the money lent to a brother and anyone *who is a fellow citizen or a fellow-countryman*, a fellow-Jew. To make money from money is like breeding yearlings from cattle, though more abhorrent. Examples of Moses' legislation on the subject are to be found in Exod. 22: 25; Deut. 23: 19; Lev. 25: 36, 37. Here we have a clear

case of laws enacted by Moses to protect his fellow-men; their poverty, which forced them to borrow, could not be exploited by greedy lenders extorting interest. Repayment of the loan alone could be asked for. In *Spec. Leg.* II.74ff. Philo suggests that lending money at interest treats the borrower like a senseless animal suffering additional hurt 'when they are deceived by a present bait'. The moneylender is no 'partner' to the borrower, but displays inhumanity in his actions, indeed a 'terrible hardness of heart'. Undoubtedly moneylending had become a transaction which did serious harm to some members of society, and it is a real sign of Moses' humanity, according to Philo, that he condemned it so fiercely. It is interesting to note that Philo concludes the section in the *De Specialibus Legibus* on the subject by saying that 'borrowers should be thought worthy of a humanity enjoined by the law, not paying back their loans and usurious interest but paying back merely the original sum lent'.

(83) *to give to those who are in need*: part of the humanitarian attitude commanded by Moses in the Law is generosity in charity. The lender should be aware that a gift to someone in need will be repaid *in better times*, and it will be done freely, without compulsion, and willingly. It has been suggested that Philo derived this teaching from Lev. 25: 35, a verse which does seem to refer only to free gifts to the poor, or from Deut. 15: 10, 'Thou shalt surely give him' (the words are followed by a promise that God will bless the giver in such a situation).

(84) *what acquisition can there be equal to these?*: free gifts to the poor do not render them helpless, as lending with interest can, and also they exonerate the giver from any blame, since he would recover only what he gave. Philo adds, *yet not 'only'!* He then explains what he means. The giver would in fact receive *interest*, though not monetary. He would receive a bonus of *the best and most honourable things among men*. Philo then lists some of them. They include mercy, neighbourliness, charity, magnanimity, a good report and a good fame. What, he asks, can rival or equal such acquisitions? The plain implication is that nothing can. Once again Moses' rules on lending protect borrowers and lenders and in fact bestow extra and unexpected benefits on lenders.

(85) *the wealth of virtue*: even a great king, Philo affirms, would appear as the poorest of men if compared with a single virtue. The reason is that wealth, without virtue, is soulless, buried in the depths of the earth. The wealth of virtue, however, lies in the

sovereign part of the soul and the purest part of existence, heaven. One is reminded by Philo's words of the saying of Jesus about 'treasure in heaven' (Matt. 19: 21). The virtuous man's treasure, according to Philo, is heavenly, belongs to heaven and to God, who is the parent of all. Ethics is the gateway to heaven and God.

The apparent wealth of the money-grabbing usurers is really of no value. Purses full of gold may seem to make men kings, but not even in their dreams do they glimpse *the wealth endowed with sight*, the wealth of wisdom and virtue.

(86) *such depths of depravity*: some men do sink to the lowest depths and lend food when they have no money, provided that they receive back more than they gave (cf. Lev. 25: 37). There is little prospect of such people giving a free meal to a pauper, when in fact they use the plight of the poor and hungry to make a profit for themselves. They *place on the scales meat and food* to make sure that they do not give away a fraction too much.

(87) *the marks of an enslaved soul*: Moses absolutely forbids members of his commonwealth, true Israelites, to engage in such practices, which only a man who is a slave to his greed and completely lacking in generosity would perform.

(88) *his hopes rest upon his payment*: Philo alludes to Lev. 19: 13 and Deut. 24: 14, 15, as setting forth one of *the commandments which prescribe humanity*, since they contain injunctions requiring that the wages of the poor are to be paid daily. This is not simply a case of immediate payment for work done, but is also because a manual worker, likened by Philo to a beast of burden, lives from day to day. Because of this, the poor man's hopes rest on his payment by his employer. To be paid cheers him and braces him for the next day's work. To remain unpaid causes him trouble, depresses him and renders him incapable of carrying on with his work.

Philo's ethics, then, involve a deep concern about the poor and some insight into their plight. Humanity, for him, involves caring for the poor and ensuring that they are at least paid promptly the pittance they earn.

(89) *it is fitting*: Moses decrees that there must be no violent acquisition of securities (see Deut. 24: 10, 11). Rather, the creditor must stand outside in the porch and ask for the pledge or security for the loan quietly. Debtors must not retain what is not theirs, since, while creditors must not abuse their position by dealing inconsiderately and insolently with borrowers, borrowers must provide a suitable surety so that they have a necessary reminder to

repay what they owe to the lender. Within the context of money-lending and borrowing, Philo, on the basis of some words in the Pentateuch, is advocating tolerant, civilised and non-violent behaviour between creditors and debtors as part of the virtue of humanity. Reasonable conduct between creditors and debtors is all part of the proper way for men to conduct their relationships with others.

(90) *fresh confidence among the poor*: here Philo deals with the injunctions about reaping and grape-picking in Lev. 19: 9 and 23: 22. Moses' words, which exhort reapers not to 'reap the corners of the field' and grape-pickers not to gather fallen grapes, elicit Philo's admiration, since they urge owners working in the fields to leave a small part of their crops ungathered. This makes the rich *magnanimous and liberal* by sacrificing something of their crops to others instead of greedily taking it all for themselves. This, at the same time, encourages the poor, who own no land, to enter the estates of the rich and reap a harvest of left-overs *as if it were their own*.

The regulations regarding gleaning came in Lev. 19, a chapter which promises the children of Israel that they will be holy since God is holy. Holiness, in the Israelite code of ethics, involves humanitarian provision by the rich, through land left unreaped, for the needs of the poor and the stranger ('for the stranger, for the fatherless and for the widow', Deut. 24: 20). The story in the Book of Ruth is perhaps the best-known example of how a stranger, Ruth, the Moabitess, benefited from such legislation.

(91) *permitting them to share*: similar regulations exist in the Mosaic Law regarding the gathering of the vine-harvest. It is forbidden to collect the grapes that have fallen to the ground (see Lev. 19: 10; cf. Deut. 24: 21). Likewise olive-pickers must leave some fruit behind (see Deut. 24: 20); no double-picking of the trees is permitted.

The humanity of the Mosaic Law is evidence of God's *mercy and pity* and that he acts *as a very loving and just father of children who have not all enjoyed the same good fortune*. It is a way of rendering more equal the condition of those who are sunk in deepest poverty and those who have prospered in life, for the former are invited to partake of what belongs to the latter *as if it were their own*, and not in any way of which they need be ashamed. Some redress of their privations is made and they become partners with their more fortunate kinsmen not only in the fruit collected but also *in the estates, at least in appearance*.

An elementary and partial form of economic socialism operates in this agricultural sector of the nation, or at least a kind of welfare state. Moses' laws at this point require a humanitarian attitude on the part of the 'haves' towards the 'have-nots'.

(92) *driven themselves to death*: that is what some, obsessed by money, have done by the amassing of wealth and property. They forget the source of their wealth, namely God, the Creator. Consequently they fail to share their own goods and crops with their fellow-creatures (as God shares his with them), gleaning olive-groves and vineyards and reaping fields of wheat and barley twice. They thus demonstrate their utter meanness and impiety. It is from a wrong attitude to God that a wrong attitude to one's fellow-men springs. It is failure to acknowledge that God is the Giver of all our possessions that leads to failure to share those possessions generously with others.

(93) *come from nature*: the rich man contributes very little to the success of his crops. It is nature that does most of the work to produce a fruitful vineyard or olive-grove with the seasonal rains she sends, the right atmospheric conditions, the gentle morning dews, the breezes, the perfectly arranged seasons of the year, summer not too hot, winter not too cold, with no harmful transitions to and from spring and autumn. These are the constant nurses of the growing plants – not the owner of the land.

Again, Philo is emphasising that humanity grows out of a proper recognition of the work of God the Father and his providential gifts to man. Philonic ethics are theological ethics.

(94) *inhumanity and impiety*: despite the observation of the phenomena just mentioned and the recognition that it is to nature that they owe their good fortune, some rich landowners take what nature gives and, as though they had been solely responsible for its production, refuse to share any of it with others less fortunate than themselves. They thus demonstrate their gross *inhumanity and impiety* (the two linked again), requiring God, since they do not seek to live a virtuous life freely, to summon them to such a life by means of the *holy laws*, obeyed willingly by the good and unwillingly by the bad.

(95) *hymns composed in honour of God*: the law of first-fruits (Num. 15: 18–20), dealt with fully in *Spec. Leg.* I.132ff., where the subject is the privilege of priests (cf. *ibid.* IV.99, where the practice of offering first-fruits is treated as a lesson in self-denial), is treated here as required humanity towards the nation's priests, but a humanity, as always, linked with piety. The gifts are to be

accompanied with hymns of praise to God (recorded for them in Deut. 26: 1–11; cf. *Spec. Leg.* II.215–20). There are also to be animal first-fruits of oxen, sheep and goats so that by the practice of honouring the Godhead by refraining from taking *everything as gain*, men may be adorned with the queens of virtue, *piety and humanity*.

(96) *natural feelings of neighbourliness*: a lost or strayed animal is to be restored to its owner and, if he is away, guarded until his return, when it can be returned to him. The subject is dealt with in Deut. 22: 1. Philo's comments, however, show some evidence of the influence of the language of the Septuagint: for example, the use of the verb *apodidōmi* (give back).

(97) *gifts of nature*: that is how Philo describes the produce of land uncultivated during the sabbatical years decreed by Moses (see Exod. 23: 10, 11; Lev. 25: 3ff.). A full treatment of the subject is to be found in *Spec. Leg.* II.86–109, where the same aspect of the law treated here is dealt with in the final six sections. Such a practice, Philo argues, is both *humane and merciful*. It is further evidence of the emphasis placed on humanity in the Mosaic Law.

(98) *produce . . . from the generosity of God*: these are things which grow on the land while it is left uncultivated by its owners. They go to those who have no possessions or money. The law enshrines the principle that it is unjust for some to labour only and others to have an exclusive claim to the products of their labour. Since, in the sabbatical year, there is no cultivation of anything that grows, it belongs to God, not to the owners, and he may use it to meet the wants of the needy. This custom, ascribed to laziness by Tacitus (*Hist.* V.4), goes back to very ancient times (see Hos. 10: 12; Jer. 4: 3; Prov. 13: 23) and was still practised in the time of Alexander the Great (Josephus, *Ant.* XI. 8.6), in the time of the Hasmoneans (*ibid.* XIII.8.1: cf. 1 Macc. 6: 49, 53), and in the time of the Herods (Josephus, *Ant.* XIV.16.2). It probably reflects an ancient fallowing custom but, as Exod. 23: 11 suggests, was also part of an attempt to deal, as were the laws on usury, with the serious and widespread problem of poverty.

(99) *the same excess of humanity*: this is to be found, Philo declares, in all the laws relating to the Jubilee year (the year of the Ram, so-called because of the command to blow the 'loud trumpet' made from a ram's horn). The regulations relating to the Jubilee year are to be found in Lev. 25: 8–55. The word Jubilee comes from the word *yobhel*, which means ram, *via* the

Vulgate *jubilaeus*. In that kind of year, Philo says, the highest point of humanity could not fail to be experienced by anyone if he had feasted abundantly and revelled in the sweet and lovely principles of the Law and not merely tasted and sipped its contents. As shown by the requirements of the Law – to be touched on briefly below, but also dealt with in *Spec. Leg.* II.111ff. (cf. *ibid.* IV.179) – the year of Jubilee requires a display of humanity, of the love of man for man, of the highest order.

(100) *others which are even greater*: such are the measures added in the case of a Jubilee year to those applicable in the case of a sabbatical year. A Jubilee year is a year of liberty, of amnesty, and, in particular, possessions given to others, under *circumstances beyond his control*, are to be returned to their original owner. According to Lev. 25: 10, every man is to return to his possessions and his family. Lev. 25: 13 requires that 'ye shall return every man to his possession'. No wrong shall be done in selling or buying (Lev. 25: 14). This, Philo says, is to bar *the road to covetousness* and *to curb that treacherous passion, the source of all evils, desire*. He repeats his view that the Jubilee year prevents the original owners being deprived permanently of what belonged to them, and so being penalised for their poverty, something which should not be punished but should meet with compassion. The poor man, the pauper, is to receive *pity*. The Jubilee laws, contained in the Law of Holiness (Lev. 17–26) are part of a set of provisions requiring Israel's life to be holy in every part. Special attention is paid again (Lev. 25: 47–55) to the harsh treatment of slaves, which Moses strictly forbids, and the general social problem of poverty. This is an important element in the Philonic virtue of humanity, the humane and caring treatment of man by man. Slaves, for example, must be treated well because the Israelites as a whole are slaves, slaves of God and treated by him with the kindness he expects them to show to others.

(101) *as a suitable sample*: Philo observes that the particular enactments relating, for example, to the year of Jubilee are more numerous than those he has had time to deal with, some of which, however, he has commented on *in my previous works*. He contents himself, therefore, with those touched on which he has added to those in the other treatises, in order to prove his point. This is that piety requires humanity, that Moses' Law gives a very special place among the virtues to philanthropy, the love of man for man, since philanthropy is the twin sister of piety and the virtue closest to it (see above, para. 51).

Philo's discussion of philanthropy extends for another 73 paragraphs, and then he turns to examine two other virtues, repentance and nobility (courage or manliness being dealt with in paras. 1–50).

CONCERNING REPENTANCE (*Virt.* 175–86 (XXXIII–XXXIV))

(175) The most holy Moses, who was a lover of virtue and goodness and especially of his fellow men, expects all men everywhere to be zealous for piety and justice, offering to penitent sinners, as conquerors, the great reward of participation in the best of all communal life found in the best of cities, and the enjoyment of those blessings, large
(176) and small, which it confers. Now these blessings, which are of the greatest importance in connection with the body, are health free from disease, on board ship travel free from danger, and in souls the memory, without forgetfulness, of things worth remembering. But second to these blessings are those which consist of recovery or rectification, recovery from illness, a long-desired escape from great dangers on a sea-voyage and subsequent safety, and the recollection which follows on forgetfulness. This has as its brother and close relative repentance and, although it is not in the first rank of blessings, it comes immediately after the first class and takes the second prize.
(177) For absolutely not to sin is a property of God alone, or perhaps of a divine man. But the conversion of a sinful man to a blameless life is the attribute of a wise man who has not been entirely ignorant of what is good for his life.
(178) And so when Moses assembles such people and initiates them into his mysteries, he addresses to them precepts which are conciliatory and friendly, urging them to practise sincerity and to reject pride, and to cling to truth and simplicity as vitally necessary virtues and the source of happiness, and to forsake the fictions of the myths impressed on their tender souls from their infancy by

parents and nannies and tutors and numerous of their circle of familiars, influencing them into endless error concern-
(179) ing the knowledge of the best. And what can this best of all things be but God, whose honours they have attributed to those who were not gods at all and glorified them beyond measure, while those empty-minded men forget him altogether? Therefore, all those who did not at first acknowledge their duty to revere the Creator and Father of the universe, yet afterwards embraced monotheism, belief in the rule of one, in place of polytheism, belief in the rule of many, we should accept as our dearest friends and closest kinsmen, since they displayed the nature which God loves, which is the greatest of all bonds in cementing friendship and intimacy; and we ought therefore to rejoice with them: even if, as men might say, they were previously blind, they have now recovered their sight, are capable now of seeing the most brilliant lights, having
(180) escaped from the profoundest darkness. We have now described the first and most important form of repentance, but let a man repent not only of the errors by which he was for a long time deceived when he revered created things before the uncreated Being who is their Maker, but also in the other important things in life, by forsaking that worst of all forms of bad government, mob-rule, for democracy, the form of government which possesses the best laws. This involves passing from ignorance to a knowledge of those things which it is disgraceful not to know, from folly to wisdom, from lack of self-control to self-control, from
(181) injustice to justice, from cowardice to courage. For it is excellent and expedient to desert, without looking back, to the ranks of virtue and to abandon vice, that wicked mistress. And as surely as in sunshine the shadow follows the body, so also where honour is given to the God who
(182) IS, the whole fellowship of virtues must follow. The proselytes immediately become temperate, masters of

themselves, modest, gentle, kind, humane, reverent, just, magnanimous, lovers of truth, superior to all considerations of money and pleasure. Conversely, those who rebel against the holy laws of God are ill-disciplined, shameless, unjust, irreverent, companions of falsehood and false witness, who have sold their freedom for good food, good wine, delicacies and the beauty of the opposite sex, in pursuit of the pleasures of the stomach and the organs below the stomach, which in the end cause serious
(183) damage both to the body and the soul. Admirable exhortations to repentance are also given, by which we are taught to change the shape of our life from an irregular and disorderly course into a better state. He says that this task is not too onerous nor removed to a distant place, neither in the air far above us, nor at the ends of the earth, nor beyond the great sea, so that we are rendered incapable of accepting it; but very near, residing in three parts of us, mouth, heart and hands, symbolic respectively of our words, our wills and our actions, for the mouth is the symbol of speech, the heart of intentions and the hands of
(184) actions, and in these three happiness consists. For whenever our thoughts match our words and our actions match our intentions, life is praiseworthy and perfect, but whenever they are in conflict, it is imperfect and blameworthy. If anyone does not forget to maintain this harmony, he will be well pleasing to God and will be at once God-loving and God-beloved. And so, in complete agreement with what has just been said, was given this revelation: 'Thou hast chosen today God to thee, and the Lord has chosen thee today to be a people to him' [Deut.
(185) 26: 17, 18]. Splendid is this reciprocity of choice, when man is anxious to serve the Existent One, and God without delay takes the suppliant to himself as his own and anticipates the wish of him who in all honesty and sincerity enters into his service. And the true servant and

> suppliant, even though he is only one in number, is worth, in power, since he has been chosen, the whole people, is
> (186) equal in value to the whole nation. That is also the case in nature, for as in a ship the pilot is of as much importance as the rest of the crew put together, and in an army the general is of as much value as the whole of the army – since if he is killed defeat is as certain as if the whole force were annihilated – so, in the same way, the wise man can contend with the worthy of the whole nation, since he is protected by an impregnable rampart, godliness.

In this section the Jewish student of the Old Testament displaces to some extent the Greek philosopher in Philo. His exposition of the virtue of repentance is rooted in the Old Testament's teaching on the subject. For the Greek philosophers repentance, *metanoia*, was not a virtue, despite the statement of Aristotle that 'he who cannot repent cannot be cured' (*Eth. Nic.* VII.7, 1150a, 23). To Aristotle, and the Greek philosophers in general, the penitent man is a *bad* man, since the good man has nothing to repent of. Typical of Aristotle's statements on the subject is, 'bad men are full of repentance' (*ibid.* IX.4, 1166b, 24–5), a view shared by the Stoics.

Judaism, however, believed that 'there is not a righteous man upon earth, that doeth good, and sinneth not' (Eccles. 7: 20; 1 Kings 8: 46; 2 Chron. 6: 36). Repentance is for Judaism a vital virtue. 'Let the wicked forsake his way, and the unrighteous man his thoughts: let him return unto the Lord, and he will have mercy upon him, and to our God, and he will abundantly pardon' (Isa. 55: 7). Among many other Old Testament examples that could be cited, where the verbs 'turn' and 'return' in English represent a verb in the original that has the meaning of the English verb 'repent', is Ezek. 14: 6, 'Return ye, and turn yourselves from your idols; and turn away your faces from all your abominations.'

Inevitably confession came to be recognised as a Mosaic requirement (see Hos. 14: 3, LXX), though there is only a limited amount of material on confession in the Pentateuch. Later, after Old Testament times, confession came to be prescribed as a daily necessity. Even in Philo, in his life of Abraham, it is said that 'repentance occupies the second place . . . after perfection' (*Abr.* 26). In Ecclus. 18: 21 repentance and confession are both desired by

God, the one the outer expression of the other, the inner attitude (cf. Ecclus. 4: 26, 17: 25–32). Wisd. Sol. 12: 19 states that there is hope for men, since God gave 'repentance when men have sinned' (cf. Wisd. Sol. 11: 23, 12: 10).

Philo's view of repentance is linked with his belief in the sinlessness of God (see below, para. 177). It is also the logical consequence of what he says about the freedom of will, the freedom to choose good or evil, possessed by man.

One aspect of Philo's view of repentance that will be of interest to students of the New Testament who are attempting to interpret the idea of Christ's pre-existence found in some New Testament documents, is what he says about Enoch in his comments on Gen. 5: 22: namely, that Scripture says that God who, a little while before 'appointed mercy and pardon to exist, now again decrees that penitence shall exist' (*Quaest. in Gn.* 1.82). It has been pointed out that throughout the story of Creation, as Philo interprets it, everything 'decreed' or 'defined' by God has been preceded by an Idea of it. In his *De Opificio Mundi* Philo states that, when God willed to create the visible world, 'He previously formed that one which is perceptible only by the intellect.' The Ideas were first 'conceived . . . in his mind' (*Op. Mund.* 16, 19). Repentance must be added, as far as Philo is concerned, to those entities which were considered, especially by the rabbis, to have been pre-existent.

(175) *the best of cities*: because Moses urged his fellow citizens to repent, Philo felt obliged to include repentance as a virtue. Because of his love of virtue and goodness and of his fellow men, Moses urged everyone everywhere to seek piety and justice. In return he offered to the repentant, in honour of the victory over sin which repentance represents, a place in *the best of cities* and the *blessings, large and small*, which such membership *confers*.

(176) *the second prize*: Philo produces some parallels to repentance. In relation to bodily health, freedom from disease is the supreme achievement; in the case of ships, safe journeys; in souls, the recollection of things worth remembering without forgetfulness. But second to these stands *rectification* in its various forms – *recovery from illness*, delivery from danger at sea, *recollection* displacing *forgetfulness*. The last of these is akin to repentance, which, though not in the highest rank of moral values, is in the second class, taking the second prize.

(177) *absolutely not to sin is a property of God alone*: it is because of this that man needs to repent, since he is, unlike God, a sinful being.

Sinlessness is a quality of God and, possibly, of *a divine man*. In Jewish tradition Enoch is an example of repentance (Ecclus. 44: 16), since his life was not always perfect (*Genesis Rabbah* 25: 1). According to Philo Enoch was a penitent (*Abr.* 17ff.; *Praem. Poen.* 15ff.). Conversion from sin to a blameless life shows a man of wisdom who has realised what is good for him (see Isa. 6: 10 for a description of the failure, unhappily, of the people to respond to the prophet's preaching with repentance). Philo in fact states that repentance came into existence with Enoch (see Gen. 5: 22; cf. *Quaest. in Gn.* 1.82). The rabbis taught that repentance came into being with Adam's repentance (*Pirke de-Rabbi Eliezer* 20). The *Yoma* 86b affirms that redemption will come to Israel through repentance, while Philo in *Praem. Poen.* 163–4 says that, if the people are shamed into a wholehearted conversion and make a full confession of all their sins, then they will find that God is merciful and will give the signal that will cause their masters – he is thinking of apostates who have become slaves – to set them free, awed by 'the sudden and universal change to virtue' of their former servants.

(178) *precepts which are conciliatory and friendly*: when Moses invites penitents to be initiated into his mysteries it is with the kind of offers of instruction referred to that he does so, exhorting them only *to practise sincerity and to reject pride and to cling to truth and simplicity*, which are vital necessities and the source of happiness, and to rebel against *the fictions of the myths* told to them when young by parents, nurses, tutors and others, who have influenced them to go endlessly astray in their search for the knowledge of the best.

(179) *this best of all*: the supreme good is God, though men have created false gods and glorified them excessively, while neglecting the true God. Yet if polytheists later embrace monotheism, they must be held to be our best friends. In turning from polytheism to monotheism they have displayed the character God loves, friendship with God (godliness), and therefore are entitled to our friendship as well. We must rejoice with them as if, having been blind, they can now see, and as if from the deepest darkness they have emerged to behold the most radiant light (*phōs idontes*). Here repentance is turning from false belief, polytheism, to true belief in the one God.

(180) *from cowardice to courage*: this is the last of the examples of other forms of repentance which men should display. The first and

most essential kind is giving up the delusions which lead to revering the created before the Creator, but in addition men should repent (the Hebrew verb, *shubh*, to turn) by turning away from the vilest form of government to the one which best preserves good order, from *mob-rule*, ochlocracy, to *democracy*. Repentance also means passing over from ignorance to knowledge of what it is disgraceful not to know, from senselessness to good sense, from incontinence to continence, from injustice to justice, from timidity to boldness. In other words, it involves abandoning a number of vices and embracing their opposing qualities and virtues.

In this passage Philo contrasts *mob-rule* with *democracy*, the latter being the Roman Republic's form of government which Philo also embraces and approves of, though in his version of it there is a place for the ideal lawgiver, Moses. The ideal state for Philo is monarchical, aristocratic democracy. In *Spec. Leg.* IV.237 democracy is said to be the 'best regulated and most excellent of all constitutions' and to it is attributed the maintenance of equality. Equality and good order are things which Philo regarded as good, as virtues. There is a similar association between democracy and equality, law and justice in *Conf. Ling.* 108, where democracy is also opposed to mob-rule (cf. *Agric.* 45), though in *Agric.* 46 it is opposed to tyranny and in the *Deus Imm.* Philo expresses the curious idea that the world is a democracy because each nation in turn obtains supremacy.

(181) *the ranks of virtue*: Philo praises the man who deserts the ranks of vice, *that wicked mistress*, and, *without looking back*, joins the company of the virtuous. For, he adds, where God is honoured by those in *the ranks of virtue*, all the other virtues must be embraced as surely *as in sunshine the shadow follows the body*.

(182) *serious damage both to the body and the soul*: these can be avoided if a man becomes a proselyte, a penitent. He at once acquires all the virtues listed here by Philo, virtues which include gentleness, kindness and humanity, and abandons at the same time the vices which include injustice, quarrelsomeness, desire, and in particular sexual lust for beautiful women (cf. *Spec. Leg.* IV.82). The greatest stress is laid on the evil of desire, which ministers *to the pleasures of the stomach and the organs below the stomach*, delights which, Philo adds, end in the gravest injuries to the body and the soul of man.

(183) *a better state*: Philo commends the admonitions to repentance contained in the Law, since they urge men to transform their

lives. Moses affirms that such a transformation is not a distant possibility (Deut. 30: 11–14). It does not remain high above us or far from us, nor beyond the great sea, making it impossible for us to reach it. It resides in the mouth, the heart and the hands, which three parts of the body and nature of man are symbols of words, thoughts and actions. In these three, he says, lies happiness, the happiness piety and virtue bring, the life of evil being exchanged for a life of virtue and goodness.

(184) *life is praiseworthy and perfect*: this is so, Philo says, when thoughts match words and actions intentions (he means when they are good, of course; cf. *Mut. Nom.* 237–8). When it is otherwise, life is imperfect and a matter for reproach. When men remember to maintain the proper harmony they will be pleasing to God, and will become both *God-loving and God-beloved.* To reinforce and express the truth God chose the words for Moses to speak (Deut. 26: 17, 18), words which tell of Israel's decision to acknowledge God and walk in his ways, keeping his commandments.

(185) *this reciprocity of choice*: it is a glorious thing, Philo affirms, when man chooses to serve God and God accepts the man who so chooses. So glorious is the acceptance of man by God, and God by man, that one individual acquires a real value, by virtue of God's choice of him, equivalent to that of a whole nation (cf. Deut. 27, where Philo explains the use of the second person singular in the commandment as implying that one virtuous person is equal in volume to a whole people).

(186) *an impregnable rampart, godliness*: on a ship, Philo observes, the pilot is worth as much as the whole crew, in an army the general as much as all the soldiers, since if a general falls the whole army will be defeated (Philo omits to refer to the disastrous consequences for ships when pilots fail in their duties). These situations are paralleled in the life of a nation, where the wise man can hold his own against all around him, since he is protected by *an impregnable rampart, godliness*. Godliness, which is accompanied by all the other virtues, and from which they spring, is the real strength of the life of an individual or a nation. Such is the importance, for Philo, of virtue and the virtues, of which repentance, the theme of this section of the *De Virtutibus*, is one.

THE TEN WORDS (*Decal.* 121–78 (XXIV–XXXIII))

The first 17 paragraphs of this treatise deal with the subject of the law-giving on Sinai. A disquisition on the reason for there being *ten* commandments follows. Coming to the commandments themselves, Philo notes that they divide into two sets of five (paras. 50–1). He reaches the fifth commandment in paras. 106–11 and presents a very interesting exposition of it. It has a special status, he argues, because it stands on the borderline, being the last of the first set of five and the first of the second set. The second set of five commandments (the sixth to the tenth) are more concerned with what would normally be called ethics. They are dealt with in a fairly simple and straightforward way without the usual supplements of sophisticated allegorical exegesis. The first five commandments deal with subjects such as polytheism, the worship of images, reckless swearing of oaths, the need to set apart time for philosophy and, in the borderline position, the duty of giving honour to one's parents. It will be seen that some of these commandments are 'ethical' in content, so that there is no neat and tidy division between the two sections. Religion and life, piety and morality, cannot be for him sharply divided.

Actions against our Fellow Men (*Decal.* 125–53)

(121) With such philosophical comments on the honour to be
paid to parents, he completes the one series of five which is
more concerned than the other with the divine. As he
embarks upon what he has to write about the second
series, which contains the prohibiting of actions against
our fellow men, he begins with the subject of adultery,
(122) which he takes to be the greatest of crimes. For in the first
place its source is a love of pleasure which weakens the
bodies of those who indulge in it, relaxes the sinews of the
series, which contains the prohibition of actions against
touches like an unquenchable fire, and leaving nothing
(123) which affects human life undamaged. Furthermore, it
persuades the adulterer not only to do wrong but also to
teach another person to be his companion in crime by
establishing a relationship in things where no relationship
is permissible. For when violent passion has taken over, the
desires cannot achieve their goal through one person
alone, but there must of necessity be two acting in unison,

one assuming the role of teacher and the other of pupil, with the intention of setting upon a firm footing those most disgraceful of evils, intemperance and debauchery.
(124) For it is impossible to say that it is only the body of the adulteress which is corrupted, when to tell the truth we must say that her soul rather than her body becomes accustomed to estrangement, being taught in every way to
(125) turn away from her husband and hate him. And it would be a less shocking evil if this hatred were displayed openly – for it is easiest to guard against what is seen – but in fact it is suspected with difficulty and hard to detect, hidden by cunning and wicked arts and at times creating the opposite impression of love by resorting to all manner of deceitful
(126) trickery. Accordingly it creates havoc in three families, that of the man who is suffering from the breach of the marriage vows and the loss of all hope of legitimate children; and of two others, that of the adulterer, and that of his wife. For each of these families is tainted with
(127) scandal, dishonour and disgrace of the cheapest kind. And if their connections embrace a large number of people through marriage and other associations with others, then the wrong done will spread around and affect the whole
(128) city. Very painful too is the uncertainty that exists as to the legitimacy of the children. For if the wife is not chaste, there will exist doubt and uncertainty as to which man is the true father of the children. Then, if the matter remains undetected, the children born of an adulterous relationship usurp the position of the legitimate children and create a spurious generation which is not theirs by right and will receive the inheritance which appears to be that of their
(129) father, but which is really not their possession at all. The adulterer, having added insult to injury in vomiting forth his passion, and having sown his passion's seed, his lust now sated, makes off ridiculing the ignorance of the victim of his crime, who, like a blind man, knowing

nothing of the intrigue going on within his own home, will be compelled to nourish the children of his greatest
(130) enemy and cherish them as his own. But if the wrong becomes known the wretched children who have done nothing wrong will be the most unfortunate of all involved, unable to be assigned as members to either family, either to that of the husband of the adulteress or to
(131) that of the adulterer. Since, then, illicit intercourse brings about such divisions, adultery is naturally hateful and loathsome to God and was placed first in the list of transgressions.

(132) The second commandment is to commit no murder. For nature created man, the most docile of creatures, to be gregarious and sociable, and has called him to a life of fellowship and partnership by endowing him with reason, which leads to harmony and the binding of dispositions. Let him who kills someone else not be unaware that he is subverting the laws and rules of nature, which have been so harmoniously ordained for the common benefit of all.
(133) Furthermore, let him also understand that he is liable to the charge of sacrilege, the theft from its sanctuary of the most sacred of all God's possessions. For what votive offering is there, so to speak, more majestic and more to be revered than man? Gold and silver and valuable stones and other precious substances are used to decorate buildings,
(134) which are as inanimate as the ornaments. But man, the best of living creatures because of the higher part of his being, his soul, is most nearly like heaven, the purest thing in all existence and, according to current opinion, also nearest to the Father of the world, having in his mind a more faithful replica and imitation than anything else on earth of the eternal Idea and archetype.

(135) The third commandment of the second group of five forbids theft, for the man who goes around gaping after what are the belongings of others, is the common enemy

of society. He is willing to rob everybody, but is able only to deprive them of some of their goods. His covetousness extends to infinite lengths, but his relatively weak power, lagging far behind, is limited in its range, so that his
(136) activities are restricted to only a few. So, as many thieves as have the strength will rob whole cities, regardless of the punishment, because they seem to be above the laws. These are the oligarchs by nature, who are ambitious for despotic power and domination, who commit thefts on an enormous scale, concealing their robbery, as it is in reality, under the grand-sounding names of government and
(137) authority. Let a man learn then from his earliest years not to steal furtively anything that belongs to anyone else, no matter how small it may be, because custom in time is stronger than nature, and little things, if they are not checked, grow and prosper until they attain grand proportions.

(138) Having forbidden stealing, he proceeds next to prohibit false witness, knowing that false witnesses are guilty of faults numerous and serious, all of which are grave. In the first instance, they corrupt truth, which is solemn, than which there is no more sacred possession among men and which, like the sun, sheds light upon all things, so that
(139) none of them is kept in the shade. Secondly, in addition to speaking falsely, they shroud facts in night and deep darkness, and they co-operate with wrongdoers and join in attacking those who have been injured by others, affirming that they know with certainty and have a complete understanding of things which in reality they have not seen or heard, and of which they know nothing.
(140) Moreover, they commit a third transgression even more serious in its consequences than the other two. For when there is a shortage of evidence, either oral or written, those involved in litigation resort to witnesses, whose words are standards for the judges in the verdicts they are about to

give; for it is necessary for the judges to pay attention to them alone when there is nothing else by which proof can be established. It follows that those against whom the false witness is given suffer injustice when they might have won their cases, and the judges who listen to the false testimony record unjust and illegal verdicts instead of just and legal
(141) ones. Moreover, this kind of roguish act outstrips all other offences and leads to impiety, for it is not customary for judgement to be pronounced except under oath, and indeed oaths of the most fearful kind, which are broken not by those who are deceived but rather by the deceivers, since the error of the first is not intentional, whereas the others knowingly plot against them, and commit a premeditated sin and compel those in whose power it is to give the verdict to participate in their action; and, though they are not aware of what they are doing, the judges administer punishment on those who in fact are guilty of no crime. These were the reasons, I believe, why he forbade false witness.

(142) The last commandment is directed against covetousness or desire, for he knew that it is fond of subversion and treachery. For all the passions of the soul which provoke and disturb it out of its proper nature and do not allow it to remain in sound health, are hard to deal with, but desire is the hardest of all. Therefore, while each of the other passions, entering from outside and attacking the soul from within, appears involuntary, only desire which has
(143) its origin in ourselves is intentional. What in fact am I saying? The perception by the mind of something which is present and considered to be good rouses and excites the soul from its previous state of repose, just like a light suddenly flashing before the eyes. This feeling of elation in
(144) the soul is called pleasure. And when evil, the opposite of good, forces its way into the soul and inflicts a mortal wound, it immediately fills the soul, against its will, with

(145) depression and despondency. The name of this feeling is
grief. When the evil thing has not yet invaded the soul nor
yet put pressure on it, but is about to arrive and is making
its preparations, it sends ahead agitation and distress,
ominous messengers to fill the soul with alarm. The
(146) feeling in this case is called fear. But when someone
conceives an idea of something good and wants to possess
it, and pushes the soul forward a considerable distance,
striving as far as he possibly can in his eagerness to touch
the desired object, he is, as it were, stretched out on a
wheel; he is desperately anxious to grasp the object but is
unable to reach it and is in the same predicament as people
who pursue with irresistible ardour, but at a slower speed,
(147) others who are slipping from them. Something of the
same kind also appears to happen with respect to the
external senses. The eyes are frequently eager to gain a
sighting of some very distant object, straining themselves
and exerting themselves to the fullest extent; creating a
powerful impulse which exceeds their powers, they lose
themselves in a deep void without obtaining a clear notion
of the object in question, and furthermore their incessant
(148) efforts weaken and dim their powers of vision. And, again,
when an indistinct sound is carried towards us from a long
distance away, the ears are stimulated and direct themselves towards it immediately, and are eager to approach
nearer if possible in order that the sound may be distinctly
(149) apprehended by the sense of hearing. The sound, for it still
continues to be dull, does not reveal itself with any greater
clarity that would make it identifiable, and so an even
greater tenacity is given to the endless and indescribable
longing for apprehension. For desire creates a kind of
punishment like that of Tantalus; as he missed everything
just when he was about to touch it, for the man who is
dominated by desire and who always longs for things
which are not there, also remains unsatisfied and remains

(150) wallowing about among his vain appetites. And just as diseases of the type that spread over the whole body, if they were not arrested by surgery or cauterisation, would work round and take possession of the whole body's frame, leaving no part unaffected, so unless philosophical discourse did not, like a good doctor, check the flow of desire, all the affairs of life would of necessity be diverted from their natural course. For there is nothing so remote that it can escape from passion which, once it discovers itself secure and free, spreads and plunders absolutely
(151) everything throughout the whole, all in all. Perhaps it is foolish to go on at this length about the facts which are so obvious, for what man or city is ignorant that not every day but, so to speak, every hour, they provide clear proof of the truth of what I am saying? Is the love of money or of a woman or of glory or of anything else that produces
(152) pleasure the origin of minor or casual evils? Is it not on its account that kinsmen are estranged and exchange their natural good-will for irremediable hostility, why large and densely populated countries are rendered desolate by domestic revolutions, and land and sea filled with disasters which lead to a perpetual renewal of military and nautical
(153) conflicts? For the wars of the Greeks and barbarians amongst themselves and against each other, celebrated by the tragedians, issued from a single source, desire – the desire for wealth or glory or pleasure. For it is in relation to these matters, or matters such as these, that the human race suffers disasters.

(121) *the prohibition of actions against our fellow-men*: Philo introduces the second set of five commandments thus, having described the fifth (Exod. 20: 12 and see paras. 165–7 of the present treatise) as the last of those which deal with man's duty to God. The second set of five, he says, *contains the prohibition of actions against our fellow-men*. As theological sections in the New Testament epistles are followed by ethical exhortations, so Philo follows the

'theological' commandments with moral rules (in this case prohibitions). Earlier Philo had shown that no man had a right to feel superior to others, since God had bestowed his statutes and oracles equally upon all. For Philo, man's relationships with his fellows ought to be determined by the relationship God has chosen to enter into equally with all mankind (*Decal.* 41).

Philo deals here first with the crime of *adultery*, which he names *the greatest of crimes* (cf. also *Spec. Leg.* III.7–11). It is worth noting that earlier (*Decal.* 36), when Philo had been giving three examples of the prohibitions contained in the Decalogue, the first one that comes to his mind is the command 'Thou shalt not commit adultery'. This is the first in the Septuagint in the second series, and is followed by the condemnation of theft and then murder (Exod. 20: 13–15; but cf. Deut. 5: 17–19).

(122) *a love of pleasure*: adultery (cf. *Spec. Leg.* III.52ff.; see pp. 256–8) is denounced by Philo strongly for a number of reasons, the chief being that, rooted in the love of physical pleasure, it weakens the bodies of those who practise it. It also, he thinks, damages the soul and *destroys its very being*, since it acts like an unquenchable fire upon all that it touches, contaminating everything in human life.

(123) *another person to be his companion*: the love of pleasure, Philo goes on, requires one person, in the case of adultery, to cause another to share in the wrong he is doing by creating an immoral partnership (no *true* partnership is possible in such circumstances). The nature of the physical and emotional state (*violent passion*) involved requires the participation of two people (for the particular appetites involved are not self-fulfilling). The one who contemplates adultery assumes the role of teacher, as it were, the other that of pupil. The teacher's aim is to put the vilest of sins, licentiousness and lawlessness, on a firm footing, thus making adultery a particularly heinous crime because it requires the involvement of someone else in one's own sin.

(124) *the truth*: Philo condemns adultery also because it is not only the body of the woman that is corrupted. By becoming used to estrangement from her husband, she soon learns to feel complete aversion and hatred for him. That is the real and terrible truth about adultery.

(125) *hidden by cunning and wicked arts*: it would not be so serious, perhaps, if an adulterous tendency to dislike for her husband was open, since then, being out in the open, it could be guarded against.

Actually suspicion and detection are avoided by the various deceptive practices used by the adulteress to create in the husband the feeling that he is still loved.

(126) *it creates havoc in three families*: that is the extent of the damage done by adultery. The husband, together with his family, suffers because of his wife's breach of faith; his marriage vows are broken and his hopes of a family destroyed. The adulterer and the woman, together with their families, suffer also. What Philo calls *scandal, dishonour and disgrace of the cheapest kind* extend to each family.

(127) *the wrong done will spread*: if the persons involved have many connections through marriage and other associations the whole nation will be affected. Adultery in high places leaves its mark upon a broad spectrum of the community.

(128) *the uncertainty that exists as to the legitimacy of the children*: this is an extremely painful matter since, if the wife in a marriage is not chaste, there will be doubt as to the true paternity of any children born to her. If the adultery is undetected the illegitimate children will become part of their putative father's family and succeed ultimately to his heritage, to which they have no legal right.

(129) *ridiculing*: the adulterer may well, when he has satisfied his physical passion and when the woman has become pregnant, leave her and go off mocking her husband, who is blind to the sin that has been committed, but who becomes the father to a child or children of his *greatest enemy* as if fathering his own flesh and blood.

(130) *the wretched children, who have done nothing wrong*: if the sin becomes known the children of the adulterous union will suffer terribly, since they belong fully to neither family.

(131) *hateful and loathsome to God*: it is because of the tragedy just referred to and other *transgressions* it creates that Moses placed it first in his list of wrongs, as being a wrong so loathsome that it provokes God's sternest disapproval. So strong is Philo's disapproval of *illicit intercourse* that its consequences can be described by him only as *hateful and loathsome*.

(132) *commit no murder*: the second commandment in the second section of the Decalogue is the prohibition of murder (Exod. 20: 13 (=LXX 15)). Murder is prohibited, according to Philo, because by nature man was intended to be a gregarious and sociable animal and to show fellowship and a spirit of partnership (*koinōnia*) to his fellow-men. This was made possible by the gift of reason, which is

a bond *which leads to harmony and the binding of dispositions*. The murderer, or would-be murderer, should realise that murder subverts the laws and statutes of nature which were enacted for the well-being of all (on the Law in nature, see above, pp 201–2).

(133) *the charge of sacrilege*: sacrilege is also a part of the crime of murder, for murder involves taking from its sanctuary the most sacred of God's possessions, man. No votive offering is more hallowed than man himself. Gold, silver and precious stones, with which men decorate buildings are, like the buildings, lifeless. They are therefore greatly inferior to a living man made in God's image.

(134) *the best of living creatures*: this phrase describes man, and Philo goes on to affirm that it is through his possession of a soul, the superior element in his nature, that man is most *nearly like heaven*. The soul is *the purest thing in all existence* and, he says, *according to current opinion also nearest to the Father of the world*. Philo here departs from his simple explanation of the commandment to suggest that the human mind is a *more faithful replica and imitation than anything else on earth of the eternal Idea and archetype*. It is because murder destroys the possessor of such an entity within him – the soul, which makes him the sharer of true likeness to the Logos, the eternal and blessed archetype – that murder is such a serious crime. The crime is seen to be even more serious when it is understood that, while man is 'many things', 'soul and body', and 'the soul is made up of a rational part and an irrational part' (*Leg. All.* II.2), the rational part has been created by God himself (*Conf. Ling.* 179; *Fug.* 69). Philo's anthropology is too vast a subject to embark upon here, but at least, in addition to the passages referred to, it should be noted that Philo asserts that it was of 'pure material' that God created 'a sacred abode or temple for a reasonable soul', which man was 'to carry in his heart, being the most God-like of all images' (*Op. Mund.* 137). In *Det. Pot. Ins.* 83–6 Philo states that 'God is the Archetype of rational nature, and that man is the imitation of him'. Murder, therefore, involves the destruction of that God-like creation.

(135) *the common enemy of society*: that describes the thief, the man who covets what belongs to others, but is able to obtain only some of it. It is the third commandment (see Exod. 20: 15 (=LXX 14)) in the second group that condemns the enemy of society who would like to rob all if he could. His covetousness is infinite, but his capacity to translate it into robbery limited to a small number of victims. In addition to the many other things Philo says about

covetousness, which leads to robbery, is that 'of all the passions there is not one so grievous as a covetous desire of what we have not got' (*Spec. Leg.* IV.80).

(136) *thefts on an enormous scale*: more serious, however, than the petty thieves are those who have acquired the power to rob whole cities and are undeterred by the thought of punishment because their being *oligarchs by nature* in the world of criminals appears to place them above the law. They are men who yearn for power, ambitious to rule as despots and to dominate, their large-scale robberies being disguised under *the grand-sounding names of government and authority*. These are the men who obtain positions of power which they then use to acquire personal wealth.

(137) *custom in time is stronger than nature*: Moses' teaching, as interpreted by Philo, is that from childhood man should learn not to steal, because childish thefts, if not checked, *attain grand proportions* in adulthood.

(138) *they corrupt truth*: false witnesses (see Exod. 20: 16) are guilty of sin in many serious respects. They *corrupt truth*, which is the most sacred treasure men possess. Philo's description of it is striking: truth *like the sun sheds light upon all things, so that none of them is kept in the shade*.

(139) *they shroud the facts*: unlike the truth and truth-tellers, false witnesses obscure the facts *in night and deep darkness* and side with the offenders against the injured parties. They do this by asserting that they have definite knowledge of *things which in reality they have not seen or heard*.

(140) *a third transgression*: worse than the first two transgressions, described in the previous paragraphs, false witnesses also, when there is a lack of evidence, oral or written, testify in words which the judges in the court accept in reaching their verdicts. Consequently the defendants suffer injustice and lose cases they might have won. The judges, too, suffer by recording votes that are false because they are based on misleading evidence. Needless to say, the verbal evidence given by the false witnesses is entirely fictitious, invented by them to serve their own immoral ends.

(141) *this kind of roguish act*: this, Philo says, *leads to impiety*, since judges are under oath. Their oaths are not broken, though, by the judges themselves, since they do not err intentionally, while the false witnesses deliberately give evidence which demands the oaths of the judges. So judges are led astray and innocent people are convicted and receive punishment. For these reasons, Philo

concludes, God forbade false witness. The prohibition of perjury in the law-courts was also intended to prevent the injuring of a person's good name. Penalties applied to those who commit perjury are listed in Deut. 19: 16–21, the last one being stated in the form of the *lex talionis*.

(142) *subversion and treachery*: at the beginning of what is a general diatribe against the evils of emotion, this is Philo's characterisation of covetousness or desire. Philo, it will be seen, extends the meaning of a desire to include its most general sense. Thus he can embark on a discussion of the four passions of the Stoics. It is noticeable that in this paragraph Philo is dealing with emotion rather than action.

Philo considers desire to be the hardest and worst to deal with of all the passions which disturb the soul. He continues, *Therefore* . . ., which seems to suggest that, whereas all the other passions are *involuntary*, extraneous visitations, assaults from outside, *only desire which has its origin in ourselves is intentional*. Philo is attempting to show how *desire* is worse than all the other emotions. He departs, in his explanation, from Stoic teaching because his native Jewish presuppositions force him to do so. Philo's division between desire as alone voluntary and the other emotions as *from outside* and seemingly involuntary is in direct opposition to the Stoic view. To the Stoics all emotions are voluntary and are within our power. Philo's distinction between desire on the one hand and the other emotions on the other may be based upon Aristotle's teaching, but it is more likely that Philo is contributing to the discussion of desire his own personal Jewish interpretation. The free-will God has given man implies free desire (*epithumia*). This free desire had to be there if men were to be really and truly free, but it did not need to be the case that the same voluntariness existed with regard to all the emotions. The other emotions may *seem* to be voluntary, but not in the absolute sense in which desire has its origin in ourselves and is voluntary. The freedom of desire is a freedom implanted by God as a special gift and therefore different in degree from the freedom of the other emotions. It must not be overlooked, in discussions of Philo's distinction between desire and the other emotions, that desire alone is prohibited in the Decalogue (Exod. 20: 17). This prohibition implies that those to whom it is addressed possess the power of voluntary control.

(143) *like a light suddenly flashing before the eyes*: spelling out what he means, Philo says that the presentation to the mind of

something actually with us and considered to be good arouses and awakes the soul when it is at rest and, like a light flashing on the eyes, gives it a *feeling of elation*. This is Philo's attempt to describe the sensation of the soul called pleasure (*hēdonē*). It is a violent, turbulent experience, exercising a powerful fascination and attraction, and it obliterates other functions just as a powerful, flashing light blots out all other sensations. Something within our reach and at the same time felt to be highly desirable, which becomes irresistible in its fascination and attraction for us, stimulates and nurtures within us an emotion which Philo here calls pleasure, the emotion of desire.

(144) *depression and despondency*: these fill the soul at once when evil, good's antithesis, forces its way into a man's soul with a sword-like thrust. That is how Philo describes the feeling of grief or pain which the entry of evil into our lives creates. One thinks of the way in which Simeon, in the New Testament, describes the grief which Mary is one day to experience: 'Yea and a sword shall pierce through thine own soul' (Luke 2: 35). Grief, or pain, is suffering of that sharpness of intensity.

(145) *ominous messengers*: before the evil has entered into a man's soul and while it is not yet even pressing hard upon him, but is near at hand and is about to arrive on the scene, it sends advance signals, as it were, of its coming: trepidation and distress, feelings which tell of the evil to come and which sound the alarm. This sensation, another of those referred to as 'outside' passions, is called *fear*.

(146) *stretched out on a wheel*: quite different, however, is the situation of the man who thinks of some absent good he would like to possess and energetically propels his soul as far as he can in his greed to touch the desired object. In that state of emotion he is like someone *stretched out on a wheel*, desperately anxious to grasp and obtain the object but unable to reach it. He is in the same frustrating predicament as people who are pursuing with *irresistible ardour, but at a slower speed* others who retreat even faster before them. This terrible sensation, unlike the others just described, originates within and is voluntary.

(147) *to the fullest extent*: Philo sees a parallel to the phenomena he has just described in the case of the senses. The eyes, he says, often try to see beyond their proper range of vision and power, and, as it were, hit upon a void and there slip, so failing to obtain an accurate sighting of the object looked for. Also, the strength of

vision of the eyes is diminished by the intensity and ferocity of their steady gazing into space.

(148) *eager to approach nearer*: similarly the ears are attracted by an indistinct sound a long distance away and strain to hear it. They, too, strain to exceed their powers.

(149) *punishment like that of Tantalus*: the distant noises, however, become no more distinct, yet the ear strains even harder to hear them with the intensity of the *endless and indescribable longing for apprehension*. This is what desire involves and it incurs the *punishment . . . of Tantalus*, a Greek king of Lydia who, when visited by the gods, murdered his son, Pelops, and served him to them as a meal. He was punished by Zeus by being thrown into Tartarus, the depths of hell, and condemned for ever to be prey to an insatiable hunger and unquenchable thirst. But whenever, for example, he attempted to drink from the water which came up to his neck, the water always receded. And just as Tantalus did not quite manage to reach the things he desperately wanted, so the person ruled by desire is for ever thirsting for what is absent but failing to find satisfaction *and remains wallowing about among his vain appetites*.

(150) *diverted from their natural course*: Philo sees a parallel with diseases of the spreading type, as he calls them, which if not dealt with by immediate surgery or other means spread through the body and leave no organ unaffected. So also, unless philosophical reasoning, acting as the good physician, checks human desire, the whole of a man's life will become distorted from what nature intended it to be. Passion is so pervasive that nothing escapes from it, for, once secure and free, it spreads like a fire and causes universal destruction. This is a fierce denunciation of pleasure, or desire, by Philo, paralleled in some of his other works (see above, pp. 260–3). In *Spec. Leg.* IV.84 he calls desire 'the source of all evils'. In many passages pleasure is said to be the source of all sin (see, e.g., *Leg. All.* II.71–2, 77–8, III.68, 107, 112–13). In *Spec. Leg.* IV.79 Philo says categorically that 'every passion is . . . deserving of blame' and then, in the next paragraph, 'but of all passions there is not one so grievous as a covetous desire'. What Philo says may be compared with what other Jewish writings have to say on the subject. In the *M. Abot* IV.1 we read, 'Who is mighty? He that subdues his desire. Who is such? He that is content with his portion' (cf. *Letter of Aristeas* 222). That is native Judaism speaking. Philo gives voice to the same sentiments but makes use of a philosophical

language alien to the native Judaism to which in ideas he is so close.

(151) *the facts which are so obvious*: Philo feels that perhaps he has gone on for too long about the evils of desire, since the facts are so clear and unambiguous. Every man and every city provides clear proof of what he has written, every day, almost every hour. If it is not the passion for money, or a woman, or glory, whatever it is that produces pleasure by seducing man, there is no doubt in Philo's mind that the evils which desire causes are by no means *minor or casual*.

(152) *kinsmen are estranged*: this is only the first of the few examples of the evils caused by desire that Philo gives. Natural good-will turns into deadly hatred as a result of desire. Large countries and populations are devastated by internal factions. Land and sea become the stage for new calamities, the result of battles on sea and military campaigns on land. All these things happen because men and nations want to possess what is not their own.

(153) *the desire for wealth or glory or pleasure*: all wars, internal or external, involving both Greeks and barbarians, known to his readers from the works of the tragedians performed on the stage, spring from one source, desire – the desire for the fruits of money, glory and pleasure. These, Philo emphatically concludes, cause the disasters from which *the human race suffers*.

The ten words as special laws (*Decal.* 154–78)

(154) Enough has been said on that subject, but we must not ignore the fact that the Ten Commandments are chapters of the special laws which are recorded in the sacred books
(155) and which pervade the whole legislation. The first of them deals with God's monarchical rule. It affirms that there is one First Cause of the world, one Ruler and King, who holds the reins of the universe and guides all things in safety, and has expelled from heaven, the purest part of all reality, oligarchy and mob-rule, those pernicious regimes which arise among wicked men, the offspring of disorder
(156) and covetousness. The second sums up all the laws enacted relating to the things made by men's hands, such as images of the gods, wooden carvings of them and in general

statues and idols, of which painting and sculpture are the pernicious creators. It forbids the making of these and also the acceptance of the mythical fictions about the birth and marriage of the gods, with all the innumerable and
(157) troublesome evils which ensue from both. In the third commandment he limits all the situations in which oaths are required, and the things regarding which men may swear an oath, defining where and when it may be lawful and who may swear the oath, and all the details concerning those who are true to their oath and *vice versa*.

(158) The fourth commandment, which deals with the seventh day, is nothing but the summary of the regulations concerning the festivals and the ritual of the appropriate ablutions for each feast and the acceptable prayers and the
(159) perfect sacrifices which constitute the cult. By the seventh I mean also the seventh together with the six, the most creative of numbers, and that which does not include it, and which takes precedence of it and resembles the monad. Both these aspects of the hebdomad are used by him in reckoning the dates of the festivals. The monad is used to fix the holy month day (New Year's Day, the first of Tishri), which is announced by a fanfare of trumpets; and a day of fasting on which abstinence from food and drink is commanded; and the day called by the Hebrews the Passover (*Pascha*), during the course of which the whole people, individually, offer up sacrifice without waiting for a priest, because the Law has graciously allowed the whole nation for one chosen day in every year to exercise the duties of the priesthood and the right to offer sacrifices
(160) themselves personally. And also it is the monad which determines the day on which the sheaf of corn is presented as an offering of gratitude for the fertility and productiveness of the plains, as shown by the fulness of the ears of corn; and then, calculating from this day seven sevens of days, the Day of Pentecost, when it is the custom to offer

up loaves, the nature of which is indicated by their title of 'loaves of the first-fruits', since, in fact, they are the first-fruits produced as eatable crops of grain, which God has
(161) given to mankind, the most civilised of living beings. To the seventh day of the week he assigns the greatest festivals, which are celebrated for several days: two feasts, in fact, for the two equinoxes, each lasting seven days – the first in the spring to celebrate the ripeness of the crops which have been sown, the second in the autumn as a festival of thanksgiving for the gathering of the fruit of the trees. Also the seven days were naturally assigned to the seven months of each equinox, so that each month might receive, as a special privilege, one sacred day of festival consecrated to cheerfulness and the enjoyment of respite.
(162) Other laws belong to the same class – laws admirably enacted, conducive to gentleness and fellowship and simplicity and equality. Some of these are to do with the sabbatical year, as it is called, during which the land is ordered to be left entirely uncultivated, with no sowing, or ploughing, or pruning trees, or any other agricultural
(163) activity. For God thought it a good thing that when the lowlands and the uplands had been working for six years in the production of crops and the performance of the annual tasks imposed on them, they were worthy of some relaxation which would serve as a kind of breathing-space in which they could enjoy the freedom which nature left
(164) to itself would give them. And there are other laws concerning the fiftieth, Jubilee, year, which is characterised not only by what has been described above, but also – which is an altogether necessary practice – by the restoration to families of patrimonies which had originally belonged to them, a custom filled with neighbourly love and justice.

(165) The fifth commandment, which is to do with honouring parents, contains implicitly many necessary laws, laws

drawn up to deal with the relationships of old to young, masters to subjects, benefactors to beneficiaries, slaves to
(166) masters. For parents belong to the superior ranks of the above-mentioned categories those which embrace elders, rulers, benefactors and masters, while children occupy an inferior rank with the young, subjects, those who have
(167) received benefits, and slaves. And many other rules are given: to the young on courtesy towards the old, to the old on the care of the young, to recipients of benefits on responding with gratitude, to those who have taken the initiative in making gifts on not seeking for repayment or return as one does in the case of a debt, to servants on rendering affectionate service to their masters, to masters on showing that gentleness and mildness by which the inequality of their respective situations is to some extent equalised.

(168) The first series, then, is limited to these five commandments described, each forming a general heading, while the number of the special laws is not small. In the other series the first general heading is that against adultery, under which many other commandments are conveyed by implication, such as that against seducers and pederasty, against libertines who practise illicit and immodest forms
(169) of intercourse. But the lawgiver has described these different vices not merely to demonstrate how diverse and varied intemperance can be, but in order to put to shame in the most explicit way those who live an indecent life, by pouring into their ears a flood of invectives as a result of
(170) which they will be made to blush and feel ashamed. The second principle forbids murder; under it are grouped the laws, essential and universally advantageous, to do with
(171) acts of violence, insults, wounding and mutilation. The third is against stealing; under it are set out all the regulations regarding the repudiation of debts, the denial of deposits, partnerships which are not true partnerships,

shameful acts of robbery and, in general, any kinds of covetousness by which men are induced, either openly or
(172) secretly, to appropriate the belongings of others. The fourth relates to false witness and embraces numerous prohibitions. It forbids deceit, false accusations, co-operation with evil-doers, making a pretence of good faith a screen for dishonesty, all of which have been the subject
(173) of appropriate laws. The fifth wards off that fountain of all injustice, desire, from which flow the most lawless actions, public and private, great and small, to do with things sacred and secular, affecting bodies and souls and what are called external things. For, as has been already stated, nothing escapes from desire, but, like a flame in combustible material, it ravages, consumes and destroys
(174) everything. And there are a great many ordinances which come under this heading which have been drawn up in order to rebuke those who are capable of being corrected and to punish the rebellious who have lived their whole life given over to passion.

(175) That is all there is that needs to be said about the second five commandments to complete our examination of the oracles which God himself pronounced in a manner worthy of his holiness. For it was in conformity with his nature that God decreed in person the general pronouncements in which the special laws were summed up, but the particular laws by the agency of the most perfect of the prophets, whom he chose because of his merits to be the interpreter of the oracles, after having filled him with the
(176) divine spirit. After having explained these matters, let us now proceed to give the reason why God expressed the ten words or laws in the form of simple commands or prohibitions, without assigning, as is the custom of lawgivers, or defining any penalty against future transgressors. He was God and, as Lord, good, the cause only of
(177) good and of nothing evil. So, therefore, he judged that it was most in keeping with his nature to ordain his saving

commandments without mixing them or making them partake of the nature of punishment, so that men might choose the best, not unwillingly, but from a deliberate decision, not prompted by senseless fear but being guided by the good. God, therefore, did not think it fit to speak his oracles to mankind, associating them with penalties, though he did not thereby give immunity to transgressors, but knew that Justice was seated at his side and surveyed human affairs and, in virtue of her inbred hatred of evil, would not remain inactive but would assume as her
(178) appropriate office the task of punishing wrongdoers. For it is fitting that the servants and lieutenants of God, like generals in time of war, should put into operation severe punishments against deserters who abandon the ranks of justice. But it is also fitting for the Great King that the general security of the universe should be ascribed to him, that he should be the one who guards the peace and perpetually, with an unrestricted bounteousness, dispenses the good things of peace, all of them to everyone everywhere and for all time. For it is God who is really the Prince of Peace, while his subordinate ministers are his captains of war.

(154–61) *chapters of the special laws*: at this point Philo decides that he has written enough on the subject of his treatise, but reminds his readers that the Ten Commandments are summaries of the special laws of Scripture. He then briefly refers to the first, second, third and fourth commandments.

(162–3) *Other laws*: he relates them here to the commandment he has just dealt with, mentioning *laws admirably enacted* which exhort men to gentleness, fellowship, simplicity and equality. Reference is also made to the institution of the sabbatical year, interpreted as an act of kindness to the land.

(164) *the fiftieth year*. he refers again (see above, pp. 246–7) to the Year of Jubilee and the *neighbourly love and justice* in which it abounds, especially by allowing re-possession of lands by families that once owned them.

(165–7) *the relationships of old to young*: Philo here makes further comments on the fifth commandment (see above, pp. 272–3), treating it as dealing with a wide range of human relationships. Courtsey by the young to the old is commended, as also are the care of the young by the old, the promotion of the welfare of their subjects by rulers, gratitude by recipients of benefits, the acceptance by donors of the view that gifts do not create debts and the need for servants to render affectionate loyalty to their masters and for masters to show that gentleness and kindness which helps to make equal those who are socially not equal. This is a good example of how Philo gives a broad ethical interpretation of the Ten Commandments.

(168–74) *the other series*: the first five commandments having been dealt with, Philo again treats of the second five and some of the matters arising out of them. Here again, he expands his exposition to show, for example, that the sixth (Exod. 20: 13, LXX) commandment is related to the laws on pederasty, dissolute living and lawless and licentious forms of intercourse, described by Moses to shame men into avoiding them.

Murder, he indicates, is linked with other violent offences: insult, outrage, wounding and mutilation. Likewise, stealing is connected with various financial frauds: defaulting debtors, repudiation of deposits, false partnerships, robberies and, in general, covetous feelings which drive men to steal the property of others.

The fourth commandment, Philo shows, also forbids deceit, false accusation, co-operation with evil-doers, using honesty as a screen for dishonesty. And all these subjects have been, he says, the *subject of appropriate laws* (172).

The fifth commandment blocks what he calls *that fountain of all injustice, desire*. It relates to that element in man which gives rise to the most iniquitous actions, public and private, to do with things sacred and profane, affecting soul and body, and external things. There is nothing, in Philo's view, that escapes the clutches of desire. Like a forest fire it spreads and consumes everything in its path.

Many of the ordinances which are related to the fifth commandment, Philo affirms, are intended to bring about reformations of life where that is possible, or punishment where life has been surrendered permanently to passion.

(175) *all there is that needs to be said*: Philo now feels that the Ten Commandments have been dealt with adequately (though he does deal with them elsewhere in his works: for example, in *Spec. Leg.* II.224–43, to mention only one passage among many). He stresses

that they were given by God himself (though earlier, in *Decal.* 32–5, he discusses the question of whether or not God actually uttered the Commandments with his own voice, concluding that 'God is not like a man, in need of a mouth, and of a tongue, and of a wind-pipe', but that the Commandments were 'spoken' by God by an 'evidently holy miracle').

The *particular laws*, as distinct from the Ten Commandments, were given *by the agency of the most perfect of the prophets*, filled with the divine spirit and chosen to be divine interpreter, Moses.

(176) *simple commands*: Philo explains that no penalties for disobedience to the commandments were prescribed. The reason is that God, as God, is good and the cause of good, not evil.

(177) *most in keeping with his nature*: God's nature was such as to lead him to issue saving commandments, free from any admixture of punishment. Obedience to the commandments brings men salvation. Nothing in them conflicts with this saving purpose. God desired the good to be chosen for its own sake and without the fear of punishment that disobedience would entail. God wanted men to make a rational choice, not one based on fear. The separation of commandments from penalties for disobedience did not, however, mean that God granted immunity to evil-doers. For God possessed in justice one who would survey human doings and, hating evil, punish sinners.

(178) *the one who guards the peace*: God's subordinate powers are the appropriate administrators of vengeance and punishment. The *Great King*, God himself, takes charge, fittingly, of the general safety of the universe. He guards the peace of the world and supplies 'things which make for peace' (Rom. 14: 19). This he does to all persons *everywhere and for all time*. For indeed God is *the Prince of Peace*, while his subalterns are leaders of war. Here is an illustration of Philo's view that God acts indirectly upon the universe, in this case administering justice through his *servants and lieutenants*. His description of God as the God of peace has parallels in, for example, Heb. 13: 20 and in several biblical passages; both in the Old and in the New Testament peace is described as God's gift.

That which men need to create for themselves the good life, to enable them to live in accordance with the Ten Commandments at peace and in safety, God supplies for all. But if men do not choose the good, there are at work in the universe divine agents who are *his captains of war*, punishing evil, and who, in quasi-military fashion, bring *severe punishments against deserters who abandon the ranks of justice.*

JEWISH SEXUAL MORALITY AND HELLENISTIC LAXITY (*Spec. Leg.* III.8–63 (II–X))

In the first five paragraphs Philo bitterly laments the fact that involvement (perhaps that described in the *In Flaccum* and the *Legatio ad Gaium*) has kept him from 'philosophy' and 'the contemplation of the world and the things in it', though he confesses that at last 'a brief period of tranquillity and a short calm and respite from the troubles which arise from state affairs' have allowed him to return to his philosophical studies. He had been prevented from studying the sacred Scriptures. To them he now returns, 'irradiated with the light of wisdom', and it is to the second group of the Ten Commandments that he here returns (cf. *Decal.* 121ff.; see pp. 256ff.). His aim is to deal with the 'special laws' relevant to the five particular commandments in the section under scrutiny, and he is specially concerned to expound Lev. 18.

The subject is the power of bodily desire and reveals Jewish obsession with sexual immorality, marriage and family life, and Philo's with the body and its destructive desires.

The emphasis on sexual morality and immorality throughout this section is perhaps best understood in the light of the severity of Jewish teaching on sexual matters and also the sexual laxity prevailing in the hellenistic world to which Philo belonged.

Adultery and prohibited unions (*Spec. Leg.* III.8–28)

(8) The first commandment on the second tablet is this: 'Thou shalt not commit adultery.' It comes first, I imagine, because in every part of the inhabited world pleasure is a very powerful force, and no part of the world has escaped its dominion, neither things on land nor in the sea nor in the air; for all creatures of the land, fowls of the air and fish of the sea, all without exception gaze respectfully at her, and pay her court, and submit to her decrees, attentive to her least glance or nod of the head, delighting in her most

insolent caprices and all but anticipating her commands, by
(9) hurrying to offer with alacrity their service to her. Now
even natural pleasure is often greatly to blame when anyone indulges in it immoderately and insatiably – as, for example, when it takes the form of gluttony which is never satisfied, even though none of the food eaten is either forbidden or unwholesome, or again in the case of those who feel a passionate desire for sex and who in their excessive urge for intercourse act lustfully – not with the
(10) wives of other men, but with their own wives. But the
blame in most of these instances lies less with the soul than with the body, which has a considerable amount of fire inside it, which consumes the food offered to it and immediately afterwards demands a second helping. It also has an abundant reservoir of moisture, which is passed through ducts to the sexual organs, producing there
(11) ceaseless longings, irritations and sensitiveness. But those
men who are mad with passion for the wives of others, including sometimes those of their relatives and friends, and who live only to injure their neighbours, who go around attempting to adulterate whole generations, great numbers of people, and violating all kinds of marriage vows and rendering vain men's hopes of legitimate offspring – these madmen, whose souls suffer from an incurable sickness, must be punished with death as the common enemies of the whole human race, so that they may no longer live in immunity to ruin other homes, nor become teachers of others who might acquire the desire to emulate their
(12) wicked ways. Moreover, the other commandments rela-
ting to marriage laid down by the Law are excellent. For it commands men not only to abstain from the wives of others, but also from women with no husband in cases
(13) where the union is not permitted by law. For the Persian
custom it displays aversion and disgust and prohibits it as the greatest offence. The Persian magistrates marry even their

own mothers, regarding the offspring of such marriages as the most noble of men and, according to the sacred formulas, they reckon them to be worthy of assuming
(14) supreme authority. What kind of unholiness could be more impious than this: that a father's bed, which ought to be kept intact as something sacred, is dishonoured; that no respect should be shown to a mother's old age; that the same man should be both son and husband to the same woman and, conversely, that a woman should be at the same time wife and mother of the same man; that the children of the couple should be brothers of their father and grandchildren of their mother; that she should be at the same time mother and grandmother of the children, while at the same time the man should be both the father and the uterine brother [half-
(15) brother] of his offspring? These things were practised in ancient days even among the Greeks in the case of Oedipus, son of Laïus. They were done in ignorance and not deliberately, and yet this marriage produced such a harvest of evils that nothing was lacking that could produce the
(16) utmost misery. For there ensued from it a continual succession of wars, civil and foreign, to be bequeathed as an inheritance from father and ancestors to children and descendants; and there took place the destruction of the greatest cities in Greece, the destruction of national armed forces and those belonging to allied contingents called to assist either side, and the slaughter, blow by blow, of the bravest leaders on both sides, while brothers killed brothers in the deadly hate provoked by the struggle for absolute power. As a result, not only families and countries, but also the greater part of the Greek world perished in a general disaster. For cities previously densely populated were left depopulated as monuments of the disasters of Greece, and a
(17) miserable spectacle for the eyes of all the beholders. Nor indeed are the Persians, among whom such practices are frequent, able to avoid such evils, for they are always

engaged in expeditions and battles, killing and being killed. Sometimes they are invading their neighbours when they are not defending themselves against invaders. Now many enemies attack them from many quarters, since it is the nature of barbarians to be warlike and, before the sedition of the moment has been suppressed, another has broken out, so that no season of the year is ever reserved for peace and quietness, but summer and winter, day and night, they are compelled to bear arms, and so little does peace reign that they are camping miserably in the open air more often than
(18) they occupy their homes. I will make no reference to the great and magnificent succession of the mighty kings, whose first exploit when they ascend to the throne is the worst of sacrileges, fratricide, predicting a *coup d'état* on the
(19) part of their brothers as justification for the murders. All these things appear to me to be the consequences of the illicit marriages of mothers and sons, because Justice, who surveys human affairs, punishes the impious for their unholy deeds, for not only do those who commit such deeds show themselves to be impious, but also as many as associate
(20) themselves with the impious in their deeds. But our Law has taken such careful precautions in this matter that it does not even permit a son of a first marriage to marry his stepmother after the death of his father, both out of respect for the father and because the names of mother and stepmother are closely akin, even if the feelings evoked by
(21) them are quite different. For the man who has been taught to abstain from a woman unrelated to him, except that she is his stepmother, has a much stronger reason for abstaining from relations with his own natural mother. And if the memory of a father can inspire respect towards the woman who was once his father's wife, it is clear that because of the respect he feels towards both his parents it will be impossible for him to violate his mother in any way. For it would be extremely foolish to show favour towards a half-parent

while appearing to flout one whose parenthood was whole
(22) and complete. Next follows the precept against becoming engaged to one's sister, a highly moral precept which promotes continence and decency. Now Solon of Athens permitted men to marry their sisters by the same father, but prohibited marriage to sisters by the same mother. But the Lacedaemonian lawgiver on the one hand allowed brothers to marry sisters by the same mother, but on the other hand
(23) not sisters by the same father. But the lawgiver of the Egyptians, ridiculing the cautiousness of both, since their teaching stopped half-way, produced an abundant harvest of licentiousness, providing abundantly for bodies and souls an evil difficult to cure and giving full freedom to marry sisters of every degree, whether they were daughters of one of the brother's parents or of both, and also not only if they were younger than their brother, but also if they were older
(24) than he or of the same age. These practices our most holy Moses rejected with abhorrence as being quite inconsistent with and hostile to an irreproachable constitution and as encouragements and incitements to the most vile practices. Moses, then, peremptorily forbade marriage to a sister,
(25) whether the daughter of both parents or of one. For why is it necessary to mar the beauty of modesty? And why deprive maidens of modesty, when it is becoming for them to blush? Why restrict the fellowship and fellow-feeling of men with men by limiting with the restricted space of each house the great and splendid plant which ought to be extended over continents and islands and the whole inhabited world? For marriages with outsiders create new relationships which are not the least bit inferior to those
(26) which proceed from blood relationships. It is on this basis that he prohibits many other unions, proscribing marriage to a granddaughter, either a daughter's daughter or a son's daughter, and to a paternal aunt or a maternal aunt, and to someone who has been the wife of an uncle or a son or a

brother, and also to a stepdaughter, whether a widow or unmarried, not only while the wife is alive – God forbid! – but even after her death. For in principle the stepfather is in the same position as a father, and he ought, therefore, to look upon his wife's daughter in the same light as his own.
(27) He does not allow the same man to marry two sisters, either at the same time or at different times, even in a situation involving the repudiation of the first wife. For while the latter is still alive, either as his consort or as divorced from him, whether she remains single or has taken another husband, he took the view that it was improper to let the sister succeed to the place which the wife forfeited by her misfortune, desiring to teach her not to violate the requirements of justice, nor to use as a stepping-stone the disasters of one so closely associated with her by birth, nor to take pride in, while luxuriating in them or returning them, the attention paid by those who have shown themselves her
(28) sister's enemies. From such things as these arise bitter jealousies and feuds, bringing with them innumerable hosts of evil. It is just as if different limbs of the body were to abandon the harmony and united relationship to one another in which they were put together by nature and to quarrel with one another, thus bringing about incurable illnesses and deaths. Now sisters are like limbs, which, though separated from one another, are all adjusted to one another and formed into a single whole by virtue of nature and common birth. And jealousy, that most troublesome passion, when it breaks out, gives rise to unprecedented evils which are difficult to cure.

(8) *a very powerful force*: as he has affirmed in *Decal.* 121ff. (see pp. 256ff.), Philo, dealing with the sixth commandment (Exod. 20: 13, LXX), states that it comes first, in the second group within the ten, because *pleasure is a very powerful force*, experienced everywhere and by all. The whole world of nature is dominated by it.

(9) *immoderately and insatiably*: what Philo calls *natural pleasure*, permitted pleasure, is often, he says, blameworthy, since it is both immoderate and insatiable. This is so in the case of the hunger which turns into gluttony and of the normal sexual desire which leads to unchaste intercourse between husbands and their wives. Even normally permissible and innocent pleasures may become excessive and immoral.

(10) *less with the soul than with the body*: that, Philo believes, is where the blame really lies. He then describes the body as containing a great fire and abundant moisture. The fire consumes the material with which it is fed and quickly demands more; the moisture is passed in a stream through the genital organs, creating persistent sensations which demand repeated satisfaction.

In several passages Philo describes the body as 'earthlike' (e.g., in *Leg. All.* I.32), made of matter, disorderly and irrational, exercising power and making it difficult for the mind to subdue it. The life of man is, therefore, an unending struggle between mind and body. In *Quaest. in Gn.* III.10 Philo describes the soul of the wise man, when in the body, as in 'a land which is not his own'. The bodily passions, though they may become our helpers, are in fact our enemies, and we are constantly afflicted from within by pleasures, desires, sorrows and fears.

(11) *an incurable sickness*: those afflicted by bodily demands are not so blameworthy, Philo says, as those who madly desire other men's wives, those of friends or relatives; who create havoc among their neighbours; who father numerous illegitimate children; who make a mockery of others' prayers for married happiness and render their hope of children fruitless. The souls of such men are beyond redemption. Death is the appropriate penalty, since they are enemies of the human race. Death alone will render them incapable of inflicting further ruin on people's homes and inciting others to follow their evil example.

(12) *other commandments relating to marriage*: on this subject Moses' law, says Philo, is excellent. It forbids adultery (the Greek word 'widows' may refer to all women without a husband – mothers, stepmothers, etc.) where the union is prohibited by the Law: that is, where incest would be involved even if the relationship were not actually adulterous. The list of prohibited unions follows Lev. 18 (cf. para. 20 of the present treatise).

(13) *the Persian custom*: this, Philo says, the Law strictly forbids (see Lev. 18: 7ff.). What the Persians do, according to Philo, is to

marry their mothers and regard the children resulting from such marriages as nobles of high birth, worthy to be rulers. Various writers, including Clement of Alexandria, refer to Persian incest. Another writer referring to these alleged Persian practices – which include marriage to mothers, daughters and sisters – is Tertullian. Philo, who elsewhere expresses his admiration for the Magi, took it for granted that the Persian custom was still practised in his own day.

(14) *What kind of unholiness could be more impious than this?*: Philo lists the various immoral forms of marriage within the prohibited degrees in words which show his disgust.

(15) *a harvest of evils*: Philo refers to the great harm done, among the Greeks, by the marriage of Oedipus to his mother. Even though it was not intentional and was done in ignorance, the consequences were nevertheless extremely serious and led to the *utmost misery*.

(16) *succession of wars, civil and foreign*: this was part of the harvest of ills bequeathed by Oedipus to his descendants, especially his two sons, who became military rivals. According to the legend, fighting took place in which the great city of Thebes was sacked. Philo, it had been suggested, however, exaggerated the ordinary traditions concerning Oedipus. In one Thebes was sacked, but not the *greatest cities in Greece*. The account of the losses incurred is described over-dramatically perhaps, and it is a considerable exaggeration to state that *the greater part of the Greek world perished*. The desolated cities, *monuments of the disasters of Greece, a miserable spectacle for the eyes of all the beholders* is another case of Philonic exaggeration – the exaggeration of a moralist. But, of course, Philo is really trying to describe the enormous evil of incest, not to give an accurate history of Greece in the period concerned.

(17) *killing and being killed*: it is not only the Persians whose immoral sexual practices led to wars and slaughter. Philo may have been thinking here of the conquest of the Persians by the Parthians (*Jos.* 136; *Deus Imm.* 174). The rest of the paragraph could describe that period of Persian history, the period contemporary with Philo, though there were earlier troubles within the Persian empire of which he may have known. His main point, however, is that immorality leads to civil disorder and a loss of peace as war after war has to be fought.

(18) *the worst of sacrileges, fratricide*: this *magnificent succession*, as Philo sarcastically puts it, he will not dwell on, except to declare

that it is justified by its perpetrators on the ground that, if it is not the *first exploit* of a new king, he will be for ever afterwards in danger from his brothers.

(19) *illicit marriages*: Philo judges that all such terrible events as those described are due to incestuous marriages. The unholy deeds are avenged by Justice, who presides over the world's affairs. The impiety extends beyond the actual perpetrators of it to those who associate themselves with them.

(20) *our Law*: the Law of Moses has taken such great care in these matters that it does not even permit the son of a first marriage to marry his stepmother after the death of his father (see Lev. 18: 8). This is because of the honour due to the father, and because the names of mother and stepmother are closely akin; however, the feelings called up by the two words may differ – Philo knows of the hostility associated with the word stepmother (*mētruia*).

(21) *it would be extremely foolish*: this would be the case in acknowledging the claims of a half-parent while appearing to treat with contempt a full parent. What Philo means is that it is improper to marry one's stepmother, but even more so to marry one's real mother. Respect for one's (deceased) father should engender respect for the one who was once his wife, and the honour which, as a Jew, he gives to both parents will also prevent his violating his mother in any way.

(22) *a highly moral precept*: in a reference to Lev. 18: 9, 20: 17, Philo says that the prohibition against marrying one's sister both is an excellent law and *promotes continence and decency*. According to Philo, Solon, the Athenian lawgiver, permitted marriage with half-sisters on the father's side (though not on the mother's side). Plato (*Laws* 838A) lists brother and sister among those between whom intercourse was unlawful, so the practice allowed by the Athenian law referred to by Philo as Solonic cannot have been a common one. For Lacedaemonian practice, we have no evidence apart from Philo's statement.

(23) *an abundant harvest of licentiousness*: the lawgiver of the Egyptians, according to Philo, scorned the caution of the other two, believing that the course of action they enjoined stopped half-way. He – and we know what a low opinion Philo had of the Egyptians – allowed marriage to a sister of any and every degree – a lavish bestowal on bodies and souls of *an evil difficult to cure*. Marriages, then, like that of Isis and Osiris were not prohibited.

This meant that twins, separated at birth, could later marry, though the words wedlock and partnership did not really apply to their unions.

(24) *inconsistent with and hostile to*: the practices of Sparta and Greece just described Moses rejected as improper within the Jewish community because they encouraged and incited the vilest of customs. He prohibited the marriage of a brother to a sister absolutely (see Lev. 18: 10–16 for this and other prohibitions listed here).

(25) *the beauty of modesty*: why, asks Philo, spoil a girl's natural modesty, why banish her natural, innocent blushes? Why limit within each separate house the fellow-feeling and intercommunion of men with men, which, like a vast, beneficent plant, might spread over continents and islands, indeed the whole world? Philo, in other words, sees incestuous relationships as an improper and unfortunate restriction of that relationship between men and women which would and should embrace the world in peace and not passion. Also he sees marriage with those outside the family as creating new relationships equal to those present with existing families.

(26) *on this basis*: the same principle by which the above incestuous relationships are prohibited applies to *many other unions*, some of which Philo lists. He is particularly vehement in his condemnation of marriage to a stepdaughter, whether a widow or unmarried, especially if the man's wife is still alive. A stepfather should act like a real father and not marry his stepdaughter any more than he would marry his own daughter.

(27) *He does not allow the same man to marry two sisters*: this applies whether it is at the same time or at different times, and even if the man involved has repudiated the one he married first (here Philo follows Lev. 18: 18). A sister should, because of the Law of Holiness, not take the position formerly held by her sister. Her sister's loss should not be her gain, nor should she relax in the friendship of *her sister's enemies*.

(28) *bitter jealousies and feuds*: when marriages of the kind just described occur, all kinds of unhappy and evil consequences follow. The analogy Philo thinks of is the unnatural partnerships of members of the body and the strife, diseases and deaths this would produce.

Sisters are not wholly separate beings; they are uniquely united by nature and common parentage. The evils created by improper marriages involving sisters would create jealousy, and from that would ensue *unprecedented evils which are difficult to cure*.

Other prohibited sexual acts (*Spec. Leg.* III.29–50)

(29) But also, he says, do not enter into a marriage union with a foreigner, lest one day you be seduced into complying with the customs inconsistent with your own and stray unwittingly from the path which leads to piety and go completely astray upon a road that leads nowhere. And though you yourself may resist, strengthened by the best possible instruction continually repeated to you by your parents from your earliest years, when they taught you the holy laws, there is not a little to be feared for your sons and daughters, for it may well be that they, enticed by the spurious customs in place of the authentic ones, are in danger of unlearning the honour due to the one God, which
(30) is the beginning and end of supreme unhappiness. If also, he says, a woman separated from her husband for any reason whatever, marries another man and then is again left on her own, whether her second husband is in fact dead or is still alive, she must not return to her former husband, but may be united to any man in the world rather than to him, because she has violated the old ties, which she has forgotten, having chosen new charms in place of the old
(31) ones. And if any man is willing to form an alliance with such a woman, let him be marked out as a man with a reputation for degeneracy and loss of manhood, since he has excised from his soul, which is so essential to life, the hatred of evil, the emotion by which is assured the good running of our domestic affairs and those of our cities, and has cheerfully accepted on his character the stamp of two of the greatest of all offences, adultery and the crime of procuring. For the reconciliations which take place subsequently are

proof of both. Let him therefore suffer the death penalty together with the woman.

(32) Whenever the menstrual period occurs, a man must not touch a woman, but during that time he must refrain from sexual intercourse, showing respect for the law of nature. At the same time he must learn not to waste generative sperm for the sake of a pleasure untimely and in bad taste. For it is just the same as if a peasant, out of drunkenness or sudden insanity, should sow wheat and barley in lakes or in torrents, instead of on the plains, for the fields should become dry before the seed is sown in them if one wishes to
(33) secure an abundant harvest. Now nature cleanses the womb each month as if it were a mysteriously fertile cornfield over which, like a good farmer, he must watch for the appropriate moment, so that he can hold back his seed while it is flooded – for the seed would otherwise be swept away surreptitiously by the flood, seeing that the humidity will not merely relax the seminal powers but will utterly dissipate them. Now they are the forces which in nature's workshop, the womb, form living creatures and which, with consummate skill, perfect each part of body and soul, but if the menstrual period ceases, he may confidently sow the creative seeds without having to be afraid that subsequently the seeds he has deposited will be destroyed.

(34) They too who plough the hard and stony land must be reproached. And who could these be but those who have intercourse with infertile women? For, in the pursuit of unbridled pleasure, like the most lustful of men, they deliberately destroy their procreative sperm. For what other reason can they have for becoming engaged to such women? It cannot be in the hope of having children, a hope which they know of necessity must fail to be realised; it must rather be to gratify their excessive lust and incurable
(35) incontinence. Those men, therefore, who marry young

women ignorant at the time as to their fertility or barrenness and later find out that they are infertile because they produce no children, but nevertheless refuse to divorce them still deserve sympathy. For they are overcome by the powerful influence of familiarity and are powerless to repudiate the attraction of an old love which a long life
(36) together has imprinted in their souls. But those who marry women who have already been tested by other husbands and found to be barren, and who are content to fornicate like pigs or goats, their names deserve to be entered on the lists of those whose impiety makes them enemies of God. For while God, in his love for living creatures and for mankind, takes all imaginable care to secure the preservation and permanent survival of every species, these people who, on the contrary, make every effort to quench the life of the seed as it is ejected, are confessedly enemies of nature.

(37) A much greater evil than that just referred to has forced its way into the cities: namely, pederasty, which formerly it was a great disgrace even to mention, but now is a matter of boasting not merely to those who actively practise it, but even to those who are passive partners in it. Accustomed to suffer from the affliction of a malady which assigns to them the female role, they acquiesce in the wasting away of both their bodies and their souls, without leaving to smoulder among the ashes the least spark of masculinity. Note how conspicuously they curl and adorn their hair, and how they scrub and paint their faces with rouge and paints and the like, and anoint their skins with fragrant perfumes (for among those people who apply such embellishments to make their appearance attractive perfume is the most seductive). In fact the transformation of the male to the female nature by artificial behaviour is practised without a
(38) blush. Such persons are naturally considered worthy of death by those who obey the Law, which commands that the man–woman, who falsifies the stamp of nature, should

not be allowed to live for a day unavenged, or even an hour, since he is a disgrace to himself, to his household, to his
(39) fatherland, and to the whole human race. And let the pederast know that he is subject to the same penalty, since he pursues a form of pleasure contrary to nature, and since, as far as he is concerned, he does his best to make cities desolate and uninhabited by destroying the creative seed. And, moreover, he does not shrink from being a guide and teacher of those greatest of evils, unmanliness and effeminacy, adulterating young men when in their prime, and making them effeminate in the flower of their youth, which ought to have been trained for strength and might of body. And, finally, like a worthless husbandman, he lets the deep-soiled and fruitful fields lie sterile, by contriving that they should remain barren, and works day and night on
(40) that soil from which there can never be any return. The cause, I think, is to be located in the prizes awarded in many nations for incontinence and effeminacy. At all events these hybrids of men and women can be seen swaggering about in the crowded market-places, at the head of festal processions, appointed, unholy as they are, to serve as ministers of holy things, presiding over mysteries and
(41) initiatory rites, and celebrating the feasts of Demeter. Those of them who, desiring to prolong their youthful beauty, have desired to be completely transformed into women and have castrated themselves, and have clothed themselves in purple robes, and are surrounded by an escort like the great benefactors of their native lands, stride in front, drawing the
(42) attentions of passers-by to themselves. But if the indignation which our lawgiver felt against those who did not shrink from such conduct was shared, if they were exterminated without mercy as public enemies and a curse and pollution of his country, many other criminals would accept the warning. For relentless punishment of those who have already committed criminal acts has a not incon-

siderable deterrent effect on those who display any eagerness to commit the same crimes.

(43) But some people, imitating the lustful indulgences of the Sybarites and others even more lascivious than they, have in the first place devoted themselves to dainty living and the eating of delicacies, drinking-bouts, and other pleasures of the stomach and the regions below it, and when fully satisfied – for satiety naturally engenders insolence – go mad with passion no longer for human beings, male or female, but even for irrational animals, as they say long ago in Crete happened in the case of Pasiphaë, the wife of Minos, the
(44) king. She fell in love with a bull and in fact became wild with passion because of the impossibility of a consummation (for a frustrated passion is usually intensified), and the sad woman confided an account of the affliction which she was suffering to Daedalus, who was the best and most skilful craftsman of his time. He, being extremely ingenious in constructing contrivances to capture elusive prey, made a wooden cow and inserted Pasiphaë through one of its sides. The bull, thinking the wooden cow was a living animal of its own kind, rushed at it and mounted it. Pasiphaë became pregnant and in due course bore a creature, half-man, half-
(45) beast, called the Minotaur. And it is very likely, if passions are allowed to go uncurbed, there will be others like Pasiphaë, and there will be not only women but also men, madly in love with animals, which will give birth to abominable creatures, monsters, which will be memorials of the disgusting abominations of mankind, as a result of which possibly those creatures hitherto unborn and non-existent, except in stories, like the Hippocentaurs and the Chimaeras, will be produced.

(46) Indeed, so great are the provisions made in the Law to ensure that men should engage in no such illicit matings, that it is expressly commanded that beasts are not to be crossed with those of a different species. No Jewish

shepherd will permit a sheep to be crossed with a male goat or a ram with a she-goat, or a cow with a horse; and, if he does, he must pay the penalty for attempting to break the solemn law which has at heart the conservation of original
(47) species free from all adulteration. It is true that some people value mules more than all other beasts of burden, since their bodies are very compact and solidly muscular, and accordingly in pastures and stalls where horses are kept they also keep mules of an extraordinary size, which they call 'Celons', to breed with the mares, who then give birth to a mixed animal, the half-ass or mule. But Moses, recognising that the way the animal is produced is contrary to nature, has strictly forbidden it by a general decree, so that the mating of different kinds of animal is on no account
(48) permitted. By making these provisions, therefore, he took into account what was in accordance with nature, but also, in addition to this, he addressed, as from a far-off watch-tower, a warning to men and women alike that they should learn from these examples that they should abstain from
(49) illicit intercourse. If, therefore, a man has intercourse with a quadruped, or a woman allows herself to surrender to a quadruped, the human offenders must die and the animals also: the first because they have exceeded the bounds of licentiousness itself by inventing abnormal lusts, and because they have created odious pleasures of which even the description is terribly degrading; the animals because they have assisted at such iniquities, and to make sure that they do not bear or give birth to monstrosities which may have been expected to be the result of such abominable practices.
(50) Moreover, those who have even a slight concern for what is becoming could not continue to use their cattle for any purpose relating to life, but would regard them with aversion and abhorrence, loathing even the sight of them, and they would even take the view that they would contaminate whatever they touched. And when things

have no useful purpose in life, even if they are profitable, they have become superfluous and, as one of the poets put it, are only 'a dead weight on earth'.

(29) *a road that leads nowhere*: alluding to Exod. 34: 16 and Deut. 7: 3 (a digression from Lev. 18), Philo reminds his readers of the law against marriage to foreigners. The danger he mentions is that one day the man may be overcome by the opposing customs of his wife's country and abandon the path that leads to (Jewish) piety and wander into a wilderness without paths. Some Jews, he concedes, have a strong grounding in their own faith and would not neglect *the holy laws*, though the children of such marriages might be at risk. Attracted by *spurious customs*, and preferring them to the genuine ones, they could unlearn *the honour due to the one God*. That is *the beginning and end of supreme unhappiness*. In the end, it is the loss of reverence for God, loss of authentic monotheism, that is the most important danger that unethical behaviour contains.

(30) *new charms in place of the old ones*: no woman who has married and then separated from her husband to marry someone else, and then is left on her own again must return to her first husband. It does not matter in fact whether the second husband is alive or dead, the prohibition still applies. What she can do is to marry any other man rather than her first husband. She broke the marriage bond between herself and her first husband when she married another man and cannot now go back to him as his wife (see Deut. 24: 3–6). Philo may have regarded the intermediate marriage as proof that the remarriage would amount to adultery or that the second marriage was not pure, and this may be why he took the word 'defiled' in Deut. 24: 6 as applicable to the wife.

(31) *the stamp of two of the greatest of all offences*: the man who is willing to marry such a 'defiled' woman is both degenerate and less than a man. He has excised hatred of evil from his soul – the emotion which serves our lives so well and ensures the proper conduct of the affairs of houses and cities – and has lightly accepted the stamp of two heinous crimes, *adultery* and pandering (*proagōgeia*). The remarriage of the kind in question is proof of both. Punishment for either or both should, according to Philo, be death.

(32) *the law of nature*: Judaism took very seriously the rule, laid down in Lev. 18: 19, that a man must not have sexual relationships

with a woman during menstruation. The satisfaction of his own physical desires should not lead him to break this rule, especially as intercourse during menstruation involved a waste of the male sperm. He adds some analogies: it is as if a farmer foolishly sowed wheat or barley in ponds or mountain streams and not on the plains: *the fields should become dry before the seed is sown in them.*

In this paragraph Philo resumes his exposition of Lev. 18 and continues it (apart from paras. 34–36) to the end of para. 53. He does not deal with Lev. 18: 20, 21, on adultery and the offering of children to Molech.

(33) *a mysteriously fertile cornfield*: that is Philo's description of the womb, purged each month, as he puts it, by nature. It is also like a field in that the husband (man) must await *the appropriate moment*. During menstruation he will abstain from intercourse, since the semen will be washed away, and he expresses the opinion that *humidity* relaxes and indeed utterly paralyses the seminal nerve-forces, which, in what he calls *nature's workshop*, the womb, mould the living creature and with perfect craftsmanship consummately create each part of body and soul. But, menstruation complete, intercourse may be enjoyed, the husband no longer needing to fear that his sperm will perish.

(34) *the hard and stony land*: it is wrong to plough this: that is, it is wrong to *have intercourse with infertile women*. The quest for pleasure of a physical kind leads some men to do this deliberately and incidentally destroy the *procreative sperm*. To marry such women is not done in the hope of securing children. It is no more than an act of *excessive lust* and constitutes *incurable incontinence*. This, and the following two sections, are not based on biblical rules or laws. In this present paragraph Philo reveals his antipathy to 'pure' pleasure.

(35) *the attraction of an old love*: a man may marry a girl not knowing if she can bear children or not, but later, long after, find out that she is infertile. Such a man, Philo declares, deserves our pardon. Familiarity, a powerful influence, is too strong to allow them to extirpate the effect on them of their long companionship. In this paragraph, like the previous one not based on a biblical passage, Philo reveals the softer side of his nature and an appreciation of affection and companionship.

(36) *like pigs or goats*: those who sue for marriage with women whose infertility has been proved in their present marriages are guilty of engaging in sexual relationships like animals. Their

names, Philo thinks, should be entered on the list of the impious as enemies of God. A vice, here a serious sexual one, is treated as an affront to God. God is loving and forgiving and does all he can to preserve the human race, while those who waste and destroy human life-giving sperm are self-confessed enemies of nature.

(37) *a great disgrace*: here, treating of Lev. 18: 22, 20: 13, Philo suggests that this particular vice, pederasty (sodomy or homosexuality), a much graver sin than the one just referred to, has spread *into the cities* of the whole land. Formerly the mere mention of it was a disgrace, but now both the active and the passive partner to it boast of their practice. They have let themselves become accustomed to endure *the affliction of a malady which assigns to them the female role*, which causes both soul and body to disintegrate and leaves not even a remnant of their male sex-nature to smoulder. They braid and adorn their hair conspicuously and put make-up on their faces and apply scent to their bodies. Of all these methods used to produce an *attractive appearance . . . perfume is the most seductive*. So blatant is the current homosexuality, Philo says, that the transformation of the male into the female is a practised art and does not raise a blush. For Paul's similar severe condemnation of such practices, see Rom. 1: 24–32.

We learn here how homosexual practices appear to have increased in cities such as Alexandria. A similar treatment of the vice appears elsewhere in Philo's treatises. In *Abr.* 135–6 he states that, in the land of Sodom (see Gen. 19) 'those who were men lusted after one another, doing unseemly things and not regarding or respecting their common nature . . . and so, by degrees, the men became accustomed to be treated like women'. In *Vit. Cont.* 59–62, after a critical review of Plato's *Symposium*, where the talk is said to include the subject of the love 'felt by men for one another', Philo describes how pederasty, among other things, turns man into a hybrid of man and woman, and ruins boyhood, reducing boys to the condition of girls besieged by a lover, damaging their bodies, souls and property. The last happens because the best kind of men become scarce, sterility and childlessness ensue, and knowledge of farming is lost.

Philo's Jewishness and his thoroughly Jewish view of sexual morality, based chiefly on Lev. 18, led him to a judgement which differs from that of Plato (even if Philo is wrong, as he may be, in treating the love discussed in the *Symposium* as homosexuality).

Philo overlooks, apparently, what Plato has to say in the dialogue about the love of man for woman.

(38) *worthy of death*: Philo has no hesitation in condemning homosexuals to death, as Scripture does (Lev. 20: 13). The homosexual debases his humanity, and should perish *unavenged* and not be allowed to live *for a day . . . or even an hour.*

(39) *subject to the same penalty*: this applies to the homosexual's partner. The pleasure he seeks is unnatural and his actions render *cities desolate and uninhabited* by destroying the means of procreation, the idea being that the pederast was supposed to become impotent (cf. *Abr.* 135: 'though eager for children they were convicted by having only an abortive offspring').

Philo also laments the fact that the pederast's lover becomes a specialist in the art of maintaining *unmanliness and effeminacy* by prolonging the bloom of youthfulness and retaining as weak what should grow in strength. Also, like a bad farmer, he allows the fertile fields to lie sterile, behaving so as to prevent their use, spending his time night and day cultivating soil from which no growth can be expected. By being an unnatural partner to his pederast lover, he prevents him from having a natural relationship with a member of the opposite sex.

(40) *the prizes awarded in many nations*: this is the cause of the widespread incidence of pederasty and homosexuality, for licentiousness and effeminacy are rewarded. Philo asserts that many *hybrids of men and women*, male prostitutes, can be seen parading through the market-places. He adds that they lead the processions at feasts and that they are appointed, *unholy as they are, to serve as ministers of holy things*, superintending the mysteries and initiations and celebrating the rites of Demeter. No evidence has been found for this assertion, though Philo frequently denounces the mysteries and their associations with male prostitutes. He based his attitude no doubt upon such passages as Deut. 23: 18 (cf. Deut. 23: 17, LXX). His objection to the mysteries is that they involve 'trickery and buffoonery' and 'mystic enchantments' shared in the secrecy of the darkness with a few others (*Spec. Leg.* 1.319).

(41) *clothed themselves in purple*: some of the male prostitutes have gone so far, Philo informs us, as to desire to become women, mutilating their sexual organs in the process. They wear clothes of regal purple as the royal benefactors of their land and are attended by a bodyguard. Not surprisingly, they attract much attention.

(42) *a curse and pollution of his country*: this is the effect that male prostitution and other practices like it have in the nation, but the condemnation of these practices by Moses in strong terms is likely, Philo thinks, to deter others from participating in them.

(43) *the lustful indulgences of the Sybarites*: the Sybarites' practices are worse than those of the male prostitutes of Demeter. There are also others more lascivious than even the Sybarites. They begin by becoming experts in matters of food and drink, and indulge in the pleasures of food and sex. Then, in a frenzy of wantonness, produced by satiety, they go mad and conceive a frantic passion for *irrational animals*. The passages Philo has in mind are no doubt Lev. 18: 23 and 20: 15–16, and Exod. 22: 19. The example Philo quotes is the well-known one of Pasiphaë, wife of King Minos *long ago in Crete* (cf. Diodorus IV.77).

(44) *She fell in love with a bull*: Philo then retells the story of how, wild with passion (*frustrated passion is usually intensified*), Pasiphaë persuaded the craftsmen of Daedalus to build a wooden cow, inside which she concealed herself. The bull was deceived by the imitation and mounted it. Pasiphaë became pregnant and gave birth to the half-beast called the Minotaur.

(45) *there will be others like Pasiphaë*: this will be so if passion is allowed to go unbridled, and as well as there being women in love with animals the same will be true of men. Unnatural monsters will be produced, Philo thinks, *memorials of the disgusting abominations of mankind*. The offspring produced will include *Hippocentaurs* and *Chimaeras* and others, forms of life hitherto unknown and *non-existent, except in stories*.

(46) *men should engage in no illicit matings*: the provisions of the Law in this respect are so strict that it ordains that even cattle are not to be crossed with others of a different species (Lev. 19: 19; cf. Deut. 22: 9–11). Philo then gives examples of what is prohibited in Jewish farming; for example, matings between goat and sheep, or ram and she-goat, or between bull and mare, breaches of which rules are offences against *the solemn law*, the aim of which is to preserve the purity of the primary species and not to produce hybrids or mongrels.

(47) *the half-ass or mule*: Philo notes that some people value the mule as a beast of burden because it is compact and muscular. Such men rear huge donkeys, called Celons, to mate with the female colts, who then give birth to the hybrid animal, the mule or half-ass. But this was forbidden by Moses as unnatural, applying the

general rule forbidding the mixture of species (though mules are often referred to in the Old Testament: e.g., in Isa. 66: 20; 1 Kings 1: 33, etc.).

(48) *in accordance with nature*: this, and the demands of decency, were what Moses took into account; but also, Philo thinks, Moses was warning mankind, *as from a far-off watch-tower*, way above the ordinary life of the human community, against unlawful forms of intercourse (either for themselves or for their animals).

(49) *the bounds of licentiousness*: those who pass these in their sexual habits – a man using a dog, a woman allowing herself to be used by an animal – must be put to death, and likewise the animal involved. This is because they have exceeded the proper limits of sexual desire by creating abnormal lusts and because sexual pleasures devised by them are distasteful, shameful even to describe. The animals must be destroyed because of their part in these infamous acts and to ensure that no monstrosity is born as a result of the abominable intercourse that took place.

(50) *superfluous*: when an animal cannot be used because it is totally and horribly unclean this is what it becomes. Those who have some sense of decency cannot continue to use such beasts for purposes serviceable to life once they have been involved in unlawful sexual practices, but will abhor them, disliking the very sight of them and worrying lest what they touch should also become unclean. So, because a thing that serves no purpose in life is *superfluous* and its survival unnecessary, its continued existence is *a dead weight on earth* (a quotation from Homer, *Odyssey* XI.379; cf. *ibid.*, I.74).

The legal handling of prostitution and adultery (*Spec. Leg.* III.51–63)

(51) Again, a prostitute is not accepted within the commonwealth of Moses, since she is a stranger to decency, modesty and chastity, and all other virtues. She contaminates the souls of both men and women with her lewdness. She pollutes the immortal beauty of the mind and honours before it the ephemeral attractiveness of the body. She flings herself at the first man she meets, and sells her beauty like some commodity in the market-place, prepared

to say anything with a view to ensnaring the young men, while at the same time she incites her lovers against one another, offering herself as the disgusting prize for the one offering the most. Let her be put to death by stoning, for she is a disgrace, a plague, a pollution of the common life, corrupting the graces bestowed by nature, instead of adorning them further, as she ought, by her own nobility of
(52) life. Flagrant acts of adultery detected on the spot or proved by clear evidence are condemned by law. But in cases in which the guilt is merely suspected, the Law did not think it a good thing to have the cases investigated by men, but rather brought before the tribunal of nature. For men can arbitrate in the case of what is visible, but God can judge also in the case of what is unseen, since to him alone belongs
(53) the power to see the soul clearly. So the Law says to the husband who suspects his wife, 'Write a formal accusation, and go up to the holy city with your wife and standing before the judges lay bare the suspicious feeling which troubles you, not like a false accuser or a malicious schemer trying to win at all costs, but as one seeking to ascertain the
(54) truth accurately without sophistry.' The woman, who confronts a double danger – the first of losing her life, the second of bringing shame on her past life (something altogether more terrible than death) – must judge the matter in her own mind, and if she is pure, then she must defend herself boldly, but if she is convicted by her own conscience, let her wash her face with her tears and cover her sins with the evil of her shame. For to refuse to the bitter end
(55) to be ashamed is the height of wickedness. But if the evidence is indecisive and does not incline definitely to one side or the other, then let them go to the Temple and let them stand opposite each other, in the presence of the priest for that day, and let the husband explain his suspicions, and let him offer some barley-flour as a kind of sacrifice, to show that his accusation is not made vindictively but that his

intentions are honest and that he entertains a reasonable
(56) doubt. The priest receives the offering and hands it to the woman and removes her head-scarf, in order that she may be judged with her head bare and minus the symbol of modesty which women usually wear when they are wholly innocent. But there has to be no oil or frankincense as in the case of other sacrifices, because the intention of the sacrifice to be offered on this occasion is not joyful, but, on the
(57) contrary, exceedingly sad. The meal used is of barley, perhaps because its food value is doubtful, appropriate for irrational animals and men suffering misfortune, and thus it is a symbol that the adulteress is no different from wild animals, which indulge in mating indiscriminately and incessantly, while the wife who is innocent of the accusations brought against her is devoted to the life-style which
(58) characterises human beings. The priest, the Law continues, it to take an earthen vessel and pour into it pure water which has been collected from a spring, and place in it a lump of earth taken from the ground on which the Temple stands. These actions, likewise, refer symbolically to the search for truth. The act of adultery is symbolised by the earthen vessel because of its fragility, for death is the penalty required in the case of the adulterous; innocence of the charge is symbolised by the earth and water, since both of them are involved in the birth, growth and maturation of all things.
(59) Therefore with the two terms used the lawgiver makes a not irrelevant contribution to the picture. The water, he says, must be 'pure' and 'living', since if the woman is innocent her conduct is pure and she deserves to live; the earth is taken not from any clean place but from the 'holy' ground of the Temple, which is necessarily fertile, as also
(60) must be the chaste wife. When these preliminaries are completed, the woman is to go forward with her head uncovered, carrying with her the sacrifice of barley-meal, as has been described, and the priest, holding the earthen vessel

with the water in it, stands facing her and pronounces the
(61) following words: 'If you have not transgressed the laws of marriage, if no other man has had intercourse with you, so that you have not violated the rights of the man who is joined to you by law, be exonerated and free from the punishment. But if you have neglected your husband and burned with ardent passions, succumbing to the love of another or overcome by love for another, betraying and debasing the closest connections, do not be ignorant of the fact that you are deservedly liable to every kind of curse, the signs of which you will display on your body. Come, then, and drink the drink of testing which will reveal and lay bare
(62) what is now hidden and secret.' Having written these words on a piece of paper he will wipe them off in the water in the earthenware vessel and give it to the woman. When she has drunk the water she will depart, expecting either the reward for her chastity or the extreme punishment for her immorality. For if she has been falsely accused she may hope to conceive and become pregnant, ignoring all fears of infertility and childlessness. But if she is guilty, she should know that there is awaiting her a swelling of the abdomen, which becomes distended and inflamed, and at the same time a horrible infection in the regions around the womb, which she did not keep pure for the man with whom she had entered into a marriage contract according to ancestral
(63) customs. The Law takes such care to prevent the introduction of any innovations into the institution of marriage, that even a husband and wife who have intercourse in accordance with the legitimate practices of married life are forbidden, when they get out of bed, to touch anything as long as they have not bathed or made their ablutions, keeping them at a respectable distance from adultery or from any accusations of adultery.

(51) *a stranger to decency*: such, according to Philo, is a prostitute, who is for that reason excluded from Moses' commonwealth (see Deut. 23: 17; the death penalty is not suggested). A prostitute is also

a stranger to modesty and temperance and the other virtues, and she infects the souls of both men and women with licentiousness. She shames the undying beauty of the mind and prefers to honour *the ephemeral attractiveness of the body*. Philo describes vividly how the prostitute plies her trade, ending his description of her methods of attracting customers by describing her as a *disgrace, a plague, a pollution of the common life*. He lays down what her punishment should be – *Let her be put to death by stoning* – though this is going beyond what the Pentateuch states. She has, however, misused the benefits bestowed by nature by failing to adorn them *by her own nobility of life*.

(52) *the case of what is unseen*: adulteries (adultery is 'the greatest of crimes': *Decal.* 121; see pp. 256ff.) detected on the spot or established by clear evidence are condemned by the Law, but when that is not so and they are a matter of suspicion only, the Law lays down that they should not be tried by man but before *the tribunal of nature*. This was necessary since men can decide on open matters, but only God can determine the truth when it is hidden, for he can see into the soul (cf. pp. 220, 225).

(53) *the husband who suspects his wife*: to him the Law (see Num. 5: 12–31) instructs that he draws up a formal accusation against his wife, takes her to Jerusalem and puts his suspicions to the judges (in Num. 5 there is no preliminary hearing before judges, but only the hearing before the priests). He must do this in the spirit of one who is purely concerned with establishing the truth.

(54) *a double danger*: these, which threaten the woman, are of losing her life and of bringing shame on her past (a thing, to Philo, more grievous than death). If she is innocent, she must plead her cause courageously; if she knows she is guilty, she must submit with shame to *cover her sins*. This is advisable, since *to refuse to the bitter end to be ashamed is the height of wickedness*.

(55) *a kind of sacrifice*: the next stage in the process, according to Philo, is that, if the statements of the two are inconclusive, the couple are required to appear before the priest officiating at the Temple altar. To him the husband should *explain his suspicions*. At the same time he should bring barley-meal *as a kind of sacrifice* in order to demonstrate his lack of spite and the honesty of his intentions founded on reasonable doubt. The offering made by the husband for his wife in these circumstances is a gesture that suggests that, for all his doubts and suspicions, the man hopes his wife will be proved innocent.

(56) *minus the symbol of modesty*: the priest receives the offering

and gives it to the woman, at the same time removing her head scarf, the symbol of feminine modesty, worn by women who are innocent. No oil or frankincense is used, not for the reason given in Num. 5: 15, where it is a sacrifice calling sin to remembrance, but because the intention is that the sacrifice should not be joyful but exceedingly painful. Philo cannot accept the idea that the offering implies the guilt of the wife.

(57) *its food value is doubtful*: that is a description of the barley-meal used for the offering perhaps because it is fit only for animals and men in unhappy circumstances. It is thus an appropriate symbol for an adulteress, placing her on a level with animals which copulate freely. The innocent wife, however, has been satisfied with a life appropriate to human beings.

(58) *an earthen vessel*: the priest takes one, pours pure water into it from a spring, and then puts into it a piece of earth from the ground on which the Temple stands (or from the floor of the Temple). This, as one might expect, Philo interprets allegorically. Adultery is symbolised by the *earthen vessel* because of its fragility, for the punishment for adultery is death. Innocence is represented by the piece of earth and the pure spring water, since earth and water are involved in the birth, growth and consummation of all things.

(59) *a not irrelevant contribution to the picture*: the things mentioned, earth and water, both add to the picture, since the water must be *pure and living* (or running), an appropriate symbol of the woman's innocence, and the earth is taken from holy ground capable of fertility, which is a condition of the chaste wife.

(60) *the woman is to go forward*: this happens after the completion of the various preliminary rituals. She brings the barley-meal, and the priest stands before her holding the earthen vessel containing the pure water and the piece of Temple earth.

(61) *be exonerated and free from the punishment*: the priest pronounces that the woman is innocent if she has not broken her marriage vows and had intercourse with other men. If she is guiltless of abandoning her duties to her legitimate partner and home, she is pronounced clear of guilt and its awful consequences. However, if she has betrayed her husband and committed adultery in gratification of newly felt sexual desires, and in response to the love of another man, she has been guilty of betraying and debasing her closest ties. This will expose her to every curse, the signs of which will be exhibited in her body. She is then invited to drink

the water which is to put her to the test and reveal the hidden truth.

(62) *Having written these words on a piece of paper*: the words to be written on the paper are, according to Num. 5: 21–3, the curses indicating what will befall the guilty woman. They are then blotted out by being dipped into the water. When the woman has drunk the water she will leave expecting either to be rewarded for her chastity or punished for her unfaithfulness. If innocent, she may hope to have children and forget her fears of sterility. But if guilty, she may expect the onset of certain unpleasant physical symptoms. They will affect her abdomen and her uterus, which she has not kept pure for her husband, who married her according to ancestral custom. Here we have further evidence of Philo's Jewish regard for monogamy and his strict Jewish code of sexual ethics.

(63) *the institution of marriage*: this is so precious to Judaism that Moses in the Law made provision against the introduction of violent changes in it. Even a husband and wife, after legitimate intercourse, are not allowed to touch anything, after leaving their marriage-bed, until they have washed themselves in accordance with the regulations in Lev. 15: 18. Philo takes the view that this law implies the prohibition of adultery, or any act which leads to an accusation of adultery. In other words, if the institution is so carefully protected by the Law that husbands and wives must purify themselves after intercourse, adultery is an act from which there can be no purification and which is therefore absolutely forbidden. It is a sin which corrupts the soul as well as the body of the adulteress (*Decal.* 124; see pp. 257, 263).

Conclusion

Philo's treatises, though they present the modern reader with certain difficulties, are undoubtedly worthy of close study for their own intrinsic interest. Hellenistic Judaism in Alexandria in Philo's time was an important and powerful segment of Judaism, and Philo was a distinguished and important statesman, thinker and writer within the Alexandrian Jewish community. His life and works have a significant place within the history of Judaism (though for a long time not recognised by Judaism itself), especially its relationships with the Roman state, and, perhaps more importantly, in the development of its religious ideas with language borrowed from the ancient philosophers. Christianity took a great interest in Philo – so much so that for a long period Philo was treated as more or less one of the Christian Fathers. A distinguished New Testament scholar has said that Philo's writings provide the most significant part of the hellenistic Jewish background to the Fourth Gospel. Attempts have been made to prove that one New Testament document, Hebrews, was influenced substantially by the vocabulary, ideas and method of scriptural exegesis employed by Philo, though more recent scholarship has tended to reject this view or to accept it with severe qualifications. But certainly there is no better way for a student to begin his study of hellenistic Judaism than by reading Philo, and no better way for the student of the New Testament to embark upon the study of its background in hellenistic Judaism than by examining, for example, what Philo has to say about the Logos.

Further reading

EDITIONS OF PHILO'S WORKS

Colson, F. H., and Whitaker, G. H. *Philo* [Greek text with introductions and an English translation], 10 vols. Loeb Classical Library (London and Cambridge, Mass., 1929–62)

Marcus, R. *Philo Supplement* [translation from ancient Armenian version], 2 vols. Loeb Classical Library (London and Cambridge, Mass., 1953)

Yonge, C. D. *The Works of Philo Judaeus, the Contemporary of Josephus* [translated from the Greek], 4 vols. Bohm's Ecclesiastical Library (London, 1854–5)

Arnaldez, R., Pouilloux, J., and Mondésart, C. (eds.). *Les Œuvres de Philon d'Alexandrie* [edited individual volumes with introduction, French translation and notes], 35 vols. (Paris, 1961–73)

Cohn, L., and Wendland, P. *Philonis Alexandrini opera quae supersunt*, 6 vols. (Berlin, 1896–1915)

Leisegang, J. *Indices ad Philonis Alexandrini Opera* [Vol. VII of above] (Berlin, 1926)

Box, H. *In Flaccum* [translation and commentary] (Oxford and London, 1939)

Conybeare, F. C. (ed.). *Philo about the Contemplative Life* [critical edition] (Oxford, 1895)

Smallwood, F. M. (ed.). *Philonis Alexandrini: Legatio ad Gaium* [introduction, translation and commentary] (Leiden, 1961)

Winston, D., and Dillon, J. (eds.). *Two Treatises of Philo of Alexandria* [a commentary on *De Gigantibus* and *Quod Deus sit Immutabilis*], Brown Judaic Studies, 25 (Missoula, Mont., 1983)

BOOKS ABOUT PHILO

Arnaldez, R., Pouilloux, J., and Mondésart, C. (eds.). *Philon d'Alexandrie* (Paris, 1967)

Bréhier, E. *Les Idées Philosophiques et Religieuses de Philon*, Etudes de Philosophie Médiévale, Librairie Philosophique (Paris, 1908)

Drummond, J. *Philo Judaeus or the Jewish Alexandrian Philosophy in its Development and Completion*, 2 vols. (London, 1888)

Festugière, P. *L'Idéal religieux des Grecs et L'Evangile*, Etudes bibliques (Paris, 1932)
Goodenough, E. R. *An Introduction to Philo Judaeus* (Oxford, 1940)
Lewy, H. *Philo: Philosophical Writings*, East and West Library (Oxford, 1946)
Nairne, A. *The Alexandrian Gospel*, Liverpool Diocesan Board of Divinity Publications (Liverpool, 1917)
Sandmel, S. *Philo of Alexandria: an Introduction* (New York, 1979)
Wolfson, H. *Philo: Foundations of Religious Philosophy in Judaism, Christianity and Islam*, 2 vols. (Cambridge, Mass., 1948)

BOOKS WITH SECTIONS OR CHAPTERS ON PHILO

Copleston, F. C. *A History of Philosophy, I: Greece and Rome*, Burns, Oates and Washbourne, 1947
Dodd, C. H. *The Interpretation of the Fourth Gospel* (Cambridge, 1953)
Epstein, I. *Judaism* (Harmondsworth, 1959)
Hengel, M. *Hellenism and Judaism*, 2 vols. (London, 1974), esp. II, 99ff. and 171ff.
Kitto, H. D. F. *The Greeks* (Harmondsworth, 1951)
Knox, W. L. *St Paul and the Church of the Gentiles* (Cambridge, 1939)
Nock, A. D. *Early Gentile Christianity and its Hellenistic Background* (New York, Evanston and London, 1964)
Schürer, E. *The History of the Jewish People in the Age of Jesus Christ*, III. 2, revised and ed. by G. Vermes, F. Millar and M. Goodman (Edinburgh, 1987), pp. 809–89: J. Morris, 'The Jewish philosopher Philo'
Stone, M. E. (ed.). *Jewish Writings of the Second Temple Period: Apocrypha, Pseudepigrapha, Qumran Sectarian Writings, Philo, Josephus* (Philadelphia, 1984), chap. 6: P. Borgen, 'Philo of Alexandria'

BOOKS ON PARTICULAR ASPECTS OF PHILO

Borgen, P. *Bread from Heaven: an Exegetical Study of the Concept of Manna in the Gospel of John and the Writings of Philo* (Leiden, 1965)
Goodenough, E. R. *By Light: the Mystic Gospel of Hellenistic Judaism* (New Haven, Conn., 1935)
The Politics of Philo Judaeus (New Haven, Conn., 1938)
Katz, P. *Philo's Bible: the Aberrant Text of Bible Quotations in some Philonic writings and its Place in the Textual History of the Greek Bible* (Cambridge, 1950)
Marmorstein, A. *Philo and the Names of God* (Philadelphia, 1932); repr. from the *Jewish Quarterly Review*, n.s. 22: 3, pp. 295–306
Runia, D. T. *Philo of Alexandria and the Timaeus of Plato* (Leiden, 1986)

Siegfried, C. *Philo von Alexandria als Ausleger des Alten Testaments* (Jena, 1875)
Sowers, S. *The Hermeneutics of Philo and Hebrews* (Zürich, 1965)
Williamson, R. *Philo and the Epistle to the Hebrews* (Leiden, 1970)
As a brief introductory article on various aspects of Philo's life and work, see A. W. Argyle, *Philo, the Man and his Work, ExT.*, 75: 4 (Jan. 1974), 115–17

OTHER WORKS CITED

Bartlett, J. R. *Jews in the Hellenistic World* (Cambridge, 1985)
Leaney, A. R. C. *The Jewish and Christian World, 200 BC to AD 200* (Cambridge, 1984)
Maccoby, H. *Early Rabbinic Writings* (Cambridge, 1988)

Index

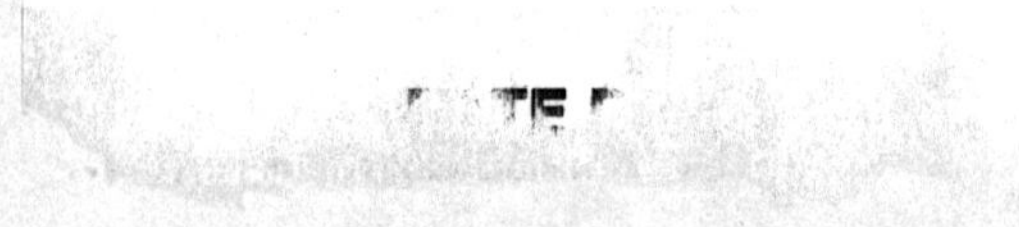